Behavioral Management Guide

BEHAVIORAL MANAGEMENT GUIDE

Essential Treatment Strategies for The Psychotherapy of Children, Their Parents, and Families

A Special Treatment Plan for Critical Incident Stress Management

Muriel Prince Warren

JASON ARONSON INC.
Northvale, New Jersey
London

This book was set in 10 pt. Goudy by Alabama Book Composition of Deatsville, AL, and printed and bound by Book-mart Press, Inc. of North Bergen, NJ.

Library of Congress Cataloging-in-Publication Data

Warren, Muriel.
   Behavioral management guide : essential treatment strategies for child psychotherapy / by Muriel P. Warren.
      p. cm.
   Includes bibliographical references and index.
   ISBN 0-7657-0354-8
   1. Child psychotherapy. 2. Group psychotherapy. 3. Family psychotherapy. I. Title.
RJ505.B4 W36 2001
618.92'8914—dc21

                                                                    2001045699

Printed in the United States of America on acid-free paper. For information and catalog write to Jason Aronson Inc., 230 Livingston Street, Northvale, NJ 07647-1726, or visit our website: www.aronson.com

For Ashleigh, Kristina, Louis, Taylor, and Kate

"Although the world is full of suffering . . . it is also full of overcoming it."

—Helen Keller

Contents

PART III
TREATMENT PLANS:
OTHER DISORDERS OF CHILDHOOD

Acknowledgments

First and always I would like to thank my publisher, Jason Aronson, who has been an unfailing source of inspiration, and Norma Pomerantz, who has held my hand through the birth of each publication. I would also like to acknowledge my husband, Howard Matus, who gives me love and support in all that I undertake. And Bill O'Hanlon for his generous contributions to this book and to my life.

Special recognition goes to Dr. David I. Perry, who spent many weekends with us researching and editing this manuscript, and to the many people who have encouraged me along the way, including Dr. Joseph Pirone, my first psychology teacher, whose brilliance has added shine to my life, and Dr. Irving Weisberg, who has taught me to keep things in perspective.

I am also grateful to Dana Salzman and Patricia Waldygo for their expert editorial assistance, Dr. Gabriel Stutman for sharing her ideas about the use of toys in working with learning disabled children, and Dr. Judith Gordon, John Reiner, and Tina Rosenbaum at the Summit School, who work with these children every day.

Most of all I am sincerely grateful to my patients and their families for all they have taught me about psychotherapy.

PART 1

INTRODUCTION

The Changing Face of Psychotherapy

MANAGED CARE AND CHILD PSYCHOTHERAPY

The language of child psychotherapy fundamentally changed when therapists contracted with insurance companies and became "service providers." The process of treating children was once regarded as play therapy or the "talking cure," in which therapy was often nondirective and the emphasis was on the relationship between the client and the therapist. The therapist provided a safe holding environment to help the child, in a nondirective way, gain insights into his or her problems and their possible causes. Although this process worked over time, it was perceived by managed care as too lengthy and too expensive. Managed care found it more expeditious to cover measurable, short-term behavioral changes, rather than long-term structural changes in the child's psyche.

Case managers have difficulty understanding how play therapy works or why they should pay a provider to "play" with their client. Many of the treatment plans in this book suggest games to use in treatment. In addition, treatment goals and interventions have been presented in cognitive, solution-focused language. The goal is to describe the treatment process in behavior-focused and measurable language, thereby allowing case managers to relate to what providers are trying to accomplish, rather than being put off by the idea of "play" therapy.

Managed care's overnight rise to dominance brought with it more than just behavioral management. A fundamental concern with cost-effectiveness led logically to the basic business techniques of project management: establishing long-term goals, choosing short-term tasks or objectives to get there, and tracking the process from start to finish. Suddenly, these terms were incorporated into the managed care lexicon and the more psychoanalytic-oriented, nondirective techniques were considered archaic. Gone were concepts such as "working through the resistance," "repetition compulsion," "maintaining a holding environment," and "exploring the underlying transference." Free association, a standard treatment mode since the early days of Freud, was replaced with specific methods that could be charted systematically along a predetermined path to the final achievement of a treatment goal.

Psychotherapists, who spent years studying the giants of psychiatry and mastering the proven techniques of maintaining a sound holding environment, listening, and intervening, suddenly discovered they could not talk to managed care case managers in terms the managers understood. The language of psychotherapy had changed. Mental disorders gave way to behavioral impairments. Patients became "clients," and psychotherapists became "service providers." Now, all terms that suggest long-term treatment, such as "psychoanalysis," "improve client's low self-esteem," or "enhance quality of life," are in danger of being labeled vague and not "medically necessary." Chances are that treatment authorization will be denied.

Managed care is concerned with Axis I impairments. These are disorders normally coded on Axis I of the Multiaxial Assessment System of the Diagnostic and Statistical Manual of Mental Disorders published by the American Psychiatric Association. Managed care does not want to pay for the treatment of irresolvable diagnoses, and Axis II diagnoses are usually considered irresolvable by insurance companies. However, if you have a client with a personality disorder, the diagnosis can legitimately be coded as Axis II, and the behavioral symptoms coded and treated as Axis I impairments. The reason for this is that most, if not all, personality disorders result in Axis I impairments as well. Managed care is also concerned that therapists treating a client for one long-term disorder may be fostering a dependent personality disorder. Therefore, if managed care case managers spot a provider with a cluster of long-term clients, they are more apt to refer future clients to other providers who provide short-term treatment. Goals that are not achievable within three months should be avoided or replaced with more focused, resolvable goals. Managed care wants quick, cost-effective change, using modalities that are consistent with the client's needs. Most insurance companies accept behavioral, solution-focused, brief dynamic, group, medication management or psychopharmacology-based treatments. Prior approvals are normally required for evaluation of medication by a psychiatrist or for psychological testing. Some companies will pay for psychological testing, biofeedback, and hypnosis, sometimes referred to as relaxation technique. Check with each company before using these terms in your outpatient treatment reports. Most insurance companies find the term *relaxation technique* more acceptable than *hypnosis*.

Another potential problem appears to be the idea of a therapeutic alliance between patient and therapist. Although many insurance case managers balk at the term *therapeutic alliance*, "research demonstrates that in successful cognitive-behavioral therapy, patients view the therapy relationship as "crucial in helping them change" (McGinn and Sanderson 1999, p. 6). The development of a positive therapeutic relationship is critical in psychotherapy and is considered most predictive of positive treatment outcome. The therapeutic relationship is even more important in the treatment of children and adolescents. "The therapist must make contact with the child, engage the child, and engender his or her trust if treatment is to be effective" (Knell 1993, p. 46). The current focus appears to be on a more active role for the client in therapy. O'Hanlon (1987) echoes the view of Milton Erickson, noted hypnotherapist, that it is the therapist's responsibility "to create a climate, an atmosphere for change in which people change themselves" (p. 19). Rossi, Ryan, and Sharp (1983) use Erickson's analogy of the starting pistol at a race: "The therapist merely initiates the race by firing the starting pistol; it is the patient who must actually run and win the race" (pp. 102–103).

In child psychotherapy, treatment often extends to parents in family sessions, with and without the child present. William O'Hanlon, author of many books on brief, solution-focused therapy and Ericksonian hypnosis (personal communication 2000), explains that it is important to involve parents of children in treatment in order to disrupt the maladaptive patterns of behavior in the family.

Insurance companies want clients to take a more active role in treatment. They encourage the use of homework assignments and self-help books, as well as referrals to self-help groups. Suggested homework assignments are included in Chapter 25 of this book, self-help books in Chapter 26, self-help groups in Chapter 27, and on-line resources in Chapter 28.

Treatment frequency is usually crisis-driven. Once a week is standard and may temporarily be increased to twice a week. Some companies also may reduce sessions to every other week or once a month as a prelude to termination. Most insurance companies will allow up to ten sessions per treatment plan. If you divide a complex goal into several simpler goals, it is more likely that a case manager will see gradual improvement and authorize further sessions. In the next treatment plan, you can request further sessions for another problem or part of the original problem that remains unresolved.

In today's managed care environment, the players may change without notice to subscribers or providers. One insurance company may gobble up another or assign a subcontractor to handle utilization review and payment or other services. Health Care Financing Administration (HCFA) forms and treatment reports now must be sent to a new company at a new address. Patients and therapists will find out about the changes eventually, but until they do, there is a great deal of confusion. There are no ground rules to cover prior notification.

For example, Aetna was managed by Merit Behavioral Health, which merged with Magellan, and Magellan has now contracted with a capitation company to manage treatment for many of its subscribers, or "covered lives," in New Jersey and Pennsylvania. Capitation companies are paid a set annual fee to handle treatment for an assigned population. The fewer services they provide, the more money the capitation company makes. Although Aetna, Merit, and Magellan may have certified you, you would not be eligible for payment unless you were now a provider for the new capitation company. In another case, one client was notified that her insurance company was bought out by another and her provider was not in the new network. She was given ninety days to find a new network provider. Upon further investigation, it was learned that the notification was a mistake. The insurance company mistakenly sent a number of letters to subscribers. Can you imagine the impact of such an error on the basic trust between client and therapist? At this point, there is no penalty for the insurance companies when they make mistakes. In contrast, when providers miss the deadline for an outpatient treatment report, they are not paid and their client's future sessions are unauthorized.

At the present time, insurance companies keep changing their mailing addresses, and it is up to the providers to keep up with the changes even though they may not have received prior notification. This author suggests making follow-up telephone calls every thirty days. This can be an extremely frustrating task, and often providers do not have the time or energy to track down insurance payments after a full day of treatment sessions.

MEDICAL NECESSITY

Medical necessity is the criterion used by managed care companies to authorize treatment sessions. There are various definitions of *medical necessity* in use today. The term and its meaning are usually published in the insurance companies' provider manuals. Value Options, one of the nation's larger behavioral management organizations, defines medical necessity treatment as "that which is intended to prevent, diagnose, correct, cure, alleviate or preclude deterioration of a diagnosable condition (*ICD*-9 or *DSM-IV*) that threatens life, causes pain or suffering, or results in illness or infirmity" (Value Options Provider Handbook 1999, p. B-2). Medical necessity is usually limited to resolvable issues. The term resolvable is vague and subject to definition by the insurance company's case manager.

There are other qualifications as well. The treatment must also be:

1. Expected to improve the client's condition or level of functioning
2. Consistent with the symptoms, diagnosis, and nationally accepted standards of care
3. Representative of a safe level of service where no effective, less expensive treatment is available

4. Not intended for the convenience of client or provider
5. No more restrictive than necessary to balance safety, effectiveness, and efficiency (Value Options Provider Handbook 1999, p. B-2)

Medical necessity is open to interpretation by a case manager, who determines what is appropriate. For example, in my private practice, one insurance company authorized thirty sessions for one patient and only ten for another with the identical diagnosis.

Frager (2000) stresses, "Medical necessity determination is not a clinical decision, nor is it a clinical concept of relevance to practice. Despite the name it is a kind of code governing the rationing of sessions [and is] open to a good deal of speculation, depending on the benefit plan of the client and the purchaser's contract with the insurance managed care company" (p. 102). She adds, "Most medical necessity guidelines specify clearly that treatment must focus on symptom-reduction and restoration of functioning or the resolution of a specific problem. . . . It is the resolvability clause that managed care companies tend to use when they think they have paid for too many sessions and are looking for a way to deny treatment" (p. 108).

If you feel the authorization decision has been unfairly made, you can usually appeal. Most insurance companies provide for at least two levels of appeal. However, the process is different for each company. It is usually outlined in the provider handbooks or available from the company's provider service center.

WHEN THE APPEAL PROCESS FAILS

It may seem as if insurance companies always have the final word, but that is not true. The National Association of Insurance Commissioners (NAIC) is an organization of insurance regulators from each of the fifty states, the four U.S. territories, and the District of Columbia. NAIC helps insurance regulators protect the interests of insurance consumers.

National Association of Insurance Commissioners
2301 McGee (Suite 800)
Kansas City, MO 64108-2604
(816) 842-3600

If you are an insurance subscriber or a provider and feel that you have been treated unfairly or have an insurance problem that defies resolution, NAIC is a good place to start. It is also available online at www.naic.org. NAIC may refer your problem to a funded consumer representative in your area or to your state insurance department. A list of state insurance departments that will handle your complaint is included in the appendix of this book. Be aware that the process will consume valuable treatment time and, consequently, few complaints are filed since providers fear they will be removed, in retribution, from the insurance company's referral list.

DEVELOPING A COMPREHENSIVE TREATMENT PLAN

This book is a guide for the development of a comprehensive treatment plan for the child, parents, and family, based on a specific diagnosis and presenting problem. It includes essential instructions for tracking patient sessions and alerting you that outpatient treatment reports (OTRs) are due. It also provides instructions for preparing the required treatment progress notes and discharge summary.

The major diagnostic categories listed in the *Diagnostic and Statistical Manual of Mental Disorders*, Fourth Edition (*DSM-IV*), published by the American Psychiatric Association, are discussed. Mental disorders are presented in terms of their manifested behavioral difficulties, since these are more readily understood and accepted by managed care case managers. A comprehensive outline of broad, long-term treatment objectives; measurable, sort-term behavioral goals to be achieved; and possible interventions for your consideration are provided. This book will take you step by step through the authorization process, show you how to monitor payments and authorization dates, and guide you through the required reports and progress notes. Separate treatment plans, not only for the child, but also for the parents or guardians and the entire family, are offered as well.

2

The Paper Trail

PAPER IS STILL KING

In this age of electronics, paper is still king. Under current state laws, the entire treatment process must be documented, from the first phone call to the final discharge summary, on paper. If it has not been well documented, it is judged to have never happened. In addition to the outpatient treatment report (OTR), discussed further on, the forms that you may need include:

1. The Psychosocial Intake Report
2. Medical Management—Psychiatrist's Report
3. Payment and Session Monitor
4. Progress Notes
5. Billing—HCFA-1500 Form
6. Discharge Summary

Chapters 29 and 30 contain a sample form for each of the previous and guidelines for its use. If you are a provider who has contracted with any of the managed care companies, be aware that they have a right to request any of these documents.

Many insurance companies follow the guidelines prepared by the National Committee for Quality Assurance or the Institute for Healthcare Quality, organizations that have researched, developed, and written position papers on each diagnosis. The papers include a description and approved treatment, usually psychotherapy and pharmacology, with a strong emphasis on the cognitive behavioral, interpersonal, and brief dynamic treatment modalities.

The Institute for Healthcare Quality, a subsidiary of Health Risk Management, develops and maintains evidence-based guidelines for clinical decisions by managed care organizations. The guidelines are available in published reports and can be accessed online by computer. The institute's QualityFIRST Behavioral Health Guideline package covers 90 percent of cases encountered in typical behavioral practices, including psychiatric and substance abuse. The guidelines, based on research findings and clinical evidence, cover over 35 behavioral health guidelines and 285 treatments. The institute maintains a staff of board-certified medical experts and allied professionals representing 63 subspecialties, who review guideline decision logic in accordance with standards developed by the Agency for Health Care Policy and Research (AHCPR) and the Institute of Medicine (IOM).

These groups advise insurance companies on the number of treatment sessions that should be authorized, under normal circumstances, for the more prevalent diagnoses. These guidelines are now integrated into the curriculum at more than a dozen medical schools in the United States, where they are changing the way psychotherapy is taught.

Some managed care companies have developed their own detailed formulas as the basis for authorizing sessions. Others say they use "medical necessity," as discussed in Chapter 1, as the criterion.

Author and former case manager Susan Frager (personal communication August 16, 2000) suggests that the number of sessions authorized depends heavily on the company that subscribes with managed care and the employee insurance coverage. No matter which insurance company manages the benefits, everything hinges on the specific policy selected and the power of the subscribing company.

THE OUTPATIENT TREATMENT REPORT

This book will guide you in the preparation of an effective outpatient treatment report. The first step is to formulate a multiaxial assessment. Based upon this assessment, you will establish both broad, long-term objectives and measurable short-term behavioral goals that can be met within a specific time frame. You must be able to estimate when you will reach a short-term behavioral goal and how far away you are from achieving that goal at any given time. There is usually more than one short-term behavioral goal for each diagnosis. The goals must be described as concrete events, since vague objectives are unacceptable.

Part III of this book includes a list of suggested objectives, behavioral goals, and therapist's interventions for each major diagnosis. You can choose those that you consider appropriate for your client. In addition, you can develop and include some of your own goals and interventions. Be sure that they have been explained in behavioral terms and are measurable (see Chapters 3–22).

Managed care companies expect treatment plans to include homework assignments and referrals to self-help groups. See Chapter 25 for suggested homework assignments and Chapter 27 for a listing of telephone numbers for major self-help groups.

By following these guidelines, you will develop a viable behavioral treatment plan for every client, a smoother relationship with behavioral case managers, and outpatient treatment reports that assure optimum treatment certification for your clients. In actual practice, of course, treatment is considerably more complicated than the plans outlined in this book. In order to begin, you must first evaluate each client and develop a multiaxial assessment.

MULTIAXIAL ASSESSMENT

The *DSM-IV* uses a multiaxial system for the comprehensive clinical evaluation of a client. It addresses mental disorders, general medical conditions, psychosocial and environmental problems, and a general level of functioning. As mentioned in Chapter 1, managed care will only pay for diagnoses that it judges to be resolvable. Therefore, the behavioral symptoms of specific Axis II diagnoses should be coded based on Axis I impairments when indicated.

AXIS I: Clinical Disorders and Other Conditions That May Be the Focus of Clinical Attention

Axis I is designated for reporting the various clinical disorders or conditions listed in the *DSM-IV* with the exception of personality disorders and mental retardation, which are reported on Axis II. Also reported on Axis I are other conditions that may be the focus of clinical attention. If a client has two or more mental disorders, they should be reported on Axis I, with the principal diagnosis listed first. If the client has both an Axis I and an Axis II disorder, it is assumed that the Axis I disorder is the principal reason for the office visit, unless otherwise noted. If no Axis II disorder is present, it is coded as V71.09.

Axis I clinical disorders include:

1. Adjustment disorders
2. Anxiety disorders
3. Delirium, dementia, amnesia, and other cognitive disorders
4. Disorders usually first diagnosed in infancy, childhood, or adolescence (*excludes mental retardation, which is coded on Axis II*)
5. Dissociative disorders
6. Eating disorders
7. Factitious disorders
8. Impulse control disorders not otherwise classified

9. Mental disorders due to a general medical condition
10. Mood disorders
11. Sexual and gender identity disorders
12. Sleep disorders
13. Somatoform disorders
14. Other conditions that may be the focus of clinical attention

AXIS II: Personality Disorders and Mental Retardation

Axis II is for reporting personality disorders and mental retardation. It may also be used for recoding maladaptive personality features and defense mechanisms that do not meet the threshold for a personality disorder. Axis II disorders include:

1. Antisocial personality disorder
2. Avoidant personality disorder
3. Borderline personality disorder
4. Dependent personality disorder
5. Histrionic personality disorder
6. Narcissistic personality disorder
7. Obsessive-compulsive personality disorder
8. Paranoid personality disorder
9. Schizoid personality disorder
10. Schizotypal personality disorder
11. Personality disorder not otherwise specified (NOS)
12. Mental retardation

AXIS III: General Medical Conditions

Axis III is provided for general medical conditions that are relevant to the understanding and management of the individual's mental disorder. When a mental disorder is considered to be the direct result of a general medical condition, it should be diagnosed on Axis I. The general medical condition should be coded on Axis III in the following manner: 316 (indicating a psychological factor) affecting *ICD-9-CM* (indicating the general medical condition). (See Appendices F and G of *DSM-IV*, American Psychiatric Association, 1994.)

When the relationship between the general medical condition and the mental symptoms is unclear or insufficient to warrant an Axis I diagnosis of mental disorder due to a general medical condition, the mental disorder should be coded on Axis I and the general medical condition coded on Axis III. If no disorder is coded on Axis III, the word *none* is acceptable. Axis III general medical conditions include:

1. Certain conditions originating in the perinatal period
2. Complications of pregnancy, childbirth, and the puerperium
3. Diseases of the blood and blood-forming organs
4. Diseases of the circulatory system
5. Diseases of the digestive system
6. Diseases of the genitourinary system
7. Diseases of the musculosketal system and connective tissue
8. Diseases of the nervous system and sense organs
9. Diseases of the skin and subcutaneous tissue
10. Endocrine, nutritional, and metabolic diseases and immunity disorders
11. Infectious and parasitic diseases
12. Injury and poisoning
13. Symptoms, signs, and ill-defined conditions

AXIS IV: Psychosocial and Environmental Problems

Psychosocial and environmental problems that may affect the diagnosis, treatment, and prognosis of Axis I and Axis II mental disorders are reported on Axis IV. If more than one psychosocial or environmental problem exists, all that are considered relevant should be listed. Psychosocial and environmental problems include:

1. Economic problems
2. Educational problems
3. Housing problems
4. Occupational problems
5. Problems related to interaction with the legal system or with the criminal justice system
6. Problems related to the social environment
7. Problems with access to health-care services
8. Problems with primary support group
9. Other psychosocial and environmental problems

AXIS V: Global Assessment of Functioning (GAF)

Axis V requires that you score the client on a special Global Assessment of Functioning (GAF) scale. This information is helpful in planning treatment, measuring impact, and predicting outcome. The GAF scale relates only to psychological, social, and occupational functioning and does not include impairment in functioning due to physical or environmental limitations. The GAF rating (1 to 100) is usually followed by the time period reflected by the rating in parenthesis: GAF (current). Usually, insurance companies consider scores lower than 50 as indicative of conditions that are irresolvable and therefore not covered. Scores of 70 or more are regarded as too high to require treatment.

THE GLOBAL ASSESSMENT OF FUNCTIONING (GAF) SCALE

Consider psychological, social, and occupational functioning on a hypothetical continuum of mental health-illness. Do not include impairment in functioning due to physical (or environmental) limitations.

THE GLOBAL ASSESSMENT OF FUNCTIONING (GAF) SCALE

Code   (**Note:** Use intermediate codes when appropriate, e.g., 45, 68, and 72.)

100   **Superior functioning in a wide range of activities, life's problems**
| **never seem to get out of hand, is sought out by others because**
91   **of his or her many positive qualities. No symptoms.**

90   **Absent or minimal symptoms** (e.g., mild anxiety before an
| exam), **good functioning in all areas, interested and involved in**
| **a wide range of activities, socially effective, generally satisfied**
| **with life, no more than everyday problems or concerns** (e.g., an
81   occasional argument with family members).

80   **If symptoms are present, they are transient and expectable**
| **reactions to psychosocial stressors** (e.g., difficulty concentrating
| after family argument); **no more than slight impairment in social,**
| **occupational, or school functioning** (e.g., temporarily falling
71   behind in schoolwork).

70   **Some mild symptoms** (e.g., depressed mood and mild insomnia)
| **OR some difficulty in social, occupational, or school func-**
| **tioning** (e.g., occasional truancy or theft within the household),
| **but generally functioning pretty well, has some meaningful**
61   **interpersonal relationships.**

60   **Moderate symptoms** (e.g., flat affect and circumstantial speech,
| occasional panic attacks) **OR moderate difficulty in social,**
| **occupational, or school functioning** (e.g., few friends, conflicts
51   with peers or co-workers).

50 | **Serious symptoms** (e.g., suicidal ideations, severe obsessional rituals, frequent shoplifting) **OR any serious impairment in social, occupational, or school functioning** (e.g., no friends,
41 | unable to keep a job).

40 | **Some impairment in reality testing or communication** (e.g., speech is at times illogical, obscure, or irrelevant) **OR major impairment in several areas, such as work or school, family relations, judgment, thinking, or mood** (e.g., depressed man avoids friends, neglects family, and is unable to work; child frequently beats up younger children, is defiant at home, and is
31 | failing in school).

30 | **Behavior is considerably influenced by delusions or hallucinations OR serious impairment in communication or judgment** (e.g., sometimes incoherent, acts grossly inappropriately, suicidal preoccupation) **OR inability to function in almost all areas** (e.g., stays in bed all day; no job, home, or friends).
21 |

20 | **Some danger of hurting self or others** (e.g., suicide attempts without clear expectation of death, frequently violent, manic excitement) **OR occasionally fails to maintain minimal personal hygiene** (e.g., smears feces) **OR gross impairment in com-**
11 | **munication** (e.g., largely incoherent or mute).

10 | **Persistent danger of severely hurting self or others** (e.g., recurrent violence) **OR persistent inability to maintain minimal personal hygiene OR suicidal act with clear expectation of**
1 | **death.**

0 | Inadequate information.

EXAMPLES OF MULTIAXIAL EVALUATION

Example 1:

Axis I	296.23	Major Depressive Disorder, Single Episode, Severe without Psychotic Features
	305.00	Alcohol Abuse
Axis II	301.6	Dependent Personality Disorder Frequent use of denial
Axis III	None	
Axis IV		Threat of job loss
Axis V	GAF = 35	(Current)

Example 2:

Axis I	300.4	Dysthymic Disorder
	315.00	Reading Disorder
Axis II	V71.09	No diagnosis
Axis III	382.9	Otitus media recurrent Victim of child neglect
Axis V	GAF = 53	(Current)

Example 3:

Axis I	293.83	Mood Disorder due to Hypothyroidism with Depressive Features
Axis II	V71.09	No diagnosis, histrionic personality features
Axis III	244.9	Hypothyroidism
	365.23	Chronic angle-closure glaucoma
Axis IV		None
Axis V	GAF = 45	(On admission)
	GAF = 65	(At discharge)

Example 4:

Axis I	V61.1	Partner Relational Problem
Axis II	V71.09	No diagnosis
Axis IV		Unemployment
Axis V	GAF = 83	(Highest level past year)

From *Diagnostic and Statistical Manual of Mental Disorders*, 4th Ed. (*DSM-IV*), copyright © 1994 American Psychiatric Association, and reprinted by permission.

PART II

THE TREATMENT PLANS
SPECIAL CHILDHOOD DISORDERS

3

Behavior Disorders

Childhood behavior disorders include Attention Deficit/Hyperactivity Disorder (314.xx), Attention Deficit/Hyperactivity Disorder NOS (314.9), Conduct Disorder (312.8), Oppositional Defiant Disorder (313.81), and Disruptive Behavior NOS (312.9).

Attention Deficit/Hyperactivity Disorder (AD/HD) (314.xx)

Specify:

Combined Type .01
Predominantly Inattentive Type .00
Predominantly Hyperactive-Impulsive Type .01

This disorder is characterized by a persistent pattern of inattention, hyperactivity, or impulsivity that is more frequent or severe than expected, given the child's level of development. Symptoms may appear singly or in combination and are usually displayed before age 7. The diagnosis must be distinguished from age-appropriate behavior of normally active children. For that reason, it is considerably more difficult to diagnose AD/HD in children younger than age 4 or 5. The disorder is substantially more frequent in males than females.

AD/HD deals with three behavioral characteristics: inattention, hyperactivity, and impulsivity, which cause impairment and distress at home, at school, and in social situations. Inattention is marked by failure to pay close attention to details and the tendency to make careless mistakes in schoolwork or other tasks. Work is often messy and without considered thought. There is no follow-through, and tasks are often left uncompleted. Hyperactivity is characterized by fidgeting or failure to remain seated in school, as well as excessive and inappropriate running or climbing. Hyperactivity varies with age and development level and should be diagnosed cautiously in younger children. Toddlers and preschoolers with this disorder are always on the go and into everything; they may dart back and forth and jump or climb on furniture. Although similar, the behavior of school-aged children is less frequent and severe. Impulsivity is manifest by impulsivity, difficulty in delaying responses or taking turns, and often interrupting or intruding on others. Psycho-stimulants are the single most effective intervention in the treatment of AD/HD. Antidepressants are also used. Nonpharmacological interventions are critical for the treatment of low self-esteem and subsequent psychosocial problems associated with the disorder.

ATTENTION DEFICIT/HYPERACTIVITY DISORDER NOS (314.9)

This diagnosis is reserved for disorders with prominent symptoms of inattention or hyperactivity-impulsivity that do not meet the criteria for Attention Deficit/Hyperactivity Disorder.

Behavioral Symptoms
Attention Deficit/Hyperactivity Disorder
Attention Deficit/Hyperactivity Disorder NOS
(severity index: 1, mild; 2, moderate; 3, intense)

<u>Severity</u>

Attention:

1. Fails to pay close attention to details in school or social situations   _____
2. Does not seem to listen when spoken to directly   _____
3. Does not follow through on instructions   _____
4. Fails to finish tasks   _____
5. Has difficulty organizing tasks and activities   _____
6. Avoids or dislikes tasks that require sustained mental effort   _____
7. Loses things that are necessary for tasks and activities   _____
8. Is easily distracted by extraneous stimuli   _____
9. Is forgetful in daily activities   _____

Hyperactivity-Impulsivity

1. Fidgets or squirms in seat _____
2. Cannot remain in seat when expected _____
3. Is inappropriately overactive _____
4. Has subjective feelings of restlessness _____
5. Has difficulty engaging appropriately in leisure activities _____
6. Feels or acts "driven by a motor" _____
7. Talks excessively _____
8. Blurts out answers before questions are completed _____
9. Has difficulty awaiting turn _____
10. Interrupts or intrudes on conversations or activities of others _____

Other Diagnostic Considerations

Conduct Disorder NOS (312.8)
Disruptive Behavior Disorder NOS (312.9)
Generalized Anxiety Disorder (300.02)
Major Depressive Disorder (296.xx)
Obsessive-Compulsive Disorder (300.3)
Oppositional Defiant Disorder (313.8)
Substance Abuse (*see Substance*)

TREATMENT PLAN
ATTENTION DEFICIT/HYPERACTIVITY DISORDER
ATTENTION DEFICIT/HYPERACTIVITY DISORDER NOS

Client: _____   Date: _____

Multiaxial Assessment

Axis I: _____
Axis II: _____
Axis III: _____
Axis IV: _____
Axis V: _____

I. OBJECTIVES OF TREATMENT
    (*select one or more*)

   1. Educate parents about this disorder.
   2. Investigate family history of the disorder.
   3. Help family develop better coping skills.
   4. Increase frustration tolerance.
   5. Reduce aggression and anxiety.
   6. Encourage compliance with educational programs and referrals.
   7. Improve self-esteem.
   8. Reduce irrational beliefs.
   9. Promote socialization.
   10. Reduce alienation.
   11. Assure compliance with medical regimen.
   12. Focus concentration for increased time span.
   13. Develop a balanced life plan.
   14. Develop a discharge plan for coping with everyday life.

II. SHORT-TERM BEHAVIORAL GOALS AND INTERVENTIONS
     (*select goals and interventions appropriate for your client*)

(Note: Separate goals and interventions are provided for A-Parents, B-Child, and C-Family.)

SHORT-TERM BEHAVIORAL GOALS, **A-PARENTS**	THERAPIST'S INTERVENTIONS
Parents collaborate with therapist in development of a treatment plan.	Establish therapeutic alliance with parents to enhance outcome of treatment.
Help therapist understand child's development to get a complete picture.	Assess problem with parents and record a comprehensive history of the child's development in order to accurately assess problems.
Become aware of the diagnosis and what to appropriately expect from the child.	Educate parents about the diagnosis.
Cooperate in building a genogram to identify familial history and its relationship to AD/HD.	Construct a genogram to better understand the family history and its impact on the child (see Genogram, Chapter 23).
Develop awareness of how your personal theory influences cognition of the problem.	Explore parental theory of the problem.
Recognize fears and feelings of negative self-blame related to the problem.	Evaluate parents' fears and negative feelings of self-blame for child's problem.
Learn to reach beyond automatic cognitive reactions in viewing the problem.	Expand parental perspective beyond limited cognitive reactions.
Undergo treatment for underlying problems that may exacerbate child's condition.	Explore for underlying problems in parents, (e.g., anxiety, depression) and treat or refer for therapy (see appropriate treatment plan in *Behavioral Management Guide: Essential Treatment Strategies for Adult Psychotherapy* in Resources for Providers, Chapter 33).
Have child evaluated for preschool special education.	Instruct parents to have preschool-age children evaluated for early intervention (see Early Intervention, Chapter 23).

Agree to allow therapist to confer with child's school to help in development of a comprehensive psycho-educational treatment plan for the child.	Request and receive parental permission to confer with child's teachers and school administrators.
Have child evaluated by neurologist and/or psychiatrist.	Provide referral for child to be seen by neurologist and/or psychiatrist for evaluation and possible medication.
Comply with referral for psychological testing of child.	Provide referral for psychological testing of child to evaluate intellectual capabilities and rule out other diagnostic considerations.
Comply with referral for medical and psychiatric evaluations.	Provide referral for medical and psychiatric evaluations if appropriate.
Buy or rent *Captain's Log* to use at home to help child reduce learning problems and improve self-esteem.	Educate parents who can afford *Captain's Log* (see Therapeutic Games, Chapter 24) on how to intervene with the computerized cognitive training system at home to improve frustration tolerance, reinforce focus, and improve self-esteem. (Note: *Captain's Log* must also be available in therapist's office.)
Learn how to help child learn.	Educate parents on how to break down seemingly impossible tasks into manageable parts and give child positive reinforcement for trying.
As alternative to *Captain's Log*, acquire "Sound Smart" or "Smart Driver" computer software programs for cognitive training at home.	As alternative to *Captain's Log* system, assign parents to use "Sound Smart" or "Smart Driver" software programs at home to improve client's cognitive skills, (i.e., sustained attention, visual tracking, rule following, and planning. See Therapeutic Games, Chapter 24.)

Meet with other parents who are experiencing similar difficulties and share solutions for coping with the problem.	Refer parents to self-help group. (See Self-Help Groups, Chapter 27.)
Read about AD/HD to better understand how to cope with the problem.	Assign reading of books on AD/HD (see *The Attention Deficit Answer Book* or *Taking Charge of ADHD*, Bibliotherapy, Chapter 26).
Make use of community resources.	Educate parents about available community resources (see Self-Help Groups, Chapter 27, and On-Line Resources, Chapter 28).
Discuss and approve termination plan. Resolve termination issues.	Develop a termination plan and discuss issues of separation: anxiety and dependency.

SHORT-TERM BEHAVIORAL GOALS, **B-CHILD**	THERAPIST'S INTERVENTIONS
Engage in play therapy	Engage client in age-appropriate play therapy.
Learn about diagnosis and develop alternate problem-solving strategies.	Educate child about the diagnosis and discuss symptomatology in order to develop alternate problem-solving strategies.
Observe puppets and how they behave. Begin to see new role models.	Shape client behavior by use of puppets (see Behavioral Techniques, Chapter 23).
Learn self-regulatory self-talk.	Have puppet model self-regulatory statements.
Mimic self-regulatory behavior of puppet or graphic.	Have puppet perform self-regulatory tasks with child.
Perform self-regulatory tasks with help of puppet/graphic.	Use puppet to guide child while he/she performs self-regulatory talk.
Develop internalized guide to help perform self-regulatory tasks.	Have puppet silently perform tasks.
Generate alternative solutions.	Use puppet to generate alternative solutions.
Learn to self-monitor behavior.	Have puppet exhibit self-monitoring behavior.
Watch how puppets express feelings.	Display socially acceptable expression of feelings using stickers with puppet.
Learn that it is okay to express feelings.	Reward puppet and praise graphic representation for expressing feelings in the right way.
Mimic puppet or graphics and express feeling.	Have client mimic the puppet or graphic representation to express his/her feelings and reward or praise.
Recognize underlying feelings of anger or depression and express appropriately.	Explore for underlying feelings of anger or depression using puppet or graphics. (See appropriate treatment plan.)

Realize others also feel bad and relate to puppet overcoming the feeling.	Investigate for feelings of low esteem related to AD/HD. Have puppets talk about how they feel and what they can do about it.
Begin to see possible solutions.	Discuss with puppets how they deal with negative feelings.
Identify irrational beliefs.	Through continued play with puppets, explore irrational beliefs about AD/HD.
Reframe beliefs about AD/HD.	Change irrational beliefs by having the puppets discuss the beliefs and develop rational alternatives.
Learn from role modeling and shape new behaviors.	Use puppets to role model appropriate behavior.
Use *Captain's Log* to enhance cognitive skills.	Play *Captain's Log* if available (see Therapeutic Games for Providers, Chapter 24), to improve frustration tolerance, reinforce focused attention, improve self-esteem, and engage in brainstorming problem-solving techniques. (Note: system must also be installed in therapist's office.)
Use "Sound Smart" or "Smart Driver" software at home to improve cognitive skills.	As alternative to *Captain's Log*, assign client to use "Sound Smart" or "Smart Driver" computer software at home. (See Therapeutic Games, Chapter 24.)
Using guided imagery or other relaxation techniques, learn to gain control over feelings.	Use relaxation techniques or guided imagery to help master anxieties. (See Using Guided Imagery to Augment the Play Therapy Process, Behavioral Techniques, Chapter 23.)
Understand anxiety and realize that avoidance does not help.	Teach client the laws of anxiety: not dangerous, not permanent, avoidance increases anxiety.

Communicate life story to therapist.	Use puppet to have client relate the story of his/her life or use *The Storytelling Card Game* (see Therapeutic Games, Chapter 24).
Express suppressed feelings in a nonthreatening environment.	Have client play *The Talking, Feeling, and Doing Game* to understand underlying processes in a nonthreatening way (see Therapeutic Games, Chapter 24).
Understand how trauma may have contributed to existing disorder.	Explore client's background for trauma that may have exacerbated the disorder.
Discuss personal coping mechanisms developed to handle the disorder.	Investigate with client possible patterns of withdrawal used to avoid AD/HD problems.
Recognize and relate how family impacts the problem.	Explore familial impact on the problem.
Significantly improve behavior.	Build client's confidence to level where he/she understands that unfocused behavior can be controlled.
Develop and use an organizational system to complete tasks.	Help client develop and implement an organizational system to help complete tasks.
Learn to prioritize tasks to assure completion of a project.	Teach client how to prioritize tasks.
Recognize triggers of impulsive behavior and learn to think before acting.	Urge client to recognize and confront triggers of impulsive behavior.
Participate in self-help group to increase understanding and control, get feedback from peers.	Refer client to self-help group.
Understand that he/she can deal with these issues and end the termination phase.	Develop a termination plan and explain issues of separation anxiety and dependency.

SHORT-TERM BEHAVIORAL GOALS, **C-FAMILY**	THERAPIST'S INTERVENTIONS
Improve communications among family members.	Conduct family sessions or refer for family therapy to reduce anger and/or alienation and improve communication skills within the family.
Cooperate in amplifying family genogram.	Amplify family genogram created in first family session to help understand family history.
Discuss genogram openly to fully understand family history as it relates to AD/HD.	Discuss genogram to reveal family history and possible family secrets dealing with AD/HD.
Demonstrate boundaries, alliances, triangles, and emotional currents that may exacerbate the problem.	Explore family boundaries using sculpturing, a useful technique for understanding triangulation, alliances, and emotional currents (see Behavioral Techniques, Chapter 23).
Shift focus from problem to possible solutions.	If appropriate, have family imagine a future without the problem and suggest actions that can be taken now to make that future possible.
Think about what treatment outcome would look like. Explain what you would like to see change in other family members when treatment is completed.	Ask family members to think about what they might want to say about each other when treatment is completed.
Family members realize they have the power to make important changes, even if these seem small.	Help family members realize they have an opportunity to do some things differently.
Members are empowered. They recognize that they can create positive change.	Ask family members to relate what they have accomplished in the past week.
Realize that major change is the result of small steps taken one at a time.	Help family identify and prioritize achievable goals.

Enhance understanding of condition and see how other families have handled similar problems.	Assign family to read *Shelly the Hyperactive Turtle* or *Jumpin Jake Settles Down*. (See Bibliotherapy, Chapter 26.)
Make use of available community resources.	Refer family to available groups in the community (see Self-Help Resources, Chapter 27).
Reduce negative communication.	Develop a system of positive reinforcement with family members to interact better with each other and reduce scapegoating.
Family members work together to develop a termination plan.	Discuss termination issues and develop a plan to terminate treatment.

CONDUCT DISORDER (312.8)

Specify: Childhood type

Conduct disorder is marked by the repeated and persistent violation of the basic rights of others or major age-appropriate societal norms or rules. This behavior takes four forms: aggressive conduct that causes or threatens physical harm to others or animals, nonaggressive conduct that causes property loss or damage, deceitfulness or theft, and serious violations of rules. In order to meet the criteria for this diagnosis, three of the four behaviors must be present for twelve months and one behavior for the past six months. The behaviors are usually found in various settings, including home, school, and community. Children with this disorder often initiate aggression and react aggressively toward others. They may bully, threaten, or intimidate others; initiate frequent fights; use a weapon that can cause serious harm (e.g., brick, bottle, knife, gun); act physically cruel to people or animals; confront a victim (e.g., mugging, purse snatching, extortion, armed robbery); force someone into sexual activity (e.g., rape), or commit assault or homicide. The destruction of others' property may include deliberate fire-setting, with intention of causing serious damage, or deliberately destroying property in other ways (e.g., school or church vandalism, smashing car windows, slashing tires). Deceitfulness and theft may include breaking into someone else's house, building, or car; lying or breaking promises to obtain goods or favors or to avoid debts or obligations; or stealing without confronting the victim (e.g., shop-lifting, forgery). Children with this disorder may also violate school and parental rules. They frequently develop a pattern before age 13 of staying out late at night, despite parental objections. There may also be a pattern of running away from home overnight or a history of truancy from school.

There are two subtypes of conduct disorder. Childhood-onset type includes at least one characteristic of the disorder before age 10. These individuals, usually male, are frequently aggressive toward others and have disturbed peer relations. Adolescent-onset type does not show characteristics of the disorder before age 10, and these individuals are less likely to display aggressive behavior or have disturbed peer relations. The ratio of males to females in this type is lower in adolescent-onset than the childhood-onset type.

Conduct Disorder is considered more serious than Oppositional Defiant Disorder, and the prognosis is not as good. Parents may tend to reinforce noncompliant behavior and ignore or punish positive behavior. They may also display antisocial behaviors. There appears to be some relation to marital discord and criticism, conflict, or inconsistency in dealing with the child.

Behavioral Symptoms
Conduct Disorder
(severity index: 1, mild; 2, moderate; 3, intense)

At least three of the following must be present for twelve months, one for the past six months.

<u>Severity</u>

Aggression:

    1. Bullies, threatens, or intimidates others   ————
    2. Initiates fights   ————
    3. Has used a dangerous weapon   ————
    4. Has been physically cruel to people   ————
    5. Has been physically cruel to animals   ————
    6. Has stolen while confronting victim   ————
    7. Has forced someone into sexual activity   ————
    8. Has committed assault or homicide   ————

Destruction of Property:

    9. Has deliberately engaged in fire-setting, with intention to do harm to others or cause serious damage   ————
    10. Has deliberately destroyed the property of others   ————

Deceitfulness/Theft:

    11. Has broken into someone else's house, building, or car   ————
    12. Often lies to obtain goods or favors or to avoid obligations   ————
    13. Has stolen items without confronting victims (shop-lifting)   ————

Rule Violation:

    14. Beginning before age 13, often stays out at night despite parents' objections   ————
    15. Has run away from home twice overnight or once for longer period   ————
    16. Has difficulties with school and may refuse to go   ————

Other Diagnostic Considerations

Adjustment Disorder (309.xx)
Antisocial Personality Disorder (301.7)
Attention-Deficit/Hyperactivity Disorder (314.xx)
Bipolar I Disorder, Manic Episode (296.0x)
Disruptive Behavior Disorder (312.9)
Oppositional Defiant Disorder (313.81)

OPPOSITIONAL DEFIANT DISORDER (313.81)

Oppositional Defiant Disorder is marked by recurrent negative, defiant, disobedient, and hostile behaviors toward authority figures. These last at least six months and are characterized by four of the following: losing temper, arguing with adults, defying adult rules or requests, deliberately doing things to annoy others, blaming others for his/her mistakes or behavior, being easily annoyed by others, being angry and resentful, and being spiteful and vindictive. This diagnosis requires that the stated behaviors occur more often than is typical of others of the same age and development level and must result in impairment in functioning at home and in school. Late onset in adolescence may be the result of normal attempts at individuation. The characteristic defiance may appear as stubbornness, resistance to directions, and unwillingness to give in, compromise, or negotiate with adults or peers. Hostility usually involves verbal aggression, without the physical aggression found in the more serious conduct disorder. Typical behaviors are usually present in the home setting, but may not be evident at school or in the community. Children with this disorder tend to justify their behavior as a response to unreasonable demands or circumstances.

Behavioral Symptoms
Oppositional Defiant Disorder
(severity index: 1, mild; 2, moderate; 3, intense)

A pattern of hostile and defiant behavior lasting six months and including at least four of the following:

	Severity
1. Often loses temper	_____
2. Often argues with adults	_____
3. Often defies adult requests or rules	_____
4. Often deliberately annoys others	_____
5. Often blames others for his/her mistakes/behaviors	_____
6. Is often easily annoyed by others	_____
7. Is often angry and resentful	_____
8. Is often spiteful and vindictive	_____

Other Diagnostic Considerations:

Antisocial Personality Disorder (301.7)
Attention-Deficit/Hyperactivity Disorder (314.xx)
Conduct Disorder (312.8)
Mental Retardation (317, 318.x, 319)

Mood Disorders (296.xx)
Psychotic Disorders (295.xx)

DISRUPTIVE BEHAVIOR DISORDER NOS (312.9)

This category is reserved for disorders with characteristics of Conduct or Oppositional Defiant Disorder that do not fully meet the diagnostic requirements for either Conduct Disorder or Oppositional Defiant Disorder, but involve significant impairment.

TREATMENT PLAN
CONDUCT DISORDER
OPPOSITIONAL DEFIANT DISORDER
DISRUPTIVE BEHAVIOR DISORDER NOS

Client: _____   Date: _____

```
Multiaxial Assessment

Axis I:    _____
Axis II:   _____
Axis III:  _____
Axis IV:   _____
Axis V:    _____
```

I. OBJECTIVES OF TREATMENT
    (*select one or more*)

    1. Educate parents about the disorder.
    2. Investigate family history of the disorder.
    3. Determine any parental psychopathology.
    4. Help family develop better parenting and coping skills.
    5. Reduce anxiety, anger, and depression related to the disorder.
    6. Encourage compliance with educational programs and referrals.
    7. Reduce parental antisocial behavior.
    8. Reduce irrational beliefs.
    9. Improve disruptive environment.
    10. Promote socialization.
    11. Reduce client's antisocial behaviors.
    12. Reduce alienation.
    13. Develop discharge plan for coping with everyday life.

II. SHORT-TERM BEHAVIORAL GOALS AND INTERVENTIONS
    (*select goals and interventions appropriate for your client*)

(Note: Separate goals and interventions are provided for A-Parents, B-Child,
and C-Family.)

SHORT-TERM BEHAVIORAL GOALS, A-PARENTS	THERAPIST'S INTERVENTIONS
Collaborate with therapist in development of a treatment plan	Attempt to establish a therapeutic alliance with parents to enhance outcome of treatment.
Help therapist understand child's development and disorder.	Assess problem with parents and record a comprehensive history of the child's development and the disorder.
Become aware of the diagnosis and what to generally expect from the child.	Educate parents about the diagnosis.
Undergo treatment for individual problems that, in turn, enhances outcome of therapy.	Explore for parental psychopathology (e.g., antisocial behaviors, marital discord, etc.) and refer for treatment or treat (see appropriate treatment plan in *Behavioral Management Guide: Essential Treatment Strategies for Adult Psychotherapy* in Resources for Providers, Chapter 33).
Undergo testing and evaluation for psychiatric medication.	If appropriate, refer parents for psychological testing and psychiatric evaluation.
Become aware of maladaptive messages you are sending to child.	Identify if and how parents model antisocial behaviors that child translates as permission to defy authority.
Recognize your ineffective or inconsistent disciplinary practices.	Assess ineffective or inconsistent practices of discipline.
Develop awareness of how your personal theory influences cognition of the problem.	Explore parental theory of the problem.
Recognize fears and negative self-blame related to the problem.	Evaluate parents' fears and negative self-blame for child's problem.
Learn to reach beyond automatic cognitive reactions in viewing the problem.	Expand parental perspective beyond limited cognitive reactions.

Request early intervention for child.	Explain importance of early intervention for children under school age (see Early Intervention, Chapter 23).
Agree to allow therapist to confer with child's school to help in development of a comprehensive psycho-educational treatment plan for the child.	Request and receive parental permission to confer with child's teachers and school officials.
Attend self-help group to improve parenting skills.	Evaluate parenting skills and, if necessary, refer to parenting skills group. (See Self-Help Groups, Chapter 27.)
Read about and improve parenting skills.	Assign reading of books on positive parenting (see *Making Families Work and What to Do When They Don't* or *Parents Do Make a Difference: How to Raise Kids with Solid Character, Strong Minds, and Caring Hearts*, Bibliotherapy, Chapter 26).
Discover simple strategies to deal with defiant behaviors.	Assign parents to read books on raising defiant children. (See *Try and Make Me* in Bibliotherapy, Chapter 26.)
Make positive use of community resources.	Educate parents about available community resources (see Self-Help Groups and 800 Numbers, Chapter 27).
Discuss termination plan and resolve termination issues.	Develop a termination plan and discuss issues of separation and dependency with parents.

SHORT-TERM BEHAVIORAL GOALS, **B-CHILD**	THERAPIST'S INTERVENTIONS
Engage in play therapy.	Engage child in therapeutic play therapy relationship.
Learn about diagnosis and develop realistic expectations of self.	Educate client about the diagnosis and discuss symptomatology so he/she can adjust self-expectations.
Observe puppets and how they behave. Begin to see new role models.	Shape client behavior by use of puppets (see Behavioral Techniques, Chapter 23).
Watch how puppet expresses feelings.	Display socially acceptable expression of feelings using puppets.
Learn that it is okay to express feelings.	Reward puppet for expressing feelings appropriately.
Mimic puppet in expressing feelings.	Have child mimic the puppet to express his/her feelings.
Recognize underlying feelings of anger or depression and express appropriately.	Explore for underlying feelings of anger or depression using puppets.
Realize others also feel bad and relate to puppet or graphics overcoming the feeling.	Investigate for feelings of low esteem related to conduct problems. Have puppets talk about how they feel and what they can do about it.
Identify irrational beliefs.	Through continued play with puppets, explore irrational beliefs about conduct disorder.
Reframe beliefs about conduct disorder.	Have puppets discuss the beliefs and develop rational alternatives.
Learn by role modeling and shape new behaviors.	Use puppets to role model appropriate behavior.
Provide insight regarding maladaptive behaviors prompted by negative emotions.	Discuss with puppet or graphics how they deal with negative feelings.

Use relaxation techniques and guided imagery to learn to gain control over feelings.	Use guided imagery and relaxation techniques to gain mastery over anxieties (See "Using Guided Imagery to Augment the Play Therapy Process," Behavioral Techniques, Chapter 23).
Understand anxiety and realize that avoidance does not help.	Teach client the laws of anxiety: not dangerous, not permanent, avoidance increases anxiety.
Communicate story of your life to therapist.	Use puppets to have client relate the story of his/her life.
Understand process that gets you into trouble, in order to control acting out.	Teach client about aggressive behavior: (1) oversensitive to hostile cues, (2) attribute hostile intentions to others, therefore, (3) solve problems with aggressive actions, and (4) become rejected by others, contributing to (5) low self-esteem.
Enter treatment for anxiety, depression, or low self-esteem.	Explore for low self-esteem, anxiety, or depression and treat appropriately (see appropriate treatment plan).
Express suppressed feelings in a nonthreatening environment.	Play *The Talking, Feeling, and Doing Game* to understand underlying processes in a nonthreatening way (see Therapeutic Games, Chapter 24).
Understand how trauma may have contributed to existing disorder.	Explore client's background for trauma that may have exacerbated the disorder.
Discuss personal coping mechanisms developed to handle the disorder.	Investigate with client possible patterns that trigger acting out.
Recognize and relate how family impacts the problem.	Explore familial impact on the problem.
Learn positive self-talk.	Teach client positive self-talk to interrupt negative patterns.

Learn new technique for dealing with anxiety.	Teach diaphragmatic breathing to control anxiety (see Behavioral Techniques, Chapter 23).
Learn new techniques for dealing with emotional difficulties.	Use the *Positive Thinking* game to teach how positive self-talk helps control emotional difficulties (see Therapeutic Games, Chapter 24).
Shift focus of attention from problem to accomplishment.	Ask client to describe accomplishments for the past week.
Feel more confident as self-esteem improves.	Compliment client to provide positive reinforcement whenever possible.
Communicate problematic feelings to develop new skills or options.	Use technique of "Pounding Away Bad Feelings" to help child release frustrations (see Behavioral Techniques, Chapter 23).
Attempt to use new control skills in school.	Urge client to use new control skills in the classroom setting.
Report results to therapist.	Provide positive reinforcement when client reports that he/she has spoken up in school. Praise attempt and reward success.
Learn positive problem solving and how famous people have overcome obstacles.	Assign to read or have parents read to child *Anyone Can Bake a Cake* or *The Mad Family Gets Their Mads Out* (see Bibliotherapy, Chapter 26).
Learn new strategies for dealing with aggressive behaviors.	For children 6 and up, assign *Attitude Adjustment in a Box, Self Control in a Box*, or *Motivation in a Box* to learn positive ways to relate to others, simple strategies to reduce acting out, and new behaviors (see Therapeutic Games, Chapter 24).
Learn methods that you can better use to advocate for yourself.	Instruct client in the technique of self-advocacy.

| Understand that he/she can deal with these issues and end treatment successfully. | Develop a termination plan and explain issues of separation anxiety and dependency. |

SHORT-TERM BEHAVIORAL GOALS, **C-FAMILY**	THERAPIST'S INTERVENTIONS
Improve communications among family members.	Conduct family sessions or refer for family therapy to reduce anger and/or alienation and improve communication skills within the family.
Cooperate in amplifying family genogram.	Amplify family genogram created in first family session to help understand family history.
Discuss genogram openly to fully understand family history as it relates to aggression.	Discuss genogram to reveal family history and possible family secrets dealing with aggression.
Demonstrate boundaries, alliances, triangles, and emotional currents that may exacerbate the problem.	Explore family boundaries using sculpturing, a useful technique for understanding triangulation, alliances, and emotional current (see Behavioral Techniques, Chapter 23).
Family members communicate how they handle aggression at home.	Explore sibling rivalry and the ways aggression is handled at home.
Learn new ways to deal with your aggressive behaviors.	Explore how parents manage their own anger and encourage prosocial behaviors to develop family cohesiveness.
Assume responsibility for changing your behavior.	Target problematic behaviors in the family and set realistic goals so family can take responsibility for changing its behaviors.
Realize that major change is the result of small steps taken one at a time.	Help family identify and prioritize achievable goals.
Shift focus from problem to possible solutions.	Have family imagine a future without the problem and suggest actions that can be taken now to make that future possible.

Reduce negative communication.	Develop a system of positive reinforcement with family members to interact better with each other and reduce scapegoating.
Think about what treatment outcome would look like. Explain what you would like to see change in other family members when treatment is completed.	Ask family members to think about what they might want to say about each other when treatment is completed.
Family members realize they have the power to make important changes, even if these seem small.	Help family members realize they have an opportunity to do some things differently.
Members are empowered. They recognize that they can create positive change.	Ask family members to relate what they have accomplished in the past week.
Helps family identify problems, confront them, and work toward new solutions.	Assign homework reading for family. (See *Homemade Books to Help Kids Cope* in Bibliotherapy, Chapter 26).
Make use of available community resources.	Refer family to available resources in the community (see Self-Help Resources, Chapter 27, or On-Line Resources, Chapter 28).
Family members work together to develop termination plan.	Discuss termination issues and develop a plan to terminate treatment.

4

Communication Disorders

Communication Disorders in children include Expressive Language Disorder—Axis I (315.31); Mixed Receptive-Expressive Language Disorder (315.31); Phonological Disorder (315.39); Stuttering (307.0); and Communication Disorder NOS (307.9).

Expressive Language Disorder and Mixed Receptive-Expressive Disorder share the same diagnostic code, 315.31 on Axis I of the *Diagnostic and Statistical Manual of Mental Disorders (DSM-IV)*. If a neurological condition or sensory or speech motor defect exists, it is coded on Axis III (see Chapter 2 for a description of the *DSM-IV* multiaxial assessment system).

EXPRESSIVE LANGUAGE DISORDER—AXIS I (315.31)

Expressive Language Disorder is marked by linguistic impairment, as measured by below normal scores of expressive language development in standardized testing of both nonverbal intellectual capacity and receptive language development. The difficulties interfere with social, as well as academic communication. The problem varies with the severity of the disorder and the age of the child and may include: limited amount of speech, limited range of vocabulary, difficulties in acquiring new words or finding words to express thoughts or ideas, vocabulary errors, shortened sentences, limited or shortened grammatical structures, and slow rate of language development.

There are two types of Expressive Language Disorders: acquired and developmental. The acquired type usually occurs as a result of a neurological or medical problem. The developmental type has no medical origin; children begin talking late in the development cycle and progress slowly.

Developmental Expressive Language Disorder is more common in males than females and is usually apparent by age 3. There may be a family history of the disorder. Culture should be considered, since children growing up in a bilingual family may have difficulty with standardized academic testing. In the acquired type of Expressive Language Disorder, progress depends primarily on the neurological or medical condition that caused the problem.

Behavioral Symptoms
Expressive Language Disorder
(severity index: 1, mild; 2, moderate; 3, intense)

Severity

1. Scores in standardized testing are significantly below normal, both verbally and intellectually   _____
2. Limited vocabulary   _____
3. Errors in tense   _____
4. Difficulty recalling words   _____
5. Difficulty in constructing sentences   _____
6. Inability to produce sentences of age-appropriate length and complexity   _____

(Note: If mental retardation is present, speech problems exceed those usually associated with this disorder.)

MIXED RECEPTIVE-EXPRESSIVE LANGUAGE DISORDER— AXIS I (315.31)

Mixed Receptive-Expressive Language Disorder is characterized by below normal scores for nonverbal or intellectual capacity in standardized testing. The deficit in comprehension distinguishes this disorder from Expressive Language Disorder. Difficulties include those previously listed for expressive language disorder, as well as problems in understanding words or sentences. These difficulties interfere with social or academic achievement. The disorder may be acquired or developed. The acquired type usually occurs because of a neurological or medical problem. In the developmental type, children begin to develop language slowly and advance slowly through the developmental stages.

As with Expressive Language Disorder, culture is an important consideration since children of bilingual families may not score well in standardized test measures.

Behavioral Symptoms
Mixed Receptive—Expressive Language Disorder
(severity index: 1, mild; 2, moderate; 3, intense)

Severity

1. Scores from standardized testing are below normal
   measures, both in receptive and in expressive language
   development   _____
2. Limited vocabulary   _____
3. Errors in tense   _____
4. Difficulty recalling words or learning new ones   _____
5. Difficulty constructing sentences   _____
6. Problems understanding words/sentences   _____
7. Interferes with social communication or academic
   achievement   _____

(Note: If mental retardation is present, the speech and language impairments are excessive for this disorder.)

PHONOLOGICAL DISORDER (315.39)
(Formerly Developmental Articulation Disorder)

Phonological Disorder is characterized by inability or failure to produce expected sounds appropriate for the child's age and dialect. It includes errors in forming, using, representing, or organizing speech sounds and may include substituting one sound for another or sound omission. The disorder significantly interferes with social communication and academic achievement. The severity may range from minor to unintelligibility. Lisping is common.

As with other communicative disorders, culture is a consideration, especially for children from bilingual families. Other problems may be associated with this disorder (e.g., mild retardation, speech motor impairment, hearing, or environmental deprivation). Intelligence, neurological, and audiometric testing are advised.

Behavioral Symptoms
Phonological Disorder
(severity index: 1, mild; 2, moderate; 3, intense)

Severity

1. Fails to produce speech sounds that are appropriate for age
   and dialect (*consider cultural impact*)   _____

2. Errors in production, use, representation, or organization of sounds _____

3. Substitution of one sound for another or omission of sounds _____

4. Interferes with social communication or academic achievement _____

(Note: If mental retardation is present, the speech and language impairments are excessive for this disorder.)

STUTTERING—AXIS I (307.0)

This disorder involves a disturbance in the flow and pattern of speech that is not age-appropriate. The disturbance is marked by frequent or prolonged repetition of sounds or syllables and may include other speech characteristics (e.g., interjections, broken words, silent or audible blocking, circumlocutions, excessive tension in producing words, and monosyllabic whole word repetitions). The disorder interferes with social communication or academic achievement. The speaker may develop a fear of the problem later on, resulting in stress or anxiety, which exacerbates the problem. Onset usually occurs between the ages of 2 and 7, with recovery before age 16. Research shows that about 80 percent of victims recover (*DSM-IV* 1994), with 60 percent recovering spontaneously. The risk of stuttering is significantly higher for children whose first-degree biological relatives have a history of stuttering.

Behavioral Symptoms
Stuttering
(severity index: 1, mild; 2, moderate; 3, intense)

Severity

1. Repetitions of sounds and syllables _____
2. Prolonged sounds _____
3. Interjections or exclamation without grammatical connection _____
4. Broken-up words _____
5. Pauses in speech that are silent or audible _____
6. Substitution of words to avoid problem sounds _____
7. Excessive tension in production of words _____
8. Repetitions of whole words (I-I-I-, he-he-he) _____

COMMUNICATION DISORDER (NOS)—AXIS I (307.9)

This category includes disorders that do not meet the criteria for any specific communication disorder (e.g., abnormal vocal pitch, loudness, tone, quality, or resonance).

Other Diagnostic Considerations

Attention Deficit/Hyperactivity Disorder (314.xx)
Posttraumatic Stress Disorder (309.81)
Separation Anxiety Disorder (309.21)
Social Phobia (300.23)

TREATMENT PLAN
COMMUNICATION DISORDERS

Client: _____   Date: _____

```
┌─────────────────────────────────────┐
│  Multiaxial Assessment               │
│  Axis I:    _____          │
│  Axis II:   _____          │
│  Axis III:  _____          │
│  Axis IV:   _____          │
│  Axis V:    _____          │
└─────────────────────────────────────┘
```

I. OBJECTIVES OF TREATMENT
    (*select one or more*)

1. Educate parents about disorder.
2. Investigate family history of the disorder.
3. Help family develop better coping skills.
4. Reduce anxiety related to this disorder.
5. Encourage compliance with educational programs and referrals.
6. Reduce irrational beliefs.
7. Promote socialization.
8. Reduce alienation.
9. Develop discharge plan for coping with everyday life.

II. SHORT-TERM BEHAVIORAL GOALS AND INTERVENTIONS
    (*select goals and interventions appropriate for your client*)

(Note: Separate goals and interventions are provided for A-Parents, B-Child, and C-Family.)

SHORT-TERM BEHAVIORAL GOALS, **A-PARENTS**	THERAPIST'S INTERVENTIONS
Collaborate with therapist in development of a treatment plan.	Establish therapeutic alliance with parents to enhance outcome of treatment.

Help therapist understand child's development and language problems.	Assess problem with parents and record a comprehensive history of the child's development and language deficits.
Become aware of the diagnosis and what to appropriately expect from the child.	Educate parents about the diagnosis.
Cooperate in building a genogram to identify familial history and its relationship to communicative disorders.	Construct a genogram to better understand the family history and its impact on the child (see Genogram, Chapter 23).
Develop awareness of how your personal theory influences cognition of the problem.	Explore parental theory of the problem.
Recognize fears and feelings of negative self-blame related to the problem.	Evaluate parents' fears and negative feelings of self-blame for child's problem.
Learn to reach beyond automatic cognitive reactions in viewing the problem.	Expand parental perspective beyond limited cognitive reactions.
Undergo treatment for underlying problems, which may exacerbate child's condition.	Explore for underlying problems in parents (e.g., anxiety, depression) and treat or refer for therapy. (See appropriate treatment plan in *Behavioral Management Guide: Essential Treatment Strategies for Adult Psychotherapy* in Resources for Providers, Chapter 33.)
Comply with referral.	If appropriate, refer parents for psychological evaluation.
Agree to allow therapist to confer with child's school to help in development of a comprehensive psycho-educational treatment plan for the child.	For younger children: Request and receive parental permission to confer with child's teachers and school administrators.
Understand importance of early intervention and have child evaluated by Early Intervention Team.	Refer and explain importance of early intervention for younger children. (See Early Intervention, Chapter 23.)

Have child evaluated by speech therapist.	Provide referral for child to be evaluated by speech therapist to determine level of impairment and need for special educational services and early intervention.
Comply with referral for psychological testing of child.	Provide referral for psychological testing of child to evaluate intellectual capabilities and rule out other diagnostic considerations.
Comply with referral for medical and psychiatric evaluations.	Provide referral for medical and psychiatric evaluations if appropriate.
Meet with other parents who are experiencing similar difficulties and share solutions for coping with the problem.	Refer parents to self-help group (see Chapter 27).
Read about communicative disorders to better understand how to cope with the problem.	Assign reading of books on parenting such as *An Ounce of Prevention* or *Good Kids, Difficult Behavior* (see Bibliotherapy, Chapter 26).
Make use of community resources.	Educate parents about available community resources (see Self-Help Groups, Chapter 27, or On-Line Resources, Chapter 28).
Discuss and approve termination plan. Resolve termination issues.	Develop a termination plan and discuss issues of separation anxiety and dependency.

SHORT-TERM BEHAVIORAL GOALS, **B-CHILD**	THERAPIST'S INTERVENTIONS
Engage in play therapy.	Engage child in a therapeutic relationship via play therapy; nonverbal, if required by speech problem.
Learn about diagnosis and develop realistic expectations of self.	Educate child about the diagnosis and discuss symptomatology so he/she can adjust self-expectations.
Observe puppets and how they behave. Begin to see new role models.	Shape client behavior using puppets (see Behavioral Techniques, Chapter 23).
Watch how puppet expresses feelings.	Display socially acceptable expression of feelings, using stickers with puppet.
Learn that it is okay to express feelings.	Reward puppet for expressing feelings in the right way. Use pantomime if necessary.
Mimic puppet and express feeling.	Have client mimic the puppet to express his/her feelings and reward or praise.
Recognize underlying feelings of anger or depression and express appropriately.	Explore for underlying feelings of anger or depression using puppet. If child is depressed or angry, treat (see appropriate treatment plan).
Realize others also feel bad and relate to puppet overcoming the feeling.	Investigate for feelings of low esteem related to communication problems. Have puppet talk about how it feels and what it can do about it.
Begin to see possible solutions.	Discuss with puppet how it deals with negative feelings.
Identify irrational beliefs.	Through continued play with puppet, explore irrational beliefs about communication disorders.
Reframe beliefs about communication disorder.	Change irrational beliefs by having the puppet discuss the beliefs and develop rational alternatives.

Learn from role modeling and shape new behaviors.	Use puppet to role model appropriate behavior.
Using relaxation and guided imagery, learn to gain control over feelings.	Use relaxation techniques and "Using Guided Imagery to Augment the Play Therapy Process," to gain mastery over anxieties (see Behavioral Techniques, Chapter 23).
Understand anxiety and realize that avoidance does not help.	Explain the laws of anxiety: not dangerous, not permanent, avoidance increases anxiety.
Communicate with therapist without using language, if necessary.	Use puppet to have client relate the story of his/her life.
Express suppressed feelings in a nonthreatening environment.	If appropriate for communicative skills, use the *Talking, Feeling, and Doing Game* to understand underlying processes in a nonthreatening way (see Therapeutic Games, Chapter 24).
Understand how trauma may have contributed to existing disorder.	Explore client's background for trauma that may have exacerbated communication disorder.
Discuss personal coping mechanisms developed to handle the disorder.	Investigate with client possible patterns of withdrawal used to avoid communication problems.
Recognize and relate how family affects the problem.	Explore familial impact on the problem.
Learn positive self-talk.	Teach client positive self-talk to interrupt negative patterns.
Learn new technique for dealing with anxiety.	Teach diaphragmatic breathing to control anxiety (see Behavioral Techniques, Chapter 23).
Visualize self with better communication skills.	Use relaxation techniques and guided imagery to help reduce tension and improve communication (see Behavioral Techniques, Chapter 23).

Learn new techniques for dealing with emotional difficulties.	Use the *Positive Thinking Game* for children 9 years old and up to teach how positive self-talk helps control emotional difficulties (see Therapeutic Games, Chapter 24).
Shift focus of attention from problem to accomplishment.	Ask client to describe accomplishments for the past week.
Feel more confident as self-esteem improves.	Compliment client to provide positive reinforcement whenever possible.
Communicate problematic feelings to develop new skills or options.	Use technique of "Pounding Away Bad Feelings" to help child release frustrations (see Behavioral Techniques, Chapter 23).
Attempt to use new communication skills in school.	Urge client to use new communication skills in the classroom setting.
Report results to therapist.	Provide positive reinforcement when client reports that he/she has spoken up in school. Praise attempt and reward success.
Learn positive problem solving and how famous people have overcome obstacles.	Read or have parents read to child *Anybody Can Bake a Cake* (see Bibliotherapy, Chapter 26), or alternate age-appropriate selection.
Learn methods that you can better use to advocate for yourself.	Instruct client in the technique of self-advocacy.
Understand that you can deal with these issues and end the termination phase.	Develop a termination plan and explain issues of separation anxiety and dependency.

SHORT-TERM BEHAVIORAL GOALS, **C-FAMILY**	THERAPIST'S INTERVENTIONS
Improve communications among family members.	Conduct family sessions or refer for family therapy to reduce anger and/or alienation and improve communication skills within the family.
Cooperate in amplifying family genogram.	Amplify family genogram created in first family session to help understand family history.
Discuss genogram openly to fully understand family history as it relates to communication disorders.	Discuss genogram to reveal family history and possible family secrets dealing with communication disorders.
Demonstrate boundaries, alliances, triangles, and emotional currents that may exacerbate the problem.	Explore family boundaries using sculpturing, a useful technique for understanding triangulation, alliances, and emotional currents, without speaking if necessary. (See Behavioral Techniques, Chapter 23.)
Shift focus from problem to possible solutions.	If appropriate, have family imagine a future without the problem and suggest actions that can be taken now to make that future possible.
Think about what treatment outcome would look like. Explain what you would like to see change in other family members when treatment is completed.	Ask family members to think about what they might want to say about each other when treatment is completed.
Family members realize they have the power to make important changes even if these seem small.	Help family members realize they have an opportunity to do some things differently.
Members are empowered. They recognize that they can create positive change.	Ask family members to relate what they have accomplished in the past week.
Realize that major change is the result of small steps taken one at a time.	Help family identify and prioritize achievable goals.

Enhance understanding of condition and see how other families have handled similar problems.	Assign homework reading that family members can read together, i.e., *The Boy Who Wouldn't Speak* or *Cats's Got Your Tongue* (see Bibliotherapy, Chapter 26).
Make use of available community resources.	Refer family to available resources in the community (see Self-Help Groups, Chapter 27 or On-Line Resources, Chapter 28).
Reduce negative communication.	Develop a system of positive reinforcement with family members to interact better with each other and reduce scapegoating.
Family members work together to develop termination plan.	Discuss termination issues and develop a plan to terminate treatment.

5

Elimination Disorders

Elimination disorders in children include Encopresis with Constipation and Incontinence—Axis I (787.6); Encopresis without Constipation and Incontinence—Axis I (307.7); and Enuresis—Axis I (308.6).

ENCOPRESIS WITH CONSTIPATION
AND INCONTINENCE—AXIS I (787.6)
ENCOPRESIS WITHOUT CONSTIPATION
AND INCONTINENCE—AXIS I (307.7)

Encopresis involves the repeated passage of feces, usually involuntary, into the individual's clothing or on some other inappropriate place. The event must occur at least once a month for three months to meet the criteria for this disorder, and occasionally it may be intentional. The chronological or developmental age of the child must be at least 4 years. There are two types of Encopresis. One involves constipation and incontinence overflow, while the other does not. Involuntary Encopresis is often related to constipation, impaction, or retention with subsequent overflow and may develop for psychological reasons (e.g., anxiety, oppositional behaviors, or fear of defecating in special places). Many therapists may be reluctant to treat children with this disorder who are less than 5 years of age, since the problem often clears up by itself.

Behavioral Symptoms
Encopresis with Constipation and Incontinence
Encopresis without Constipation and Incontinence
(severity index: 1, mild; 2, moderate; 3, intense)

(Note: Child must be 4 years old chronologically or developmentally. The condition is not due to a substance such as a laxative or a general medical condition.)

<u>Severity</u>

1. Repeated passage of feces, involuntary or intentional, into inappropriate places (e.g., clothing, floor) _____
2. Occurs once a month for at least three months _____
3. Not due exclusively to the direct physiological effects of a substance _____
4. Feelings of shame _____
5. Fear of rejection _____
6. Attempts to hide accidents _____
7. Ridiculed by peers for disorder _____
8. Socially anxious because of disorder _____
9. Problems with parents over toilet-training issues _____

TREATMENT PLAN
ENCOPRESIS

Client: _____ Date: _____

> Multiaxial Assessment
>
> Axis I: _____
> Axis II: _____
> Axis III: _____
> Axis IV: _____
> Axis V: _____

I. OBJECTIVES OF TREATMENT
    (*select one or more*)

    1. Determine if problem is psychological or organic.
    2. Reduce voluntary or involuntary inappropriate passage of feces.
    3. Reduce feelings of shame and/or anger.
    4. Educate parents about appropriate toilet training.
    5. Reduce fears associated with bowel movements.
    6. Reduce social anxieties.

Other Diagnostic Considerations

Acute Stress Disorder (308.3)
Autistic Disorder (299.00)
Conduct Disorder (312.8)
Developmental Coordination Disorder (315.4)
Dysthymia (300.4)
Generalized Anxiety Disorder (300.02)
Major Depressive Disorder (296.xx)
Mental Retardation (317, 318.0, 318.1, 318.2, 319)
Oppositional Defiant Disorder (313.81)
Reactive Attachment Disorder (313.89)
Separation Anxiety Disorder (309.21)

ENURESIS—AXIS I (308.6)
(specify if nocturnal, diurnal, or both)

Enuresis is characterized by the inappropriate voiding of urine, usually into clothing or bedding. Although usually involuntary, sometimes the urination may be intentional. The criteria for Enuresis specifies that the incontinence must occur at least twice a week for three months or must result in significant distress or impairment in important areas of functioning. The child must have reached a chronological or mental age of 5 years. The incontinence should not be related to a general medical condition or use of a substance such as diuretics. There are two general types of Enuresis. In Primary Enuresis, urinary continence has never been established. In Secondary Enuresis, the problem occurs after the child has established a history of continence. In addition, there are three subtypes. Nocturnal Enuresis is the more common subtype and may be related to a dream of urinating. Diurnal Enuresis is more common in females and usually occurs in the early afternoon on school days. It is sometimes associated with reluctance to use the school toilet facilities because of social anxiety or the preoccupation with school or play activities. The third subtype is defined as a combination of nocturnal and diurnal.

Behavioral Symptoms
Enuresis
(severity index: 1, mild; 2, moderate; 3, intense)

Note: Child must be 5 years old chronologically or developmentally. The condition is not due to a substance such as a diuretic or a general medical condition.

	Severity
1. Repeatedly voids urine into clothes or bedding	_____
2. Incident has occurred twice a week for three months	_____
3. Results in clinically significant distress	_____
4. Causes significant impairment in important areas of functioning	_____

TREATMENT PLAN
ENURESIS

Client: _____   Date: _____

Multiaxial Assessment

Axis I: _____
Axis II: _____
Axis III: _____
Axis IV: _____
Axis V: _____

I. OBJECTIVES OF TREATMENT
   (*select one or more*)

    1. Determine if problem is psychological or organic.
    2. Reduce inappropriate voluntary or involuntary urination.
    3. Reduce feelings of shame and/or anger.
    4. Educate parents about appropriate toilet training.
    5. Reduce fears associated with urination.
    6. Reduce social anxieties.

Other Diagnostic Considerations

Autistic Disorder (299.0)
Childhood Disintegrative Disorder (299.10)
Conduct Disorder (312.8)
Developmental Coordination Disorder (315.4)
Mental Retardation (317, 318.x, 319)
Oppositional Defiant Disorder (313.81)
Reactive Attachment Disorder (313.89)
Separation Anxiety Disorder (309.2)

II. SHORT-TERM BEHAVIORAL GOALS AND INTERVENTIONS
   (*select goals and interventions appropriate for your client*)

(Note: Separate goals and interventions are provided for A-Parents, B-Child, and C-Family.)

SHORT-TERM BEHAVIORAL GOALS, **A-PARENTS**	THERAPIST'S INTERVENTIONS
Have child medically evaluated.	Confirm diagnosis and provide parents with referral to have client evaluated medically to rule out organic problems and evaluate for possible medication. (Although not the technique of choice for most therapists, medication may be advisable in certain circumstances.)
Recognize you are no longer alone in facing this problem, and collaborate with therapist in helping the child.	Establish a therapeutic alliance with parents before seeing child.
Understand that treatment is blameless, and you are not being characterized as failures.	Explain advisability of seeing parents separately.
Undergo treatment for underlying disorder to enhance outcome of therapy.	Investigate for underlying problems in parents and treat or refer for therapy (see appropriate treatment plan in *Behavioral Management Guide: Essential Treatment Strategies for Adult Psychotherapy* in Resources for Providers, Chapter 33).
Provide a complete history of the disorder.	Explore problem without child present to reduce discomfort and eliminate embarrassment.
Discuss and evaluate your toilet-training skills with a professional.	Discuss toilet-training procedures with parents in a nonjudgmental manner.
Learn better toilet-training skills. Share book or videotape with child as appropriate.	Refer parents to read self-help books on toileting and parenting, i.e. *Koko Bear's New Potty* or *An Ounce of Prevention* (see Bibliotherapy, Chapter 26).

Recognize issue of control and possible negative reinforcement.	Help parents recognize that elimination problems can be control issues and that negative reinforcement or bribery is not helpful.
Help construct a genogram to better understand family history associated with elimination disorders.	Construct a genogram to better understand family patterns and interactions (see Genograms, Behavioral Techniques, Chapter 23).
Investigate self-directed anger or anger at child to help see the problem in a more rational way.	Explore parental anger at himself or herself or child and reduce irrational beliefs.
Recognize secondary gains for yourself and the child associated with this disorder.	Explore and reduce secondary gains for both the parents and child associated with the elimination disorder (e.g., control, negative attention).
Learn dry bed training techniques to deal with the elimination disorder, and become less critical, more hopeful that the problem can be overcome.	If the problem is Enuresis, teach parents dry bed training techniques (see Azrin and Fox 1974, in References section).
Attend parenting course or group to enhance their skills.	If appropriate, refer parents to a parenting skills course or self-help group (see Chapter 27).
Keep a record of successes and failures.	Instruct parents to maintain a log of urinary or fecal accidents, without being intrusive, to monitor progress.
Provide rewards to child for successful elimination control. Meet failure with understanding and encouragement to do better next time.	Teach parents to reward child for days without elimination accidents and to be understanding and encouraging about failures.
Review termination plan. Discuss and resolve issues of termination.	Discuss termination plan with parents and deal with issues of separation anxiety and dependence.

SHORT-TERM BEHAVIORAL GOALS, **B-CHILD** (*5-10 YRS*)	THERAPIST'S INTERVENTIONS
Join in therapeutic alliance with therapist.	Establish a separate therapeutic alliance with the child to enhance outcome of treatment.
Explore irrational fears and beliefs about toilet functions.	Initiate play therapy to explore irrational fears about toilet training or use of bathroom. (For girls, see Potty Dotty, which comes with its own toilet; and for boys, anatomically correct dolls. See Therapeutic Games, Chapter 24.) Play provides therapist with information younger children may not be able to verbalize.
Recognize that the doll displays no fear of the toilet.	Shape child's play by having Potty Dotty or male doll approach the toilet.
Learn by role modeling as doll uses toilet without fear or incident.	Provide role model by placing doll on the toilet without negative reaction.
Associate successful use of the toilet with reward.	Provide positive reinforcement for successful use of toilet by Potty Dotty or boy doll.
Realize you are not alone, and that accidents happen even to Potty Dotty or boy doll. Shame and guilt are reduced. Anxieties associated with toilet are ameliorated.	Simulate doll having a toilet accident, and verbalize his/her feelings about it.
Express fears and anxieties about use of the toilet. Recognize irrational beliefs and replace with reality.	Have child mimic dolls to express fears and anxieties over using the toilet. Test feelings against reality and correct irrational beliefs.

Gain added insights into toileting by reading book with parents. Relationship with parents is improved.	With parental help, have child read, or parents read to him/her in a nonthreatening way, book on toileting, i.e., *Koko Bear's New Potty*; if child is encopretic, assign *Clocks and Clowns* or *Dry All Night* (see Bibliotherapy, Chapter 26).
Develop pride in cleanliness and self-control. Feel better about yourself.	Reinforce toileting success and encourage pride in cleanliness and control.
Review termination plans, and resolve associated issues.	Develop termination plan and explain the related issues of separation and dependency.

SHORT-TERM BEHAVIORAL GOALS, **C-FAMILY**	THERAPIST'S INTERVENTIONS
Family communication is improved. Client feels less alienated.	Conduct family sessions or refer for family therapy to improve communications and reduce anger.
Help create a genogram to track history of elimination disorders in family. (About 75% of children with Enuresis have first-degree biological relatives with a history of the disorder.)	Expand and enhance genogram constructed in parental sessions (see Genograms, Behavioral Techniques, Chapter 23).
Learn better ways of coping with this disorder.	Educate family about the disorder and teach new coping skills.
Cooperate in family sculpturing exercise.	Explore family boundaries, alliances, triangles, and emotional currents through family sculpturing (see Family Sculpturing, Behavioral Techniques, Chapter 23).
Shift focus from problem to possible solutions.	If appropriate, have family imagine a future without the problem and suggest actions that can be taken now to make that future possible.
Think about what treatment outcome would look like. Explain what you would like to see change in other family members when treatment is completed.	Ask family members to think about what they might want to say about each other when treatment is completed.
Family members realize they have the power to make important changes, even if these seem small.	Help family members realize they have an opportunity to do some things differently.
Enhance understanding of condition and see how other families have handled similar problems.	Assign homework reading that can help the entire family deal with elimination problems, i.e., *Don't Worry Bear* or *Dry All Night* (see Bibliotherapy, Chapter 26).
Make use of available community resources.	Refer family to available resources in the community (see Self-Help Groups, Chapter 27).

Reduce negative communication.	Develop a system of positive reinforcement with family to interact better with each other and reduce scapegoating.
Family members work together to develop termination plan.	Discuss termination issues and develop plan to terminate treatment.

6

Learning Disorders

Childhood learning disorders include Reading Disorder (315); Mathematics Disorder (315.1); Disorder of Written Expression (315.2); and Learning Disorder NOS (315.9).

Learning disorders are determined by performance that is substantially below expectations on standardized tests in reading, mathematics, or written expression, given the child's age, intelligence level, and education. The problem substantially interferes with academic or social achievement. Although various statistical methods are used to determine when a deficit is significant, "substantially below" is commonly defined as a difference of more than two standard deviations between achievement and IQ. Special care must be taken in individualized testing to ensure that the individual's ethnic or cultural background is considered. If a sensory deficit is present, the learning difficulties should be in excess of those usually associated with it. It is common for Mathematics Disorder and Disorder of Written Expression to occur in combination with Reading Disorder. If more than one learning disorder is present, they should all be coded on Axis I. If a general medical condition, sensory deficit, or neurological problem exists, it should be coded on Axis III.

Reading Disorder, also called dyslexia, is characterized by distortions, omissions, or substitutions of letters or words, resulting in slowness and lack of comprehension. In Mathematics Disorder, various skills may be impaired, including linguistic, perception, attention, or mathematics. In Disorder of Written Expression, various difficulties may exist, such as grammatical and punctuation errors within sentences, poor paragraph organization, multiple spelling errors, and excessively poor handwriting. Poor handwriting or spelling errors, alone, do not rate a diagnosis of Disorder of Written Expression. With the exception of spelling, standardized tests for this are far less advanced than in other learning disorders. In Learning Disorder NOS, problems in reading, mathematics, or written expression may not be sufficient to meet the criteria for a specific disorder, but taken together significantly interfere with academic achievement. Learning disorders must be differentiated from normal variations in academic achievement, as well as academic problems due to lack of opportunity, poor teaching, or cultural factors.

Behavioral Symptoms
Learning Disorders
(severity index: 1, mild; 2, moderate; 3, severe)

<u>Severity</u>

Mathematics Disorder

1. Has difficulty understanding mathematical terms, operations, or concepts   _____
2. Has difficulty translating written problems into mathematical symbols   _____
3. Has difficulty reading or recognizing numerical symbols and arithmetic signs and clustering objects into groups   _____
4. Has difficulty copying numbers or figures correctly, remembering to add in "carried" numbers, and paying attention to operational signs   _____

Reading Disorder

5. Reading is marred by distortions, omissions, or substitutions   _____
6. Reads slowly   _____
7. Reading marked by errors in comprehension   _____

Disorder of Written Expression

8. Excessive grammatical and punctuation errors   _____
9. Poor paragraph organization   _____
10. Multiple spelling errors   _____
11. Excessively poor handwriting   _____

Other Diagnostic Considerations

Communication Disorders
Developmental Coordination Disorder (315.4)
Impaired Vision or Hearing
Mental Retardation (317, 318.x, 319)
Pervasive Development Disorders

TREATMENT PLAN
LEARNING DISORDERS

Client: _____ Date: _____

```
┌─────────────────────────────────────┐
│  Multiaxial Assessment               │
│                                      │
│  Axis I:   _____           │
│  Axis II:  _____           │
│  Axis III: _____           │
│  Axis IV:  _____           │
│  Axis V:   _____           │
└─────────────────────────────────────┘
```

I.   OBJECTIVES OF TREATMENT

1. Educate parents about disorder.
2. Investigate family history of the disorder.
3. Help family develop better coping skills.
4. Reduce anxiety related to this disorder.
5. Encourage compliance with educational programs and referrals.
6. Reduce irrational beliefs.
7. Promote socialization.
8. Reduce alienation.
9. Develop discharge plan for coping with everyday life.

II.   SHORT-TERM BEHAVIORAL GOALS AND INTERVENTIONS
(*select goals and interventions appropriate for your client*)

(Note: Separate goals and interventions are provided for A-Parents, B-Child, and C-Family.)

SHORT-TERM BEHAVIORAL GOALS, **A-PARENTS**	THERAPIST'S INTERVENTIONS
Collaborate with therapist in development of a treatment plan.	Establish therapeutic alliance with parents to enhance outcome of treatment.
Help therapist understand child's learning disorder.	Assess problem with parents and record a comprehensive history of the child's learning disorder.

Become aware of the diagnosis and what to appropriately expect from the child.	Educate parents about the diagnosis.
Cooperate in building a genogram to identify familial history and its relationship to communicative disorders.	Construct a genogram to better understand the family history and its impact on the child (see Genogram, Chapter 23).
Help identify other factors that may contribute to the disorder.	Explore for other possible disorders (e.g., ADHD, depression, anxiety). See appropriate treatment plan.
Develop awareness of how your personal theory influences cognition of the problem.	Explore parental theory of the problem.
Recognize fears and feelings of negative self-blame related to the problem.	Evaluate parents' fears and negative feelings of self-blame for child's problem.
Learn to reach beyond automatic cognitive reactions in viewing the problem.	Expand parental perspective beyond limited cognitive reactions.
Undergo treatment for underlying problems that may exacerbate child's condition.	Explore for underlying problems in parents (e.g., anxiety, depression), and treat or refer for therapy (see appropriate treatment plan in *Behavioral Management Guide: Essential Treatment Strategies for Adult Psychotherapy* in Resources for Providers, Chapter 33).
Comply with referral.	If appropriate, refer parents for psychological evaluation.
Be evaluated for early intervention (preschool special education).	Refer preschool-age children for early intervention (see Early Intervention, Chapter 23).
Agree to allow therapist to confer with child's school to help in development of a comprehensive psycho-educational treatment plan for the child.	For school-age children: Request and receive parental permission to confer with child's teachers and school administrators.

Have child evaluated by school.	Provide referral for child to be evaluated by the school to determine level of impairment and need for special educational services.
Comply with referral for psychological testing of child.	Provide referral for psychological testing of child to evaluate intellectual capabilities and rule out other diagnostic considerations.
Comply with referral for medical and psychiatric evaluations.	Provide referral for medical and psychiatric evaluations, if appropriate.
Buy or rent *Captain's Log* to use at home to help child reduce learning problems and improve self-esteem.	Educate parents who can afford *Captain's Log* (see Therapeutic Games, Chapter 24) on how to intervene with the computerized cognitive training system at home to improve frustration tolerance, reinforce focus, and improve self-esteem. (Note: *Captain's Log* must also be available in therapist's office.)
Learn to help child learn.	Educate parents on how to break down "impossible" tasks into manageable parts and give child positive reinforcement for trying.
As alternative to *Captain's Log*, acquire "Sound Smart" or "Smart Driver" computer software programs for cognitive training at home.	As alternative to *Captain's Log* system, assign parents to use "Sound Smart" or "Smart Driver" software programs at home to improve client's cognitive skills (i.e., sustained attention, visual tracking, rule following, and planning. See Therapeutic Games, Chapter 24.)
Meet with other parents who are experiencing similar difficulties and share solutions for coping with the problem.	Refer parents to self-help group.

Read about learning disorders to better understand how to cope with the problem.	Assign reading of books on learning disorders, *How to Talk So Kids Can Learn* or *Common Solutions for the Uncommon Child* (see Bibliotherapy, Chapter 26).
Make use of community resources.	Educate parents about available community resources (see Self-Help Groups, Chapter 27, or On-Line Resources, Chapter 28).
Discuss and approve termination plan. Resolve termination issues.	Develop a termination plan and discuss issues of separation anxiety and dependency.

SHORT-TERM BEHAVIORAL GOALS, **B-CHILD**	THERAPIST'S INTERVENTIONS
Engage in play therapy	Engage client in a play therapy therapeutic relationship to help develop sustained attention, increase memory, and enhance sensory motor integration (see *Simon* or *Bop It*, Therapeutic Games, Chapter 24).
Learn about diagnosis and develop realistic expectations of self.	Educate client about the diagnosis and discuss symptomatology so he/she can adjust self-expectations.
Observe puppets and how they behave. Begin to see new role models.	Shape client behavior by use of puppets (see Behavioral Techniques, Chapter 23).
Watch how puppet expresses feelings.	Display socially acceptable expression of feelings using puppet.
Learn that it is okay to express feelings.	Reward puppet for expressing feelings in the right way.
Mimic puppet and express feeling.	Have client mimic the puppet to express his/her feelings. Reward or praise.
Recognize underlying feelings of anger or depression and express appropriately.	Explore for underlying feelings of anger or depression using puppet and treat (see appropriate treatment plan).
Realize others also feel bad and relate to puppets in overcoming the feelings.	Investigate for feelings of low esteem related to learning disorder. Have puppets talk about how they feel and what they can do about it.
Begin to see possible solutions.	Discuss with puppets how they deal with negative feelings.
Identify irrational beliefs.	Through continued play with puppets, explore irrational beliefs about learning disorders.
Reframe beliefs about communication disorder.	Change irrational beliefs by having the puppets discuss the beliefs and develop rational alternatives.

Learn from role modeling and shape new behaviors.	Use puppets to role model appropriate behavior.
Using guided imagery or relaxation technique, learn to gain control over feelings.	Use guided imagery or relaxation techniques to gain mastery over anxieties (see "Using Guided Imagery to Augment the Play Therapy Process," Behavioral Techniques, Chapter 23).
Understand anxiety and realize that avoidance does not help.	Teach client the laws of anxiety: not dangerous, not permanent, avoidance increases anxiety.
Communicate with therapist without using language, if necessary.	Use puppet to have client relate the story of his/her life.
Express suppressed feelings in a nonthreatening environment.	If appropriate, use the *Talking, Feeling, and Doing Game* to understand underlying processes in a nonthreatening way (see Therapeutic Games, Chapter 24).
Understand how trauma may have contributed to existing disorder.	Explore client's background for trauma that may have exacerbated the learning disorder.
Discuss personal coping mechanisms developed to handle the disorder.	Investigate with client possible patterns of withdrawal used to avoid learning problems.
Develop tools that make you a better learner.	Educate client on how self-instructional training helps increase skills (e.g., ask self-silent questions about the problem you are trying to solve. What is the most effective way to solve it? Rate the accuracy and quality of performances.)
Learn by imitating therapist.	Demonstrate self-instruction for client to imitate.
Learn problem-solving strategies and feel better about your abilities.	Teach client problem-solving strategies (e.g., silent verbal rehearsals and/or organizational rehearsals).

Have parents work with you around targeted behavior.	Discuss behaviors to be targeted. Have client record targeted behaviors as they affect academic capability.
Learn new techniques for dealing with emotional difficulties.	Use the *Positive Thinking Game* for children 9 years old and up to teach how positive self-talk helps control emotional difficulties (see Therapeutic Games, Chapter 24).
Shift focus of attention from problem to accomplishment.	Ask client to describe accomplishments for the past week.
Feel more confident as self-esteem improves.	Compliment client to provide positive reinforcement whenever possible.
Communicate problematic feelings to develop new skills or options.	Use technique of "Pounding Away Bad Feelings" to help child release frustrations (see Behavioral Techniques, Chapter 23).
Attempt to use new skills in school.	Urge client to use new skills in the classroom setting.
Report results to therapist.	Provide positive reinforcement when client reports that he/she has displayed new learning capabilities in school. Praise attempt and reward success.
Learn positive problem solving and how famous people have overcome obstacles.	For children ages 6 to 12, read or assign to read *Anybody Can Bake a Cake* or *Don't Pop Your Cork on Mondays* (see Bibliotherapy, Chapter 26).
Learn methods that you can better use to advocate for yourself.	Instruct client in the technique of self-advocacy.
Understand that you can deal with these issues and end the termination phase.	Develop a termination plan and explain issues of separation anxiety and dependency.

SHORT-TERM BEHAVIORAL GOALS, **C-FAMILY**	THERAPIST'S INTERVENTIONS
Improve communications among family members.	Conduct family sessions or refer for family therapy to reduce anger and/or alienation and improve communication skills within the family.
Cooperate in amplifying family genogram.	Amplify family genogram created in first family session to help understand parental design.
Discuss genogram openly to fully understand family history as it relates to learning disorders.	Discuss genogram to reveal family history and possible family secrets dealing with learning disorders.
Demonstrate boundaries, alliances, triangles, and emotional currents that may exacerbate the problem.	Explore family boundaries using sculpturing, a useful technique for understanding triangulation, alliances, and emotional currents (see Behavioral Techniques, Chapter 23).
Shift focus from problem to possible solutions.	If appropriate, have family imagine a future without the problem and suggest actions that can be taken now to make that future possible.
Think about what treatment outcome would look like. Explain what you would like to see change in other family members when treatment is completed.	Ask family members to think about what they might want to say about each other when treatment is completed.
Family members realize they have the power to make important changes even if they seem small.	Help family realize they have an opportunity to do some things differently.
Family members are empowered. Recognize you can create positive change.	Ask family members to relate what they have accomplished in the past week.
Realize that major change is the result of small steps taken one at a time.	Help family identify and prioritize achievable goals.

Enhance understanding of condition and see how other families have handled similar problems.	Assign family to read *How to Help Your Child with Homework* or *The Seven Habits of Highly Effective Families* (see Bibliotherapy, Chapter 26).
Make use of available community resources.	Refer family to available resources in the community (see Self-Help Groups, Chapter 27).
Reduce negative communication.	Develop a system of positive reinforcement with family to interact better with each other and reduce scapegoating.
Family works together to develop termination plan.	Discuss termination issues and develop plan to terminate treatment.

7

Development Disorders

Developmental disorders of childhood include Asperger's Disorder—Axis I (299.80); Autistic Disorder—Axis I (299.00); Childhood Disintegrative Disorder—Axis I (200.10); Rett's Disorder—Axis I (299.80); and Pervasive Development Disorder NOS—Axis I (299.80).

These disorders are usually evident during the first years of life and are usually associated with mental retardation. (Mental Retardation is coded on Axis II of the *DSM-IV* multiaxial assessment system.) These disorders involve severe impairment of various areas of development, such as social interaction or communication, as well as the existence of stereotyped behavior, interests, and activities that are inappropriate for the individual's age or development level. They may also be associated with a range of general medical conditions (e.g., chromosomal abnormalities, congenital infections, and structural abnormalities of the central nervous system). These may be coded on Axis III of the *DSM-IV* system.

Children with pervasive development disorders are usually treated in dedicated educational settings. The focus of therapy with these disorders is usually limited to interventions with the parents to help them cope with the problem.

ASPERGER'S DISORDER—AXIS I (299.80)

Asperger's Disorder is characterized by severe impairment in social interaction and limited, repetitive patterns of behavior, interests, and activities. The disorder causes severe impairment in social and educational functioning. There are no significant delays in language, cognitive development, or the development of age-appropriate self-help skills and adaptive behavior. The disorder is more common in males and appears to have a later onset than Autistic Disorder.

Behavioral Symptoms
Asperger's Disorder
(severity index: 1, mild; 2, moderate; 3, intense)

Impairment in social interaction, including at least two of the following:

	Severity
1. Multiple nonverbal behaviors are impaired (body posture, eye-to-eye contact, facial expressions, and use of gestures to regulate social interaction)	_____
2. Inability to develop appropriate peer relationships	_____
3. Fails to spontaneously seek the sharing of enjoyment, interests, or achievements with others	_____
4. Lacks social or emotional reciprocity	_____
5. Preoccupation with one or more stereotyped patterns	_____
6. Interest that is abnormal in focus or intensity	_____
7. Inflexibility in adherence to nonfunctional routines	_____
8. Stereotyped, repetitive motor mannerisms	_____
9. Persistent preoccupation with parts of objects	_____
10. Significant impairment in social and school functioning	_____

AUTISTIC DISORDER—AXIS I (299.00)

Autistic Disorder is marked by abnormal development in communication and social interaction, with a severely restricted range of interests and activities. Approximately 75 percent of children with Autistic Disorder function at a retarded level (IQ 35–50). The disorder is four to five times more prevalent in males, but females with this disorder are more likely to be severely retarded. Although some signs may appear earlier, usual onset is at approximately age 3.

Behavioral Symptoms
Autistic Disorder
(severity index: 1, mild; 2, moderate; 3, intense)

This diagnosis requires six or more of the following symptoms, including at least two from Group A and one each from Groups B and C.

<u>Severity</u>

Group A:

   1. Marked impairment in nonverbal behaviors (e.g.,
      eye-to-eye contact, facial and body postures, gestures to
      regulate social interaction)   _____
   2. Failure to establish peer relationships appropriate for
      developmental level   _____
   3. Lacks ability to share spontaneously with others   _____
   4. Lacks ability for social or emotional interchange   _____

Group B:

   5. Spoken language delayed or nonexistent, with no
      attempt to compensate by other means   _____
   6. Inability to initiate or carry on conversation with others   _____
   7. Repetitive or stereotyped use of language   _____
   8. Lack of ability for spontaneous, age-appropriate play   _____

Group C:

   9. Preoccupied with limited, stereotyped patterns of interest
      of abnormal intensity   _____
  10. Inflexible adherence to non-functional routines   _____
  11. Repetitive motor mannerisms (e.g., body movements,
      finger twisting)   _____

CHILDHOOD DISINTEGRATIVE DISORDER—
AXIS I (200.10)

This disorder is characterized by marked regression, following two years of normal development, in multiple areas of functioning, including: verbal and nonverbal communication, expressive and receptive language, social skills, bowel and bladder control, play, and motor skills. Onset is typically after age 2 and before age 10. Children with disintegrative disorder display many of the deficits seen in autistic disorder, including impairment in social interaction and communication and the development of restricted, stereotyped patterns of behavior and interests. The disorder may be associated with abnormal EEGs and seizure disorders. It is thought to be caused by an insult to the central nervous system.

Behavioral Symptoms
Childhood Disintegrative Disorder
(severity index: 1, mild; 2, moderate; 3, intense)

<u>Severity</u>

1. Normal development from birth to age 2 _____
2. Loss, before age 10, of previous skills, including at least two of the following:

   Expressive or receptive language _____
   Social skills _____
   Adaptive behavior _____
   Bowel or bladder control _____
   Play _____
   Motor skills _____

3. Abnormal functioning in at least two of the following areas:

   Impairment in social interaction _____
   Impairment in communications _____
   Restricted, stereotyped patterns of behavior _____

RETT'S DISORDER—AXIS I (299.80)

Rett's Disorder, usually associated with mental retardation, is characterized by multiple deficits following a period of normal functioning after birth. Following normal psychomotor development through the first five months of life, head growth degenerates and there is a loss of previous hand skills, with the development of stereotyped hand movements. Interest in social interaction gradually diminishes and may later redevelop. Coordination problems develop, and expressive and receptive language developments are severely impaired with psychomotor retardation. Rett's Disorder has been reported only in females and may be accompanied by increased frequency of EEG (electroencephalogram) abnormalities and seizure disorders.

Behavioral Symptoms
Rett's Disorder
(severity index: 1, mild; 2, moderate; 3, intense)

<u>Severity</u>

Birth to age five months:

    1. Normal natal and perinatal development   _____

    2. Normal psychomotor development through age five
       months   _____

    3. Normal head circumference at birth   _____

After age five months:

    4. Deceleration of head growth   _____

    5. Loss of previously acquired hand skills   _____

    6. Stereotypical hand movements (e.g., wringing, washing)   _____

    7. Lack of social interaction   _____

    8. Poor coordination (e.g., gait, trunk movements)   _____

    9. Severely impaired expressive and receptive language
       development   _____

  10. Psychomotor retardation   _____

PERVASIVE DEVELOPMENT DISORDER NOS—AXIS I (299.80)

This category is used for disorders that do not meet the criteria for specific pervasive developmental disorders, but involve severe and pervasive impairment in the development of verbal and nonverbal communication or reciprocal social interaction or the existence of stereotyped behavior, interests, and activities. The disorder may lack the necessary criteria because of age at onset or atypical symptomatology.

Other Diagnostic Considerations

Avoidant Personality Disorder (301.82)
Mental Retardation (317)
Mental Retardation, Severity Unclassified—Axis II (319)
Schizoid Personality Disorder—Axis II (301.20)
Schizophrenia (295.xx)

TREATMENT PLAN
DEVELOPMENT DISORDERS

Client: _____   Date: _____

```
┌─────────────────────────────────────┐
│  Multiaxial Assessment               │
│                                      │
│  Axis I:   _____           │
│  Axis II:  _____           │
│  Axis III: _____           │
│  Axis IV:  _____           │
│  Axis V:   _____           │
└─────────────────────────────────────┘
```

I.   OBJECTIVES OF TREATMENT
     (*select one or more*)

     1. Increase client's social skills.
     2. Reduce bizarre behaviors.
     3. Decrease anxiety, depression.
     4. Reduce ritualistic behaviorisms.
     5. Enhance familial communication.
     6. Reduce scapegoating of "identified client."
     7. Increase social interactions.
     8. Increase positive coping skills.
     9. Teach client to advocate for self.
     10. Control or decrease destructive habits.
     11. Reduce distorted thinking.
     12. Enhance problem-solving ability.
     13. Provide information on resources and self-help groups.

II. SHORT-TERM BEHAVIORAL GOALS AND INTERVENTIONS
     (*select goals and interventions appropriate for your client*)

(NOTE: Separate goals and interventions are provided for A-Parents, B-Child, and C-Family.)

SHORT-TERM BEHAVIORAL GOALS, **A-PARENTS**	THERAPIST'S INTERVENTIONS
Collaborate with therapist to develop a treatment plan and reduce feelings of alienation.	Establish a therapeutic alliance with parents to enhance treatment outcome.
Help therapist understand child's disorder.	Assess problem with parents and take a detailed developmental history of the child to better understand the nature of the disorder.
Cooperate in building genogram.	Construct a genogram to identify familial history of the disorder. Determine if other members had similar problems and how they were handled in the family of origin (see genograms, Behavioral Techniques, Chapter 23).
Become aware of how your personal theory of the problem shapes your cognitions of the problem.	Investigate parents' personal theory of the problem.
Learn to reach beyond limited cognitive reactions to a new perspective on the problem.	Help parents develop a deeper perspective on the problem.
Follow up with referrals.	Refer for medical, neurological, and psychiatric evaluations.
Take medication as prescribed and report side effects.	If medications are prescribed, confirm that prescription has been filled and regimen is followed. Have dosage adjusted if necessary.
Maintain medication journal to help comply with schedule.	Assign parents to keep a medication journal.
Receive treatment for anxiety or depression as necessary.	Explore for underlying problems (e.g., anxiety, depression) and treat if necessary (see appropriate treatment in *Behavioral Management Guide: Essential Treatment Strategies for Adult Psychotherapy* in Resources for Providers, Chapter 33).

Give therapist permission to confer with school officials.	Get permission from parents to confer with child's teachers and school officials.
Help in formulating a psycho-educational program for the child.	Develop a psycho-educational program for the child.
Have child evaluated for early intervention.	If child is not in school, refer for early intervention. (See Early Intervention, Chapter 23.)
Reduce fear and feelings of self-blame.	Explore parental fears and negative feelings of self-blame.
Child becomes less alienated.	Urge parents to include child in family activities.
Siblings learn better ways of dealing with the disorder.	Teach siblings new ways to deal with the problem.
Learn what resources are available and make full use of them.	Educate parents about available community resources to help deal with the problem (see Self-Help Groups and 800 Numbers, Chapter 27, or On-Line Resources, Chapter 28).
Read self-help books to better understand the problem and learn how other parents have dealt with it.	Assign self-help books to help parents deal with the disorder, i.e., *The Hidden Child* or *Keys to Parenting a Child with Autism*. (See Bibliotherapy, Chapter 26.)
Attend self-help group to meet other parents with similar problems. Alienation is reduced.	Refer to self-help group as appropriate. (See Self-Help Groups, Chapter 27.)
Discuss and resolve termination issues with therapist.	Develop termination plan and address issues of separation anxiety and dependency.

SHORT-TERM BEHAVIORAL GOALS, **B-CHILD**	THERAPIST'S INTERVENTIONS
Begin to relate to therapist according to developmental ability.	Attempt to develop therapeutic alliance with child.
View puppets appropriately and imitate the behavior.	Start shaping behavior using puppets.
Start to understand that it is okay to express feelings.	Show puppets expressing feelings.
Realize that there is an appropriate way to express feelings.	Reward or praise puppet for appropriate behavior.
Recognize your irrational beliefs about the disorder.	Using play with puppets, identify irrational beliefs about disorder.
See how puppets reframe their beliefs and copy them.	Have puppets discuss irrational beliefs, test them against reality, and change them.
Learn from role modeling and shape some new behaviors. Develop hope that a solution may be possible.	Use puppets to model other appropriate behaviors.
Undergo treatment for anger, anxiety, or depression.	Explore for underlying feelings of anger, rage, anxiety, or depression (see appropriate treatment plan).
Learn new solutions for dealing with situations that hurt you or make you angry.	If developmentally appropriate, use "Pounding Away Bad Feelings" game to help client express feelings, and develop new solutions (see Behavioral Techniques, Chapter 23). Provide ideas for solutions, if necessary.
Learn new behaviors to deal with problems and also discover how famous people have overcome obstacles.	Select self-help books for parents to read to child, i.e., *My Best Friend Is Me* or *Anybody Can Bake a Cake* (see Bibliotherapy, Chapter 26).
Learn and practice more positive self-talk.	Investigate irrational self-destructive thoughts.
Through play therapy, learn how positive self-talk helps control emotional difficulties.	Play the *Positive Thinking Game* (see Therapeutic Games, Chapter 24).

Describe your relationship with your brother or sister and understand how it impacts your lives.	If appropriate, investigate sibling relations.
Understand and successfully handle termination issues.	Develop a termination plan and explain issues of separation anxiety and dependency, in order to bring treatment to a successful closure.

SHORT-TERM BEHAVIORAL GOALS, **C-FAMILY**	THERAPIST'S INTERVENTIONS
Improve family communication and reduce alienation.	Conduct family sessions, including client and sibling/s, or refer to family therapist.
Help create genogram and describe family history.	Construct genogram (see Behavioral Techniques, Chapter 23) or expand and discuss genogram from parental session to help understand family history and bring hidden issues into the open.
Participate in family sculpturing to better understand relationships.	Explore family boundaries through sculpturing (see Behavioral Techniques, Chapter 23) and identify triangles and emotional currents.
Realize and verbalize hidden feelings.	Explore feelings of rage or shame over family problems and issues.
Recognize the feelings of other family members	Conduct family role-playing exercises to clarify relationships and family dynamics.
Family members realign themselves to reflect how they would like the family to be.	Investigate how the family would like to change the system, and have family members realign themselves within the structure.
Focus on solutions instead of problems.	Have family members imagine how they would like to function when treatment is completed.
Recognize what life would be like at the end of treatment and understand how the lives of all family members will change.	Ask family members to verbalize three things they would like to say about each family member when therapy is completed.
Use family outing to practice new knowledge and insights and enhance relationships.	Assign family outings to include all family members.
Discuss termination issues.	Develop a treatment plan with family and discuss issues of termination.

8

Selective Mutism—Axis I (313.23)

Selective Mutism is characterized by the persistent failure to speak in certain situations (e.g., school, social interaction) in which speech is expected. Children with this disorder usually communicate by gestures or in monosyllables or short utterances. The condition must exist for more than one month to meet the criteria for this disorder, excluding the first month of school, where many children are reluctant to talk up. In addition, the problem should not be related to stuttering, pervasive development disorders, or psychiatric disorders. Other features of the disorder may include shyness, social embarrassment, isolation, clinging, compulsive traits, oppositional behavior, or temper tantrums. Children with this disorder usually have normal language skills.

There are two general types of Selective Mutism. The first is withdrawn, shy, or manipulative. The other type is tense and anxious. The disorder may be related to general medical problems. Selective Mutism is less common in females than males. Onset is commonly at about age 5 and usually persists for a few months, but in some cases may continue for longer periods.

Behavioral Symptoms
Selective Mutism
(severity index: 1, mild; 2, moderate; 3, intense)

<u>Severity</u>

1. Persistent failure to speak in certain social situations, despite being able to speak in others   _____

2. Condition has persisted for more than one month, excluding the first month of school
3. Client appears shy and withdrawn   _____
4. Client appears tense and anxious   _____
5. Client is compulsive or clinging   _____
6. Communicates with gestures or monosyllables   _____
7. Displays oppositional behaviors or temper tantrums   _____

Other Diagnostic Considerations

Autistic Disorder (299.0)
Childhood Disintegrative Disorder (219.10)
Conduct Disorder (312.8)
Developmental Coordination Disorder (315.4)
Expressive Language Disorder (315.31)
Mental Retardation (317, 318.xx, 319)
Mixed Receptive-Expressive Language Disorder (315.31)
Oppositional Defiant Disorder (315.81)
Phonological Disorder (315.19)
Stuttering (307.0)

TREATMENT PLAN
SELECTIVE MUTISM

Client: _____   Date: _____

```
┌─────────────────────────────────────┐
│  Multiaxial Assessment              │
│                                     │
│  Axis I:   _____          │
│  Axis II:  _____          │
│  Axis III: _____          │
│  Axis IV:  _____          │
│  Axis V:   _____          │
│                                     │
└─────────────────────────────────────┘
```

I.   OBJECTIVES OF TREATMENT
     (*select one or more*)

     1. Reduce fear of speaking.
     2. Eliminate interpersonal fears.
     3. Increase positive coping skills.
     4. Control shame or fear of ridicule.
     5. Enhance familial communication.
     6. Increase client's social skills.
     7. Strengthen self-esteem.
     8. Reduce scapegoating of "identified client."
     9. Reduce excessive shyness.
     10. Develop feelings of adequacy in social situations.
     11. Increase positive coping skills.
     12. Teach parents how to deal with the child's problem.
     13. Provide information on resources and self-help groups.

II. SHORT-TERM BEHAVIORAL GOALS AND INTERVENTIONS
     (*select goals and interventions appropriate for your client*)

(Note: Separate goals and interventions are provided for A-Parents, B-Child, and C-Family.)

SHORT-TERM BEHAVIORAL GOALS, **A-PARENTS**	THERAPIST'S INTERVENTIONS
Collaborate with therapist in establishing a therapeutic alliance.	Establish therapeutic alliance with parents to enhance outcome of treatment.
Help therapist understand child's problem.	Assess problem and develop a detailed history of the child's mutism.
Become aware of the diagnosis and what to appropriately expect from the child.	Educate parents about the diagnosis.
Cooperate in building a genogram to identify familial history and its relationship to communicative disorders.	Construct a genogram to better understand the family history and its impact on the child (see Genogram, Behavioral Techniques, Chapter 23).
Cooperate in investigation of possible disorders and undergo treatment as required.	Evaluate parents for underlying disorders (e.g., anxiety, depression), and treat as required. (See appropriate treatment plan in *Behavioral Management Guide: Essential Treatment Strategies for Adult Psychotherapy* in Resources for Providers, Chapter 33).
Get a better understanding of your underlying feelings about the child's problem. Relate situations in which the symptoms seem to appear.	Explore parents' view of the underlying feelings about Selective Mutism and determine the times and places that the symptoms seem to appear.
Curtail questioning child about refusal to talk and reduce pressure on the child.	Encourage parents not to question child about refusal to talk and reduce pressure on the child.
Realize that mutism is often a way for the child to gain control over his/her environment.	Educate parents that mutism is often a child's way to control his/her threatening environment.
Take child for medical examination to rule out other diagnoses.	Refer for medical and hearing examination, including neurological studies, to rule out other diagnoses.

Develop awareness of how your personal theory influences cognition of the problem.	Explore parental theory of the problem.
Recognize fears and feelings of negative self-blame related to the problem.	Evaluate parents' fears and negative feelings of self-blame for child's problem.
Learn to reach beyond automatic cognitive reactions in viewing the problem.	Expand parental perspective beyond limited cognitive reactions.
Comply with referral.	If appropriate, refer parents for psychiatric evaluation.
Understand importance of early intervention.	Explain importance of early intervention for younger children (see Early Intervention, Chapter 23).
Agree to allow therapist to confer with child's school to help in development of a comprehensive psycho-educational treatment plan for the child.	Request and receive parental permission to confer with child's teachers and school administrators, if age-appropriate.
Comply with referral for psychological testing of child.	Provide referral for psychological testing of child to evaluate intellectual capabilities and rule out other diagnostic considerations.
Meet with other parents who are experiencing similar difficulties and share solutions for coping with the problem.	Refer parents to self-help group (see Chapter 27).
Read about parenting to better understand how to cope with the problem.	Assign reading of books on parenting, such as *How to Talk So Kids Will Listen and Listen So Kids Will Talk* or *It's Nobody's Fault* (see Bibliotherapy, Chapter 26).
Make use of community resources.	Educate parents about available community resources (see Self-Help Groups, Chapter 27, or On-Line Resources, Chapter 28).

Discuss and approve termination plan. Resolve termination issues.	Develop a termination plan and discuss issues of separation anxiety and dependency.

SHORT-TERM BEHAVIORAL GOALS, **B-CHILD**	THERAPIST'S INTERVENTIONS
Engage in play therapy.	Engage client in a therapeutic play therapy relationship, nonverbal if necessary.
Learn about diagnosis and develop realistic expectations of self.	Educate client about the diagnosis and discuss symptomatology so he/she can adjust self-expectations.
Undergo treatment for underlying disorder as necessary.	Explore for underlying disorders (e.g., anxiety, depression) and treat as necessary (see appropriate treatment plan).
Through play, enhance relationship with therapist while developing sensory motor integration and other skills.	With children over 8 years old, play *Bop It* to enhance the relationship, develop sensory motor integration, and increase sustained attention and cognitive flexibility without the use of language (see Therapeutic Games, Chapter 24).
Recognize that talking may be hard at first, but will get progressively easier.	Explain to puppets that talking may be difficult at first, but will get easier.
Become involved in treatment while increasing skills.	Play *Simon* with children over 7 (see Therapeutic Games, Chapter 24).
Learn new ways to deal with anxiety.	Use guided imagery and relaxation techniques to help master anxiety (see "Using Guided Imagery to Augment the Play Therapy Process," Behavioral Techniques, Chapter 23).
Read or have parents read self-help books to you.	Assign client to read or have parents read to him/her *Anybody Can Bake a Cake, Getting Along with Myself,* or *My Best Friend Is Me* (see Bibliotherapy, Chapter 26).

SHORT-TERM BEHAVIORAL GOALS, **C-FAMILY**	THERAPIST'S INTERVENTIONS
Improve communications among family members.	Conduct family sessions or refer for family therapy to reduce anger and/or alienation and improve communication skills within the family.
Cooperate in amplifying family genogram.	Amplify family genogram, created in first family session, to help understand parental history.
Discuss genogram openly to fully understand family history as it relates to the disorder.	Discuss genogram to reveal family history and possible family secrets dealing with Selective Mutism.
Demonstrate boundaries, alliances, triangles, and emotional currents that may exacerbate the problem.	Explore family boundaries using sculpturing, a useful technique for understanding triangulation, alliances, and emotional currents, without speaking if necessary (see Behavioral Techniques, Chapter 23).
Family members share feelings about the problem and explore possible solutions.	Explore each family member's personal view of the problem and possible solutions.
Shift focus from problem to possible solutions.	If appropriate, have family imagine a future without the problem and suggest actions that can be taken now to make that future possible.
Think about what treatment outcome would look like. Explain what you would like to see change in other family members when treatment is completed.	Ask family members to think about what they might want to say about each other when treatment is completed.
Family members realize they have the power to make important changes, even if these seem small.	Help family members realize they have an opportunity to do some things differently.
Members are empowered. They recognize that they can create positive change.	Ask family members to relate what they have accomplished in the past week.

Realize that major change is the result of small steps taken one at a time.	Help family identify and prioritize achievable goals.
Read assigned book and schedule activities to reduce alienation of the "identified patient."	Assign as homework reading *Museum Visits and Activities for Family Life Enrichment* (see Bibliotherapy, Chapter 26).
Make use of available community resources.	Refer family to available resources in the community. (See Self-Help Groups, Chapter 27, or On-Line Resources, Chapter 28.)
Reduce negative communication.	Develop a system of positive reinforcement with family members to interact better with each other and reduce scapegoating.
Family members work together to develop termination plan.	Discuss termination issues and develop plan to terminate treatment.

9

Separation Anxiety Disorder

Specify: Early Onset (before age 6)

Separation Anxiety Disorder involves excessive anxiety about being separated from home or a major attachment figure. The anxiety is beyond that considered appropriate for the child's development level. It must occur before age 18 and persist for at least four weeks to meet the requirements for this diagnosis.

Children with this disorder often fear being lost and never returning to their parents. They are usually uncomfortable traveling by themselves away from home or other familiar areas and may be reluctant or refuse to go to school or camp, visit or sleep at the house of a friend, or go on errands alone. These children may be unable to stay in a room by themselves and may display clinging behavior or shadow a parent around the house. Their refusal to attend school leads to major academic difficulties, as well as to social withdrawal.

They typically have difficulty at bedtime and may insist that someone stay with them until they fall asleep. If they awaken during the night, they may make their way to the bed of their parents or a sibling. Nightmares usually focus on fear of destruction of the family by catastrophe. If separation is imminent, physical complaints usually include headaches, nausea, or vomiting in younger children. Palpitations, dizziness, or feeling faint are more common in older children.

Children with this disorder may be demanding, intrusive, and in need of constant attention. Their demands may lead to parental frustration, as well as to resentment and conflict in the family.

This diagnosis should not be made if the anxiety occurs exclusively during the course of a Pervasive Development Disorder, Schizophrenia, or other Psychotic Disorder in children or is better accounted for by Panic Disorder with Agoraphobia in adolescents.

Behavioral Symptoms
Separation Anxiety Disorder
(severity index: 1, mild, 2, moderate, 3, intense)

Severity

1. Excessive and inappropriate anxiety when separated from home or major attachment figure _____
2. Persistent fear of losing major attachment figures or of harm coming to them _____
3. Persistent worry that a catastrophic event will result in separation from attachment figure _____
4. Reluctance or refusal to leave home or go to school due to fear of separation _____
5. Fear of being alone _____
6. Fear of going to sleep without closeness of an attachment figure _____
7. Repeated nightmares focused on separation by catastrophe _____
8. Somatization in anticipation of imminent separation _____
9. Symptoms persist for four weeks or more _____
10. Symptoms cause significant distress in academic and social functioning _____

Other Diagnostic Considerations

Generalized Anxiety Disorder (300.02)
Panic Disorder with Agoraphobia (300.21)
Pervasive Development Disorder (299.80)
Psychotic Disorders (298.9)
Schizophrenia (295.xx)

TREATMENT PLAN
SEPARATION ANXIETY DISORDER

Client: _____ Date: _____

```
Multiaxial Assessment

Axis I:    _____
Axis II:   _____
Axis III:  _____
Axis IV:   _____
Axis V:    _____
```

I. OBJECTIVES OF TREATMENT
(*select one or more*)

1. Educate parents about the disorder.
2. Determine family history of the disorder.
3. Help family develop better coping skills.
4. Reduce pervasive anxiety and worry.
5. Diminish symptoms of anxiety.
6. Encourage compliance with educational programs and referrals.
7. Reduce irrational beliefs, fears of loss, and catastrophe.
8. Reduce fear of being alone, promote socialization.
9. Encourage school attendance, reduce alienation.
10. Eliminate nightmares, establish normal bedtime routine.
11. Restore child and family to optimum level of functioning.
12. Develop discharge plan for coping with everyday life.

II. SHORT-TERM BEHAVIORAL GOALS AND INTERVENTIONS
(*select goals and interventions appropriate for your client*)

(Note: Separate goals and interventions are provided for treatment of A-Parents, B-Child, and C-Family.)

SHORT-TERM BEHAVIORAL GOALS **A-PARENTS**	THERAPIST'S INTERVENTIONS
Parents collaborate with therapist in the development of a treatment plan.	Establish therapeutic alliance with parents to enhance outcome of treatment.

Help therapist understand child's development of anxiety problems.	Assess problem with parents and record a comprehensive history of the child's development and separation anxiety problems.
Become aware of the diagnosis and what to appropriately expect from the child.	Educate parents about the diagnosis.
Cooperate in building a genogram to identify familial history and its relationship to separation anxiety problems.	Construct a genogram to better understand the family history and define how family deals with separation anxiety and its impact on the child (see Behavioral Techniques, Chapter 23).
Enter treatment for Anxiety Disorder, if appropriate, to enhance outcome of child's therapy.	Evaluate parents for anxiety and social phobia problems and treat or refer for treatment as appropriate (for treatment plan see *Behavioral Management Guide: Essential Treatment Strategies for Adult Psychotherapy*, Resources for Providers, Chapter 33).
Develop awareness of how your personal theory influences cognition of the problem in child.	Explore parental theory of the problem.
Parents are treated and educated about developmentally appropriate separation anxiety.	Explore extent of problem to rule out developmentally appropriate anxiety. If positive, abort interventions with child and instead treat parents.
Recognize fears and feelings of negative self-blame related to the problem.	Evaluate parents' fears and negative feelings of self-blame for child's problem.
Learn to reach beyond automatic cognitive reactions in viewing the problem.	Expand parental perspective beyond limited cognitive reactions.
Identify fears you may have in "letting go" of the child.	Explore parental anxieties and secondary gains of not encouraging child to separate appropriately.

Learn how to help your child deal with stressors.	Teach parents the laws of anxiety: not permanent, not dangerous, and reduced by child confronting the problem. Exposure can produce growth.
Read about how to stop emotional and behavioral symptoms before they become major problems.	Assign parents to read *An Ounce of Prevention: How Parents Can Stop Childhood Behavioral and Emotional Problems before They Start* (see Bibliotherapy, Chapter 26).
Learn how to deal with child's sleep disorder.	Investigate for sleep problems in child and teach parents how to deal with it (see Sleep Disorders, Chapter 24).
Confront thoughts of exaggerated and unrealistic consequences—"What ifs?"	Guide parents in confronting distorted reactions to trigger situations.
Identify cognitive distortions.	Weigh the reactions against evidence-based reality.
Restructure distortions with evidence-based consequences.	With parents, reframe distortions with reality-based reactions to stressors.
Learn diaphragmatic breathing as a relaxation technique and teach child to help in relaxation.	Teach parents diaphragmatic breathing to assist child in relaxation (see Behavioral Techniques, Chapter 23).
Comply with referral for psychological testing of child.	Provide referral for psychological testing of child to evaluate intellectual capabilities and rule out other diagnostic considerations.
Understand importance of early intervention.	Explain importance of and refer for early intervention when child is preschool age (see Early Intervention, Chapter 23).

Agree to allow therapist to confer with child's school to help in development of a comprehensive psycho-educational treatment plan for the child.	Request and receive parental permission to confer with child's teachers and school administrators.
Comply with referral for medical and psychiatric evaluations.	Provide referral for medical and psychiatric evaluations, if appropriate.
Parents read to child, improving their relationship while learning new coping skills.for dealing with anxiety.	Assign parents books they can read to their child to enhance their relationship while increasing their coping skills, such as *Sometimes I'm Afraid* or *Linda Saves the Day* (see Bibliotherapy, Chapter 26).
Parents develop new parenting skills.	Assign parents to read books on how to deal with their anxiety and increase parenting skills, such as *Making Families Work and What to Do When They Don't* and others (see Bibliotherapy, Chapter 26).
Monitor child's medication schedule and report all reactions or failures to take meds.	If child is on meds, instruct parents on need for a regular schedule and feedback that may indicate need for revised dosage.
Meet with other parents who are experiencing similar difficulties, and share solutions for coping with the problem.	Refer parents to self-help group or group on parenting skills (see Chapter 27).
Read about anxiety disorders to better understand how to cope.	Assign books on anxiety disorders, such as *Your Anxious Child* (see Bibliotherapy for Parents, Chapter 26).
Discuss termination plan and resolve related issues.	Develop a termination plan and discuss issues of separation anxiety and dependency.

SHORT-TERM BEHAVIORAL GOALS, **B-CHILD**	THERAPIST'S INTERVENTIONS
Engage in play therapy.	Engage child in a therapeutic relationship via play therapy. (Note: Child may need attachment figure in room during early stages of treatment.)
Undergo treatment for sleep disorder.	Investigate for sleep disorder and treat if necessary (see appropriate treatment plan).
Understand underlying dynamics that lead to maladaptive behavior and stress.	Explore ways in which anxieties manifest themselves (e.g., fear of leaving home, catastrophe befalling parents or other attachment figure, etc.).
Realize that human beings are not perfect, and reduce stressors imposed on self.	Teach child that human beings are not perfect.
Recognize underlying feelings of anger or depression and express appropriately.	Explore for underlying feelings of anger or depression, using puppet or graphics (see appropriate treatment plan).
Observe puppets and how they behave. Begin to see how new role models deal with anxieties.	Shape client behavior by use of puppets (see Behavioral Techniques, Chapter 23).
Watch how puppet expresses feelings about anxieties.	Display socially acceptable expression of feelings about anxieties, using stickers with puppet.
Learn new ways to handle fears.	Use puppet to role model successful ways to deal with fears.
Realize others also feel bad and relate to puppets overcoming the feeling.	Investigate for feelings of low esteem related to anxiety. Have puppets talk about how they feel and what they can do about it.
Begin to see possible solutions.	Discuss through puppets how they deal with negative feelings.

Identify irrational beliefs.	Through continued play with puppets, explore irrational beliefs about fears and anxieties.
Reframe beliefs about fears and anxieties.	Change irrational beliefs by having the puppets discuss the beliefs and develop rational alternatives.
Learn from role modeling and shape new behaviors.	Use puppets to role model appropriate behavior.
Using relaxation techniques and guided imagery, learn to gain control over feelings.	Teach relaxation techniques and guided imagery to master anxieties (see "Using Guided Imagery to Augment the Play Therapy Process," Behavioral Techniques, Chapter 23).
Understand anxiety and realize that avoidance does not help.	Teach child the dynamics of anxiety: It is not dangerous, not permanent, avoidance increases anxiety. Exposure can promote change.
Communicate life story to therapist.	Use puppet to have child relate the story of his/her life or play *Lifestories* (see Therapeutic Games, Chapter 24).
Express suppressed feelings in a nonthreatening environment.	Play the *Talking, Feeling, and Doing Game* to understand underlying processes in a nonthreatening way (see Therapeutic Games, Chapter 24).
Understand how trauma may have contributed to existing disorder.	Explore client's background for trauma that may have exacerbated the disorder.
Discuss personal coping mechanisms developed to avoid anxieties and stay at home or with parents.	Investigate with child possible patterns of withdrawal used to avoid anxieties and stay with parents.
Recognize and relate how family affects the problem.	Explore familial impact on the problem.

Somatization problems are treated.	Explore for somatization problems and treat (see appropriate treatment plan).
Learn positive self-talk.	Teach child positive self-talk to interrupt negative patterns.
Learn new technique for dealing with anxiety.	Teach diaphragmatic breathing to control anxiety (see Behavioral Techniques, Chapter 23).
Learn to nurture yourself and deal with emotional difficulties.	Play the *Anxiety Management Game* or *The Ungame* to teach ways positive self-talk helps control emotional difficulties (see Therapeutic Games, Chapter 24).
Shift focus of attention from problem to accomplishment.	Ask client to describe accomplishments for the past week.
Feel more confident as self-esteem improves.	Compliment client to provide positive reinforcement whenever possible.
Communicate problematic feelings to develop new skills or options.	Use technique of "Pounding Away Bad Feelings" *and* game *Don't Break the Ice* to help child release frustrations (see Behavioral Techniques, Chapter 23).
Attempt to use new control skills in school.	Urge child to use new control skills in the classroom setting.
Report results to therapist.	Provide positive reinforcement when client reports that he/she has challenged anxiety-provoking situations. Praise attempt and reward success.
Learn positive problem solving and how famous people have overcome obstacles.	Assign to read *Don't Be Afraid, Tommy* or *The Lion Who Lost His Roar* (see Bibliotherapy, Chapter 26).
Learn new strategies for dealing with aggressive behaviors.	Assign to read or have parents read to child *Anybody Can Bake a Cake* (see Bibliotherapy, Chapter 26).

Learn methods that you can use to advocate for yourself.	Instruct client in the technique of self-advocacy.
Understand that you can deal with these issues and end treatment successfully.	Develop a termination plan and explain issues of separation anxiety and dependency.

SHORT-TERM BEHAVIORAL GOALS, **C-FAMILY**	THERAPIST'S INTERVENTIONS
Improve communications among family members to reduce familial anxiety.	Conduct family sessions or refer for family therapy to reduce anger and/or alienation and improve communication skills within the family.
Cooperate in amplifying family genogram.	Amplify family genogram created in first family session to help understand family history.
Discuss genogram openly to fully understand family history as it relates to anxiety.	Discuss genogram to reveal family history and possible family secrets dealing with anxiety.
Demonstrate boundaries, alliances, triangles, and emotional currents that may exacerbate the anxieties.	Explore family boundaries using sculpturing, a useful technique for understanding triangulation, alliances, and emotional currents (see Behavioral Techniques, Chapter 23).
Shift focus from problem to possible solutions.	Have family imagine a future without the problem and suggest actions that can be taken now to make that future possible.
Think about what treatment outcome would look like. Explain what you would like to see change in other family members when treatment is completed.	Ask family members to think about what they might want to say about each other when treatment is completed.
Family members realize they have the power to make important changes, even if these seem small.	Help family members realize they have an opportunity to do some things differently.
Members are empowered. They recognize that they can create positive change.	Ask family members to relate what they have accomplished in the past week.
Realize that major change is the result of small steps taken one at a time.	Help family identify and prioritize achievable goals.

Enhance understanding of condition and see how other families have handled similar problems.	Assign as homework reading *Making Families Work and What to Do When They Don't* (see Bibliotherapy, Chapter 26).
Make use of available community resources.	Refer family to available resources in the community. (See Self-Help Groups, Chapter 27.)
Reduce negative communication.	Develop a system of positive reinforcement with family members to interact better with each other and reduce scapegoating.
Family members work together to develop termination plan.	Discuss termination issues and develop a plan to terminate treatment.

PART III

TREATMENT PLANS:
OTHER DISORDERS OF CHILDHOOD

10

Anxiety Disorders

ACUTE STRESS DISORDER (308.3)

Acute Stress Disorder is marked by anxiety, dissociation, and other symptoms within one month after an extreme traumatic sensor, including at least three of the following: a sense of numbing, detachment, lack of emotional responsiveness, a reduction in awareness of his/her surroundings, derealization, depersonalization, or dissociative amnesia. The traumatic event is persistently re-experienced, and situations that may trigger a remembrance of the event are actively avoided. The disturbance lasts for at least two days and usually does not endure for more than four weeks. During that time, the disorder may significantly interfere with the individual's normal functioning. Posttraumatic Stress Disorder requires a history of more than one month. If the symptoms of Acute Stress Disorder persist, a revised diagnosis should be considered.

Behavioral Symptoms
Acute Stress Disorder
(severity index: 1, mild; 2, moderate; 3, intense)

	Severity
1. Numbing or lack of emotion	_____
2. Feels dazed or disconnected	_____
3. Derealization or depersonalization	_____

4. Inability to recall an important part of the traumatic event   _____
5. Recurring images, thoughts, dreams, or flashbacks of the event   _____
6. Distress at reminders of the event   _____
7. Avoids people, places, and things associated with the event   _____
8. Sleep problems, anxiety, irritability, lack of concentration, restlessness, exaggerated vigilance   _____
9. Major impairment of daily activities   _____

Other Diagnostic Considerations

Posttraumatic Stress Disorder (309.81)
Adjustment Disorders (309.xx)
Major Depressive Episode (296.2)
Brief Psychotic Disorder (298.8)
Malingering should be ruled out.

TREATMENT PLAN
ACUTE STRESS DISORDER

Client: _____ Date: _____

```
┌─────────────────────────────────┐
│ Multiaxial Assessment           │
│                                 │
│ Axis I:    _____       │
│ Axis II:   _____       │
│ Axis III: _____        │
│ Axis IV:  _____         │
│ Axis V:   _____         │
└─────────────────────────────────┘
```

I. OBJECTIVES OF TREATMENT
   (*select one or more*)

   1. Educate parents about the disorder.
   2. Investigate family history of the disorder.
   3. Help family develop better coping skills.
   4. Reduce anxiety related to the disorder.
   5. Reduce other symptoms: restlessness, sleep problems, irritability, poor concentration, and excessive vigilance.
   6. Encourage compliance with educational programs and referrals.
   7. Reduce irrational beliefs.
   8. Restore realization and personification.
   9. Promote socialization.
   10. Eliminate need for avoidance of people, places, or things reminiscent of the trauma.
   11. Reduce alienation.
   12. Restore to optimum level of functioning.
   13. Develop discharge plan for coping with everyday life.

II. SHORT-TERM BEHAVIORAL GOALS AND INTERVENTIONS
   (*select goals and interventions appropriate for your client*)

(Note: Separate goals and interventions are provided for the treatment of A-Parents, B-Child, and C-Family.)

SHORT-TERM BEHAVIORAL GOALS, **A-PARENTS**	THERAPIST'S INTERVENTIONS
Parents collaborate with therapist in development of a treatment plan.	Establish therapeutic alliance with parents to enhance outcome of treatment.
Undergo treatment for individual problems, which, in turn, enhances outcome of therapy.	Explore for parental psychopathology (e.g., anxiety disorder, marital discord, etc.) and refer for treatment or treat (see appropriate treatment plan in *Behavioral Management Guide: Essential Treatment Strategies for Adult Psychotherapy* in Resources for Providers, Chapter 33).
Recognize how the family is also affected by this disorder.	Review parents' methods for dealing with anxiety. If other children are also afflicted, treat or refer for treatment as appropriate.
Undergo testing and evaluation for psychiatric medication.	If appropriate, refer parents for psychological testing and psychiatric evaluation.
Become aware of maladaptive messages you are sending to child.	Identify how parents deal with stress or anxiety.
Develop awareness of how your personal theory influences cognition of the problem.	Explore parental theory of the problem.
Learn the laws of anxiety: not dangerous, not permanent, and reduced by confrontation.	Teach parents the laws of anxiety.
Examine distortions in reaction to the traumatic event stressors.	Discuss reactions to identify exaggerations and distortions.
Replace exaggerated reactions with positive reactions, using evidence-based reality.	Reframe negative reactions with positive, reality-based reactions.

Help child practice coping skills in real-life situations. Report reactions and reward successes.	Instruct parents on how to help child challenge persons, places, things, and activities related to the traumatic event and record reactions. Reward successes.
Learn to reach beyond automatic cognitive reactions in viewing the problem.	Expand parental perspective beyond limited cognitive reactions.
Request early intervention for child.	Explain importance of early intervention for preschool children (see Early Intervention, Chapter 23).
Agree to allow therapist to confer with child's school to help in development of a comprehensive psycho-educational treatment plan for the child.	If appropriate, request and receive parental permission to confer with child's teachers and school officials.
Attend self-help group to improve parenting skills.	Evaluate parenting skills and, if necessary, refer to parenting skills group (see Self-Help Groups, Chapter 27).
Read about and improve parenting skills.	Assign reading of *An Ounce of Prevention: How Parents Can Stop Childhood Behavioral and Emotional Problems before They Start* and other selections (see Bibliotherapy, Chapter 26, and Videotapes, in Resources for Providers, Chapter 33).
Make positive use of community resources.	Educate parents about available community resources (see Self-Help Groups and 800 Numbers, Chapter 27).
Discuss termination plan and resolve termination issues.	Develop a termination plan and discuss issues of separation and dependency with parents.

SHORT-TERM BEHAVIORAL GOALS, **B-CHILD**	THERAPIST'S INTERVENTIONS
Engage in play therapy.	Engage client in therapeutic relationship, via play therapy.
Learn about diagnosis and develop realistic expectations of self.	Educate client about the diagnosis and discuss symptomatology so he/she can adjust self-expectations.
Through play therapy, relate terror during event.	Investigate with child his/her reaction to the traumatic event.
Observe puppets and how they behave. Begin to see new role models.	Shape client behavior by use of puppets (see Behavioral Techniques, Chapter 23).
Watch how puppet expresses feelings.	Display socially acceptable expression of feelings, using stickers with puppet.
Learn that it is okay to express feelings.	Reward puppet for expressing feelings appropriately.
Mimic puppet and express feeling.	Have client mimic the puppet to express his/her feelings and reward or praise.
Recognize underlying feelings of anger or depression and express appropriately.	Explore for underlying feelings of anger or depression, using puppet, and treat (see appropriate treatment plan).
Realize others also feel bad and relate to puppet overcoming the feeling.	Investigate for feelings of low self-esteem related to Acute Stress Disorder. Have puppet talk about how it feels and what it can do about it.
Begin to see possible solutions.	Discuss with puppet how it deals with anxieties.
Identify irrational beliefs.	Through continued play with puppet, explore irrational beliefs.
Reframe beliefs about stress.	Change irrational beliefs by having the puppet discuss the beliefs and develop rational alternatives.

Learn from role modeling and shape new behaviors.	Use puppet to role model appropriate behavior.
Using guided imagery to augment the play therapy process, learn to gain control over feelings.	Use guided imagery and relaxation techniques to gain mastery over anxieties (see "Using Guided Imagery to Augment the Play Therapy Process," Behavioral Techniques, Chapter 23).
Understand anxiety and realize that avoidance does not help.	Teach client the laws of anxiety: not dangerous, not permanent, avoidance increases anxiety.
Communicate with therapist without using language, if necessary.	Use puppet to have client relate the story of his/her life.
Express suppressed feelings in a nonthreatening environment.	Play the *Talking, Feeling, and Doing* game to understand underlying processes in a nonthreatening way (see Therapeutic Games, Chapter 24).
Understand how trauma may have contributed to existing disorder.	Explore client's background for trauma that may have exacerbated acute stress.
Discuss personal coping mechanisms developed to handle anxieties.	Investigate with client possible patterns of withdrawal used to avoid anxiety.
Understand how you misinterpreted events.	Explore for misinterpretations of environmental events and correct.
Recognize and relate how family affects the problem.	Explore familial impact on the problem.
Learn positive self-talk.	Teach client positive self-talk to interrupt negative patterns.
Learn new technique for dealing with anxiety.	Teach diaphragmatic breathing to control anxiety (see Behavioral Techniques, Chapter 23).
Identify sleep problems.	Explore for sleep problems and treat if necessary. (See appropriate treatment plan.)

Learn that you can control nightmares and other sleep problems.	If client has sleep problems, use technique called "Bad Dreams" (see Behavioral Techniques, Chapter 23).
Learn to develop self-esteem through positive self-talk.	Assign to read *Don't Feed the Monster on Tuesdays* or alternate selection (see Bibliotherapy, Chapter 26).
Understand that fear diminishes when it is discussed, rather than hidden.	Assign reading of *Sometimes I'm Afraid* or alternate selection for older children (see Bibliotherapy, Chapter 26).
Learn new techniques for dealing with emotional difficulties.	Use the *Positive Thinking Game* for children 9 years old and up to teach how positive self-talk helps control emotional difficulties (see Therapeutic Games, Chapter 24).
Shift focus of attention from problem to accomplishment.	Ask client to describe accomplishments for the past week.
Feel more confident as self-esteem improves.	Compliment client to provide positive reinforcement whenever possible.
Communicate problematic feelings to develop new skills or options.	Use technique of "Pounding Away Bad Feelings" to help child release frustrations (see Behavioral Techniques, Chapter 23).
Attempt to use new behavioral skills in school.	Urge client to use new behavioral skills in the classroom setting.
Report results to therapist.	Provide positive reinforcement when client reports that he/she has developed new ways to handle stressors. Praise attempt and reward success.
Learn positive problem solving and how famous people have overcome obstacles.	For children ages 6 through 12, read or assign to read *Anybody Can Bake a Cake* (see Bibliotherapy, Chapter 26, and alternate selections for other children).

Learn methods that you can better use to advocate for yourself.	Instruct client in the technique of self-advocacy.
Understand that he/she can deal with these issues and successfully end treatment.	Develop a termination plan and explain issues of separation anxiety and dependency.

SHORT-TERM BEHAVIORAL GOALS, **C-FAMILY**	THERAPIST'S INTERVENTIONS
Improve communications among family members.	Conduct family sessions or refer for family therapy to reduce anxieties and/or alienation, and improve communication skills within the family.
Explore methods you use as a family to deal with anxieties.	Identify methods family uses to cope with anxieties, and if maladaptive, create new solutions.
Cooperate in amplifying family genogram.	Amplify family genogram created in early parental session to help understand ways family deals with anxiety.
Discuss genogram openly to fully understand family history as it relates to aggression.	Discuss genogram to reveal family history and possible family secrets dealing with anxiety.
Demonstrate boundaries, alliances, triangles, and emotional currents that may exacerbate the problem.	Explore family boundaries using sculpturing, a useful technique for understanding triangulation, alliances, and emotional currents (see Behavioral Techniques, Chapter 23).
Shift focus from problem to possible solutions.	Have family imagine a future without the problem and suggest actions that can be taken now to make that future possible.
Think about what treatment outcome would look like. Explain what you would like to see change in other family members when treatment is completed.	Ask family members to think about what they might want to say about each other when treatment is completed.
Family members realize they have the power to make important changes, even if these seem small.	Help family members realize they have an opportunity to do some things differently.
Members are empowered. They recognize that they can create positive change.	Ask family members to relate what they have accomplished in the past week.

Realize that major change is the result of small steps taken one at a time.	Help family identify and prioritize achievable goals.
Enhance understanding of the condition and see how other families have handled similar problems.	Assign as homework reading *Smart Guide to Relieving Stress, The Worry Control Workshop*, or *Do One Thing Different* to find new solutions (see Bibliotherapy, Chapter 26).
Make use of available community resources.	Refer family to available resources in the community. (See Self-Help Resources, Chapter 27.)
Family members work together to develop termination plan.	Discuss termination issues and develop a plan to terminate treatment.

CRITICAL INCIDENT STRESS MANAGEMENT

This is not a DSM-IV classification, but many of the symptoms of this disorder fall into Axis I behavioral impairments, and the diagnosis probably should be Posttraumatic Stress Disorder or Bereavement, depending on how the incident affected your client. If your client is suffering from the loss of a loved one, you will probably be dealing with both diagnoses.

Critical Incident Stress Management, in itself, is not psychotherapy, but a system of interventions designed to prevent or mitigate adverse psychological reactions. If crises and disasters become epidemic, we will need immediate, effective strategies to deal with our clients. Individual, family, and group interventions will be needed, at any time and any place, with the goal of reducing fear and returning to normal functioning as much as possible.

Behavioral Symptoms

In Critical Incident Stress Management, the client has witnessed or experienced an actual or threatened event that placed him/her or another person in danger of death or serious injury, and reacted with feelings of intense horror, fear, or helplessness. No one who experiences a disaster in person or sees it on television is untouched by it. After a disaster, most people will pull together, but their effectiveness will be diminished. Many will not see the need for mental health services and may reject assistance of all types. This is a special time, and therapists need to put aside their usual methods and use a more practical, active outreach approach that is appropriate for each phase of the disaster.

Clients may react to disaster in a wide range of ways. They need to be reminded that grief reactions or disaster stress reactions are normal in times of crisis. In the beginning, people will need more practical advice than psychological help. There are four waves of assistance:

1. Coping and Stabilization with a focus on basic needs and safety;
2. Stress Management, including arousal reduction strategies and coping with current and future life circumstances;
3. Resolution of grief and trauma; and
4. Accommodation, Adaptation, Transformation, and Reconnection.

Behavioral Symptoms
(severity index: 1, mild; 2, moderate; 3, intense)

<u>Severity</u>

Emotional:

1. Overwhelming fear or anxiety _____
2. Feels lost or overwhelmed _____
3. Depression _____
4. Guilt, grief _____
5. Excessive death anxiety _____
6. Feels detached from others _____
7. Range of feelings is restricted _____
8. Has increased sense of limited future _____
9. Irritable, displays outbursts of anger _____

Behavioral:

10. Withdraws from others _____
11. Sleep disturbances _____
12. Unusual behaviors _____
13. Changes in eating patterns _____
14. Excessive silence or problems in communication _____
15. Changes in work habits _____
16. Persistently re-experiences traumatic event as a dream or recollection _____
17. Has flashbacks of the event _____
18. Displays intense distress at cues reminiscent of the event _____
19. Avoids people, places, activities, and thoughts associated with the event _____

Cognitive:

20. Poor concentration _____
21. Memory problems, poor attention span _____
22. Difficulty making decisions _____
23. Slowed problem solving _____
24. Difficulties with calculations _____
25. Unable to remember an important aspect of the event _____
26. Interest in usual activities is diminished _____
27. Is easily startled _____

Physical:

28. Muscle tremors   _____
29. Chest pains   _____
30. Gastro-intestinal distress   _____
31. Difficulty breathing   _____
32. Headaches   _____
33. Elevated blood pressure   _____

Other Diagnostic Considerations

Adjustment Disorders
Acute Stress Disorder (308.3)
Obsessive-Compulsive Disorder (300.3)
Posttraumatic Stress Disorder (309.81)
Bereavement (V62.82)

TREATMENT PLAN
CRITICAL INCIDENT STRESS
MANAGEMENT

Client: _____ Date: _____

I. OBJECTIVES OF TREATMENT
(select one or more)

1. Identify if basic needs are being met (i.e., safety, food, shelter, etc.).
2. If necessary, refer to FEMA (Federal Emergency Management Assistance).
3. Educate parents or caretakers about the cognitive, emotional, behavioral, and physical symptoms associated with being involved in a critical incident.
4. If child has lost a loved one, use the Bereavement Plan or Post-Traumatic Stress Disorder Plan in addition to this one.
5. Help family regain internal and external control.
6. Reduce cognitive, behavioral, emotional, and physical stress symptoms.
7. Diminish symptoms of anxiety or survivor guilt.
8. Help mourners through the grieving process.
9. Teach strategies to reduce stressors to critical events.
10. Identify stress reactions of significant others.
11. Resolve feelings of despair and hopelessness.
12. Help each family member to tell his/her story and identify how they are dealing with trauma.
13. Eliminate sleep disturbances and nightmares.
14. Demonstrate appropriate communication skills (active listening, questioning, mirroring, paraphrasing).
15. Restore appetite, stop weight loss.
16. Teach the Phoenix Model of dealing with bereavement and crisis (i.e., Impact, Chaos, Adaptation, Equilibrium, and Transformation or Self-Actualization).
17. Encourage compliance with educational programs and referrals.
18. Develop personal rituals to ensure safety and empowerment.
19. Reframe irrational beliefs.
20. Promote socialization, reconnection, reduce alienation.
21. If appropriate, encourage family to develop spiritual side for grounding.
22. Develop discharge plan for coping with everyday life.

II. SHORT-TERM BEHAVIORAL GOALS AND INTERVENTIONS
(select the goals and interventions appropriate for your client)

Note: Separate goals and interventions are provided for the treatment of A-Parents, B-Child, and C-Family.)

SHORT-TERM BEHAVIORAL GOALS, **A-PARENTS**	THERAPIST'S INTERVENTIONS
Collaborate with therapist to reduce stressors immediately associated with the event.	Establish therapeutic alliance with parents, child, or family as soon as possible to help them deal with overwhelming stressors of traumatic event/s.
Relate, in detail, the traumatic event and your reactive feelings to it.	Investigate with the parents the impact of the traumatic event and how it is affecting them.
Parents and family are treated for bereavement plus Critical Incident Stress Management.	Assess problem with parents, and if anyone in their family has died, revise diagnosis and see Bereavement plan to use with CISM.
Explain needs to therapist.	Investigate if basic needs are being met (i.e., food, clothing, shelter, safety., etc.).
Follow-up with referral.	Refer to FEMA, Federal Emergency Management Assistance (see On-Line Resources, Chapter 27).
Describe flashbacks and their intensity.	Explore for flashbacks and assess intensity.
Understand the different types of trauma.	Help parents understand the different types of trauma. Type 1—Single unpredictable event. Type 2—On-going world event, sexual abuse, or domestic violence. Individual—A brutal blow to psyche that breaks through one's defenses. Collective—A blow that damages social life and bonds between people.

Become aware of ways to reduce stress during critical incidents or disasters.	Educate parents about ways to reduce stressors to the critical event.
Learn how to reduce stressors to the critical event.	1. Structure time. Keep busy. 2. Don't label yourself crazy. It's normal to feel crazy under stress. 3. Talk to others. 4. Understand that attempting to numb pain with drugs, alcohol, or excessive food will just complicate problems. 5. Reach out and connect with others. 6. Show feelings. 7. Help co-workers and let them help you. 8. Write your feelings in a journal, especially during sleepless hours. 9. Do things that feel good. 10. Do not begin hoarding out of fear. It will cause more trouble for everyone. 11. Do not make any major life decisions. 12. Do not fight flashbacks. Talk about them. Realize they will become less painful over time. 13. Do things that help you feel you have some control over your life. 14. Listen carefully to traumatized persons. 15. Do not deny reality, but reduce the time listening to radio and watching TV to avoid re-infecting yourself.
Learn to identify symptoms of stress reaction: emotional, behavioral, cognitive, or physical.	Help parents identify the stress reactions they and their children are having to the traumatic event/s.

Help yourselves and your family move through a transitional period toward greater development.	Educate parents to understand the phases of the Phoenix Model: Rising from the Ashes of Grief. 1. Impact 2. Chaos 3. Adaptation 4. Equilibrium 5. Transformation (See Bibliotherapy, Chapter 26, and Resources for Providers, Chapter 33.)
Identify the Phoenix developmental stage your children are in to help deal with the crisis.	Help parents identify where they are in the Phoenix Model, and what to expect from themselves and their children.
Understand you need to maintain stability, establish security measures, and begin to belong or reach out to others.	During the Impact stage, help them to understand the needs for food, shelter, sleep, safety, security, and preliminary belonging. Guide them in designing a support system.
Recognize the need to maintain physiological stability while acknowledging and expressing grief while resisting isolation.	During the Chaos stage there is still a need for food, shelter, sleep, safety, and security, but the major task is to maintain physiological stability and be able to talk about and acknowledge grief while staying connected and resisting isolation.
Understand that during times of crisis and fear, there can also be growth.	The following stage of Adaptation is aimed at normalization. Remind clients that "although the world is full of suffering . . . it is also full of overcoming it" (Helen Keller). Create a realistic outline to live in today's world while encouraging the expression of feelings.
Develop proactive strategies to reduce helplessness and hopelessness.	Help parents gain equilibrium and develop proactive strategies for living in the new world.

Look for ways to create meaning from the tragedy.	Help parents through the transformation stage by creating meaning from the grief and loss of life.
Confront thoughts of unrealistic or exaggerated consequences.	Guide parents in confronting distorted reactions to trigger situations.
Identify cognitive distortions.	Weigh the actions against evidence-based reality.
Learn to self-soothe rather than catastrophize.	Help clients develop coping mechanisms that are soothing rather than frightening (i.e., staying in the here and now). Even though this may be very difficult during times of critical disaster, help them see that what they worry about often doesn't happen, and what they don't know to worry about may happen.
Enter treatment to help deal with your trauma and enhance outcome of child therapy.	Evaluate parents for anxiety problems related to traumatic event and refer for treatment or treat if appropriate (see *Behavioral Management Guide: Essential Treatment Strategies for Adult Psychotherapy* in Resources for Providers, Chapter 33).
Develop awareness of how your personal theory influences cognition of the problem in child.	Explore parental theory of the crisis.
Learn to reach beyond automatic cognitive reactions in viewing the problem.	Expand parental perspective beyond limited cognitive reactions.
Learn how to help child deal with stressors.	Teach parents the laws of anxiety: not permanent, not dangerous, running away from problem increases anxiety rather than reducing it. Attempt to help them normalize life as much as possible.

Undergo treatment for individual problems which, in turn, enhances outcome of child's therapy.	Explore for parental psychopathology (i.e., anxiety, depression, marital discord, etc.) and refer for treatment or treat as appropriate (see Treatment Plan, *Behavioral Management Guide: Essential Treatment Strategies for Adult Psychotherapy* in Resources for Providers, Chapter 33).
Parents learn how to deal with child's sleep disorder.	Investigate for sleep problems in child and teach parents how to deal with the problem.
Learn diaphragmatic breathing as relaxation technique and teach child to help in relaxation.	Teach parents diaphragmatic breathing to assist child in relaxation (see Behavioral Techniques, Chapter 23).
Agree to allow therapist to confer with child's school to help in development of a comprehensive psycho-educational treatment plan for the child.	After interviewing child, and with permission of the parents and the child, confer with teachers and school administrators.
Comply with referrals for medical and psychiatric evaluations.	Provide referral for medical and psychiatric evaluations, if appropriate.
Develop new coping strategies.	Assign parents to read books to enhance coping skills such as *I Can't Get Over It, Life After Trauma: A Workbook for Healing* or *The Phoenix Phenomenon: Rising from the Ashes of Grief* (see Bibliotherapy, Chapter 26).
Cultivate new parenting skills and learn how to deal with child's anxiety.	Assign parents to read *Making Families Work and What to Do When They Don't* and *Trust After Trauma* (see Bibliotherapy, Chapter 26).

Monitor child's medication schedule and report all reactions or failures to take meds.	If child is on meds, instruct parents on need for a regular schedule and feedback that may indicate the need for revised dosage.
Resolve separation and dependency issues and terminate.	Address issues of separation and dependency and terminate.

SHORT-TERM BEHAVIORAL GOALS, **B-CHILD**	THERAPIST'S INTERVENTIONS
Develop a therapeutic relationship to help him/her through the traumatic event or loss of loved one.	Engage child in therapeutic relationship to help deal with the traumatic event.
Identify how you are attempting to deal with the traumatic event.	Investigate the impact of the traumatic event and how the child is affected by it.
Get help to deal with the crisis if you need it.	Determine if basic needs are being met (i.e., food, clothing, shelter, safety.) If necessary, refer to FEMA (Federal Emergency Management Assistance). (See On-Line Resources, Chapter 28 or Resources for Providers, Chapter 33.)
Realize you can look to others for support.	Explore available support systems. Are there aunts, uncles, other relatives, friends available to help child adjust to the emotional shock wave?
Understand the stages of trauma and be reassured that you will get through the grieving process.	Educate child about the stages of trauma: 1. shock, denial, disbelief. 2. anger, "why did it happen?" 3. chaos, despair "how can it ever get better?" 4. bargaining, "If I am a better person, things will improve?" Help child reorganize and create a new life in order to reduce the effects of trauma.
Learn to identify the symptoms you are experiencing and recognize them as a response to trauma.	Help child to identify his/her stress reactions, emotional, behavioral, cognitive, physical.
Undergo treatment for symptoms.	See appropriate treatment plans for indicated disorders.
Realize that human beings are not perfect and reduce stressors imposed on self.	Teach the child that human beings are not perfect.

Determine the impact of the trauma on schoolwork.	Explore for academic problems related to the trauma and treat accordingly (refer to appropriate treatment plan).
Become aware of ways to reduce stress during critical incidents or disasters.	Educate child about ways to reduce stressors to the critical event.
Learn how to reduce stressors to the critical event.	1. Structure time. Keep busy. 2. Don't label yourself crazy. It's normal to feel crazy under stress. 3. Talk to others. 4. Understand that attempting to numb pain with drugs, alcohol, or excessive food just creates problems. 5. Reach out and connect with others. 6. Show feelings. 7. Help others and let them help you. 8. Write your feelings in a journal, especially during sleepless hours. 9. Do things that feel good. 10. Do not begin hoarding out of fear. It will cause more trouble for everyone. 11. Do not make any major life decisions. 12. Do not fight flashbacks. Talk about them. Realize they will be less painful over time. 13. Do things that help you feel you have some control over life. 14. Listen carefully to other traumatized persons. 15. Do not deny reality, but reduce the time spent listening to radio or watching TV to avoid reinfecting yourself.

Learn how to manage the stages of grief	Teach child to understand the phases of the Phoenix Model: Rising from the Ashes of Grief. 1. Impact, 2. Chaos, 3. Adaptation, 4. Equilibrium, 5. Transformation. (See Bibliotherapy, Chapter 26.)
Learn to identify the Phoenix development stage you are in.	Help child identify where he/she is in the Phoenix Model and what can be expected at this stage.
Recognize that you need to maintain stability and safety, and begin reaching out to others.	During the Impact Stage, help child understand the need for food, clothing, shelter, safety. sleep. Start a support system.
Recognize the need for psychological stability while being able to express grief.	During the Chaos Stage, basic needs continue but the major task is to maintain physiological stability and be able to talk about and acknowledge grief, while staying connected and resisting isolation.
Develop proactive strategies for living in the new world.	Help child regain equilibrium after the trauma by developing proactive strategies for reducing helplessness and hopelessness.
Look for ways to find meaning in the tragedy.	Guide child through the Transformation Phase by attempting to find meaning in the grief and loss of life.
Understand that during times of crisis and fear, there can also be growth.	The following stage of Adaptation is aimed at normalization. Remind the child of Helen Keller's words, "although the world is full of suffering, it is also full of overcoming it." Develop a realistic outline to live in today's world while encouraging the expression of feelings.

Confront thoughts of unrealistic or exaggerated consequences.	Guide child in confronting distorted reactions to trigger situations.
Identify cognitive distortions.	Weigh the actions against evidence-based reality.
Learn to self-soothe rather than catastrophize.	Help client develop coping mechanisms that are soothing rather than frightening (i.e. staying in the here and now). Even though this may be difficult during times of critical disaster, help them realize that what we worry about often doesn't happen and what we don't know to worry about may happen.
Realize that others also feel bad when critical trauma incidents occur.	Explore for low self-esteem or survivor guilt, and explain it as a normal reaction to trauma.
Identify irrational beliefs.	Explore irrational beliefs about death.
Reframe beliefs about fears and anxieties.	Discuss the beliefs and develop rational alternatives.
Using relaxation techniques and guided imagery, learn to gain control over feelings.	Teach relaxation techniques and guided imagery to master anxieties (see Behavioral Techniques, Chapter 23).
Understand anxiety and realize that avoidance does not help.	Teach child the dynamics of anxiety: not dangerous, not permanent, confrontation can promote change.
Communicate life story to therapist.	Have the child relate the story of his/her life.
Express suppressed feelings about saying goodbye to a loved one.	If appropriate, play the *Goodbye Game* to dispel myths and false ideas about death (see Therapeutic Games, Chapter 24).
Discuss personal coping mechanisms developed to handle stressful situations.	Investigate with child possible patterns of social withdrawal or becoming overly active as a way of dealing with feelings about trauma.

Recognize and discuss how the family affects the problem.	Explore the family's impact on the problem. Are they supportive? Do they talk about the tragedy or pretend it never happened? Remind the child that anxiety and uncertainty are normal parts of grief.
Learn positive self-talk.	Teach child positive self-talk to interrupt negative patterns.
Learn new techniques for relaxing and dealing with anxieties.	Teach diaphragmatic breathing to help the child relax and reduce stress (see Behavioral Techniques, Chapter 23).
Agree to allow therapist to confer with school to help in development of a comprehensive psycho-educational treatment plan.	Interview child to determine if he/she thinks the school should also be involved in helping.
Comply with referrals for medical and psychiatric evaluations.	Provide referrals for medical and psychiatric evaluations, if appropriate.
Develop new coping strategies.	Assign parents to read *I Can't Get Over It* or *Trust After Trauma* to child (see Bibliotherapy, Chapter 26).
Identify ways you have changed.	Investigate ways in which the child has changed in attempt to create meaning for what he/she has gone through.
Shift focus of attention from problems to accomplishments.	Ask client to describe accomplishments of past week.
Feel more confident as self-esteem improves.	Compliment child to provide positive reinforcement whenever possible.
Learn that grieving is a natural process and learn skills to cope.	Assign child to read or have parents read to him/her *Effective Grief Management for Children* or *The Hyena Who Lost Her Laugh* (see Bibliotherapy, Chapter 26).

Learn positive problem-solving techniques and how famous people have overcome obstacles.	Assign child to read or have parents read to him/her *Anybody Can Bake a Cake* or *Don't Despair on Thursdays* (see Bibliotherapy, Chapter 26).
Learn methods you can use to advocate for yourself.	Instruct client in the technique of self-advocacy.
Understand that you can deal with these issues and bring treatment to a successful conclusion.	Develop termination plan and resolve issues of separation anxiety and dependency. Let child know you will be available should he/she ever need further counseling.

SHORT-TERM BEHAVIORAL GOALS, **C-FAMILY**	THERAPIST'S INTERVENTIONS
Improve communications among family members to reduce familial anxiety.	Conduct family sessions, to reduce alienation, improve communication skills, and enhance understanding of the trauma on the entire family.
Identify unsatisfied needs and get help.	Explore how basic needs are being met, (i.e., food, clothing, shelter, safety, etc) and if necessary refer family for Federal Emergency Management Assistance (FEMA) (see On-Line Resources, Chapter 28).
Identify outside sources that can lend temporary support during the grieving process.	Identify if there are members of the extended family who can provide additional support.
Each family member shares his/her reaction to the loss.	Explore individual reactions to the trauma. See how each family member felt before and after the loss.
Family members understand the normal stages of grieving and what to expect from each other.	If the rest of the family is unfamiliar with the stages of grief, explain them using the Kubler-Ross Model: Denial, Anger, Bargaining, Depression, and Acceptance, or the Phoenix Model: Impact, Chaos, Adaptation, Equilibrium, and Transformation (see Bibliotherapy, Chapter 26).
Each family member shares his/her unique reaction to the critical incident.	Have each member explore his/her individual feelings and response to the critical incident to give his/her sorrow words which can be cathartic.
Identify methods of coping with the disaster.	Discuss methods of coping.

Identify irrational thoughts related to death.	Explore irrational methods of coping in all family members. Do they feel guilty for the death? Blame each other?
Each family member identifies their unfinished business with the deceased and psychodynamically works through relevant issues that are unresolved.	If any family members died in the critical incident, use role-playing with an empty chair representing the deceased. Ask family members to express what they would like to relate to the dead person. Include any unfinished business they would like to complete (see Behavioral Techniques, Chapter 23).
Learn how to reduce stressors to the critical event.	1. Structure time. Keep Busy 2. Don't label yourself crazy. It's normal to feel crazy under stress. 3. Talk to others. 4. Understand that attempting to numb pain with alcohol, drugs, or excessive food will just complicate problems. 5. Reach out and connect with others. 6. Show feelings. 7. Help others and let them help you. 8. Write your feelings in a journal especially during sleepless hours. 9. Do things that feel good. 10. Do not begin hoarding out of fear. It will cause more trouble. 11. Do not make any major life decisions 12. Do not fight flashbacks. Talk about them. Realize they will become less painful over time. 13. Do things that help you feel you have some control over life.

Continue with actions to reduce stressors to critical event.	14. Listen carefully to other traumatized people. 15. Do not deny reality, but reduce the time listening to radio or watching TV to avoid reinfecting yourself.
Expose hidden blame in order to resolve it.	Explore for hidden blame among family members.
Family members disclose survivor's guilt.	Investigate for survivor's guilt and educate family members that it is a normal part of the grieving process.
Family realizes they can find hope through growth and adaptation.	Educate family about the phase of adaptation and help them realize their old life has ended. Help them to let go and see that this process can be the birthplace of hope and transition.
Family members are empowered by realizing by trial and error they can take on new roles and grow.	Assist family to establish equilibrium by taking on new roles and planning a life even in time of crisis.
Stay in the here and now to reduce stress.	Realize that staying in the here and now will calm you down.
Recognize the uselessness of worry.	Reassure family members that worry is useless since what we worry about very rarely happens.
Each family member strengthens himself by developing new, productive roles.	Help each family member build self-confidence through actual realistic achievements.
Learn the principles of problem-solving.	Teach clients the principles of problem-solving: 1. stay calm, take a deep breath 2. think about what is bothering you 3. create a SMART action plan: Small, Measurable, Achievable, Realistic, Timely

	4. select three different solutions, pick the best one, do the best you can, if it doesn't work, try again. Remember perseverance works (see Change, Behavioral Techniques, Chapter 23).
Family members recognize they have the power to make important changes even if they seem small.	Help family members realize they have an opportunity to do some things differently.
Realize that major change is the result of small changes taken one at a time.	Help family members identify and prioritize achievable goals.
Identify individual transformation.	Have each member identify ways they have transformed since the tragedy.
Discuss the books to enhance your understanding of grief.	Assign reading of *The Phoenix Phenomenon: Rising from the Ashes of Grief* and *Living Beyond the Loss: Death in the Family* (see Bibliotherapy, Chapter 26).
Make use of available community resources.	Refer family to available community groups (see Self-Help Groups and 800 Numbers, Chapter 27, and On-Line Resources, Chapter 28).
Reduce negative communication.	Develop a system of positive reinforcement with family to help members interact better with each other and reduce scapegoating.
Work together to develop a termination plan.	Discuss termination issues and develop a plan to terminate treatment.

GENERALIZED ANXIETY DISORDER (300.02)

Generalized Anxiety Disorder is characterized by excessive anxiety and worry about various events and activities over a six-month period. In children, the anxiety and worry are accompanied by one additional symptom to qualify for this diagnosis, including restlessness, irritability, tires easily, difficulty concentrating, muscle tension, or disturbed sleep. Usually, the duration or intensity of the anxiety or worry is out of proportion with the likelihood of the anticipated or feared event. Children with this disorder tend to worry about their competence or the quality of their performance in routine activities at school, at sporting events, or at home. Concerns may focus on punctuality or catastrophic events like earthquakes or nuclear war. Children may be insecure, overly conforming, and perfectionistic. They are often overanxious in seeking approval and require constant reassurance. Individuals with Generalized Anxiety Disorder frequently also suffer from major depression or other anxiety disorders. In addition, certain medical conditions can mimic Generalized Anxiety Disorder, making differential diagnosis difficult.

Behavioral Symptoms
Generalized Anxiety Disorder
(severity index: 1, mild; 2, moderate; 3, intense)

Excessive anxiety or worry more days than not for six months or more, PLUS one of the following:

	Severity
1. Feels restless	_____
2. Fatigues easily	_____
3. Has difficulty concentrating	_____
4. Is often irritable	_____
5. Displays muscular tension	_____
6. Has difficulty getting to sleep and staying asleep	_____
7. Complains about multiple physical problems	_____
8. Symptoms impair child's daily activities	_____

Other Diagnostic Considerations

Adjustment Disorder (*see Subtypes*)
Anorexia Nervosa (307.1)
Anxiety Disorder due to a General Medical Condition (293.84)
Hypochondriasis (300.7)
Mood Disorders (*see Subtypes*)
Obsessive-Compulsive Disorder (300.3)
Panic Disorder (not codable)
Posttraumatic Stress Disorder (309.81)
Psychotic Disorders (*see Subtypes*)
Separation Anxiety (309.21)
Social Phobia (300.23)
Somatization Disorder (300.81)
Substance-Induced Anxiety Disorder (*Substance Specific*)

TREATMENT PLAN
GENERALIZED ANXIETY DISORDER

Client: _____ Date: _____

```
┌─────────────────────────────────────┐
│                                      │
│   Multiaxial Assessment              │
│                                      │
│   Axis I:   _____          │
│   Axis II:  _____          │
│   Axis III: _____          │
│   Axis IV:  _____          │
│   Axis V:   _____          │
│                                      │
└─────────────────────────────────────┘
```

I. OBJECTIVES OF TREATMENT
    (*select one or more*)

    1. Educate parents about disorder.
    2. Investigate family history of the disorder.
    3. Help family develop better coping skills.
    4. Reduce pervasive anxiety and worry.
    5. Diminish symptoms of anxiety:

        Restlessness
        Fatigue
        Difficulty concentrating
        Irritability
        Somatization
        Sleep disturbance

    6. Encourage compliance with educational programs and referrals.
    7. Reduce irrational beliefs.
    8. Promote socialization.
    9. Reduce alienation.
    10. Restore child and family to optimum level of functioning.
    11. Develop discharge plan for coping with everyday life.

II. SHORT-TERM BEHAVIORAL GOALS AND INTERVENTIONS
    (*select goals and interventions appropriate for your client*)

(Note: Separate goals and interventions are provided for treatment of A-Parents, B-Child, and C-Family.)

SHORT-TERM BEHAVIORAL GOALS, **A-PARENTS**	THERAPIST'S INTERVENTIONS
Parents collaborate with therapist in development of a treatment plan.	Establish therapeutic alliance with parents to enhance outcome of treatment.
Help therapist understand child's development of anxiety problems.	Assess problem with parents and record a comprehensive history of the child's development and anxiety problems.
Become aware of the diagnosis and what to appropriately expect from the child.	Educate parents about the diagnosis.
Cooperate in building a genogram to identify familial history and its relationship to anxiety problems.	Construct a genogram to better understand the family history and define how family deals with anxiety and its impact on the child (see Behavioral Techniques, Chapter 23).
Enter treatment for Generalized Anxiety Disorder, if appropriate, to enhance outcome of child's therapy.	Evaluate parents for anxiety problems and treat or refer for treatment (see *Behavioral Management Guide: Essential Treatment Strategies for Adult Psychotherapy* in Resources for Providers, Chapter 33).
Develop awareness of how your personal theory influences cognition of the problem in child.	Explore parental theory of the problem.
Recognize fears and feelings of negative self-blame related to the problem.	Evaluate parents' fears and negative feelings of self-blame for child's problem.
Learn to reach beyond automatic cognitive reactions in viewing the problem.	Expand parental perspective beyond limited cognitive reactions.
Parents learn how to help their child deal with stressors.	Teach parents the laws of anxiety: not permanent, not dangerous, and reduced by child confronting the problem. Exposure can produce growth.

Parents learn to deal with child's sleep disorder.	Investigate for sleep problems in child, and teach parents how to deal with problem.
Confront thoughts of exaggerated and unrealistic consequences—"What ifs?"	Guide parents in confronting distorted reactions to trigger situations.
Identify cognitive distortions	Weigh the reactions against evidence-based reality.
Restructure distortions with evidence-based consequences	With parents, reframe distortions with reality-based reactions to stressors.
Learn diaphragmatic breathing as a relaxation technique and teach child to help in relaxation.	Teach parents diaphragmatic breathing to assist child in relaxation (see Behavioral Techniques, Chapter 23).
Comply with referral for psychological testing of child.	Provide referral for psychological testing of child to evaluate intellectual capabilities and rule out other diagnostic considerations.
Understand importance of early intervention.	Explain importance of and refer for early intervention for young children under school age (see Behavioral Techniques, Chapter 23).
Agree to allow therapist to confer with child's school to help in development of a comprehensive psycho-educational treatment plan for the child.	Request and receive parental permission to confer with child's teachers and school administrators.
Comply with referral for medical and psychiatric evaluations.	Provide referral for medical and psychiatric evaluations, if appropriate.
Parents read to child, improving their relationship while learning new coping skills.	Assign parents books they can read to their child to enhance their relationship, while increasing their coping skills, such as *Don't Feed the Monster on Tuesdays!* or *The Bear Who Lost His Sleep* (see Bibliotherapy, Chapter 26).

Parents develop new parenting skills.	Assign parents to read books on how to deal with their anxiety and increase parenting skills, such as *Making Families Work and What to Do When They Don't* and others (see Bibliotherapy, Chapter 26).
Monitor child's medication schedule and report all reactions or failures to take medications.	If child is on medications, instruct parents on need for a regular schedule and feedback that may indicate need for revised dosage.
Meet with other parents who are experiencing similar difficulties, and share solutions for coping with the problem.	Refer parents to self-help group or group on parenting skills (see Self-Help Groups, Chapter 27).
Read about anxiety disorders to better understand how to cope.	Assign books on anxiety disorders such as *Your Anxious Child* (see Bibliotherapy, Chapter 26).
Discuss termination plan and resolve related issues.	Develop a termination plan and discuss issues of separation anxiety and dependency.

SHORT-TERM BEHAVIORAL GOALS, **B-CHILD**	THERAPIST'S INTERVENTIONS
Engage in play therapy.	Engage child in a therapeutic relationship, via play therapy.
Learn about diagnosis and develop realistic expectations of self.	Educate client about the diagnosis and discuss symptomatology so he/she can adjust self-expectations.
Undergo treatment for sleep disorder.	Investigate for sleep disorder and treat if necessary. See appropriate treatment plan.
Understand underlying dynamics that lead to maladaptive behavior and stress.	Explore ways in which anxieties manifest themselves (e.g., need for perfection, worry about nuclear war or catastrophe, over-conformance), and clarify underlying dynamics.
Realize that human beings are not perfect, and reduce stressors imposed on self.	Teach child that human beings are not perfect.
Recognize underlying feelings of anger or depression and express appropriately.	Explore for underlying feelings of anger or depression, using puppet or graphics (see appropriate treatment plan).
Observe puppets and how they behave. Begin to see new role models deal with anxieties.	Shape client behavior by use of puppets (see Behavioral Techniques, Chapter 23).
Watch how puppet expresses feelings about anxieties.	Display socially acceptable expression of feelings about anxieties, using stickers with puppet.
Learn new ways to handle fears.	Use puppet to role model successful ways to deal with fears.
Realize others also feel bad and relate to puppets overcoming the feeling.	Investigate for feelings of low esteem related to anxiety. Have puppets talk about how they feel and what they can do about it.
Begin to see possible solutions.	Discuss with puppets how they deal with negative feelings.

Identify irrational beliefs.	Through continued play with puppets, explore irrational beliefs about fears and anxieties.
Reframe beliefs about fears and anxieties.	Change irrational beliefs by having the puppets discuss the beliefs and develop rational alternatives.
Learn from role modeling and shape new behaviors.	Use puppets to role model appropriate behavior.
Using guided imagery to augment the play therapy process, learn to gain control over feelings.	Teach relaxation techniques and "Using Guided Imagery to Augment the Play Therapy Process" to master anxieties (see Behavioral Techniques, Chapter 23).
Understand anxiety and realize that avoidance does not help.	Teach child the laws of anxiety: not dangerous, not permanent, avoidance increases anxiety. Exposure can promote change.
Communicate life story to therapist.	Use puppet to have child relate the story of his/her life.
Express suppressed feelings in a nonthreatening environment.	Play the *Talking, Feeling, and Doing Game* to understand underlying processes in a nonthreatening way (see Therapeutic Games, Chapter 24).
Understand how trauma may have contributed to existing disorder.	Explore client's background for trauma that may have exacerbated the disorder.
Discuss personal coping mechanisms developed to handle the disorder.	Investigate with child possible patterns of withdrawal used to avoid anxieties.
Recognize and relate how family affects the problem.	Explore familial impact on the problem.
Learn positive self-talk.	Teach child positive self-talk to interrupt negative patterns.
Learn new technique for dealing with aggression.	Teach diaphragmatic breathing to control anxiety (see Behavioral Techniques, Chapter 23).

Learn new techniques to nurture yourself and deal with emotional difficulties.	Use the *Positive Thinking Game*, the *Anxiety Management Game*, or *The Ungame* to teach ways positive self-talk helps control emotional difficulties (see Therapeutic Games, Chapter 24).
Shift focus of attention from problem to accomplishment.	Ask client to describe accomplishments for the past week.
Feel more confident as self-esteem improves.	Compliment client to provide positive reinforcement whenever possible.
Communicate problematic feelings to develop new skills or options.	Use technique of "Pounding Away Bad Feelings" and game *Don't Break the Ice* to help child release frustrations (see Behavioral Techniques, Chapter 23).
Attempt to use new control skills in school.	Urge child to use new control skills in the classroom setting.
Report results to therapist.	Provide positive reinforcement when client reports that he/she has challenged anxiety-provoking situations. Praise attempt and reward success.
Learn positive problem solving and reduce anxiety by confronting your feelings.	Assign to read *Don't Be Afraid, Tommy* or *Linda Saves the Day* (see Bibliotherapy, Chapter 26).
Learn how famous people have overcome their problems.	Assign to read or have parents read to child *Anybody Can Bake a Cake* (see Bibliotherapy, Chapter 26).
Learn methods that you can better use to advocate for yourself.	Instruct client in the technique of self-advocacy.
Understand that you can deal with these issues and end treatment successfully.	Develop a termination plan and explain issues of separation anxiety and dependency.

SHORT-TERM BEHAVIORAL GOALS, **C-FAMILY**	THERAPIST'S INTERVENTIONS
Improve communications among family members to reduce levels of anger and alienation.	Conduct family sessions or refer for family therapy to reduce anger and/or alienation and improve communication skills within the family.
Cooperate in amplifying family genogram.	Augment genogram created in an early parental session to help understand structure of family and spell out physical and emotional boundaries, including toxic issues.
Discuss genogram openly to fully understand family history as it relates to anxiety over medical issues.	Discuss genogram to reveal family history and possible family secrets and defenses surrounding illness.
Demonstrate boundaries, alliances, triangles, and emotional currents that may exacerbate the anxieties.	Explore family boundaries using sculpturing, a useful technique for understanding triangulation, alliances, and emotional currents (see Behavioral Techniques, Chapter 23).
Negative interactions (i.e., jealousy, competition, enmity) are reduced to establish homeostasis.	Investigate sibling rivalries and reduce negative interactions.
Shift focus from problem to possible solutions.	Have family imagine a future without the problem and suggest actions that can be taken now to best approximate that possibility.
Think about what treatment outcome would look like. Explain what you would like to see change in other family members when treatment is completed.	Ask family members to think about what they might want to say about each other when treatment is completed.
Family members realize they have the power to make important changes, even if these seem small.	Help family members realize they have an opportunity to do some things differently.

Members are empowered. They recognize that they can create positive change.	Ask family members to relate what they have accomplished in the past week.
Realize that major change is the result of small steps taken one at a time.	Help family identify and prioritize achievable goals.
Enhance understanding of condition and see how other families have handled similar problems.	Assign as homework reading *Making Families Work, and What to Do When They Don't* or *An Ounce of Prevention: How Parents Can Stop Childhood Behavioral and Emotional Problems before They Start* (see Bibliotherapy, Chapter 26).
Make use of available community resources.	Refer family to available resources in the community. (See Self-Help Groups or 800 Numbers, Chapter 27.)
Reduce negative communication.	Develop a system of positive reinforcement with family members to interact better with each other and reduce scapegoating.
Family members work together to develop termination plan.	Discuss termination issues and develop a plan to terminate treatment.

OBSESSIVE-COMPULSIVE DISORDER (300.3)

Obsessive-Compulsive Disorder is marked by persistent and time-consuming obsessions or compulsions that cause significant distress or impairment in everyday activities. Obsessions are inappropriate and intrusive (ego-dystonic) ideas, thoughts, impulses, and images that cause anxiety or distress. These may take the form of thoughts about contamination, repeated doubts, and the need for a specific pattern of order, sexual imagery, or aggressive impulses. Compulsions are repetitive behaviors or mental acts designed to relieve anxiety or distress or to prevent a dreaded event. Common compulsions including washing and cleaning, counting, checking, and other repeated actions. Most adults realize that the obsessions or compulsions are excessive and unrealistic. However, children may not have the cognitive ability to make that judgment. Although the disorder may begin in childhood, it is more common in adolescence or early adulthood, appearing earlier in males than in females.

Behavioral Symptoms
Obsessive-Compulsive Disorder
(severity index: 1, mild; 2, moderate; 3, intense)

Severity

Obsessions:

1. Client has intrusive, inappropriate thoughts, impulses, or images that cause anxiety or distress. _____
2. The thoughts, impulses, or images are not just excessive worries about real-life problems. _____
3. Client wards off or suppresses these stimuli by ritualized thought or action. _____
4. Client recognizes the stimuli as the products of his/her own mind. _____

Compulsions:

1. Client is driven to act out repetitive physical or mental
   tasks to reduce or eliminate distress or to prevent a
   dreaded event.   _____

2. The behavior is not connected in a realistic way with the
   event.   _____

3. The client recognizes that the obsessions or compulsions
   are excessive or unrealistic.   _____

4. The obsessions and compulsions are time-consuming,
   cause distress, and interfere with client's daily activities.   _____

THE TREATMENT PLAN
OBSESSIVE-COMPULSIVE DISORDER

Client: _____ Date: _____

```
┌─────────────────────────────────────────┐
│  Multiaxial Assessment                    │
│                                           │
│  Axis I:   _____                  │
│  Axis II:  _____                  │
│  Axis III: _____                  │
│  Axis IV:  _____                  │
│  Axis V:   _____                  │
│                                           │
└─────────────────────────────────────────┘
```

I. OBJECTIVES OF TREATMENT
    (*select one or more*)

1. Educate parents about the disorder.
2. Investigate family history of the disorder.
3. Help family develop better coping skills.
4. Reduce anxiety related to the disorder.
5. Ameliorate obsessional thoughts, impulses, and images that cause anxiety or distress.
6. Encourage compliance with educational programs and referrals.
7. Reduce or eliminate the excessive and unrealistic compulsions that interfere with the client's daily activities.
8. Reduce irrational beliefs.
9. Promote socialization.
10. Reduce alienation.
11. Restore client to optimal level of functioning.
12. Develop discharge plan for coping with everyday life.

II. SHORT-TERM BEHAVIORAL GOALS AND INTERVENTIONS
    (*select goals and interventions appropriate for your client*)

(Note: Separate goals and interventions are provided for treatment of A-Parents, B-Child, and C-Family.)

SHORT-TERM BEHAVIORAL GOALS, **A-PARENTS**	THERAPIST'S INTERVENTIONS
Parents collaborate with therapist in development of a treatment plan.	Establish therapeutic alliance with parents to enhance outcome of treatment.
Help therapist understand child's development and accurately assess problem.	Discuss problem with parents and record a comprehensive history of the child's development in order to assess Obsessive-Compulsive Disorder.
Become aware of the diagnosis and what to appropriately expect from the child.	Educate parents about the diagnosis.
Cooperate in building a genogram to identify familial history and its relationship to the disorder.	Construct a genogram to better understand the family history and its impact on the child (see Genogram, Chapter 23).
Develop awareness of how your personal theory influences cognition of the problem.	Explore parental theory of the problem.
Recognize fears and feelings of negative self-blame related to the problem.	Evaluate parents' fears and negative feelings of self-blame for child's problem.
Learn to reach beyond automatic cognitive reactions in viewing the problem.	Expand parental perspective beyond limited cognitive reactions.
Undergo treatment for underlying problems that may exacerbate child's condition.	Explore for underlying problems in parents (e.g., anxiety, depression) and treat or refer for therapy (see *Behavioral Management Guide: Essential Treatment Strategies for Adult Psychotheray* in Resources for Providers, Chapter 33).
Comply with referral.	If appropriate, refer parents for psychological evaluation.
Understand importance of early intervention and follow through with referral.	Refer preschool children for early intervention (see Early Intervention, Chapter 23).

Agree to allow therapist to confer with child's school to help in development of a comprehensive psycho-educational treatment plan for the child.	Request and receive parental permission to confer with child's teachers and school administrators.
Comply with referral for psychological testing of child.	Provide referral for psychological testing of child to determine intellectual capabilities and rule out other diagnostic considerations.
Agree to psychiatric evaluation, if necessary, after child is interviewed.	Provide referral for psychiatric evaluation and possible medication, if indicated.
Meet with other parents who are experiencing similar difficulties and share solutions for coping with the problem.	Refer parents to self-help group.
Read about parenting skills and Obsessive-Compulsive Disorder to better understand how to cope with the problem.	Assign reading of *The OCD Workbook* or alternate book on Obsessive-Compulsive Disorder (see Bibliotherapy, Chapter 26).
Make use of community resources.	Educate parents about available community resources (see Self-Help Groups, Chapter 27, or On-Line Resources, Chapter 28).
Discuss and approve termination plan. Resolve termination issues.	Develop a termination plan and discuss issues of separation anxiety and dependency.

SHORT-TERM BEHAVIORAL GOALS, **B-CHILD**	THERAPIST'S INTERVENTIONS
Engage in play therapy.	Engage client in a therapeutic play therapy relationship.
Communicate the story of your life.	Use puppets to have client relate the story of his/her life.
Learn about diagnosis and develop realistic expectations of self.	Educate client about the diagnosis and discuss symptomatology so he/she can understand nature of Obsessive-Compulsive Disorder.
Mimic puppet in identifying automatic thoughts and behaviors.	Have puppets list their automatic thoughts and ritualized behaviors.
Evaluate automatic thoughts for cognitive distortions.	Have puppets analyze their cognitive distortions and ritualized actions.
Replace distorted thinking with evidence-based reality.	Use puppets to reframe the distortions, based on available evidence.
Identify ritualized actions you use to ward off anxiety.	Identify and monitor client's ritualized actions.
Understand anxiety and realize that avoidance does not help.	Teach client the laws of anxiety: not dangerous, not permanent, avoidance increases anxiety.
Observe puppets and how they behave. Begin to see new role models.	Shape client behavior by use of puppets. (See Behavioral Techniques, Chapter 23.)
Watch how puppet expresses feelings.	Display socially acceptable expression of feelings, using puppets.
Learn that it is okay to express feelings.	Reward puppets for expressing feelings appropriately.
Mimic puppets in expressing feelings.	Have client mimic the puppet to express his/her feelings.

Recognize underlying feelings of anger or depression and express appropriately.	Explore for underlying feelings of anger or depression, using puppet or graphics, and treat as necessary (see appropriate treatment plan).
Realize others also feel bad and overcome the feeling.	Investigate for feelings of low esteem related to Obsessive-Compulsive Disorder.
Begin to see possible solutions.	Discuss with puppets how they deal with obsessions and compulsions.
Identify irrational beliefs.	Through continued play with puppets, explore irrational beliefs about the disorder.
Reframe irrational thoughts and develop rational alternatives.	Have puppets discuss the irrational beliefs and develop rational alternatives.
Learn from role modeling and shape new behaviors.	Use puppets to role model appropriate behavior.
Use relaxation techniques or guided imagery to gain control over feelings and visualize self with better control.	With parents' permission, teach relaxation techniques and guided imagery to reduce obsessive-compulsive behaviors. (See Behavioral Techniques, Chapter 23.)
Express suppressed feelings in a nonthreatening environment.	Play the *Talking, Feeling, and Doing Game* to understand underlying processes in a nonthreatening way (see Therapeutic Games, Chapter 24).
Understand how trauma may have contributed to existing disorder.	Explore client's background for trauma that may have exacerbated the disorder.
Discuss personal coping mechanisms developed to handle the disorder.	Investigate with client possible patterns of withdrawal used to avoid Obsessive-Compulsive Disorder.
Recognize and relate how family affects the problem.	Explore familial impact on the problem.
Learn positive self-talk.	Teach client positive self-talk to interrupt obsessions/compulsions.

Learn new technique for dealing with aggression.	Teach diaphragmatic breathing to control anxiety (see Behavioral Techniques, Chapter 23).
Learn new techniques for dealing with emotional difficulties.	Use *The Social Skills Game* to teach how positive self-talk helps control emotional difficulties (see Therapeutic Games, Chapter 24).
Shift focus of attention from problem to accomplishment.	Ask client to describe accomplishments for the past week.
Feel more confident as self-esteem improves.	Compliment client to provide positive reinforcement whenever possible.
Communicate problematic feelings to develop new skills or options.	Use technique of "Pounding Away Bad Feelings" to help child release frustrations (see Therapeutic Games, Chapter 24).
Attempt to use new control skills in school.	Urge client to use new control skills in the classroom setting.
Report results to therapist.	Provide positive reinforcement when client reports that he/she has exercised control in school. Praise attempt and reward success.
Learn positive problem solving and how other people have overcome obstacles.	Assign child to read or have parents read to him/her *I Like Me, Anybody Can Bake a Cake*, or alternate (see Bibliotherapy, Chapter 26).
Learn methods that you can use to advocate for yourself.	Instruct client in the technique of self-advocacy.
Understand that you can deal with these issues and successfully end treatment.	Develop a termination plan and explain issues of separation anxiety and dependency.

SHORT-TERM BEHAVIORAL GOALS, **C-FAMILY**	THERAPIST'S INTERVENTIONS
Improve communications among family members.	Conduct family sessions or refer for family therapy to reduce anger and/or alienation, and improve communication skills within the family.
Cooperate in amplifying family genogram.	Amplify family genogram created in first family session to help understand parental session.
Discuss genogram openly to fully understand family history as it relates to Obsessive-Compulsive Disorder.	Discuss genogram to reveal family history and possible family secrets dealing with Obsessive-Compulsive Disorder.
Demonstrate boundaries, alliances, triangles, and emotional currents that may exacerbate the problem.	Explore family boundaries using sculpturing, a useful technique for understanding triangulation, alliances, and emotional currents (see Behavioral Techniques, Chapter 23).
Shift focus from problem to possible solutions.	Have family imagine a future without the problem and suggest actions that can be taken now to make that future possible.
Think about what treatment outcome would look like. Explain what you would like to see change in other family members when treatment is completed.	Ask family members to think about what they might want to say about each other when treatment is completed.
Family members realize they have the power to make important changes, even if these seem small.	Help family members realize they have an opportunity to do some things differently.
Members are empowered. They recognize that they can create positive change.	Ask family members to relate what they have accomplished in the past week.
Realize that major change is the result of small steps taken one at a time.	Help family identify and prioritize achievable goals.

Enhance understanding of condition and learn how to survive and break free.	Assign as homework reading, e.g., *Obsessive Compulsive Disorder* or *The OCD Workbook* (see Bibliotherapy, Chapter 26).
Make use of available community resources.	Refer family to available resources in the community (see Self-Help Group, Chapter 27, or On-Line Resources, Chapter 28).
Reduce negative communication.	Develop a system of positive reinforcement with family to interact better with each other and reduce scapegoating.
Family members work together to develop termination plan.	Discuss termination issues and develop a plan to terminate treatment.

POSTTRAUMATIC STRESS DISORDER (309.81)

Specify:

Acute: < three months
Chronic: > three months
Delayed onset: after six months

Posttraumatic Stress Disorder is characterized by development of typical stress symptoms following the experience of an event that involves potentially severe personal injury or loss of life. The symptoms may also be triggered by witnessing such a life-threatening event happening to another person, especially a close friend or relative. The individual's response to the event includes intense fear, helplessness, or horror. In children, the response may include disorganized or agitated behavior. Other symptoms include the persistent re-experience of the event, persistent avoidance of stimuli associated with the event, the numbing of general responsiveness (emotional anesthesia), or increased arousal. Traumatic events may include violent personal attack, physical or sexual attack, mugging, robbery, severe auto accidents, natural disasters, or being diagnosed with a life-threatening illness. In children, traumatic events may include sexual experience that is developmentally inappropriate without threat of injury or death. The symptoms must persist for more than a month and cause significant distress or impairment in important areas of functioning. Studies show that children whose parents do not overreact fare better in treatment.

Behavioral Symptoms
Posttraumatic Stress Disorder
(severity index: 1, mild; 2, moderate; 3, intense)

	Severity
1. Persistently re-experiences the traumatic event as a recollection or dream	_____
2. Has flashbacks of the event	_____
3. Displays intense distress at cues that are reminiscent of the event	_____
4. Avoids people, places, activities, and thoughts associated with the event	_____
5. Unable to remember an important aspect of the event	_____
6. Interest in usual activities is diminished	_____
7. Feels detached from others	_____
8. Range of feelings is restricted	_____
9. Has increased sense of limited future	_____
10. Has problem falling asleep or maintaining sleep	_____
11. Irritable, displays outbursts of anger	_____
12. Unable to concentrate	_____
13. Is easily startled	_____

Other Diagnostic Considerations

Adjustment Disorders
Acute Stress Disorder (308.3)
Obsessive-Compulsive Disorder (300.3)

(Malingering should be ruled out.)

TREATMENT PLAN
POSTTRAUMATIC STRESS DISORDER

Client: _____ Date: _____

+---+
| Multiaxial Assessment |
| |
| Axis I: _____ |
| Axis II: _____ |
| Axis III: _____ |
| Axis IV: _____ |
| Axis V: _____ |
+---+

I. OBJECTIVES OF TREATMENT
    (*select one or more*)

    1. Educate parents about disorder.
    2. Investigate how family deals with anxiety.
    3. Reduce pervasive anxiety and worry.
    4. Help family develop better coping skills.
    5. Eliminate stressors associated with the traumatic event.
    6. Diminish symptoms associated with the event (i.e., restlessness, fatigue, difficulty concentrating, irritability, somatization, sleep disturbance).
    7. Encourage compliance with educational programs and referrals.
    8. Reduce irrational beliefs.
    9. Promote socialization.
    10. Reduce alienation.
    11. Restore child and family to level of functioning before the event.

II. SHORT-TERM BEHAVIORAL GOALS AND INTERVENTIONS
    (*select goals and interventions that are appropriate for your client*)

(Note: Separate goals and interventions are provided for treatment of A-Parents, B-Child, and C-Family.)

SHORT-TERM BEHAVIORAL GOALS, **A-PARENTS**	THERAPIST'S INTERVENTIONS
Collaborate with therapist in development of a treatment plan.	Establish therapeutic alliance with parents to enhance outcome of treatment.
Relate in detail the traumatic event and your reactive feelings to it.	Investigate with parents the traumatic event and their feelings and reactions.
Help therapist understand child's development of anxiety related to the traumatic event.	Assess problem with parents and record a comprehensive history of the event.
Describe child's flashbacks and their intensity.	Explore for flashbacks in child and assess intensity.
Become aware of the diagnosis and what to appropriately expect from the child.	Educate parents about Posttraumatic Stress Disorder.
Cooperate in building a genogram to identify familial history and its relationship to anxiety problems.	Construct a genogram to better understand the family history and define how family deals with anxiety and its impact on the child (see Behavioral Techniques, Chapter 23).
Enter treatment to help you deal with child's trauma and enhance outcome of child's therapy.	Evaluate parents for anxiety problems related to traumatic event and treat or refer for treatment. (*Behavioral Management Guide: Essential Treatment Strategies for Adult Psychotherapy* in Resources for Providers, Chapter 33.)
Develop awareness of how your personal theory influences cognition of the problem in child.	Explore parental theory of the problem.
Recognize fears and feelings of negative self-blame related to the problem.	Evaluate parents' fears and negative feelings of self-blame for child's problem.
Learn to reach beyond automatic cognitive reactions in viewing the problem.	Expand parental perspective beyond limited cognitive reactions.

Learn how to help child deal with stressors.	Teach parents the laws of anxiety: not permanent, not dangerous, and reduced by child confronting the problem. Exposure can produce growth.
Undergo treatment for individual problems, which, in turn, enhances outcome of child's therapy.	Explore for parental psychopathology (e.g., anxiety, depression, marital discord, etc.) and refer for treatment (see appropriate treatment plan, *Behavioral Management Guide: Essential Treatment Strategies for Adult Psychotherapy* in Resources for Providers, Chapter 33).
Parents learn to deal with child's sleep disorder.	Investigate for sleep problems in child, and teach parents how to deal with problem.
Confront thoughts of exaggerated and unrealistic consequences.	Guide parents in confronting distorted reactions to trigger situations.
Identify cognitive distortions.	Weigh the reactions against evidence-based reality.
Restructure distortions with evidence-based consequences.	With parents, reframe distortions with reality-based reactions to stressors.
Learn diaphragmatic breathing as relaxation technique and teach child to help in relaxation.	Teach parents diaphragmatic breathing to assist child in relaxation (see Behavioral Techniques, Chapter 23).
Comply with referral for psychological testing of child.	Provide referral for psychological testing of child to estimate acute and chronic event-related stress (i.e., Trauma Symptom Inventory [TSI], or Beck Anxiety Disorder [BAD]).
Agree to allow therapist to confer with child's school to help in development of a comprehensive psycho-educational treatment plan for the child.	Request and receive parental permission to confer with child's teachers and school administrators.

Comply with referral for medical and psychiatric evaluations.	Provide referral for medical and psychiatric evaluations if appropriate.
Understand importance of early intervention.	Explain importance of and refer for early intervention for preschool children. (See Early Intervention, Chapter 23.)
Parents read to child, improving their relationship while learning new coping skills.	Assign parents books they can read to their child to enhance their relationship while increasing their coping skills, such as *Stress Can Really Get on Your Nerves*. (See Bibliotherapy, Chapter 26.)
Develop new coping strategies.	Coach parents in developing new strategies for coping with their child's problem.
Parents develop new parenting skills and understand how to deal with their child's anxiety.	Assign parents to read books on how to deal with their anxiety and increase parenting skills, such as *Making Families Work and What to Do When They Don't, I Can't Get Over It*, and others (see Bibliotherapy, Chapter 26).
Monitor child's medication schedule and report all reactions or failures to take medications.	If child is on medications, instruct parents on need for a regular schedule and feedback that may indicate need for revised dosage.
Meet with other parents who are experiencing similar difficulties, and share solutions for coping with the problem.	Refer parents to self-help group or group on parenting skills (see Self-Help Groups, Chapter 27).
Discuss termination plan and resolve related issues.	Develop a termination plan and discuss issues of separation anxiety and dependency.

SHORT-TERM BEHAVIORAL GOALS, **B-CHILD**	THERAPIST'S INTERVENTIONS
Engage in play therapy.	Engage child in a therapeutic relationship, via play therapy.
Learn about diagnosis and develop realistic expectations of self.	Educate client about the diagnosis and discuss symptomatology so he/she can adjust self-expectations.
Cooperate in evaluation of symptomatology.	Refer for or administer to child the Trauma Symptom Checklist for Children (TSCC) to evaluate symptomatology.
Undergo treatment for sleep disorder.	Investigate for sleep disorder and treat if necessary. (See appropriate treatment plan.)
Understand underlying dynamics, which lead to maladaptive behavior and stress.	Explore ways in which flashbacks manifest themselves and discuss and clarify underlying dynamics.
Recognize cues and use appropriate cognitive strategies to deal more effectively with anxiety.	Teach child to recognize signs of anxious arousal to use as cues, and train in cognitive strategies to avoid flashbacks or panic attacks.
Realize that human beings are not perfect, and reduce stressors imposed on self.	Teach child that human beings are not perfect.
Recognize underlying feelings of anger or depression and express appropriately.	Explore for underlying feelings of anger or depression, using puppet or graphics (see appropriate treatment plan).
Observe puppets and how they behave. Begin to see new role models deal with anxieties.	Shape client behavior by use of puppets (see Behavioral Techniques, Chapter 23).
Watch how puppet expresses feelings about anxieties.	Display socially acceptable expression of feelings about anxieties, using stickers with puppet.
Learn new ways to handle fears.	Use puppet to role model successful ways to deal with fears.

Realize others also feel bad and relate to puppets overcoming the feeling.	Investigate for feelings of low esteem related to trauma. Have puppets talk about how they feel and what they can do about it.
Discuss flashbacks and bad dreams to lessen their impact.	Explore flashbacks and analyze dreams to reduce their impact on the child.
Learn new methods for dealing with flashbacks.	Desensitize child to flashbacks using relaxation techniques or hypnosis, with parents' permission. (See Behavioral Techniques, Chapter 23.)
Begin to see possible solutions.	Discuss with puppets how they deal with negative feelings.
Identify irrational beliefs.	Through continued play with puppets, explore irrational beliefs about the traumatic event.
Reframe beliefs about fears and anxieties.	Change irrational beliefs by having the puppets discuss the beliefs and develop rational alternatives.
Learn from role modeling and shape new behaviors.	Use puppets to role model behaviors to deal with stress.
Using guided imagery and relaxation techniques, learn to gain control over feelings.	Teach relaxation techniques and guided imagery to master anxieties (see "Using Guided Imagery to Augment the Play Therapy Process," Behavioral Techniques, Chapter 23).
Understand anxiety and realize that avoidance does not help.	Teach child the laws of anxiety: not dangerous, not permanent, avoidance increases anxiety. Exposure can promote change.
Communicate life story to therapist.	Use puppet to have child relate the story of his/her life.

Express suppressed feelings in a nonthreatening environment.	Play the *Talking, Feeling, and Doing Game* to understand underlying processes in a nonthreatening way (see Therapeutic Games, Chapter 24).
Learn new methods of coping with trauma.	Shape behavior by having puppets talk about how they have dealt with a trauma in their lives.
Discuss personal coping mechanisms developed to handle the disorder.	Investigate with child possible patterns of withdrawal used to avoid anxieties.
Recognize and relate how family affects the problem.	Explore familial impact on the problem.
Learn positive self-talk.	Teach child positive self-talk to interrupt negative patterns.
Learn new technique for dealing with aggression.	Teach diaphragmatic breathing to control anxiety (see Behavioral Techniques, Chapter 23).
Learn new techniques to nurture yourself and deal with emotional difficulties.	Use the *Positive Thinking Game*, *Bounce Back*, or *The Coping Skills Game* to teach ways positive self-talk helps control emotional difficulties (see Therapeutic Games, Chapter 24).
Shift focus of attention from problem to accomplishment.	Ask client to describe accomplishments for the past week.
Feel more confident as self-esteem improves.	Compliment client to provide positive reinforcement whenever possible.
Communicate problematic feelings to develop new skills or options.	Use technique of "Pounding Away Bad Feelings" and game *Don't Break the Ice* to help child release frustrations (see Behavioral Techniques, Chapter 23).

Report results to therapist.	Provide positive reinforcement when client reports that he/she has challenged anxiety-provoking situations. Praise attempt and reward success.
Learn new coping skills to deal with the trauma.	Assign to read or have parents read to child, *I Saw It Happen* for children who have witnessed violence (see Bibliotherapy, Chapter 26).
Learn new strategies for dealing with anxiety.	Assign to read or have parents read to child *Don't Feed the Monster on Tuesdays* or *The Lion Who Lost His Roar* (see Bibliotherapy, Chapter 26).
Learn methods that you can use to advocate for yourself.	Instruct client in the technique of self-advocacy.
Understand that you can deal with these issues and end treatment successfully.	Develop a termination plan and explain issues of separation anxiety and dependency.

SHORT-TERM BEHAVIORAL GOALS, **C-FAMILY**	THERAPIST'S INTERVENTIONS
Improve communications among family members to reduce familial anxiety.	Conduct family sessions or refer for family therapy to reduce anxiety and improve communication skills within the family.
Family members share their feelings surrounding the trauma and their responses to it. Work together to deal with the issues. "Identified patient" is less alienated.	Have family members explain their personal view of the trauma and its impact on each one of them. If other siblings were involved, see individually or refer for treatment.
Cooperate in amplifying family genogram.	Amplify family genogram created in first family session to help understand parental session.
Discuss genogram openly to fully understand family history as it relates to anxiety.	Discuss genogram to reveal family history and possible family secrets dealing with trauma and anxiety.
Demonstrate boundaries, alliances, triangles, and emotional currents that may exacerbate the anxieties.	Explore family boundaries using sculpturing, a useful technique for understanding triangulation, alliances, and emotional currents (see Behavioral Techniques, Chapter 23).
Shift focus from problem to possible solutions.	If possible, have family imagine a future without the problem and suggest actions that can be taken now to make that future possible.
Think about what treatment outcome would look like. Explain what you would like to see change in other family members when treatment is completed.	Ask family members to think about what they might want to say about each other when treatment is completed.
Family members realize they have the power to make important changes, even if these seem small.	Help family members realize they have an opportunity to do some things differently.
Members are empowered. They recognize that they can create positive change.	Ask family members to relate what they have accomplished in the past week.

Realize that major change is the result of small steps taken one at a time.	Help family identify and prioritize achievable goals.
Enhance understanding of condition and see how other families have handled similar problems.	Assign as homework reading *Making Families Work, and What to Do When They Don't* (see Bibliotherapy, Chapter 26).
Make use of available community resources.	Refer family to available resources in the community. (See Self-Help Groups, Chapter 27, or On-Line Resources, Chapter 28.)
Reduce negative communication.	Develop a system of positive reinforcement with family members to interact better with each other and reduce scapegoating.
Family members work together to develop termination plan.	Discuss termination issues and develop a plan to terminate treatment.

SOCIAL PHOBIA (300.23)

Social Phobia is marked by a persistent fear of social situations where evaluation by others is possible. The individual is afraid of acting in an embarrassing or humiliating manner and often reacts to social interaction with a panic attack. Usually, the individual recognizes the fear as excessive and unreasonable. Typically, the onset of this disorder is in the mid-teens after a childhood of shyness.

Social Phobia appears as excessive shyness or fearfulness in children. Children appear excessively timid in unfamiliar settings and shrink away from contact with people they do not know. They typically do not participate in group play or other social activities and cling to a familiar adult. In extreme cases, mutism may be present. There must be evidence of the child's capacity to interact with familiar people and failure to interact in peer settings or with unfamiliar adults. Children with Social Phobia usually do poorly in school, may be school phobic, and avoid age-appropriate social activities.

When onset is in adolescence, Social Phobia leads to decreased ability to function academically. Despite contrary evidence in some clinical samples, the disorder is more prevalent in girls than in boys.

Behavioral Symptoms
Social Phobia
(severity index: 1, mild; 2, moderate; 3, intense)

Severity

1. Persistent fear of social interactions where evaluation by others is possible _____

2. School phobic _____

3. Fear of acting in social situations in an embarrassing or humiliating way _____

4. Exposure to social situations leads to panic attacks _____

5. Feared social situations are avoided or endured under duress _____

6. The fear and duress interfere with the child's activities of daily living _____

(Note: Behavioral symptoms for related panic attack and agoraphobia are listed in the following sections. These symptoms may occur with Social Phobia and other disorders, but are not themselves *DSM-IV* codable.)

Panic Attack Symptoms

Panic attacks are characterized by intense fear, in which four of the following develop quickly and increase to peak intensity within minutes:

1. Palpitations, pounding heart, increased pulse rate
2. Perspiration
3. Trembling, shaking
4. Feeling of choking or smothering
5. Chest pain
6. Nausea, dizziness
7. Derealization, depersonalization
8. Fear of losing control, going crazy, or dying
9. Numbness or tingling
10. Chills or hot flashes

Symptoms of Agoraphobia

1. Anxiety of being in a situation or place where escape may be difficult or impossible
2. Anxiety over being in a place where a panic attack would be embarrassing
3. Anxiety over being in a place where help may not be available in case of a panic attack
4. The situation or place is avoided or endured with duress
5. The situation or place is endured with the help of a friend or companion

TREATMENT PLAN
SOCIAL PHOBIA

Client: _____ Date: _____

Multiaxial Assessment

Axis I: _____

Axis II: _____

Axis III: _____

Axis IV: _____

Axis V: _____

I.   OBJECTIVES OF TREATMENT
     (*select one or more*)

   1. Educate parents about the disorder.
   2. Determine family history of the disorder.
   3. Help family develop better coping skills.
   4. Reduce pervasive anxiety and worry.
   5. Diminish symptoms of shyness.
   6. Diminish fear of social situations.
   7. Eliminate school phobia.
   8. Reduce and eliminate fear of embarrassment in social interactions.
   9. Control and eliminate panic attacks.
   10. Eliminate need for avoidance of social interactions.
   11. Encourage compliance with educational programs and referrals.
   12. Reduce irrational beliefs.
   13. Promote socialization.
   14. Reduce alienation.
   15. Restore child and family to optimum level of functioning.
   16. Develop discharge plan for coping with everyday life.

II. SHORT-TERM BEHAVIORAL GOALS AND INTERVENTIONS
     (*select goals and interventions appropriate for your client*)

(Note: Separate goals and interventions are provided for the treatment of
A-Parents, B-Child, and C-Family.)

SHORT-TERM BEHAVIORAL GOALS, **A-PARENTS**	THERAPIST'S INTERVENTIONS
Collaborate with therapist in development of a treatment plan.	Establish therapeutic alliance with parents to enhance outcome of child's treatment.
Help therapist understand child's development of anxiety problems.	Assess problem with parents and record a comprehensive history of child's development of excessive shyness or social phobias.
Become aware of the diagnosis and what to appropriately expect of the child.	Educate parents about the diagnosis.
Cooperate in building a genogram to identify family history and its relationship to social phobias.	Construct a genogram to better understand the family history of social phobias or excessive shyness and the methods the family has used to deal with it.
Enter treatment for anxiety or social phobias to support child's therapy.	Evaluate parents for anxiety problems or social phobia and treat or refer for treatment (see *Behavioral Management Guide: Essential Treatment Strategies* in Resources for Providers, Chapter 33).
Develop awareness of how your personal theory influences cognition of the problem in the child.	Explore parental history of the problem.
Recognize situational triggers for child's avoidance behavior.	Have parents identify situational triggers for social avoidance behavior.
Recognize fears and self-blame related to the problem.	Evaluate parents' fears and negative feelings of self-blame for child's problem.
Learn to reach beyond automatic cognitive reactions in viewing the problem.	Expand parental perspective beyond cognitive reactions.

Learn how to help child deal with stressors.	Teach parents the laws of anxiety: not permanent, not dangerous, and reduced by confrontation. Exposure can produce growth.
Learn how to empower child, rather than provide secondary gains for avoidance behavior.	Help parents realize and teach child that most people are afraid of something, but each time they face their fear they become stronger. Avoidance weakens.
Learn how to deal with child's sleep problems.	Investigate for sleep problems and teach parents how to deal with them (see appropriate treatment plan).
Confront thoughts of exaggerated or unrealistic expectations in social situations.	Guide parents in confronting distorted reactions to social situations.
Identify cognitive distortions.	Weigh the reactions against evidence-based reality.
Restructure distortions with evidence-based consequences.	With parents, reframe distortions with reality-based reactions to stressors.
Learn diaphragmatic breathing as a relaxation technique and teach child.	Teach parents diaphragmatic breathing to assist child in relaxation (see Behavioral Techniques, Chapter 23).
Comply with referral for psychological testing of child.	Provide referral for psychological testing of child to evaluate intellectual capabilities and rule out other disorders.
Agree to allow therapist to confer with school officials to help in development of a comprehensive psycho-educational program for the child.	Get parental permission to confer with school officials.
Comply with referrals for medical and psychiatric evaluation.	Provide referral for medical and psychiatric evaluations, if appropriate.

Read assigned books to learn new coping skills to develop a stronger parent–child bond.	Assign parents to read to their child *The Shy Little Girl, A Tiger Called Thomas,* or *Linda Saves the Day* to learn new coping skills (see Bibliotherapy, Chapter 26).
Develop new parenting skills.	Assign parents to read *Making Families Work and What to Do When They Don't* or *It's Nobody's Fault* to increase their parenting skills (see Bibliotherapy, Chapter 26).
Monitor child's medication schedule and report all reactions and failures to take medications.	If child is on medication, instruct parents on need for a regular schedule and feedback that might indicate a need for dosage adjustment.
Meet with other parents who are experiencing similar difficulties and share solutions for coping with the problem.	Refer parents to self-help group or group on parenting skills.
Read about anxiety disorders and further enhance your coping skills.	Assign parents to read *Your Anxious Child* (see Bibliotherapy, Chapter 26).
Discuss termination plan and resolve related issues.	Develop a termination plan and discuss issues of separation anxiety and dependency.

SHORT-TERM BEHAVIORAL GOALS, **B-CHILD**	THERAPIST'S INTERVENTIONS
Engage in play therapy.	Engage child in a therapeutic relationship via play therapy. Child may need parent to be included in early sessions.
Learn about diagnosis and develop realistic perceptions of self.	Educate child about the disorder and discuss symptomatology so he/she can adjust self-expectations.
Undergo treatment for sleep problems.	Investigate for sleep disturbance and treat as necessary (see appropriate treatment plan).
Understand underlying dynamics that lead to maladaptive behavior and Social Phobia.	Explore ways in which Social Phobia manifests itself, and clarify underlying dynamics.
Realize that human beings are not perfect. Reduce self-imposed stressors.	Teach child that human beings are not perfect.
Cooperate in building genogram and identify patterns of interaction.	Construct genogram to better understand family interrelationships.
Recognize underlying feelings of anger and/or depression and express appropriately.	Explore for underlying feelings of anger and/or depression, using puppets (see appropriate treatment plan).
Comply with referral.	Refer child for medical and psychiatric evaluations, if appropriate.
Verbalize feelings toward evaluations and medications, if prescribed.	Investigate child's feelings about evaluations and, if appropriate, how he/she reacts to medications.
Observe puppets and how they behave. Begin to see how new role models deal with anxieties.	Shape client behavior with use of puppets (see Behavioral Techniques, Chapter 23).
Watch how puppets express feelings about Social Phobia.	Have puppets display acceptable expression of feelings about Social Phobia.

Become aware of situational triggers and avoidance behavior.	Identify situational triggers for phobia and resulting avoidance behavior.
Learn new ways to handle fears.	Use puppets to role model successful ways to deal with Social Phobia and other fears.
Realize that others also feed bad and relate to puppets in overcoming feelings of shyness.	Investigate for feelings of low self-esteem related to Social Phobia. Have puppets talk about how they feel and what they can do about it.
Work out your fears psychodynamically. Through role play, see what it feels like to master your fear.	Have child role play with puppets. Have child act out his/her fears with the puppets. Then have child act socially without fear.
Begin to see possible solutions.	Discuss with puppets how they deal with negative feelings.
Learn to face social fear rather than run from it.	Have puppets discuss how much better they feel when they face their fears, rather than avoid them.
Identify irrational beliefs.	Through continued play with puppets, explore irrational beliefs about fears and anxieties.
Reframe beliefs about fears and phobia.	Have puppets discuss the irrational beliefs and develop evidence-based alternatives.
Gain confidence and overcome fears that cause Social Phobia.	Encourage child to externalize his/her positive role-playing.
Learn from role modeling and shape new behavior.	Use puppets to role model appropriate behavior by confronting their social fears.
Using relaxation techniques and guided imagery, learn to master social fears.	Teach relaxation techniques and "Using Guided Imagery to Augment the Play Therapy Process" to help master Social Phobia (see Behavioral Techniques, Chapter 23).

Understand anxiety and realize that avoidance does not help.	Teach child the laws of anxiety: not dangerous, not permanent, avoidance increases anxiety, exposure can produce growth.
Learn that anxieties are diminished by confrontation and increased by avoidance.	Instruct child to confront anxiety, rather than run from it.
Communicate life story to therapist.	Use puppet to have child relate the story of his/her life.
Express suppressed feelings in a nonthreatening environment.	Play the *Talking, Feeling, and Doing Game* to understand the underlying processes in a nonthreatening way (see Therapeutic Games, Chapter 24).
Learn to focus on task and not the audience.	Help child to ignore audience and focus on the task.
Understand how trauma may have contributed to existing disorder.	Explore client's background for trauma that may have caused or exacerbated the disorder.
Discuss personal coping mechanisms developed to handle Social Phobia.	Investigate with child possible patterns of withdrawal used to avoid Social Phobia and anxieties.
Evaluate beliefs for negative consequences and reframe them.	Help child examine and reframe irrational beliefs for positive consequences.
Recognize and relate how family affects the problem of Social Phobia.	Explore familial impact on the problem.
Learn positive self-talk.	Teach child positive self-talk to interrupt the negative patterns.
Learn new technique for handling anxiety.	Instruct child in diaphragmatic breathing to control anxiety (see Behavioral Techniques, Chapter 23).
Children learn how to handle stress.	Recommend that parents read *Ready . . . Set . . . R.E.L.A.X.* (see Bibliotherapy, Chapter 26).

Learn new techniques to nurture yourself and deal with emotional difficulties.	Use the *Positive Thinking Game, Bounce Back,* or *Clear Thinking* to teach ways positive self-talk helps control negative emotions (see Behavioral Techniques, Chapter 23).
Shift focus of attention from problem to accomplishment.	Ask client to describe accomplishments of the past week.
Feel more confident as self-esteem improves.	Whenever possible, compliment child to provide positive reinforcement.
Communicate problematic feelings to develop new skills or options.	Use technique of "Pounding Away Bad Feelings" and game *Don't Break the Ice* to help child release frustrations (see Behavioral Techniques, Chapter 23).
Attempt to use new control skills in school.	Urge client to use new control skills in classroom setting.
Report results to therapist.	Provide positive reinforcement. Praise attempt, reward success.
Learn positive problem solving while increasing self-esteem.	Have parents read to child *Don't Be Afraid, Tommy* or *Full Esteem Ahead: 100 Ways to Build Self-Esteem in Children and Adults* (see Bibliotherapy, Chapter 26).
Learn effective technique for dealing with phobias.	Provide homework assignment from *Forms for Helping the Socially Fearful Child* (see Resources for Providers, Chapter 33).
Learn new strategies for controlling fears.	Assign to have parents read to child *The Lion Who Lost His Roar* or *A Tiger Called Thomas* (see Bibliotherapy, Chapter 26).
Learn methods that you can use to advocate for yourself.	Instruct client in self-advocacy.
Resolve separation and dependency issues and successfully end treatment.	Develop a termination plan and discuss issues of separation anxiety and dependency.

SHORT-TERM BEHAVIORAL GOALS, **C-FAMILY**	THERAPIST'S INTERVENTIONS
Improve communication among family members to reduce familial anxiety.	Conduct family sessions or refer for family therapy to reduce anger and/or alienation, and improve communication.
Cooperate in amplifying existing genogram.	Expand genogram created in parental session to determine personal views and understand family history of phobia.
Demonstrate family boundaries, alliances, triangles, and emotional currents that may exacerbate Social Phobia.	Using family sculpturing, explore family boundaries (see Behavioral Techniques, Chapter 23).
Identify secondary gains generated by the disorder.	Explore for secondary gains within family that reinforce the disorder.
Situational triggers are identified.	Identify situational triggers that may cause episodes of Social Phobia.
Family clarifies feelings of shame or guilt.	Investigate familial feelings of shame or guilt over Social Phobia.
Negative hidden messages are exposed and reduced.	Explore for hidden messages family uses to create further problems for "identified patient."
Realize you have the power to make important changes, even if they seem small.	Have family members realize they have an opportunity to do some things differently.
Think about what treatment outcome would look like. Explain what you would like to see change in other family members.	Ask family members what they want to say about each other when treatment is complete.
Imagine future without the problem.	Have family members imagine a future without the problem or with the problem controlled. Suggest actions that can be taken now to make that future possible.
Realize you can create positive change.	Empower family members to create positive change.

Realize that major change is the result of many small steps taken one at a time.	Help family identify and prioritize achievable goals.
Enhance understanding of Social Phobia and see how other families have handled similar problems.	Assign as homework reading for family members *Making Families Work and What to Do When They Don't* (see Bibliotherapy, Chapter 26).
Make use of available community resources.	Refer family to available resources in the community (see Self-Help Groups, Chapter 27, or On-Line Resources, Chapter 28).
Reduce negative communication.	Develop system of positive reinforcement within family to improve interaction.
Work together to develop and implement termination plan.	Discuss termination issues and develop a viable plan to end treatment.

SPECIFIC PHOBIA (300.29)

Specify:

Animal: cued by insects or animals, usually begins in early childhood.

Natural Environment: cued by environment elements (i.e., hurricanes, storms, floods, etc.), usually begins in childhood.

Blood-Injection: cued by blood and injury, highly familial.

Situational: cued by specific situations (i.e., public transportation, tunnels, bridges, elevators, etc.) highly familial and bimodal, onset in early childhood to mid-twenties.

Other: cued by fear or avoidance of situations that might lead to choking, vomiting, or contracting an illness; "space" phobia; and childhood fears of loud noises or costumed characters.

Specific Phobia involves the persistent, excessive, and unreasonable fear of objects or situations that provoke an immediate anxiety response characterized as a panic attack. In children, the anxiety may be expressed by crying, tantrums, freezing, or clinging. Fear of animals is common and usually transitory. Although adults and adolescents may realize that the fear is excessive or unreasonable, children clearly may not. Usually, the object or situation is avoided, but sometimes may be endured under duress. For children under 18 years of age, the situation must persist for more than six months to qualify for the diagnosis of Specific Phobia. The phobia must significantly interfere with the individual's daily scholastic or social activities. There are several types of Specific Phobia that should be specified with the diagnosis, including Animal, Natural Environment, Blood-Injection, Injury, Situational, and Other. Such fears are common in children, but the level of impairment is usually insufficient to warrant a diagnosis.

(Note: Agoraphobia and Panic Attack occur with several other disorders, but are not codable disorders in themselves. Behavioral symptoms for both of these conditions are included in the following sections.)

Behavioral Symptoms
Specific Phobia
(severity index: 1, mild; 2, moderate; 3, intense)

<u>Severity</u>

1. Excessive and unreasonable fear of an object or situation   _____
2. Immediate anxiety upon exposure to object or situation   _____
3. Excessively clingy   _____
4. Throws tantrums or cries a great deal   _____
5. Freezes   _____
6. Fails to recognize unreasonable nature of fear   _____
7. The object or situational trigger is avoided or endured   _____
8. The avoidance or distress significantly interferes with the client's daily life   _____

Panic Attack Symptoms
(not *DSM-IV* codable)

Intense fear or discomfort, in which at least four of the following develop quickly and reach peak intensity within minutes:

1. Palpitations, pounding heart, increased pulse rate
2. Perspiration
3. Trembling or shaking
4. Shortness of breath
5. Feeling of smothering or choking
6. Chest pain
7. Nausea
8. Dizziness
9. Derealization or depersonalization
10. Fear of losing control, going crazy, or dying
11. Numbness or tingling
12. Chills or hot flashes

Symptoms of Agoraphobia
(not *DSM-IV* codable)

1. Anxiety over being in a situation or place where escape may be difficult or impossible
2. Anxiety over being in a place where a panic attack would be embarrassing
3. Anxiety over being in a situation or place where help may not be available in case of panic attack

4. The situation or place is avoided or endured with distress
5. The situation or place is endured with support of a companion

Other Diagnostic Considerations

Panic Disorder with Agoraphobia (300.21)
Agoraphobia without History of Panic Disorder (300.22)
Social Phobia (300.23)
Separation Anxiety Disorder (309.21)
Obsessive-Compulsive Disorder (300.3)
Posttraumatic Stress Disorder (309.81)
Avoidant Personality Disorder (301.82)

Panic Attack, as a reaction to a substance or medication, or as a general medical condition, should be ruled out.

TREATMENT PLAN
SPECIFIC PHOBIAS

Client: _____   Date: _____

Multiaxial Assessment

Axis I: _____
Axis II: _____
Axis III: _____
Axis IV: _____
Axis V: _____

I.   OBJECTIVES OF TREATMENT
     (*select one or more*)

     1. Educate parents about disorder.
     2. Determine family history of the disorder.
     3. Help family develop better coping skills.
     4. Reduce pervasive anxiety and worry.
     5. Diminish excessive fear of object or situation.
     6. Decrease anxiety when exposed to object or situation.
     7. Eliminate need to avoid or endure object or situation.
     8. Eliminate interference with activities of daily living.
     9. Encourage compliance with educational programs and referrals.
    10. Reduce irrational beliefs.
    11. Promote socialization and reduce alienation.
    12. Restore client to optimum level of functioning.
    13. Develop discharge plan for coping with everyday life.

II. SHORT-TERM BEHAVIORAL GOALS AND INTERVENTIONS
     (*select goals and interventions appropriate for your client*)

(Note: Separate goals and interventions are provided for the treatment of
A-Parents, B-Child, and C-Family.)

SHORT-TERM BEHAVIORAL GOALS, **A-PARENTS**	THERAPIST'S INTERVENTIONS
Collaborate with therapist in development of a treatment plan.	Establish therapeutic alliance with parents to enhance outcome of treatment.
Help therapist understand development of the child's specific phobia.	Assess problem with parents, identify specific phobia, and record a comprehensive history of the child's disorder.
Explore and understand origin of child's fears.	Explore with parents the original source of fear in the child.
Become aware of the diagnosis and what to appropriately expect from the child.	Educate parents about the diagnosis.
Cooperate in building a genogram to identify familial history and its relationship to phobias.	Construct a genogram to better understand the family history of phobias and define how family deals with them and their impact on the child (see Behavioral Techniques, Chapter 23).
Reduce severity of fear.	Examine with parents both their fears and the child's fears, and look at related reality issues.
Enter treatment for phobias or anxiety, if appropriate, to enhance outcome of child's therapy.	Evaluate parents for phobia or anxiety problems and treat or refer for treatment, as appropriate (see *Behavioral Management Guide: Essential Strategies for Adult Psychotherapy*, in Resources for Providers, Chapter 33).
Develop awareness of how your personal theory influences cognition of the problem in child.	Explore parental theory of the problem.
Recognize fears and feelings of negative self-blame related to the problem.	Evaluate parents' fears and negative feelings of self-blame for child's problem.

Learn to reach beyond automatic cognitive reactions in viewing the problem.	Expand parental perspective beyond limited cognitive reactions.
Agree to allow therapist to confer with child's school to help in development of a comprehensive psycho-educational treatment plan for the child.	Request and receive parental permission to confer with child's teachers and school administrators.
Comply with referral for medical and psychiatric evaluations.	Provide referral for medical and psychiatric evaluations, if appropriate.
Parents develop new parenting skills.	Assign parents to read books on how to deal with their anxiety and increase parenting skills, such as *Making Families Work and What to Do When They Don't, Mastering Your Special Phobias*, and other selections (see Bibliotherapy, Chapter 26).
Monitor child's medication schedule and report all reactions or failures to take medications.	If child is on medications, instruct parents on need for a regular schedule and feedback that may indicate need for revised dosage.
Meet with other parents who are experiencing similar difficulties, and share solutions for coping with the problem.	Refer parents to self-help group or group on parenting skills.
Read about anxiety disorders to better understand how to cope.	Assign books on anxiety disorders, such as *Your Anxious Child* (see Bibliotherapy, Chapter 26).
Discuss termination plan and resolve related issues.	Develop a termination plan and discuss issues of separation anxiety and dependency.

SHORT-TERM BEHAVIORAL GOALS, **B-CHILD**	THERAPIST'S INTERVENTIONS
Engage in play therapy.	Engage client in therapeutic relationship, via play therapy.
Recognize cues that trigger phobias.	Identify the persons, places, and things that cue phobias (e.g., animals, environment, blood, situational, other, etc.).
Learn about diagnosis and develop realistic expectations of self.	Educate client about the diagnosis and discuss symptomatology so he/she can adjust self-expectations.
Understand origins of your fears.	If possible, explore the original source of the child's phobia, what, when, and why.
Through play therapy, explore reactions to phobias.	Investigate with child his/her reaction to phobias.
Observe puppets and how they behave. Begin to see new role models.	Shape client behavior by use of puppets (see Behavioral Techniques, Chapter 23). Have puppets act out new reactions to cues.
Watch how puppet expresses feelings.	Display socially acceptable expression of feelings using stickers with puppet.
Learn that it is okay to confront fears.	Reward puppet for confronting phobic situation.
Mimic puppet and express feeling.	Have client mimic the puppets to express his/her fears and reward or praise.
Join in play therapy and imagine you are exposed to feared situation or event, to reduce actual fear when exposed to real event.	Via play therapy, expose puppets to feared situation and discuss feelings and reactions.
Recognize underlying feelings of anger or depression and express appropriately.	Explore for underlying feelings of anger or depression using puppet and treat (see appropriate treatment plan).

Realize others also feel bad and relate to puppet overcoming the feeling.	Investigate for feelings of low self-esteem. Have puppet talk about how it feels and what it can do about it.
Begin to see possible solutions.	Discuss with puppet how it deals with anxieties.
Identify irrational beliefs.	Through continued play with puppet, explore irrational beliefs.
Reframe beliefs about stress.	Change irrational beliefs by having the puppet discuss the beliefs and develop rational alternatives.
Learn from role-modeling and shape new behaviors.	Use puppets to role model appropriate behavior.
Using guided imagery and relaxation techniques, learn to gain control over phobias.	Use guided imagery and relaxation techniques to gain mastery over phobias (see "Using Guided Imagery to Augment the Play Therapy Process," Behavioral Techniques, Chapter 23).
Slowly become desensitized to phobias.	Gradually desensitize child to feared situation or event through relaxation techniques or hypnosis (see Behavioral Techniques, Chapter 23).
Communicate story of your life to therapist without using language, if necessary.	Use puppets to have client relate the story of his/her life.
Express suppressed feelings in a nonthreatening environment.	Play the *Talking, Feeling, and Doing Game* to understand underlying processes in a nonthreatening way (see Therapeutic Games, Chapter 24).
Understand how trauma may have contributed to existing disorder.	Explore client's background for trauma that may have exacerbated acute stress.

Discuss personal coping mechanisms developed to handle anxieties.	Investigate with client possible patterns of withdrawal used to avoid situations or event that trigger phobias.
Understand how you misinterpreted events.	Explore for misinterpretations of environmental events and correct.
Recognize and relate how family affects the problem.	Explore familial impact on the problem.
Learn positive self-talk.	Teach client positive self-talk to interrupt negative patterns.
Learn new technique for dealing with anxiety.	Teach diaphragmatic breathing to control anxiety (see Behavioral Techniques, Chapter 23).
Learn that you can control nightmares and other sleep problems.	If client has sleep problems, use technique called "Bad Dreams" (see Behavioral Techniques, Chapter 23).
Learn new relaxation techniques.	Assign to read *Ready . . . Set . . . Relax* or alternate selection (see Bibliotherapy, Chapter 26).
Read about new ways to avoid and work through fears.	Assign reading of *Let's Talk About Feeling Afraid* or alternate selection for older children (see Bibliotherapy, Chapter 26).
Learn new techniques for dealing with emotional difficulties.	Use the *Positive Thinking* game for children 9 years old and up to teach how positive self-talk helps control emotional difficulties (see Therapeutic Games, Chapter 24).
Shift focus of attention from problem to accomplishment.	Ask client to describe accomplishments for the past week.
Feel more confident as self-esteem improves.	Compliment client to provide positive reinforcement whenever he/she confronts anxieties that lead to phobias.
Communicate problematic feelings to develop new skills or options.	Use technique of "Pounding Away Bad Feelings" to help child release frustrations (see Behavioral Techniques, Chapter 23).

Attempt to use new behavioral skills in school.	If appropriate, urge client to use new behavioral skills in the classroom setting.
Report results to therapist.	Provide positive reinforcement when client reports that he/she has developed new ways to handle phobias. Praise attempt and reward success.
Learn causes and effects of stress, positive problem solving, and methods to deal with stressors and see how other people have overcome obstacles.	For children ages 6 through 12, assign to read *Anybody Can Bake a Cake* or *Don't Pop Your Cork on Monday* (see Bibliotherapy, Chapter 26, and alternate selections for other children).
Learn methods that you can use to advocate for yourself.	Instruct client in the technique of self-advocacy.
Understand that you can deal with these issues and successfully end treatment.	Develop a termination plan and explain issues of separation anxiety and dependency.

SHORT-TERM BEHAVIORAL GOALS, **C-FAMILY**	THERAPIST'S INTERVENTIONS
Improve communications among family members to reduce familial anxiety.	Conduct family sessions or refer for family therapy to reduce anger and/or alienation and improve communication skills.
Understand family history of phobias and your personal view of the family.	Amplify family genogram created in early parental session and compare with child's view of family history of phobias.
Discuss genograms openly to fully understand family history as it relates to anxiety.	Discuss genograms to reveal family history and possible family secrets dealing with anxiety.
Demonstrate boundaries, alliances, triangles, and emotional currents that may exacerbate the anxieties.	Explore family boundaries using sculpturing, a useful technique for understanding triangulation, alliances, and emotional currents (see Behavioral Techniques, Chapter 23).
Share coping styles and uncover irrational beliefs.	Explore with each family member the ways he/she deal with his/her personal fears and explore for irrational beliefs.
Replace irrational reactions to triggers.	Replace irrational family belief system with rational beliefs.
Improve communication skills.	Teach family principles of assertiveness—equal respect for self and others.
Recognize that avoidance increases anxiety, and enhance ability to help "identified patient" cope.	Instruct family on laws of anxiety: avoidance increases anxiety, confrontation lessens it. Panic is not dangerous, never permanent.
Shift focus from problem to possible solutions.	If possible, have family imagine a future without the problem and suggest actions that can be taken now to make that future possible.

Think about what the treatment outcome would look like. Explain what you would like to see change in other family members when treatment is completed.	Ask family members to think about what they might want to say about each other when treatment is completed.
Family members realize they have the power to make important changes even if they seem small.	Help family members realize they have an opportunity to do some things differently.
Family members are empowered. They recognize that they can create positive change.	Ask family members to relate what they have accomplished in the past week.
Realize that major change is the result of small steps taken one at a time.	Help family identify and prioritize achievable goals.
Enhance understanding of condition and see how other families have handled similar problems.	Assign as homework reading *Making Families Work and What to Do When They Don't* (see Bibliotherapy, Chapter 26).
Make use of available community resources.	Refer family to available resources in the community. (See Self-Help Groups, Chapter 27, or On-Line Resources, Chapter 28.)
Reduce negative communication.	Develop a system of positive reinforcement with family members to interact better with each other and reduce scapegoating.
Family members work together to develop termination plan.	Discuss termination issues and develop a plan to terminate treatment.

11

Bipolar Disorders

Bipolar Disorders include recurrent mood disorders in which episodes of mania occur, with or without major depression. Included in this category are Bipolar I Disorder (296.xx); Bipolar II Disorder (296.89); Bipolar Disorder NOS (296.80); and Cyclothymia (301.13).

BIPOLAR I DISORDER (296.xx)

Specify:

Single manic episode (296.0x)
Most recent episode:
    Depressed (296.5x)
    Hypomanic (296.40)
    Mixed (296.4x)
    Unspecified (296.7)

Bipolar I Disorder is characterized by one or more manic episodes, or mixed (manic-depressive) episodes. Often, clients have had one or more major depressive episodes as well. There are six subsets of Bipolar I Disorder, depending on whether the individual is experiencing a first episode, characterized as a Single Manic Episode, or a recurrence. Recurrence may be marked by a shift in polarity (Major Depressive Episode to a Manic or Mixed Episode, or a Manic

Episode into a Depressive or Mixed Episode). A Hypomanic Episode that evolves into a Manic or Mixed Episode, or vice versa, is considered a single episode. The first episode in males is more likely to be manic, while the first episode in females is usually depressive. Recurrent Bipolar I Disorders are specified by the current or most recent episode as follows:

> *Depressed*, characterized by depressive symptoms for a two-week period, with at least one previous Manic or Mixed Episode. Impairment is clinically significant. The first episode in females is usually depressive.

> *Hypomanic*, characterized by manic symptoms for at least four days, without significant impairment in social or occupational functioning. Presence of at least one previous Manic or Hypomanic Episode.

> *Manic*, characterized by manic symptoms for one week or requiring hospitalization, with at least one previous Manic, Major Depressive, or Mixed Episode. Marked impairment in functioning. The first episode in males is more likely to be manic.

> *Mixed*, characterized by both manic and depressive symptoms nearly every day for one week, with significant impairment in functioning or requiring hospitalization. Mixed episodes are more likely to appear in adolescents than adults.

> *Single Manic Episode*, characterized by manic symptoms for one week or requiring hospitalization, with no past Depressive Episodes. Marked impairment in functioning.

> *Unspecified*, characterized by manic, hypomanic, mixed, or depressive symptoms but not meeting the duration criteria listed previously. Presence of at least one previous Manic or Mixed Episode. Impairment is clinically significant.

Genetics and gender contribute to the incidence and severity of bipolar symptoms. The incidence of Bipolar I Disorder or Major Depressive Disorder among first-degree biological relatives of individuals with Bipolar I Disorder may be as high as 24 percent. More than 90 percent of individuals who have experienced a single Manic Episode will go on to have future episodes. More than 60 percent of Manic Episodes occur immediately before or after a Major Depressive Episode. Completed suicides occur in 10–15 percent of individuals with Bipolar I Disorder.

Most individuals with Bipolar I Disorder return to a functional level. However, some 20–30 percent continue to exhibit interpersonal and occupational difficulties. Although medication is the primary treatment modality for Bipolar Disorders, a biopsychosocial approach that incorporates therapy, medication, and psychoeducation is most productive and effective. The therapeutic alliance among the patient, family, and clinician is important in managing the disorder. Mood swings may alter a patient's willingness to comply with a treatment plan (including medication). An assessment of the patients' risk to themselves or others must determine the appropriate level of care. Patients experiencing a severe Manic Episode are often hospitalized. After hospitalization, regular outpatient sessions are necessary to fine-tune medication.

Manic and Depressive Episodes are defined as follows:

Manic Episode

A Manic Episode is marked by an abnormal and persistent elevated or irritable mood, including at least three of the following symptoms and lasting for one week or requiring hospitalization. In the case of irritable mood, four of the following are necessary to meet the criteria. Social or academic functioning is impaired. There are psychotic features. Hospitalization may be required to preclude harm to self or others.

1. Abnormally talkative, pressured speech
2. Flight of ideas or racing thoughts
3. Marked increase in goal-directed activity
4. Psychomotor agitation
5. Easily distracted by external stimuli
6. Excessive involvement in pleasurable activities with a high potential for negative consequences
7. Decreased need for sleep
8. Inflated self-esteem or grandiosity

Depressive Episodes

A Major Depressive Episode is marked by five or more of the following symptoms in a two-week period that mark a change in usual functioning. The symptoms must include depressed mood (or irritable mood in adolescents or children) or loss of interest.

1. Depressed mood most of the day
2. Decreased pleasure or interest in activities
3. Significant weight change (+/− 5 percent) in past thirty days
4. Insomnia or hypersomnia
5. Retardation or psychomotor agitation
6. Fatigue or loss of energy
7. Feelings of worthlessness or excessive guilt
8. Diminished ability to think or concentrate
9. Recurrent thoughts of death

10. Recurrent suicidal ideations, with or without a specific plan
11. Suicide attempt

Behavioral Symptoms
Bipolar I Disorder—Single Manic Episode
(severity index: 1, mild; 2, moderate; 3, intense)

Abnormal, persistent elevated, expansive or irritable mood lasting for one week, including three of the following and causing significant impairment in social or academic functioning or the need for hospitalization. There are psychotic features.

	Severity
1. Abnormally talkative, pressured speech	_____
2. Flight of ideas or racing thoughts	_____
3. Marked increase in goal-directed activity	_____
4. Psychomotor agitation	_____
5. Easily distracted by external stimuli	_____
6. Excessive involvement in pleasurable activities with a high potential for negative consequences	_____
7. Decreased need for sleep	_____
8. Inflated self-esteem or grandiosity	_____

TREATMENT PLAN
BIPOLAR I DISORDER—SINGLE MANIC EPISODE

Client: _____ Date: _____

```
┌─────────────────────────────────────────┐
│                                           │
│  Multiaxial Assessment                    │
│                                           │
│  Axis I:   _____                │
│  Axis II:  _____                │
│  Axis III: _____                │
│  Axis IV:  _____                │
│  Axis V:   _____                │
│                                           │
└─────────────────────────────────────────┘
```

I.   OBJECTIVES OF TREATMENT
     (*select one or more*)

1. Educate parents about disorder.
2. Determine family history of the disorder.
3. Help family develop better coping skills.
4. Reduce pervasive anxiety and worry.
5. Instruct parents about stress management.
6. Control pressurized speech.
7. Reduce psychomotor agitation.
8. Increase ability to maintain concentration.
9. Control potentially destructive activities.
10. Restore normal sleep pattern.
11. Reduce grandiosity.
12. Increase ability to focus on a single thought or task.
13. Encourage compliance with educational programs and referrals.
14. Work with educators to facilitate learning.
15. Reduce irrational beliefs.
16. Promote socialization, reduce alienation.
17. Restore child and family to optimum level of functioning.
18. Develop discharge plan for coping with everyday life

Other Diagnostic Considerations

ADHD (314.01, 314.00, 314.9)
Bipolar II Disorder (286.89)
Bipolar Disorder NOS (296.80)
Cyclothymic Disorder (301.13)

Mood Disorder due to a General Medical Condition (293.83)
Mood Disorder NOS (296.90)
Substance-Induced Mood Disorder (293.83)

Behavioral Symptoms
Bipolar I Disorder—Depressed
(severity index: 1, mild; 2, moderate; 3, intense)

Depressed mood or loss of pleasure or interest and three or more of the following for a two-week period:

                                                                    Severity

1. Depressed mood most of the day   _____
2. Decreased pleasure or interest in activities   _____
3. Significant weight change (+/- 5 percent) in past thirty days   _____
4. Insomnia or hypersomnia   _____
5. Retardation or psychomotor agitation   _____
6. Fatigue or loss of energy   _____
7. Feelings of worthlessness or excessive guilt   _____
8. Diminished ability to think or concentrate   _____
9. Recurrent thoughts of death   _____
10. Recurrent suicidal ideations, with or without a specific plan   _____
11. Suicide attempt   _____

TREATMENT PLAN
BIPOLAR I DISORDER, DEPRESSED

Client: _____   Date: _____

```
┌─────────────────────────────────────┐
│  Multiaxial Assessment               │
│                                      │
│  Axis I:    _____          │
│  Axis II:   _____          │
│  Axis III:  _____          │
│  Axis IV:   _____          │
│  Axis V:    _____          │
│                                      │
└─────────────────────────────────────┘
```

I. OBJECTIVES OF TREATMENT
    (*select one or more*)

    1. Educate parents about disorder.
    2. Determine family history of the disorder.
    3. Help family develop better coping skills.
    4. Reduce pervasive anxiety and worry.
    5. Reduce persistent depression.
    6. Restore interest in former pleasurable activities.
    7. Restore normal sleep and eating patterns.
    8. Eliminate feelings of worthlessness, guilt.
    9. Improve energy level.
    10. Eliminate or control suicidal ideations.
    11. Encourage compliance with educational programs and referrals.
    12. Reduce irrational beliefs.
    13. Promote socialization, reduce alienation.
    14. Restore child and family to optimum level of functioning.
    15. Develop discharge plan for coping with everyday life.

Behavioral Symptoms
Bipolar I Disorder—Hypomanic
(severity index: 1, mild; 2, moderate; 3, intense)

Abnormal, persistent elevated, expansive, or irritable mood lasting for four days and clearly different from the usual nondepressed mood. Three of the following symptoms persist (four, if only irritable mood). There is *no* significant impairment in social or academic functioning or the need for hospitalization. There are no psychotic features.

	Severity
1. Abnormally talkative, pressured speech	_____
2. Flight of ideas or racing thoughts	_____
3. Marked increase in goal-directed activity	_____
4. Psychomotor agitation	_____
5. Easily distracted by external stimuli	_____
6. Excessive involvement in pleasurable activities, with a high potential for negative consequences	_____
7. Decreased need for sleep	_____
8. Inflated self-esteem or grandiosity	_____

TREATMENT PLAN
BIPOLAR I DISORDER—HYPOMANIC

Client: _____ Date: _____

```
┌─────────────────────────────────────┐
│ Multiaxial Assessment               │
│                                     │
│ Axis I:    _____          │
│ Axis II:   _____          │
│ Axis III: _____           │
│ Axis IV:   _____          │
│ Axis V:    _____          │
└─────────────────────────────────────┘
```

I. OBJECTIVES OF TREATMENT
    (*select one or more*)

1. Educate parents about disorder.
2. Determine family history of the disorder.
3. Help family develop better coping skills.
4. Reduce pervasive anxiety and worry.
5. Instruct parents about stress management.
6. Control pressurized speech.
7. Reduce psychomotor agitation.
8. Increase ability to maintain concentration.
9. Control potentially destructive activities.
10. Restore normal sleep pattern.
11. Reduce grandiosity.
12. Increase ability to focus on a single thought or task.
13. Encourage compliance with educational programs and referrals.
14. Work with educators to facilitate learning.
15. Reduce irrational beliefs.
16. Promote socialization, reduce alienation.
17. Restore child and family to optimum level of functioning.
18. Develop discharge plan for coping with everyday life.

Other Diagnostic Considerations

ADHD (314.01, 314.00, 314.9)
Bipolar II Disorder (286.89)
Bipolar Disorder NOS (296.80)

Cyclothymic Disorder (301.13)
Mood Disorder due to a General Medical Condition (293.83)
Mood Disorder NOS (296.90)
Substance-Induced Mood Disorder (293.83)

Behavioral Symptoms
Bipolar I Disorder—Mixed Episode
(severity index: 1, mild; 2, moderate; 3, intense)

Symptoms for *both* Manic and Depressive Episodes (listed previously); persisting almost every day for one week.

BIPOLAR II DISORDER (296.89)
(Specify: Hypomanic or Depressed)

Bipolar II Disorder is characterized by one or more Major Depressive Episodes, in conjunction with at least one Hypomanic Episode. The most recent episode should be specified as Hypomanic or Depressed. The existence of a Manic or Mixed Episode would preclude the diagnosis of Bipolar II Disorder. The symptoms must cause significant distress or impairment in social, occupational, or other areas of functioning. Completed suicide occurs in 10–15 percent of cases of Bipolar II Disorder.

Behavioral Symptoms
Bipolar II Disorder—Depressive Episode
(severity index: 1, mild; 2, moderate; 3, intense)

Depressed mood or loss of pleasure or interest and three or more of the following for a two-week period:

Severity

1. Depressed mood most of the day. _____
2. Decreased pleasure or interest in usual activities _____
3. Significant weight change (+/– 5 percent) in past thirty days _____
4. Insomnia or hypersomnia _____
5. Retardation or psychomotor agitation _____
6. Fatigue or loss of energy _____
7. Feelings of worthlessness or excessive guilt _____
8. Diminished ability to think or concentrate _____
9. Recurrent thoughts of death _____

10. Recurrent suicidal ideations, with or without a specific plan   _____
11. Suicide attempt   _____

Other Diagnostic Considerations

Bipolar I Disorder (296.xx)
Bipolar Disorder NOS (296.80)
Cyclothymic Disorder (301.13)
Dysthymia (300.4)
Major Depressive Disorder (296.xx)
Mood Disorder due to a General Medical Condition (293.83)
Mood Disorder NOS (296.90)
Psychotic Disorders (298.xx)
Substance-Induced Mood Disorder (293.83)

TREATMENT PLAN
BIPOLAR II DISORDER—DEPRESSED

Client: _____ Date: _____

I. OBJECTIVES OF TREATMENT
   (*select one or more*)

   1. Reduce persistent depression.
   2. Restore interest in former pleasurable activities.
   3. Restore normal eating pattern.
   4. Restore normal sleep pattern.
   5. Eliminate feelings of worthlessness or guilt.
   6. Improve energy level.
   7. Eliminate or control suicidal ideations.

Behavioral Symptoms
Bipolar II Disorder—Hypomanic Episode
(severity index: 1, mild; 2, moderate; 3, intense)

An elevated, expansive, or irritable mood persisting for at least four days and including three of the following, four with only irritable mood. The episode is not acute enough to cause major impairment in educational or social functioning or to require hospitalization. There are no psychotic features.

	Severity
1. Abnormally talkative, pressured speech	_____
2. Flight of ideas or racing thoughts	_____
3. Marked increase in goal-directed activity	_____
4. Psychomotor agitation	_____
5. Easily distracted by external stimuli	_____
6. Excessive involvement in pleasurable activities, with a high potential for negative consequences	_____
7. Decreased need for sleep	_____
8. Inflated self-esteem or grandiosity	_____

TREATMENT PLAN
BIPOLAR II DISORDER—HYPOMANIC EPISODE

Client: _____ Date: _____

I. OBJECTIVES OF TREATMENT
(*select one or more*)

   1. Control pressurized speech.
   2. Reduce psychomotor agitation.
   3. Increase ability to maintain concentration.
   4. Curtail potentially destructive activities.
   5. Restore normal sleep pattern.
   6. Reduce grandiosity.
   7. Increase ability to focus on a single thought or task.

CYCLOTHYMIC DISORDER (301.13)

Cyclothymic Disorder is a chronic fluctuating mood disturbance persisting for at least two years and characterized by periods of hypomanic and periods of depressive symptoms. The individual is not without symptoms for more than two months out of the twenty-four. The symptoms cause significant distress or impairment in social or educational functioning. The hypomanic symptoms are insufficient to meet the criteria for a Manic Episode and the depressive symptoms are insufficient to meet those for a Major Depressive Episode. The diagnosis is contingent upon the absence of Major Depressive, Manic, or Mixed Episodes over the initial two-year period. After the initial period, Manic or Mixed Episodes (Bipolar I Disorder) and Major Depressive Episodes (Bipolar II Disorder) can be superimposed on the Cyclothymic Disorder in a dual diagnosis.

Behavioral Symptoms
Cyclothymic Disorder
(severity index: 1, mild; 2, moderate; 3, intense)

(Note: Cyclothymic Disorder should *not* fully meet the following criteria sets for hypomanic or depressive symptoms.)

Hypomanic Symptoms:

Three or more of the following, but not severe enough to cause impairment in social or educational functioning or to require hospitalization. No psychotic features are present:

1. Grandiosity, inflated self-esteem   _____
2. Diminished need for sleep   _____
3. Talkative, pressurized speech   _____
4. Flight of ideas, feels that thoughts are racing   _____
5. Easily distracted by external stimuli   _____
6. Psychomotor agitation   _____
7. Increase in goal-directed activity   _____
8. Excessive involvement in pleasurable activities
   that have a high destructive potential   _____
9. Symptoms cause distress or impairment in
   social or educational functioning   _____

Depressive Symptoms:

Five or more of the following present in a two-week period: One symptom must be depressed mood or loss of interest.

1. Depressed mood   _____
2. Diminished pleasure or interest in all or most
   all activities   _____
3. Significant weight change (+/-5 percent)   _____
4. Insomnia or hypersomnia   _____
5. Psychomotor agitation or retardation   _____
6. Fatigue or loss of energy   _____
7. Feelings of worthlessness or excessive guilt   _____
8. Indecisiveness, inability to concentrate   _____
9. Recurrent thoughts of death   _____
10. Suicidal ideations, with or without a plan   _____
11. Attempted suicide   _____
12. Symptoms cause major distress or impairment
    in social or occupational functioning   _____

Other Diagnostic Considerations

Bipolar I Disorder (296.xx)
Bipolar II Disorder (296.89)
Borderline Personality Disorder (301.83)
Mood Disorder due to a General Medical Condition (293.9)
Substance-Induced Mood Disorder (*see specific substance*)

TREATMENT PLAN
CYCLOTHYMIC DISORDER

Client: _____   Date: _____

I. OBJECTIVES OF TREATMENT
    (*select one or more*)

    1. Diminish grandiosity.
    2. Restore normal sleep pattern.
    3. Reduce pressurized speech.
    4. Control flight of ideas.
    5. Increase ability to concentrate.
    6. Ease psychomotor agitation.
    7. Eliminate pleasurable activities with negative consequences.
    8. Ease depression.
    9. Restore interest in usual activities.
    10. Restore normal eating pattern, weight.
    11. Reduce fatigue.
    12. Increase self-esteem.
    13. Diminish guilt feelings.
    14. Control suicidal ideations.
    15. Prevent suicide.
    16. Prevent relapse.

BIPOLAR DISORDER NOS (296.80)

Bipolar Disorder Not Otherwise Specified includes those disorders with bipolar features that do not meet the specifications for other specific Bipolar Disorders. Bipolar Disorder NOS is characterized by quick alternating manic and depressive symptoms, usually over a matter of days, that do not meet the duration requirements for a Manic Episode (one week) or a Major Depressive Episode (two weeks.) The symptoms cause major impairment in functioning.

The objectives of treatment are identical to those previously listed for cyclothymic disorder.

Other Diagnostic Considerations

Bipolar I Disorder (296.xx)
Bipolar II Disorder (296.89)
Cyclothymic Disorder (301.13)

II. SHORT-TERM BEHAVIORAL GOALS AND INTERVENTIONS
(select goals and interventions appropriate for your client)

(Note: Separate goals and interventions are provided for treatment of A-Parents, B-Child, and C-Family.)

SHORT-TERM BEHAVIORAL GOALS, **A-PARENTS**	THERAPIST'S INTERVENTIONS
Collaborate with therapist in development of a treatment plan.	Establish therapeutic alliance with parents to enhance outcome of treatment.
Help therapist understand child's development of bipolar or cyclothymic problems.	Assess problem with parents and record a comprehensive history of the child's development of bipolar or cyclothymic problems.
Identify child's symptoms and how you deal with them.	Explore, with parents, the symptoms they are dealing with and the techniques they use to help child.
Become aware of the diagnosis and what to appropriately expect from the child.	Educate parents about the diagnosis.
Cooperate in building a genogram to identify familial history and its methods for dealing with the "identified patient."	Construct a genogram to better understand the family history since there is a high likelihood that biological relatives share the disorder and to determine how the family has dealt with the disorder in the past. (See Behavioral Techniques, Chapter 23.)
Understand possible need for hospitalization.	Explain to parents the possible need for hospitalization of child to reduce anxiety and blame.
Agree with need for immediate hospitalization.	If parents believe child is actively suicidal, refer child for immediate hospitalization.

Comply with referral for psychological testing of child.	If child is not actively suicidal, provide referral for psychological testing of child or get parental permission to administer test to assess the disorder and the level of mania or depression.
Comply with medical referral.	Refer client for medical evaluation to rule out symptoms that mimic the disorder.
Have client treated for medical problem.	Confirm or revise diagnosis. Rule out Disorder due to a General Medical Condition.
Follow through with psychiatric evaluation to assess need for medication and possible anti-suicide measures.	Provide referral for psychiatric evaluation and follow up to confirm appointment was kept.
Maintain regular medication schedule and report urges to ignore or discontinue meds.	If medication is prescribed, confirm that prescription is filled and meds are taken on schedule.
Undergo evaluation of sexual abuse and, if necessary, enter treatment.	Evaluate for or rule out sexual abuse. If necessary, have parents treated (see *Behavioral Management Guide: Essential Treatment Strategies for Adult Psychotherapy* in Resources for Providers, Chapter 33).
Understand underlying dynamics that lead to maladaptive behavior.	Explore ways in which disorder manifests itself (i.e., pressurized speech, flight of ideas, psychomotor agitation, etc.) and clarify underlying dynamics.
Learn new strategies for dealing with stress interpersonally and intrapersonally.	Teach parents about stress management to reduce potential precipitants to negative events.
Have child referred for early intervention.	Explain the benefits of early intervention to parents.

Allow therapist to confer with school officials to develop a comprehensive psycho-educational treatment plan for the child.	If appropriate, request and receive parental permission to confer with child's teachers and school administrators.
Identify sleep problems and receive treatment.	Investigate with parents for sleep disorder or nightmares. Read to child *Can't You Sleep, Little Bear?* (see Bibliotherapy, Chapter 26).
Enter treatment for psychological problems, if appropriate, to enhance outcome of adolescent's therapy.	Evaluate parents for psychological problems (i.e., bipolar disorder, depression, cyclothymia, anxiety, etc.) and refer for treatment, if appropriate (see *Behavioral Management Guide: Essential Treatment Strategies for Adult Psychotherapy* in Resources for Providers, Chapter 33).
Become aware of how your personal theory influences cognition of the problem in the child.	Explore parental theory of the problem.
Recognize fears and feelings of self-blame related to the child's disorder.	Evaluate parents' fears and negative feelings of self-blame for the child's problem.
Learn to reach beyond automatic cognitive reactions in viewing the problem.	Expand parental perspective beyond limited cognitive reactions.
Learn how to help your child deal with stressors.	Instruct parents in laws of anxiety: not permanent, not dangerous, and reduced by child confronting the problem. Exposure can produce growth.
Confront thoughts of exaggerated and unrealistic consequences—"What ifs?"	Guide parents in confronting distorted reactions.
Identify cognitive distortions.	Weigh the reactions against evidence-based reality.
Restructure distortions with evidence-based consequences.	With parents, reframe distortions with reality-based reactions to stressors.

Learn innovative techniques for helping your child.	Assign parents to read *Survival Strategies for Parenting Children with Bipolar Disorder and Bipolar Disorders* (see Bibliotherapy, Chapter 26).
Learn diaphragmatic breathing as a relaxation technique and teach child to help in relaxation.	Teach parents diaphragmatic breathing to assist child in relaxation (see Behavioral Techniques, Chapter 23).
Develop new parenting skills.	Assign parents to read books on how to deal with their anxiety about child's disorder and increase parenting skills, such as *Making Families Work and What to Do When They Don't or Wonderful Ways to Have a Child* or *Try and Make Me: A Revolutionary Program for Raising Your Defiant Child without Losing Your Cool* (see Bibliotherapy, Chapter 26).
Meet with other parents who are experiencing similar difficulties and share solutions for coping with the problem.	Refer parents to self-help group or group on parenting skills.
Discuss termination plan and resolve related issues.	Develop a termination plan and discuss issues of separation anxiety and depression.

SHORT-TERM BEHAVIORAL GOALS, **B-CHILD**	THERAPIST'S INTERVENTIONS
Engage in play therapy.	Engage child in a therapeutic relationship, via play therapy.
Learn about diagnosis and develop realistic expectations of self.	Educate client about the diagnosis and discuss symptomatology so he/she can adjust self-expectations.
Undergo treatment for sleep disorder.	Investigate for sleep disorder and treat if necessary (see appropriate treatment plan).
Learn self-comforting techniques from suggested reading.	Read to child *Can't You Sleep, Little Bear?* (see Bibliotherapy, Chapter 26).
Understand triggers that lead to maladaptive behavior and stress.	Explore triggers that lead to maladaptive behavior.
Realize that human beings are not perfect, and reduce stressors imposed on self.	Teach child that human beings are not perfect.
Recognize underlying feelings of mania or depression and express appropriately.	Explore for underlying feelings of mania or depression using puppets.
Observe puppets and how they behave, or what they can do when depressed or manic. Begin to see new role models deal with anxieties.	Shape client behavior by use of puppets to role model ways they deal with mania or depression. (See Behavioral Techniques, Chapter 23.)
Watch how puppets express feelings of anger or mania.	Puppets display socially acceptable expression of feelings when angry or manic.
Learn new ways to handle fears.	Use puppet to role model successful ways to deal with fears.
Realize others also feel bad and relate to puppets overcoming the feeling.	Investigate for feelings of low esteem related to the disorder. Have puppets talk about how they feel and what they can do about it.

Identify how the disorder manifests itself.	Explore with puppets the ways the disorder manifests itself (i.e., pressurized speech, flight of ideas, agitation, excessive activity, etc.).
Identify with puppets and learn new methods for dealing with stressors.	Have puppets identify what stressors precipitate negative events and what actions to take to avoid destructive behaviors.
See puppets role model appropriate behaviors to deal with frustration.	Have puppets discuss what they can do when they want what they want and cannot have it.
Begin to see possible solutions.	Discuss with puppets how they deal with negative feelings.
Identify irrational beliefs and grandiose ideas.	Through continued play with puppets, explore irrational beliefs and grandiose ideas.
Reframe beliefs about self to more realistic beliefs.	Change irrational beliefs and grandiose ideas by having the puppets discuss the beliefs and develop rational alternatives.
Learn from role modeling and shape new behaviors.	Use puppets to role model appropriate behavior, such as slowing down speech if child suffers from pressurized speech.
Use guided imagery and relaxation techniques, to gain control over feelings.	Teach relaxation techniques and guided imagery to master anxieties (see "Using Guided Imagery to Augment Play Therapy," Behavioral Techniques, Chapter 23).
Understand anxiety and realize that avoidance does not help.	Teach child the laws of anxiety: not dangerous, not permanent, avoidance increases anxiety. Exposure can promote change.
Communicate life story to therapist.	Use puppet to have child relate the story of his/her life.

Express suppressed feelings in a nonthreatening environment.	Play the *Talking, Feeling, and Doing Game* to understand underlying processes in a nonthreatening way (see Therapeutic Games, Chapter 24).
Understand how trauma may have contributed to existing disorder.	Explore client's background for trauma that may have exacerbated the disorder.
Discuss personal coping mechanisms developed to handle the disorder.	Investigate with child possible patterns of withdrawal used to avoid others due to manic or depressive episodes.
Recognize and relate how family impacts the problem.	Explore familial impact on the problem.
Learn positive self-talk.	Teach child positive self-talk to interrupt negative patterns.
Learn new technique for dealing with anxiety.	Teach diaphragmatic breathing to control anxiety (see Behavioral Techniques, Chapter 23).
Learn new techniques to nurture yourself and deal with emotional difficulties.	Use the *Positive Thinking Game*, *Clear Thinking*, *The Anger Control Game*, or *The Ungame* to teach ways positive self-talk helps control emotional difficulties (see Therapeutic Games, Chapter 24).
Learn the consequences of your actions and develop solutions to problems as well as self-discipline.	Play the *Stop, Think, and Go Bears* self-control game to help child control impulses (see Therapeutic Games, Chapter 24).
Shift focus of attention from problem to accomplishment.	Ask client to describe accomplishments for the past week.
Feel more confident as self-esteem improves.	Compliment client to provide positive reinforcement whenever possible.

Communicate problematic feelings to develop new skills or options.	Use technique of "Pounding Away Bad Feelings" and game *Don't Break the Ice* to help child release frustrations (see Behavioral Techniques, Chapter 23).
Attempt to use new control skills in school.	Urge child to use new control skills in the classroom setting.
Report results to therapist.	Provide positive reinforcement when client reports back that he/she has challenged a manic or depressive episode. Praise attempt and reward success.
Learn positive problem-solving and new ways to handle these problems.	Assign to read *The Self Control Patrol Workbook* or *The Problem Solving Workbook* (see Bibliotherapy, Chapter 26).
Learn new strategies for dealing with aggressive behaviors.	Assign to read or have parents read to child *The Penguin Who Lost Her Cool* (see Bibliotherapy, Chapter 26).
Learn methods that you can use to advocate for yourself.	Instruct client on the technique of self-advocacy.
Understand that you can deal with these issues and bring treatment to an end successfully.	Develop a termination plan and explain issues of separation anxiety and dependency.

SHORT-TERM BEHAVIORAL GOALS, **C-FAMILY**	THERAPIST'S INTERVENTIONS
Improve communications among family members to reduce familial anxiety.	Conduct family sessions or refer for family therapy to reduce anger and/or alienation and improve communication skills.
Accept the fact that a family member has a chronic disorder.	Educate family about the chronic nature of the disorder to reduce denial, anger, and blame.
Cooperate in amplifying family genogram.	Amplify family genogram created in first parental session to help understand family history.
Discuss genogram openly to fully understand family history as it relates to the disorder.	Discuss genogram to reveal family history and possible family secrets dealing with the disorder.
Demonstrate boundaries, alliances, triangles, and emotional currents that may exacerbate the anxieties.	Explore family boundaries using sculpturing, a useful technique for understanding triangulation, alliances, and emotional currents (see Behavioral Techniques, Chapter 23).
Improve communications among family members.	Identify interpersonal problems among family members and work toward promoting healthier interactions and reducing stress.
Shift focus from problem to possible solutions.	Have family imagine solutions to the problem that can be implemented to deal with the disorder when it manifests itself.
Think about what treatment outcome would look like. Explain what you would like to see change in other family members when treatment is completed.	Ask family members to think about what they might want to say about each other when treatment is completed.
Learn problem-solving techniques and begin working as a team.	Assign as family reading *13 Steps to Help Families Stop Fighting* (see Bibliotherapy, Chapter 26).

Family members realize they have the power to make important changes, even if these seem small.	Help family members realize they have an opportunity to do some things differently.
Family members are empowered. They recognize that they can create positive change.	Ask family members to relate what they have accomplished in the past week.
Realize that major change is the result of small steps taken one at a time.	Help family identify and prioritize achievable goals.
Enhance understanding of condition and see how other families have handled similar problems.	Assign as homework reading *Making Families Work and What to Do When They Don't* (see Bibliotherapy, Chapter 26).
Plan trips together to become more cohesive.	Assign family outings to reduce alienation (i.e., museums, picnics, etc.) to enrich family life (see Bibliotherapy, Chapter 26).
Make use of available community resources.	Refer family to available resources in the community (see Self-Help Groups, Chapter 27, and On-Line Resources, Chapter 28).
Reduce negative communication.	Develop a system of positive reinforcement within family members to interact better with each other and reduce scapegoating.
Family members work together to develop termination plan.	Discuss termination issues and develop a plan to terminate treatment.

12

Depressive Disorders

MAJOR DEPRESSIVE DISORDER (296.xx)

Specify:

Single Episode (296.2x)
Recurrent Episode (296.3x)

Specifiers coded in the sixth digit:

1—Mild
2—Moderate
3—Severe without Psychotic Features
4—Severe with Psychotic Features
5—In Partial Remission
6—In Full Remission

Major Depressive Disorder is characterized by one or more major depressive episodes without a history of Manic, Mixed, or Hypomanic Episodes. If Manic, Mixed, or Hypomanic Episodes occur, the diagnosis should be revised to Bipolar Disorder. Although the *DSM-IV* states that individuals diagnosed with severe Major Depressive Disorder die by suicide, the figure may be much lower in children. The disorder occurs twice as frequently in girls as in boys. The symptoms in children appear as irritability, somatic complaints, and social withdrawal, rather than motor retardation, delusions, or hypersomnia These symptoms occur with other diagnostic disorders, such as Conduct Disorder, Anxiety Disorders, Attention Deficit Disorder, Eating Disorders, and Substance Abuse. Major Depressive Disorder may be preceded by Dysthymic Disorder and may co-exist with other disorders.

Behavioral Symptoms
Major Depressive Disorder
(severity index: 1, mild; 2, moderate; 3, intense)

Single Episode specifier requires five or more of the following occurring in a two-week period. Symptoms occur most all day, almost every day. Recurrent episodes require two consecutive months between episodes.

Severity

1. Depressed mood (as observed by parents or others) _____
2. Diminished interest or pleasure in almost all activities, socially withdrawn _____
3. Significant weight loss or gain, increase or decrease in appetite _____
4. Insomnia or hypersomnia _____
5. Psychomotor agitation or retardation _____
6. Irritable _____
7. Somatic complaints _____
8. Fatigue, loss of energy _____
9. Feelings of worthlessness, excessive guilt _____
10. Diminished ability to think or concentrate _____
11. Recurrent thoughts of death _____
12. Recurrent suicidal ideations, with or without a plan _____
13. Attempted suicide _____

DYSTHYMIC DISORDER (300.4)

Specify:

Early onset: before age 21.

Between 5 and 10 percent of all Americans suffer from Major Depression or Dysthymia every year. Dysthymia has fewer symptoms and is less severe than Major Depression. It is differentiated from a normal nonclinically depressed mood by the intensity and pervasiveness of the symptoms, which are in excess of those considered normal reactions to the difficulties of life. The adolescent must have experienced depressed mood and at least two of the following listed symptoms for a period of two years to meet the requirements for this diagnosis.

Dysthymic Disorder occurs equally in boys and girls and usually impairs school performance and interpersonal relations. Children and adolescents with this disorder typically display low self-esteem, are cranky and irritable, and tend to be pessimistic. In adulthood, women are two to three times more likely than men to suffer from this disorder. Clients with Dysthymia are vulnerable to Major Depression. Studies have shown that psychotherapy is an effective treatment. If no progress is apparent, the child should be re-evaluated for medication.

Behavioral Symptoms
Dysthymic Disorder (300.4)
(severity index: 1, mild; 2, moderate; 3, intense)

	Severity
1. Pervasive depressed mood	_____
2. Generalized loss of interest	_____
3. Feelings of helplessness or hopelessness	_____
4. Fatigue	_____
5. Irritability, excessive anger	_____
6. Decreased activity, productivity, or effectiveness	_____
7. Poor concentration	_____
8. Low self-esteem	_____
9. Insomnia, hypersomnia	_____
10. Difficulty making decisions	_____
11. Excessive or inappropriate guilt	_____
12. Poor appetite	_____
13. Overeating	_____
14. Thoughts of suicide or death	_____

DEPRESSIVE DISORDER NOS (311)

Included in this category are disorders with depressive features that do not meet the requirements for Major Depressive Disorder, Dysthymic Disorder, or related mood disorders. Examples include premenstrual dysmorphic disorder, minor depressive disorder, recurrent brief depressive disorder, post-psychotic depressive disorder, and a major depressive episode superimposed on Delusional or Psychotic Disorder.

Other Diagnostic Considerations

Bipolar I Disorder (296.0x)
Bipolar II Disorder (296.89)

TREATMENT PLAN
MAJOR DEPRESSIVE DISORDER
DYSTHYMIA
DEPRESSIVE DISORDER NOS

Client: _____   Date: _____

Multiaxial Assessment

Axis I: _____
Axis II: _____
Axis III: _____
Axis IV: _____
Axis V: _____

I. OBJECTIVES OF TREATMENT
    (*select one or more*)

    1. Educate parents about the disorder.
    2. Determine family history of the disorder.
    3. Help family develop better coping skills.
    4. Reduce persistent depression, diminish symptoms.
    5. Reduce pervasive anxiety and worry.
    6. Eliminate suicide plans, control suicidal ideations.
    7. Eliminate feelings of worthlessness, guilt.
    8. Restore normal eating patterns.
    9. Encourage compliance with educational programs and referrals.
    10. Improve energy level.
    11. Reduce irrational beliefs.
    12. Restore interest in former pleasurable activities.
    13. Promote socialization, reduce alienation.
    14. Restore adolescent and family to optimum level of functioning.

II. SHORT-TERM BEHAVIORAL GOALS AND INTERVENTIONS
    (*select goals and interventions appropriate for your client*)

(Note: Separate goals and interventions are provided for treatment of A-Parents,
B-Child, and C-Family.)

SHORT-TERM BEHAVIORAL GOALS, **A-PARENTS**	THERAPIST'S INTERVENTIONS
Parents collaborate with therapist in development of a treatment plan.	Establish therapeutic alliance with parents to enhance outcome of treatment.
Help therapist understand child's development of depression.	Assess problem with parents and record a comprehensive history of the child's development of depression.
If actively suicidal, hospitalize child immediately to preclude harm to self.	If child is actively suicidal, have parents hospitalize child immediately.
Undergo immediate evaluation to determine possible need for hospitalization.	If parents report that child has suicidal ideations, evaluate immediately to determine need for hospitalization.
Become aware of the diagnosis and what to appropriately expect.	Educate parents about the diagnosis. Explain chronicity of the disorder and the contagious nature of depression.
Realize that anger is a pitfall.	Inform parents that family members often become angry with the depressed patient.
Cooperate in building a genogram to identify familial history and its relationship to depression.	Construct a genogram to better understand the family history and define how family deals with depression and its impact on the child (see Behavioral Techniques, Chapter 23).
Enter treatment for depression or other existing disorders to enhance child's treatment.	Evaluate parents for depression or other psychiatric problems and treat or refer out for treatment (see *Behavioral Management Guide: Essential Treatment Strategies for Adult Psychotherapy*, Resources for Providers, Chapter 33).
Develop awareness of how your personal theory influences cognition of the problem in child.	Explore parental theory of the problem.

Identify other problems associated with a Major Depressive Disorder.	Investigate other problems that may be associated with Major Depressive Disorder (i.e., sleep disorders, somatization, eating disorders, guilt, worthlessness, fatigue).
Recognize fears and feelings of negative self-blame related to the problem.	Evaluate parents' fears and negative feelings of self-blame for child's problem.
Have child tested to confirm diagnosis and determine level of intensity of depression.	Refer child for psychological testing or test child in individual session, using Beck's Depression Inventory (BD1-11) to confirm diagnosis and determine level of intensity of depression.
Learn to reach beyond automatic cognitive reactions in viewing the problem.	Expand parental perspective beyond limited cognitive reactions.
Parents learn to deal with sleep disorder of child.	Investigate for sleep problems in child, and teach parents how to deal with problem.
Have child evaluated for medical problems and treated, if necessary.	Refer child for medical evaluation to rule out Disorder due to a General Medical Condition.
Be evaluated by psychiatrist for medication.	If child does not improve in treatment, refer to psychiatric evaluation and possible medication.
If sexual abuse is confirmed, have child placed in protected environment and treated.	Evaluate and rule out sexual abuse. If it is suspected that parents are abusers, refer for treatment and notify appropriate authorities.
Identify existing triggers that may cause depression.	Investigate with parents underlying feelings and identify issue that may cause or contribute to depression.
Learn diaphragmatic breathing as a relaxation technique and teach child to help in relaxation.	Teach parents diaphragmatic breathing to assist child in relaxation (see Behavioral Techniques, Chapter 23).

Understand importance of early intervention and comply with referral.	Explain importance of early intervention for pre-school children and refer (see Early Intervention, Behavioral Techniques, Chapter 23).
Agree to allow therapist to confer with child's school to help in development of a comprehensive psycho-educational treatment plan for the child.	Request and receive parental permission to confer with child's teachers and school administratators.
Develop new parenting skills to deal with depression.	Assign parents to read books on how to deal with their anxiety and increase parenting skills, such as *Making Families Work and What to Do When They Don't* (see Bibliotherapy, Chapter 26).
Learn how to identify the symptoms and strategies to help child.	Assign parents to read *The Depression Workbook* (see Bibliotherapy, Chapter 26).
Play audiotape to learn new methods of dealing with depression.	Have parents read *Depression and Anxiety Management* in order to learn new methods of dealing with child's depression (see Bibliotherapy, Chapter 26).
Read to child to enhance relaxation and teach strategies for dealing with depression.	Assign parents books they can read to child to help their relationship while reducing the depression, such as *The Cat at the Door* or *The Hyena Who Lost Her Laugh* (see Bibliography, Chapter 26).
Monitor child's medication schedule and report all reactions or failures to take meds.	If child is on meds, instruct parents on need for a regular schedule and feedback that may indicate need for revised dosage.
Meet with other parents who are experiencing similar difficulties, and share solutions for coping with the problem.	Refer parents to self-help group or group on parenting skills. (See Self-Help Groups, Chapter 27.)

Read about anxiety disorders to better understand how to cope.	Assign books on depressive disorders such as *Depression: A Parent' Guide to Suicidal and Depressed Teens* (see Bibliotherapy, Chapter 26).
Discuss termination plan and resolve related issues.	Develop a termination plan and discuss issues of separation anxiety and dependency.

SHORT-TERM BEHAVIORAL GOALS, **B-CHILD**	THERAPIST'S INTERVENTIONS
Engage in play therapy.	Engage child in a therapeutic relationship, via play therapy.
Learn about diagnosis and develop realistic expectations of self.	Educate client about the diagnosis and discuss symptomatology so he/she can adjust self-expectations.
Undergo treatment for sleep disorder.	Investigate for sleep disorder and treat, if necessary (see appropriate treatment plan).
Identify symptoms related to the disorder.	Explore ways in which depression manifests itself (irritability, somatization, guilt, feelings of worthlessness, fatigue, etc.).
Have medical exam. If necessary, be treated medically.	Refer for medical exam to rule out Disorder due to a General Medical Condition. If positive, change diagnosis and refer client for medical treatment.
Follow up with referral for psychological testing.	Refer for psychological evaluation and possible medication.
Discuss with therapist your reactions to psych evaluation and meds.	Discuss child's reaction to evaluation and medication, if prescribed.
Realize that human beings are not perfect, and reduce stressors imposed on self.	Teach child that human beings are not perfect.
Be hospitalized to protect yourself from harm.	Explore for suicidal feelings. If child has an active suicide plan, notify parents and hospitalize immediately.
Willingly enter into "suicide pact" with therapist—agree to inform therapist before taking any action.	If child is clearly not suicidal, but has ideations, implement a "suicide pact."
Recognize and clarify underlying feelings of depression.	Explore and clarify underlying feelings of depression, using puppets (see Therapeutic Games, Chapter 24).

Your depression is confirmed and intensity defined.	Refer for or administer Beck's Depression Inventory (BDI-II) to confirm existence of the disorder and the level of intensity.
Observe puppets and how they behave. Begin to see new role models deal with anxieties.	Shape client behavior by use of puppets (see Bibliotherapy, Chapter 33).
Watch how puppet expresses feelings about depression.	Display socially acceptable expression of feelings about depression, using puppets.
Realize others also feel bad and relate to puppets overcoming the feeling.	Investigate for feelings of low esteem related to depression. Have puppets talk about how they feel and what they can do about it.
Undergo treatment for sexual abuse. Be relocated to safe environment if parents are abusers.	Investigate for sexual abuse. If child is being abused, notify authorities and treat or refer for treatment (see appropriate treatment plan. See *Behavioral Management Guide: Essential Strategies for Adult Psychotherapy*, in Resources for Providers, Chapter 33.) If parents are abusers, have child removed to safe environment.
Begin to see possible solutions.	Discuss with puppets how they deal with negative feelings.
Recognize existing triggers that cause depression.	Through continued play with puppets, explore issues and feelings that lead to depression.
Recognize and express feelings of self-rage and anger.	Have puppets share their rage and anger at themselves to help child realize his own rage and anger.
Learn from role modeling and shape new behaviors.	Use puppets to role model appropriate behavior.
Replace negative self-talk.	Explain self-talk and encourage child to replace negative self-talk with positive affirmations.

Using guided imagery to augment the play therapy process, learn to gain control over feelings.	Teach relaxation techniques and guided imagery to master anxieties and depression (see "Using Guided Imagery to Augment the Play Therapy Process," Behavioral Techniques, Chapter 23).
Understand anxiety and realize that avoidance does not help.	Teach child the laws of anxiety: not dangerous, not permanent, avoidance increases anxiety. Exposure can promote change.
Communicate life story to therapist.	Use puppet to have child relate the story of his/her life, or play *Lifestories* with children 6 and over (see Therapeutic Games, Chapter 24).
Express suppressed feelings in a nonthreatening environment.	Play the *Talking, Feeling, and Doing Game* to understand underlying processes in a nonthreatening way (see Therapeutic Games, Chapter 24).
Understand how trauma may have contributed to existing disorder.	Explore client's background for trauma that may have exacerbated the depression.
Discuss personal coping mechanisms developed to handle the disorder.	Investigate with child possible patterns of withdrawal used to avoid anxieties.
Recognize and relate how family impacts the problem.	Explore familial impact on the problem.
Learn new technique for dealing with anxiety.	Teach diaphragmatic breathing to control anxiety (see Behavioral Techniques, Chapter 23).
Learn new techniques to nurture yourself and deal with emotional difficulties.	Use the *Positive Thinking Game*, *Bounce Back* or *The Ungame* to teach ways positive self-talk helps control emotional difficulties (see Therapeutic Games, Chapter 24).
Shift focus of attention from problem to accomplishment.	Ask client to describe accomplishments for the past week.

Feel more confident as self-esteem improves.	Compliment client to provide positive reinforcement whenever possible.
Communicate problematic feelings to develop new skills or options.	Use technique of "Pounding Away Bad Feelings" and game *Don't Break the Ice* to help child release frustrations (see Behavioral Techniques, Chapter 23).
Build new assertiveness skills.	Teach child the principles of assertiveness—equal respect for self and others.
Report results to therapist.	Provide positive reinforcement when client reports back that he/she has challenged anxiety or depression-provoking situations. Praise attempt and reward success.
Learn new techniques for dealing with depression.	With parents' permission, use hypnosis, visualization, or relaxation techniques to coach child to handle triggers of depression. Provide audiotape for home use (see Behavioral Techniques, Chapter 23, or Bibliotherapy, Chapter 26).
Learn the secret of optimistic thinking to change attitudes and behavior.	Assign to read *Don't Be Afraid, Tommy* or *The Hyena Who Lost Her Laugh* (see Bibliotherapy, Chapter 26).
Learn positive problem-solving and how famous people have overcome obstacles.	Assign to read *Don't Be Afraid, Tommy* or *The Feelings Story Book* (see Bibliotherapy, Chapter 26).
Learn methods that can be used to advocate for yourself.	Instruct client in the technique of self-advocacy.
Diminish need to "hide out" because of guilt and/or shame over being depressed.	Gradually build child's self-confidence to a point where avoidance behavior is no longer a rational response.
Realize that you are more than just a disorder and can use your unique skills to deal with problems.	Empower child by reinforcing skills and strengths.

| Understand that you can deal with these issues and bring treatment to an end successfully. | Develop termination plan and explain issues of separation anxiety and dependency. |

SHORT-TERM BEHAVIORAL GOALS, **C-FAMILY**	THERAPIST'S INTERVENTIONS
Improve communications among family members to reduce familial anxiety.	Conduct family sessions or refer for family therapy to reduce anger and/or alienation, and improve communication skills.
Cooperate in amplifying parental genogram.	Amplify genogram created in first parental session to help understand family history.
Demonstrate boundaries, alliances, triangles, and emotional currents that may exacerbate the anxieties.	Explore family boundaries using sculpturing, a useful technique for understanding triangulation, alliances, and emotional currents (see Behavioral Techniques, Chapter 23).
Explain how depression impacts your life and suggest strategies for dealing with it.	Explore with each family member how depression affects him or her and possible strategies for dealing with it.
Shift focus from problem to possible solutions.	Have family imagine a future without the problem and suggest actions that can be taken now to make that future possible.
Other family members are treated.	Determine if other family members have Major Depressive Disorder and treat or refer for treatment (see appropriate treatment plan).
Understand that it is normal, but counterproductive, to get angry at depressed family member.	Explain dynamics of depression cycle. Depression triggers anger in others, which, in turn, exacerbates the depression.
Family members realize they have the power to make important changes, even if these seem small.	Help family members realize they have an opportunity to do some things differently.
Learn new ways to deal with unpleasant feelings.	Encourage prosocial behaviors to develop family cohesiveness.

Family members are empowered. They recognize that they can create positive change.	Ask family members to relate what they have accomplished in the past week.
Realize that major change is the result of small steps taken one at a time.	Help family identify and prioritize achievable goals.
Focus on strengths rather than weaknesses.	Have each family member identify strengths he or she sees in the other members.
Enhance understanding of depression and learn how other families have dealt with this disorder.	Assign homework reading of *Making Families Work and What to Do When They Don't* or *Mind over Matter* (see Bibliotherapy, Chapter 26).
Make use of available community resources.	Refer family to available resources in the community (see Self-Help Groups, Chapter 27, and On-Line Resources, Chapter 28).
Read monograph to develop ideas of what to do together to reduce alienation.	Encourage family outings to reduce alienation. Have members read *Museum Visits and Other Activities for Family Life Enhancement* (see Bibliotherapy, Chapter 26).
Reduce negative communication.	Develop a system of positive reinforcement with family members to interact better with each other and reduce scapegoating.
Family members work together to develop termination plan.	Discuss termination issues and develop a plan to terminate treatment.

13

Dissociative Disorders

Dissociative Disorders are usually marked by a disruption in the functions of consciousness, perception, memory, or identity. The disorder can be gradual or sudden or transient or chronic. Included in the category of Dissociative Disorders are: Dissociative Amnesia (300.12); Dissociative Fugue (300.13); Dissociative Identity Disorder (300.14); Depersonalization Disorder (300.6); and Dissociative Disorder NOS (300.15). Dissociative symptoms may also be found in Acute Stress Disorder, Posttraumatic Stress Disorder, and Somatization Disorder.

In some societies, dissociative states are an accepted expression of cultural activities or religious experience. They do not lead to significant impairment or distress and are not considered pathological.

This is a difficult diagnosis to make in pre-adolescence, since the disorder can be confused with Learning Disorders, Conduct Disorders, Anxiety Disorders, and Childhood Amnesia before age 5. The agreement of several examiners is required for an accurate diagnosis.

DEPERSONALIZATION DISORDER (300.6)

This disorder is characterized by a persistent feeling of being detached from one's body or mental processes that is accompanied by intact reality testing.

Behavioral Symptoms
Depersonalization Disorder
(severity index: 1, mild; 2, moderate; 3, intense)

Severity

1. Persistent or recurrent feeling of being detached from
   one's mind or body   _____
2. Reality testing remains intact   _____
3. The symptoms cause significant distress or impairment in
   the activities of daily living (ADL)   _____

The symptoms do not occur exclusively during the course of another mental disorder and are not the result of a substance or general medical condition.

DISSOCIATIVE AMNESIA (300.12)

Dissociative Amnesia is characterized by the inability to recall important personal information that is too extensive to be explained by simple forgetfulness. The disorder involves a reversible memory impairment in which the individual cannot retrieve, or hold in consciousness, memories of personal experience in verbal form. It usually appears as a reported gap in the recollection of all aspects in a person's life history, with the gap associated with a traumatic or stressful event. In localized amnesia, a person fails to recall events during a specific time period, usually following a traumatic event. In selective amnesia, the person can recall some, but not all, of what happened. Other forms of amnesia, including generalized, continuous, and systematized, are quite rare.

Behavioral Symptoms
Dissociative Amnesia (300.12)
(severity index: 1, mild; 2, moderate; 3, intense)

Severity

1. Excessive age-appropriate inability to recall important
   personal information not explainable as simple
   forgetfulness   _____
2. Significant stress or impairment in the activities of daily
   living (ADL)   _____

The symptoms do not occur during the course of Dissociative Identity Disorder, Dissociative Fugue, Posttraumatic Stress Disorder, Acute Stress Disorder, or Somatization Disorder and are not due to a substance or medical condition.

DISSOCIATIVE FUGUE (300.13)

This disorder is marked by sudden, unexpected travel away from home or other usual locations, the inability to recall one's past, and confusion about personal identity.

Behavioral Symptoms
Dissociative Fugue
(severity index: 1, mild; 2, moderate; 3, intense)

	Severity
1. Sudden, unexpected travel away from home or school	_____
2. Inability to recall past	_____
3. Identity confusion or assumption of new identity	_____
4. Significant stress or impairment in activities of daily living (ADL)	_____

The symptoms do not occur exclusively during the course of Dissociative Identity Disorder and are not due to a substance or general medical condition.

DISSOCIATIVE IDENTITY DISORDER (300.14)

Formerly called Multiple Personality Disorder, this disorder is characterized by the existence of two or more distinct identities or personality states that recurrently take control of the person's behavior. The disorder also involves the inability to recall important personal information that is too extensive to be explained as simple forgetfulness.

Behavioral Symptoms
Dissociative Identity Disorder
(severity index: 1, mild; 2, moderate; 3, intense)

	Severity
1. The existence of two or more distinct personalities, each with their own pattern of thinking and relating to the environment, self and others	_____
2. Each of the personalities recurrently takes control of the person's behavior	_____

3. Inability to recall important personal information (not simple forgetfulness)   _____

The symptoms are not due to a substance or a general medical condition.

DISSOCIATIVE DISORDER NOS (300.15)

Disorders in which the major feature is a dissociative symptom, but do not meet the criteria for a specific dissociative disorder, are included in this category.

Behavioral Symptoms
Dissociative Disorder NOS
(severity index: 1, mild; 2, moderate; 3, intense)

Similar to, but does not meet the full criteria for, Dissociative Identity Disorder.

	Severity
1. Derealization without depersonalization	_____
2. Client subjected to prolonged and extensive coercive persuasion	_____
3. Dissociative trance related to locations or cultures	_____
4. Possession trance, control by a new identity attributed to a spirit, deity, power, or person	_____
5. Loss of consciousness, not the result of a general medical condition	_____

Other Diagnostic Considerations

Acute Stress Disorder (308.3)
Age-Related Cognitive Decline (780.9)
Amnestic Disorder due to a General Medical Condition (294.0)
Amnestic Disorder due to Brain Injury (294.0)
Anxiety Disorders
Conduct Disorders
Delirium (293.1)
Dementia (290.4)
Learning Disorders
Posttraumatic Stress Disorder (309.81)
Seizure Disorders
Somatization Disorder (300.81)
Substance-Induced Persisting Amnestic Disorder (*see substance*)
Substance Intoxication (*see substance*)

TREATMENT PLAN
DISSOCIATIVE DISORDERS

Client: _____ Date: _____

I. OBJECTIVES OF TREATMENT
(*select one or more*)

1. Educate parents about the disorder.
2. Investigate family history of the disorder.
3. Help family develop better comforting and coping skills.
4. Reduce pervasive anxiety and worry.
5. Identify environmental stressors, help child and family build a stress-free environment.
6. Reduce acute symptomatology.
7. Integrate primary personality and alters.
8. Reduce associated depression, anxiety, and mood swings.
9. Reduce irrational beliefs.
10. Help child accept trauma or abuse that may have led to dissociation.
11. Reduce depersonalization.
12. Encourage compliance with educational programs and referrals.
13. Help child develop self-comforting skills.
14. Promote socialization.
15. Reduce alienation.
16. Restore child and family to optimum level of functioning.
17. Develop discharge plan for coping with everyday life.

II. SHORT-TERM BEHAVIORAL GOALS AND INTERVENTIONS
(*select the goals and interventions that are appropriate for your client*)

(Note: Separate goals and interventions are provided for treatment of A-Parents, B-Child, and C-Family.)

SHORT-TERM BEHAVIORAL GOALS, **A-PARENTS**	THERAPIST'S INTERVENTIONS
Parents collaborate with therapist in development of a treatment plan.	Establish therapeutic alliance with parents to enhance outcome of treatment.

Help therapist understand child's development of dissociative disorder and other associated emotional problems.	Assess problem with parents and record a comprehensive history of the child's development and dissociative disorder and explore accompanying emotional problems (i.e., anxiety, depression, mood swings).
Have child evaluated by multiple examiners to confirm an accurate diagnosis. (Examiners may include psychiatrist, teacher, counselor, etc.)	Explain to parents importance of having three to five examiners evaluate the child to determine diagnosis and not confuse it with other possible disorders (i.e., conduct, learning, opposition, etc.). Provide necessary referrals.
Help identify other symptoms associated with the disorder.	Explore with parents the symptomatology of the disorder, such as amnesia, derealization, depersonalization, identity confusion or alternation, or insomnia, and time lapse in child's consciousness.
Identify triggers that touch off aberrant behavior.	Investigate with parents known triggers that result in aberrant behavior.
Learn new skills for coping with child's trigger points.	Teach parents stress reduction or relaxation techniques to help child deal with trigger points (see Behavioral Techniques, Chapter 23).
Become aware of the diagnosis and what to appropriately expect from the child.	Educate parents about the diagnosis and how a stress-free environment aids healing.
Accept diagnosis and use available resources to live more comfortably with it.	Help parents overcome denial and fully accept the disorder.
Agree to investigate the possibility of a structured environment or residential treatment center for the child.	If child is severely disturbed, explore with parents the possibility of a residential treatment center or group home for the child.

Treatment services for child are provided through the school.	If child is between ages 3 and 5, this diagnosis will probably not be made. However, if it is, refer child for early intervention (see Behavioral Techniques, Chapter 23).
Help identify trauma or abuse that may have led to dissociative disorder in child.	Explore for trauma or abuse in child.
Cooperate in building a genogram to identify familial history and its relationship to the disorder.	Construct a genogram to better understand the family history and define how family deals with the disorder and its impact on the child (see Behavioral Techniques, Chapter 23).
Undergo treatment as sexual abusers.	If sexual abuse is suspected, have parents evaluated immediately and treated if necessary. Report to authorities as mandated by law.
Enter treatment for psychological problems, if appropriate, to enhance outcome of child's therapy.	Evaluate parents for psychological problems and treat or refer for treatment if appropriate. (See *Behavioral Management Guide: Essential Strategies for Adult Psychotherapy*, in Resources for Providers, Chapter 33.)
Develop awareness of how your personal theory influences cognition of the problem in child.	Explore parental theory of the problem.
Recognize fears and feelings of negative self-blame related to the problem.	Evaluate parents' fears and negative feelings of self-blame for child's problem.
Learn to reach beyond automatic cognitive reactions in viewing the problem.	Expand parental perspective beyond limited cognitive reactions.
Parents learn to deal with sleep problems of child.	Investigate for sleep problems in child, and teach parents how to deal with problem.

Learn a range of comforting techniques to help child.	Assign parents to read to child *Can't You Sleep, Little Bear?* or alternate selection (see Bibliotherapy, Chapter 26).
Confront thoughts of exaggerated and unrealistic consequences—"What ifs?"	Guide parents in confronting distorted reactions to trigger situations.
Learn how to comfort child and act as role model for comforting skills child needs to learn.	Teach parents the importance of developing comforting skills to deal with their child.
Identify cognitive distortions.	Weigh the reactions against evidence-based reality.
Restructure distortions with evidence-based consequences.	With parents, reframe distortions with reality-based reactions to stressors.
Learn how to help the child deal with stressors.	Teach parents how to build a stress-free environment.
Comply with referral for psychological testing of child.	Provide referral for psychological testing of child to evaluate intellectual capabilities and rule out other diagnostic considerations.
Agree to allow therapist to confer with child's school to help in development of a comprehensive psycho-educational treatment plan for the child.	Request and receive parental permission to confer with child's teachers and school administratators.
Comply with referral for medical and psychiatric evaluations.	Provide referral for medical and psychiatric evaluations, if appropriate. Child may need meds to deal with anxiety, depression, or other problems.
Understand need for hospitalization of child during times of crisis.	Discuss with parents possible need for hospitalization and resolve their fears.

Develop new parenting skills.	Assign parents to read books on how to deal with their anxiety and increase parenting skills, such as *Making Families Work and What to Do When They Don't, Wonderful Ways to Love a Child* and others (see Bibliotherapy, Chapter 26).
Monitor child's medication schedule and report all reactions or failures to take meds.	If child is on meds, instruct parents on need for a regular schedule and feedback that may indicate need for revised dosage.
Learn how to help child build a mission statement.	Teach parents how to help child build a positive mission statement (i.e., You are safe today, etc.), designed to bring wholeness to the detached parts of the child's personality.
Feel enabled to help child deal with dissociative episodes.	Help parents develop distraction techniques to cope with any dissociative episode (i.e., play cards, go for a bike ride, etc.).
Learn to help child fight destructive thoughts and urges with positive self-talk.	Instruct parents how to help child counter destructive thoughts and urges with positive talk, drawing on successful experiences from child's past.
Become alert for child wandering, and reduce risks of injury/harm.	Involve parents in developing awareness of wandering behavior in child, and reduce risk factors.
Meet with other parents who are experiencing similar difficulties, and share solutions for coping with the problem.	Refer parents to self-help group or group on parenting skills.
Read about anxiety to better understand how to cope.	Assign books on anxiety such as *Homecoming: Reclaiming and Championing Your Inner Child* (see Bibliotherapy, Chapter 26).

Reduce alienation and promote socialization of child.	Suggest to parents some family activities they can do together. Assign parents to read *Museum Visits and Activities for Family Life Enrichment* (see Bibliotherapy, Chapter 26).
Discuss termination plan and resolve related issues.	Develop a termination plan and discuss issues of separation anxiety and dependency.

SHORT-TERM BEHAVIORAL GOALS, **B-CHILD**	THERAPIST'S INTERVENTIONS
Engage in play therapy.	Engage child in an age-appropriate therapeutic relationship via play therapy that is stress-free to assure healing.
Learn about diagnosis and develop realistic expectations of self.	Educate child about the diagnosis and discuss symptomatology so that he/she can adjust self-expectations.
Follow up and comply with medical and psychiatric recommendations.	Refer child for medical and psychiatric evaluations.
Understand need for hospitalization during times of crisis and resolve any fears.	Evaluate need for hospitalization and resolve patient fears of hospital.
Comply with regular meds schedule and report urges to ignore or overdose.	When medication is prescribed, confirm that prescription has been filled and meds are taken on a regular schedule.
Provide prompt feedback on effectiveness of medication and side effects. Discuss feelings about meds.	If necessary, refer to psychiatrist for dosage adjustment or control of side effects.
Understand dangers of mixing medication and other drugs.	Instruct child on dangers of mixing medication and other drugs.
Understand underlying dynamics that lead to depersonalization, identity confusion, dissociative symptoms, or out of body experiences.	Explore triggers that exacerbate dissociative symptoms.
Communicate life story to therapist.	Use puppets to have child relate the story of his/her life.
Enter treatment for sexual, physical, or emotional abuse. Parents are reported and treated.	Explore in a nonthreatening way, using anatomical dolls for sexual, physical, or emotional abuse, and treat immediately. Report to the appropriate protection agency (see appropriate treatment plan).

Recognize underlying feelings of anger or depression and express appropriately.	Using puppets, explore for underlying feelings of anger or depression.
Undergo treatment for sleep problems.	Investigate for sleep problem and treat accordingly (see appropriate treatment plan).
Learn a range of comforting skills to help you sleep.	Assign books on sleep disorders to comfort child, i.e., *Can't You Sleep, Little Bear?* (See Bibliotherapy, Chapter 26.)
Observe puppets and how they behave. Begin to see how new role models deal with anxieties.	Use puppets to shape child's behavior (see Behavioral Techniques, Chapter 23).
Identify with puppets and see ways to coordinate fragmented parts or personality.	Have puppets identify internal fragments and coordinate them to reduce identity confusion.
Explore feelings and memories using the puppets.	Have puppets share feelings and explore memories to reduce amnesia.
Learn new ways to handle fears.	Use puppets to role model successful ways to deal with fears.
Develop a repertoire of self-comforting skills.	Have puppets build a repertoire of skills to comfort themselves each day.
Realize others also feel bad, and mirror the puppets in overcoming the feeling.	Investigate for feelings of low self-esteem related to anxiety. Have puppets talk about how they feel and what they can do about it.
Learn to distinguish past from present events to prevent trauma response and reduce derealization.	Have puppets talk about how they distinguish past from present and avoid derealization.
Copy the puppets and open a dialogue with your fragmented parts to clear up cognitive distortions.	Have puppets open a dialogue with their fragmented parts to clear up cognitive distortions.
Identify alter/alters under hypnosis.	With parental permission, use hypnosis or relaxation techniques to help identify alter personalities (see Behavioral Techniques, Chapter 23).

Integrate split personalities.	Establish a therapeutic alliance with each personality and work toward integration.
Begin to see possible solutions.	Discuss with puppets how they deal with negative feelings.
Recognize that the parts can cooperate and eventually become cohesive.	Have puppets play the different parts of the child's personality and share their feelings to break the silence between parts.
Identify irrational beliefs.	Through continued play with the puppets, explore irrational beliefs about fears and anxieties.
Reframe beliefs about fears and anxieties.	Change irrational beliefs by having puppets discuss them and develop rational alternatives.
Child becomes more integrated.	Have puppets call a meeting of all parts to reduce identity confusion. Alters become more integrated through communication.
Learn from role modeling and shape new behaviors that build a positive inner voice to counter rage.	Use puppets to role model appropriate behavior and build an inner voice that responds to the negative voice of fear, rage, and sadness that resulted from trauma.
Gain mastery over anxieties by guided imagery and relaxation techniques.	Teach relaxation techniques and guided imagery to master anxieties (see "Using Guided Imagery to Augment the Play Therapy Process," Behavioral Techniques, Chapter 23).
Build positive statements to help deal with trauma.	Have puppets build a mission statement (i.e., "I am safe today," "Nobody can hurt me today") aimed at bringing wholeness to the detached parts.
Understand anxiety and realize that avoidance does not help.	Teach child the laws of anxiety: not dangerous, not permanent, exposure can promote change.

Recognize pattern of wandering and involve parents in reducing risk of harm or injury.	Investigate for issue of wandering, and if necessary, have child involve family to prevent harm and reduce risk.
Express suppressed feelings in a nonthreatening environment.	Play the *Talking, Feeling and Doing Game* to understand the underlying processes in a nonthreatening way (see Therapeutic Games, Chapter 24).
Understand how trauma may have contributed to existing disorder.	Explore child's background for trauma that may have exacerbated the disorder.
Discuss personal coping mechanisms developed to handle the disorder.	Investigate with child possible patterns of withdrawal used to avoid anxieties.
Recognize and relate how family impacts the problem.	Explore familial impact on the problem and ways the members deal with dissociation.
Learn positive self-talk.	Teach child positive self-talk to interrupt negative patterns.
Learn new technique for dealing with anxiety.	Teach diaphragmatic breathing to control anxiety (see Behavioral Techniques, Chapter 23).
Understand how stress triggers emergence of hidden parts and learn how to develop self-confidence.	Teach child how hidden parts emerge under stress and help build a lengthy repertoire of self-confidence skills.
Have internal dialogue with parts and clear up cognitive distortions.	Help child conduct a dialogue with the parts in order to correct distortions.
Disassociated memories and feelings are integrated to reduce identity alternation.	Call a meeting of the parts in session to reduce identity alternation and integrate the parts through communications. Silence between the parts is reduced.
Shift focus of attention from problem to accomplishment.	Ask child to describe accomplishments of past week.

Feel more confident as self-esteem improves.	Compliment child at every opportunity to provide positive reinforcement for positive accomplishments.
Communicate problematic feelings to develop new skills or opinions.	Use the technique of "Pounding Away Bad Feelings" and the game *Don't Break the Ice* to help release frustrations (see Therapeutic Games, Chapter 24).
Learn positive problem solving and how famous people have overcome obstacles.	Assign child to have parents read to him/her *Don't Be Afraid, Tommy* or *The Feelings Story Book* (see Bibliotherapy, Chapter 26).
Learn new strategies for dealing with uncertainty.	Have parents read to child *Anybody Can Bake a Cake* (see Bibliotherapy, Chapter 26).
Learn methods that you can use to advocate for yourself.	Instruct child in the technique of self-advocacy.
Explore separation and dependency issues and end treatment.	Develop a termination plan and resolve issues of separation and dependency.

SHORT-TERM BEHAVIORAL GOALS, **C-FAMILY**	THERAPIST'S INTERVENTIONS
Improve communications among family members to reduce familial anxiety.	Conduct family sessions or refer for family therapy to reduce alienation and improve communication skills.
Cooperate in amplifying family genogram.	Amplify family genogram created in a parental session to help understand family history.
Discuss genogram openly to fully understand family history of dissociative disorder.	Discuss genogram to reveal family history and possible secrets related to dissociative disorder.
Demonstrate boundaries, alliances, triangles, and emotional currents that may exacerbate the disorder.	Explore family boundaries using sculpturing, a useful technique for understanding triangulation, alliances, and emotional currents (see Behavioral Techniques, Chapter 23).
Shift focus from problem to possible solutions.	Have family imagine a future without the problem and suggest actions that can be taken now to make that future possible.
Think about what treatment outcome would look like. Explain what you would like to see change in other family members when treatment is completed.	Ask family members to think about what they might want to say about each other when treatment is completed.
Family members realize they have the power to make important changes, even if these seem small.	Help family members realize they have an opportunity to do some things differently.
Family members are empowered. They recognize that they can create positive change.	Ask family members to relate what they have accomplished in the past week.
Realize that major change is the result of small steps taken one at a time.	Help family identify and prioritize achievable goals.

Enhance understanding of condition and see how other families have handled similar problems.	Assign as homework reading *Making Families Work and What to Do When They Don't* (see Bibliotherapy, Chapter 26).
Make use of available community resources.	Refer family to available resources in the community. (See Self-Help Groups, Chapter 27, and On-Line Resources, Chapter 28.)
Reduce negative communication.	Develop a system of positive reinforcement with family members to interact better with each other and reduce scapegoating.
Family members work together to develop termination plan.	Discuss termination issues and develop a plan to terminate treatment.

14

Eating Disorders

Included in this category are Anorexia Nervosa and Bulimia Nervosa.

ANOREXIA NERVOSA (307.1)

Anorexia Nervosa is characterized by an abnormal drive toward thinness and perfection, an intense fear of gaining weight or becoming fat, and a refusal to maintain a normal body weight. The onset usually begins in adolescence with a disturbance in the way individuals think about the size and weight of their bodies. Females are twice as likely as males to be affected by this disorder. The norms of Western society, cognitive distortions, and family obsessions have been identified as contributing factors. Anorexia is increasingly found in younger children, mainly because of cultural pressures that extol thinness (i.e., fashion models, TV actresses, Barbie). The disorder is often related to certain athletic activities such as ballet dancing, gymnastics, and ice skating.

There are two subtypes of this disorder: Restricting and Purging. The restricting type reduces body weight by controlling calories and is usually obsessed with food intake and feelings of superiority because of his or her food control. The binge-eating, purging type controls weight by vomiting and using laxatives and/or diuretics. Unlike bulimic clients, this type does not regularly overeat, but will purge even small amounts of food.

Behavioral Symptoms
Anorexia Nervosa (307.1)
(severity index: 1, mild; 2, moderate; 3, intense)

	Severity
1. Body weight is significantly below (85 percent) normal	_____
2. Intense fear of gaining weight or becoming fat	_____
3. Clings to the shelter of childhood	_____
4. Amenorrea—absence of three consecutive menstrual cycles	_____
5. Denies seriousness of low body weight	_____
6. Restricts calorie intake; obsessed with low-calorie, low-fat foods	_____
7. Overeats and purges by vomiting or use of laxatives, enemas, or diuretics	_____
8. Uses excessive exercise to control weight	_____
9. Feels superior to others because of food control	_____
10. Extremely self-critical; needs to be perfect	_____

Other Diagnostic Considerations

Bulimia Nervosa (307.51)
Body Dysmorphic Disorder (300.7)
Major Depressive Disorder (296.xx)
Narcissistic Personality Disorder (301.81)
Obsessive-Compulsive Disorder (301.4)
Schizophrenia (295.xx)
Social Phobia (300.23)

TREATMENT PLAN
ANOREXIA NERVOSA

Client: _____ Date _____

```
┌─────────────────────────────────┐
│ Multiaxial Assessment           │
│                                 │
│ Axis I:    _____        │
│ Axis II:   _____        │
│ Axis III: _____         │
│ Axis IV:  _____         │
│ Axis V:   _____         │
└─────────────────────────────────┘
```

I.   OBJECTIVES OF TREATMENT
     (*select one or more*)

1. Educate parents about the disorder.
2. Determine family history of the disorder.
3. Evaluate and reduce idiosyncratic beliefs related to food and weight.
4. Help family develop better coping skills.
5. Reduce preoccupation with food, promote weight gain.
6. Reduce stressors that cause client to undereat.
7. Reduce irrational fears of becoming fat.
8. Eliminate purging by self-induced vomiting or laxative abuse.
9. Eliminate compulsive exercise.
10. Restore normal eating patterns.
11. Mitigate need for perfection.
12. Decrease need to control environment and be superior.
13. Promote socialization.
14. Restore adolescent and family to optimum level of functioning.
15. Develop discharge plan for coping with everyday life.

II. SHORT-TERM BEHAVIORAL GOALS AND INTERVENTIONS
     (*select goals and interventions appropriate for your client*)

(Note: Separate goals and interventions are provided for A-Parents, B-Child, and C-Family.)

SHORT-TERM BEHAVIORAL GOALS, **A-PARENTS**	THERAPIST'S INTERVENTIONS
Parents collaborate with therapist in development of a treatment plan.	Establish therapeutic alliance with parents to enhance outcome of treatment.
Help therapist understand child's development of eating disorder.	Assess problem with parents and record a comprehensive history of the child's development of eating problems.
Comply with referral for psychiatric and/or medical evaluation.	Provide referral for psychiatric and/or medical evaluation as appropriate.
Comply with referral for dental evaluation.	If adolescent is vomiting to control weight, refer for dental evaluation to assess and treat damage to teeth.
Become aware of the diagnosis and what to appropriately expect from the child.	Educate parents about the diagnosis.
Understand seriousness of child's condition and comply with immediate hospitalization.	If child is significantly underweight, refer for immediate hospitalization.
Identify dysfunctional attitudes or cognitive distortions within family system.	Explore for maladaptive assumptions, expectations, tacit beliefs, or cognitive distortions related to eating.
Identify maladaptive ways you role model weight control.	Discuss methods used by parents to control weight (i.e., diet pills, laxatives, etc.).
Cooperate in building a genogram to identify familial history and its relationship to eating disorder.	Construct a genogram to better understand the family history and define how family deals with food and its impact on the child's eating patterns (see Behavioral Techniques, Chapter 23).

Enter treatment for identified problems to enhance outcome of adolescent therapy.	Evaluate parents for anxiety, depression, eating problems, or marital discord and treat or refer for treatment as appropriate (see *Behavioral Management Guide: Essential Treatment Strategies for Adult Psychotherapy* in Resources for Providers, Chapter 33).
Develop awareness of how your personal attitudes influence cognition of the problem in child.	Explore parental theory of the problem and impact it has on the child's problem (i.e., need for perfection, negative reaction to obesity, etc.).
Identify and discuss societal and family obsession with thinness.	Investigate parental issues that reinforce pathological eating patterns.
Learn to reach beyond automatic cognitive reactions in viewing the problem.	Expand parental perspective beyond limited cognitive reactions.
Recognize your expectations of child and pressures you exert for compliance with them.	Explore parental expectations of their child and pressures they exert on child for perfection or compliance.
Mitigate pressures on child.	Guide parents in alleviating identified pressures on child.
Explore fears of allowing adolescent to grow up and move through a healthy separation-individuation process.	Explore parental need to maintain adolescent childlike and tacit induction of fear of growing up.
Confront and clarify mixed messages given to child.	Help parents confront distorted reactions and clarify mixed messages given to the child.
Replace irrational ideas concerning weight with more rational goals.	Explore for irrational expectations about weight.
Learn not to reinforce secondary gains of the adolescent's disorder.	Discuss secondary gains of eating disorder (i.e., feelings of superiority, admiration for control, etc.).

Agree to allow therapist to confer with school to help in development of a comprehensive psycho-educational treatment plan for the child.	If appropriate, request and receive parental permission to consult with child's teachers and school officials.
Identify others who exacerbatc the disorder and reduce their impact.	Explore outside pressures that may exacerbate the disorder (i.e., pressure from coach, instructor, parents) and discuss ways to reduce negative forces in child's life.
Expand parenting skills and develop new techniques for coping with child's disorder.	Assign parents to read books on dealing with anxiety and increasing parenting skills, such as *Making Families Work and What to Do When They Don't, The Eating Illness Workbook*, and other selections (see Bibliotherapy, Chapter 26).
Monitor child's medication schedule and report all reactions or failures to take meds.	If child is on meds, instruct parents on need for a regular schedule and feedback that may indicate need for revised dosage.
Meet with other parents who are experiencing similar difficulties, and share solutions for coping with the problem.	Refer parents to self-help group or group on parenting skills. (See Self-Help Groups, Chapter 27.)
Discuss termination plan and resolve related issues.	Develop a termination plan and discuss issues of separation anxiety and dependency.

SHORT-TERM BEHAVIORAL GOALS, **B-CHILD**	THERAPIST'S INTERVENTIONS
Agree with therapist on target problems.	Create treatment plan and agree with client on target problems.
Join in therapeutic alliance or collaborative treatment relationship.	Cultivate a therapeutic alliance or collaborative relationship to build trust and enhance treatment outcome.
Discuss underlying dynamics and possible causes of the disorder.	Encourage client to discuss feelings about self and clarify underlying dynamics that have created or contributed to eating disorder.
Follow up with referrals and comply with recommendations.	Refer adolescent for psychiatric, medical, and dental evaluations.
Discuss and resolve fear of hospitalization.	Explain need for hospitalization and refer client for in-patient treatment, if necessary.
Explore possible mood disorders that may contribute to Anorexia.	Evaluate possible mood disorders that may contribute significantly to Anorexia and treat (see appropriate treatment plan).
Identify means used to control weight besides limited food intake.	Explore use of diet pills, laxatives, or diuretics to control weight.
Communicate life story to therapist.	Have client relate life's story.
Maintain daily journal of eating patterns, feelings, triggers, and reactions. Discuss with therapist.	Assign client to keep daily journal of eating patterns and reactions and discuss with you.
Explore irrational beliefs about becoming fat.	Examine client's beliefs about fatness and its consequences.
Cooperate in constructing genogram to identify familial eating problems.	Construct genogram to identify family eating problems from adolescent's viewpoint.
Investigate societal and family obsessions with thinness.	Investigate family issues and attitudes that reinforce pathological eating pattern.

Realize that human beings are not perfect and reduce stressors imposed on self.	Teach child that human beings are not perfect.
Recognize underlying feelings of anger or depression and express appropriately.	Explore for underlying feelings of anger or depression and treat (see appropriate treatment plan).
Identify fear of becoming sexual.	Explore for sexual fears or fears of becoming an adult.
Understand that you use disorder to avoid separation-individuation and delay the move into adulthood.	Discuss fears of becoming an adult or the need to hide behind the shelter of childhood and avoid separation-individuation.
Undergo treatment for sexual dysfunction.	If appropriate, treat for sexual disorder (see appropriate treatment plan).
Recognize and replace cognitive distortions and explore issue in family therapy, if required.	Correct cognitive distortions and refer client to family therapy, if necessary. Treat or refer family for treatment.
Replace abnormal weight goals with realistic goals.	Investigate client need to have unrealistic goals for weight and replace with more realistic ones.
Recognize the underlying need for perfection and how it started.	Address with client the need for perfection and its origins.
Accept lower expectations of self as "good enough." Live more comfortably within self.	Teach client that "good enough" is acceptable.
Recognize "secondary gains" (control, attention, feelings of superiority, avoidance of adulthood) and replace them with new coping skills.	Point out to client the secondary gains of food control and replace them with new coping skills.
Diminish and eliminate purging behavior.	Evaluate purging behavior and replace with new coping skills.
Client builds confidence in relating to others, reduces pathological interactions.	Teach client more appropriate ways of interacting with others at home and school.

Confront and eliminate need to control family and others by passive-aggressive behavior (i.e., refusing to eat).	Point out any passive-aggressive need to use food to control family and others.
Learn new ways to handle fears.	Role model successful ways to deal with fears of getting fat.
Realize that others also feel bad and overcome the feeling.	Investigate for feelings of low esteem related to anxiety.
Begin to see possible solutions.	Discuss how to deal with negative feelings.
Understand how trauma may have contributed to this disorder.	Explore client's background for trauma that may have exacerbated the eating disorder.
Discuss personal coping mechanisms developed to handle the disorder.	Investigate with client possible patterns of withdrawal and isolation caused by the disorder.
Recognize and relate how family impacts the problem.	Explore familial impact on the problem.
Express underlying feelings in a nonthreatening environment.	Play the *Talking, Feeling, and Doing Game* to understand underlying processes in a nonthreatening way (see Therapeutic Games, Chapter 24).
Learn positive self-talk.	Teach client positive self-talk to interrupt negative eating patterns.
Learn new technique for dealing with anxiety.	Teach diaphragmatic breathing to control anxiety (see Behavioral Techniques, Chapter 23).
Learn new techniques to nurture yourself and deal with emotional difficulties.	Use the *Positive Thinking Game*, *Clear Thinking*, or *The Ungame* to teach ways positive self-talk can help control emotional difficulties (see Therapeutic Games, Chapter 24).

Have assigned books read to you and discuss in session.	Assign client to have books on eating disorders read to him/her, *The Deadly Diet* or *The Fasting Illness Workbook* (see Bibliotherapy, Chapter 26).
Shift focus of attention from problem to accomplishment.	Ask client to describe accomplishments for the past week.
Use audio tape to increase self-esteem and develop better eating behavior.	With parental permission, use hypnosis or relaxation techniques to reduce stress and increase self-esteem. Provide audio tape for home use (see Behavioral Techniques, Chapter 23).
Feel more confident as self-esteem improves.	Compliment client to provide positive reinforcement whenever possible.
Report results to therapist.	Assign client to challenge anxieties by eating a complete meal. Provide reinforcement by praising attempt and rewarding success.
Learn methods that can be used to advocate for yourself.	Instruct client in the technique of self-advocacy.
Understand that you can deal with these issues and bring treatment to an end successfully.	Develop termination plan and explain issues of separation anxiety and dependency.

SHORT-TERM BEHAVIORAL GOALS, **C-FAMILY**	THERAPIST'S INTERVENTIONS
Improve communications among family members to reduce familial anxiety.	Conduct family sessions or refer for family therapy to reduce anger and/or alienation and improve communication skills.
Understand family history and relate personal views of the disorder.	Amplify family genogram created in parental session and compare personal views of eating disorders in the family.
Discuss genogram openly to fully understand family history.	Discuss genogram to reveal family history and possible family secrets related to the disorder.
Demonstrate boundaries, alliances, triangles, and emotional currents that may exacerbate the anxieties.	Explore family boundaries using sculpturing, a useful technique for understanding triangulation, alliances, and emotional currents (see Behavioral Techniques, Chapter 23).
Clarify and share your feelings about the problem.	Explore family members' views of the problem and identify feelings toward "identified patient."
Identify pathological family eating rituals and replace with alternatives.	Explore family eating rituals that are pathological and replace with healthy alternatives.
Identify methods other family members use to control weight.	Explore possible family use of diet pills, laxatives, diuretics, or excessive exercise to control weight.
Pathological behaviors are identified to correct poor eating habits.	Explore how family eats together and identify pathology that contributes to anorexia.
Understand how food is used to control family.	Discuss control issues associated with food in family.

Other family members with eating problems are treated.	Identify other family members who may have eating disorder and immediately treat or refer for treatment (see appropriate treatment plan).
Explain your personal theory of the problem.	Ask family members to share their theories of why the eating problems exist.
Identify sibling rivalries and their impact on perfectionism in the family.	Discuss sibling rivalry issues and how they impact on need for perfection.
Shift focus from problem to possible solutions.	Have family imagine a future without the problem and suggest actions that can be taken now to make that future possible.
Think about what the treatment outcome would look like. Explain what you would like to see change in other family members when treatment is completed.	Ask family members to think about what they might want to say about each other when treatment is completed.
Family members realize they have the power to make important changes, even if these seem small.	Help family members realize they have an opportunity to do some things differently.
Family members are empowered. They recognize that they can create positive change.	Ask family members to relate what they have accomplished in the past week.
Realize that major change is the result of small steps taken one at a time.	Help family identify and prioritize achievable goals.
Enhance understanding of condition and see how other families have handled similar problems.	Assign as homework reading *Making Families Work and What to Do When They Don't*, *The Eating Illness Workbook*, or other selections (see Bibliotherapy, Chapter 26).
Make use of available community resources.	Refer family to available resources in the community (see Self-Help Groups, Chapter 27, and On-Line Resources, Chapter 28.)

Reduce negative communication.	Develop a system of positive reinforcement with family members to interact better with each other and reduce scapegoating.
Family members work together to develop termination plan.	Discuss termination issues and develop a plan to terminate treatment.

BULIMIA NERVOSA (307.51)

Bulimia Nervosa is marked by binge eating followed by inappropriate compensatory methods to prevent weight gain, such as purging, excessive exercise, and use of laxatives, enemas, or diuretics. Body size and weight excessively influence self-esteem. The disorder typically begins in adolescence or early adulthood, predominantly in females. It usually begins between ages 12 and 25. However, increasingly, this disorder is being found in younger children because of cultural pressures that extol thinness (i.e., fashion models, TV actresses, Barbie dolls). For that reason, a treatment plan for Bulimia in younger children is included here. The disorder is often related to certain athletic activities, such as ballet dancing, gymnastics, and ice skating. Binge eating usually occurs in secrecy and is accompanied by a feeling of lack of control. Dysmorphic mood, interpersonal stressors, or intense hunger following a prolonged period of dieting usually trigger binge eating. Clients are typically reluctant to discuss symptoms, as the result of embarrassment or ambivalence toward bingeing. Some evidence of pathology in the family of origin exists, and it is possible that the disorder is linked to sexual abuse. There are two subtypes of Bulimia Nervosa: Purging and Non-Purging. The latter relies on fasting and overexercising to control weight.

Behavioral Symptoms
Bulimia Nervosa
(severity index: 1, mild; 2, moderate; 3, intense)

Severity

1. Recurrent binge eating _____
2. Feeling of loss of control during binge _____
3. Inappropriate use of vomiting, laxatives, enemas, or diuretics _____
4. Overexercising _____
5. Exhibits low self-esteem _____
6. Overconcern with body weight and fatness _____
7. Extremely self-critical _____
8. Depressed and/or anxious _____
9. Difficulties with family of origin _____
10. Poor interpersonal skills _____

Other Diagnostic Considerations

Anorexia Nervosa (307.1)
Borderline Personality Disorder (301.83)
Major Depressive Disorder (296.xx)

TREATMENT PLAN
BULIMIA NERVOSA

Client: _____ Date _____

+---+
| Multiaxial Assessment |
| |
| Axis I: _____ |
| Axis II: _____ |
| Axis III: _____ |
| Axis IV: _____ |
| Axis V: _____ |
+---+

I. OBJECTIVES OF TREATMENT
    (*select those appropriate for your client*)

    1. Enhance parental knowledge of the disorder.
    2. Determine family history of the disorder.
    3. Identify idiosyncratic beliefs related to food and weight.
    4. Improve family's coping skills.
    5. Reduce pervasive anxiety and worry related to food and body size.
    6. Eliminate stressors that cause client to binge and purge.
    7. Establish healthy eating and exercise patterns.
    8. Eliminate irrational fears of fatness.
    9. Abandon purging, excessive exercise, and other compensatory actions.
    10. Identify and treat sexual abuse.
    11. Make full use of available community resources.
    12. Mitigate need to be perfect.
    13. Promote socialization and reduce alienation.
    14. Restore child and family to optimum level of functioning.
    15. Develop discharge plan for coping with everyday life.

II. SHORT-TERM BEHAVIORAL GOALS AND INTERVENTIONS
    (*select goals and interventions appropriate for your client*)

(Note: Separate goals and interventions are provided for treatment of A-Parents, B-Child, and C-Family.)

SHORT-TERM BEHAVIORAL GOALS, **A-PARENTS**	THERAPIST'S INTERVENTIONS
Collaborate with therapist in development of a treatment plan.	Establish therapeutic alliance with parents to enhance outcome of treatment.
Help therapist understand child's development of eating disorder.	Assess parental view of eating problems and record a comprehensive history of the child's development of eating disorder.
Comply with referral for psychiatric, medical, and dental evaluations.	If appropriate, refer for psychiatric, medical, and dental evaluations.
Have child hospitalized, if necessary.	If child is in danger, provide referral for hospitalization.
Cooperate in building a genogram to identify family history and its relationship to eating disorder.	Construct a genogram to better understand family history of eating disorders, while defining impact on child's eating patterns (see Behavioral Techniques, Chapter 23).
Enter treatment for personal eating problems, if appropriate, to enhance outcome of child's therapy.	Evaluate parents for anxiety problems or eating disorders and treat or refer for treatment, if appropriate (see *Behavioral Management Guide: Essential Treatment Strategies for Adult Psychotherapy*, in Resources for Providers, Chapter 33).
Develop awareness of how your personal theory influences cognition of the problem in child.	Explore parental theory of the problem and its impact on the child.
Recognize fears and feelings of negative self-blame related to the problem.	Evaluate parents' fears and negative feelings of self-blame for child's problem.
Identify pathological weight control methods you role model for the child. And realize the need to rectify.	Investigate parents' methods of weight control. Are they overconcerned with their own weight? Do they take diet pills; use laxatives, diuretics, etc.; or exercise excessively?

Identify societal and parental obsessions with thinness.	Investigate parental issues that reinforce pathological eating and purging.
Learn to reach beyond automatic cognitive reactions in viewing the problem.	Expand parental perspective beyond limited cognitive reactions.
Discuss and reduce expectations of your child.	Explore parental expectations of the child and pressures they may impose on him/her.
Confront thoughts of exaggerated and unrealistic messages transmitted to child.	Guide parents in confronting distorted reactions to eating patterns and clarify mixed messages given to child.
Identify cognitive distortions about food and body weight.	Explore for irrational weight goals and beliefs about food, body size, and weight.
Control negative interactions that pressure child to continue pathological weight control measures.	Investigate for outside pressures for child to be thin (e.g., coach, dance instructor, personal trainer, etc.).
Recognize secondary gains of child's eating disorder and replace them with better coping skills.	Discuss possible secondary gains of the disorder in child (i.e., control, negative attention, etc.).
Agree to allow therapist to confer with child's school to help in development of a comprehensive psycho-educational treatment plan for the child.	If appropriate, request and receive parental permission to confer with child's teachers and school administratators.
Develop new parenting skills.	Assign parents to read books on how to deal with their anxiety and increase parenting skills, such as *Making Families Work and What to Do When They Don't, Overcoming Eating Disorders: A Cognitive Behavioral Treatment for Bulimia Nervosa and Binge Eating Disorders*, and others (see Bibliotherapy, Chapter 26).

Meet with other parents who are experiencing similar difficulties, and share solutions for coping with the problem.	Refer parents to self-help group or group on parenting skills.
Discuss termination plan and resolve related issues.	Develop a termination plan and discuss issues of separation anxiety and dependency.

SHORT-TERM BEHAVIORAL GOALS, **B-CHILD**	THERAPIST'S INTERVENTIONS
Engage in play therapy.	Engage child in a therapeutic relationship, via play therapy.
Understand internal and external causes of eating disorder.	Explore with child and identify internal and external pressures that contribute to the eating problems.
Realize that human beings are not perfect, and reduce stressors imposed on self.	Teach child that human beings are not perfect.
Recognize underlying feelings of anger or depression and express appropriately.	Explore for underlying feelings of anger or depression, using puppet or graphics (see appropriate treatment plan).
Observe puppets and how they eat.	Shape client behavior by use of puppets (see Behavioral Techniques, Chapter 23).
Learn new ways to eat.	Use puppet to role model healthy eating.
Realize others also feel bad and relate to puppets overcoming the eating disorder.	Investigate for feelings of low esteem related to eating problems. Have puppets talk about how they feel and what they can do about it.
Begin to see possible solutions.	Discuss with puppets how they deal with negative feelings.
Play game to experience positive self-talk.	Play *The Positive Thinking Game* to improve positive self-talk and control emotional responses (see Therapeutic Games, Chapter 24).
Learn positive self-talk.	Teach child positive self-talk to interrupt negative patterns.
Identify irrational beliefs.	Through continued play with puppets, explore irrational beliefs about their bodies.
Reframe beliefs about fears and food.	Change irrational beliefs by having the puppets discuss the beliefs and develop rational eating plans.

Using guided imagery and relaxation techniques, learn to gain control over feelings.	Teach relaxation techniques and guided imagery to master anxieties (see "Using Guided Imagery to Augment the Play Therapy Process," Behavioral Techniques, Chapter 23).
Communicate life story to therapist.	Use puppets to have child relate the story of his/her life.
Express suppressed feelings in a nonthreatening environment.	Play the *Talking, Feeling, and Doing Game* to understand underlying processes in a nonthreatening way (see Therapeutic Games, Chapter 24).
Understand how trauma may have contributed to eating disorder.	Explore client's background for trauma that may have triggered or exacerbated the eating disorder.
Discuss personal coping mechanisms developed to handle the eating disorder (i.e., purging behavior, refusal to eat).	Investigate with child possible patterns of withdrawal used to avoid anxieties related to the disorder.
Recognize and relate how family impacts the problem.	Explore familial impact on the problem.
Learn new technique for dealing with anxiety.	Teach diaphragmatic breathing to control anxiety (see Behavioral Techniques, Chapter 23).
Learn new techniques to nurture yourself and deal with emotional difficulties.	Use the *Positive Thinking Game, I Can, The Anxiety Management Game*, or *The Ungame* to teach ways positive self-talk helps control emotional difficulties (see Therapeutic Games, Chapter 24).
Shift focus of attention from problem to accomplishment.	Ask client to describe accomplishments for the past week.
Feel more confident as self-esteem improves.	Compliment client to provide positive reinforcement whenever possible.

Communicate problematic feelings to develop new skills or options.	Use technique of "Pounding Away Bad Feelings" and game *Don't Break the Ice* to help child release frustrations (see Behavioral Techniques, Chapter 23).
Report results to therapist.	Provide positive reinforcement when client reports that he/she has challenged his/her eating disorder. Praise attempt and reward success.
Maintain eating diary to monitor step-by-step progress and identify pitfalls.	If child is old enough, have him/her keep a diary of eating behavior. Use positive reinforcement for healthy eating.
Understand the disorder and develop new ways to deal with it.	Have parents read with child *Why I Can't Stop Eating* or *The Eating Illness Workbook* (see Bibliotherapy, Chapter 26).
Learn how famous people overcame seemingly impossible obstacles.	Assign to read or have parents read to child *Anybody Can Bake a Cake* (see Bibliotherapy, Chapter 26).
Learn methods that you can use to advocate for yourself.	Instruct client in the technique of self-advocacy.
Understand that you can deal with these issues and bring treatment to an end successfully.	Develop a termination plan and explain issues of separation anxiety and dependency.

SHORT-TERM BEHAVIORAL GOALS, **C-FAMILY**	THERAPIST'S INTERVENTIONS
Improve communications among family members to reduce familial anxiety.	Conduct family sessions or refer for family therapy to reduce anger and/or alienation and improve communication skills.
Understand familial history and personal view of the problem.	Ask family members to relate personal views of the eating problem and compare.
Discuss genogram openly to fully understand family history as it relates to binge-eating.	Have family members discuss genogram to reveal family history and possible family secrets dealing with binge-eating.
Identify pathological rituals and replace.	Explore family rituals that are pathological and replace with healthy alternatives.
Identify if and how other family members participate in binge eating and/or purging.	Explore whether other family members participate in or enable binge eating and/or purging.
Demonstrate boundaries, alliances, triangles, and emotional currents that may exacerbate the anxieties.	Explore family boundaries using sculpturing, a useful technique for understanding triangulation, alliances, and emotional currents (see Behavioral Techniques, Chapter 23).
Clarify and share your feelings about the problem.	Explore family members' views of the problem and identify feelings toward "identified patient."
Understand how food is used to control family.	Discuss control issues associated with food in family.
Other family members with eating problems are treated.	Identify other family members who may have eating disorder and immediately treat or refer for treatment (see appropriate treatment plan).
Explain your personal theory of the problem.	Ask family members to share their theories of why the eating problems exist.

Identify sibling rivalries and their impact on perfectionism in the family.	Discuss sibling rivalry issues and how they impact on need for perfection.
Shift focus from problem to possible solutions.	Have family imagine a future without the problem and suggest actions that can be taken now to make that future possible.
Think about what the treatment outcome would look like. Explain what you would like to see change in other family members when treatment is completed.	Ask family members to think about what they might want to say about each other when treatment is completed.
Family members realize they have the power to make important changes, even if these seem small.	Help family members realize they have an opportunity to do some things differently.
Family members are empowered. They recognize that they can create positive change.	Ask family members to relate what they have accomplished in the past week.
Realize that major change is the result of small steps taken one at a time.	Help family identify and prioritize achievable goals.
Enhance understanding of condition and see how other families have handled similar problems.	Assign as homework reading *Making Families Work and What to Do When They Don't, Why I Can't Stop Eating, Bulimia: A Guide for Family and Friends*, or alternate selections (see Bibliotherapy, Chapter 26).
Make use of available community resources.	Refer family to available resources in the community (see Self-Help Groups, Chapter 27, and On-Line Resources, Chapter 28.)
Reduce negative communication.	Develop a system of positive reinforcement with family members to interact better with each other and reduce scapegoating.
Family members work together to develop termination plan.	Discuss termination issues and develop a plan to terminate treatment.

15

Factitious Disorders

FACTITIOUS DISORDER (300.xx)

Specify:

.16   With predominantly psychological symptoms
.19   With predominantly physical symptoms
.19   With combined psychological and physical symptoms

The essential feature of Factitious Disorder is the deliberate production of psychological or physical symptoms in order to assume the sick or patient role. The disorder must be distinguished from Malingering, which feigns psychological or physical symptoms for secondary gains (i.e., special attention, excused from school, etc.). Typically, the symptoms may include vague, subjective complaints, exaggeration or exacerbation of a preexisting medical condition, or feigning of a grand mal seizure by a child with a previous seizure history. When investigations of the complaints prove negative, new symptoms are usually presented. These children may engage in pathological lying about any aspect of their history or symptoms. The disorder is usually chronic, and there may be a pattern of repeated hospitalizations. Although the disorder can appear in childhood, typical onset is in early adulthood, often after a hospitalization for a general medical condition or other mental disorder.

Behavioral Symptoms
Factitious Disorder
(severity index: 1, mild; 2, moderate; 3, intense)

<u>Severity</u>

1. Feigns physical or psychological symptoms to assume the sick role _____
2. Fabricates vague or subjective complaints _____
3. Presents with self-induced or self-inflicted condition _____
4. Exaggerates or exacerbates preexisting medical condition _____

Other Diagnostic Considerations

Malingering
Somatoform Disorders
True General Medical Condition
True Mental Disorders

TREATMENT PLAN
FACTITIOUS DISORDER

Client: _____ Date _____

```
┌─────────────────────────────────┐
│ Multiaxial Assessment           │
│                                 │
│ Axis I:    _____       │
│ Axis II:   _____       │
│ Axis III:  _____       │
│ Axis IV:   _____       │
│ Axis V:    _____       │
└─────────────────────────────────┘
```

I.   OBJECTIVES OF TREATMENT
     (*select one or more*)

1. Determine parental or caregivers' involvement in the disorder.
2. Determine family history of the disorder.
3. Investigate possible acting out for mother.
4. Explore possible collusion between parent and child.
5. Review history of past hospitalization and attraction to "sick fole."
6. Rule out or treat substance abuse.
7. Eliminate need for psychoactive or other drugs.
8. Restore child and family to optimum level of functioning.
9. Develop a discharge plan for coping with everyday life without factitious symptoms.

II. SHORT-TERM BEHAVIORAL GOALS AND INTERVENTIONS
     (*select goals and interventions appropriate for your client*)

(Note: Separate goals and interventions are provided for treatment of A-Parents, B-Child, and C-Family.)

SHORT-TERM BEHAVIORAL GOALS, **A-PARENTS**	THERAPIST'S INTERVENTIONS
Parents collaborate with therapist in development of a treatment plan.	Attempt to establish therapeutic alliance with parents to enhance outcome of treatment.

Help therapist understand child's development of physical and psychological problems.	Assess problem with parents and record a comprehensive history of the child's development of psychological and physical symptoms.
Become aware of the diagnosis and what to appropriately expect from the child.	Educate parents about the diagnosis.
Cooperate in revealing past patterns of illness.	Explore history of medical and psychiatric treatment (i.e., hospitals, clinics, physicians, etc.).
Sign releases.	Request necessary release to collect child and parent records from all sources.
Cooperate in building a genogram to identify familial history and its relationship to illness.	Construct a genogram to better understand the family history and define how family deals with illness and its impact on the child (see Behavioral Techniques, Chapter 23, or Resources for Providers, Chapter 33).
Enter treatment for Factitious Disorder, if appropriate, to enhance outcome of child therapy.	Evaluate parents for pathology related to Factitious Disorder and treat or refer for treatment, if appropriate (see *Behavioral Management Guide: Essential Treatment Strategies for Adult Psychotherapy*, in Resources for Providers, Chapter 33).
Develop awareness of how your personal theory influences cognition of the problem in child.	Explore parental theory of the problem.
Parents identify or deny secondary gains. Investigate possible malingering, if appropriate.	Investigate for secondary gains in parents. If positive, treat or refer for treatment (see *Behavioral Management Guide: Essential Treatment Strategies for Adult Psychotherapy*, Resources for Providers, Chapter 33).

Recognize fears and feelings of negative self-blame related to the problem.	Evaluate parents' fears and negative feelings of self-blame for child's problem.
Identify pathological behavior.	Assess parents' understanding of their or other caregivers' pathological behaviors that interfere with child's functioning.
Learn to reach beyond automatic cognitive reactions in viewing the problem.	Expand parental perspective beyond limited cognitive reactions.
Understand your need to have a child in the sick role.	Urge parents to understand and challenge their need to have a sick child.
Identify cognitive distortions.	Weigh reactions against evidence-based reality.
Restructure distortions with evidence-based consequences.	With parents, reframe distortions with reality-based reactions to stressors.
Learn diaphragmatic breathing as a relaxation technique and teach child.	Teach parents diaphragmatic breathing to assist child in relaxation (see Behavioral Techniques, Chapter 23).
Comply with referral for psychological evaluation of child.	Provide referral for psychological testing of child to rule out other diagnostic considerations.
Allow therapist to confer with school to help develop a comprehensive psycho-educational treatment plan for the child.	If appropriate, request and receive parental permission to confer with child's teachers and school administrators.
Comply with referral for medical and psychiatric evaluations	Provide referral for medical and psychiatric evaluations of child.
Read to child, improving your relationship while teaching new coping skills.	Assign parents to read to child *Cool Cats, Calm Kids* or *Earth Light* (see Bibliotherapy, Chapter 26).

Develop new parenting skills.	Assign parents to read *Making Families Work and What to Do When They Don't* or *Wonderful Ways to Love a Child* (see Bibliotherapy, Chapter 26).
Monitor child's medication schedule and report all reactions or failures to take meds.	If child is on meds, instruct parents on need for a regular schedule and feedback that can indicate need for dosage adjustment.
Meet with other parents who are experiencing similar difficulties and share solutions for coping with your problems.	Refer parents to self-help group or group on parenting skills. (See Self-Help Groups, Chapter 27.)
Realize how you can change.	Assign parents to read books on how to change, such as *Do One Thing Different* (see Bibliotherapy, Chapter 26).
Discuss termination plan and resolve related issues.	Develop a termination plan and discuss separation anxiety and dependency.

SHORT-TERM BEHAVIORAL GOALS, **B-CHILD**	THERAPIST'S INTERVENTIONS
Engage in play therapy.	Attempt to engage child in a therapeutic relationship via play therapy.
Learn about diagnosis and develop realistic expectations of self.	Educate child about the diagnosis and discuss symptomatology so he/she can adjust self-expectations.
Determine comprehensive history of treatment.	Explore history of treatment (hospitalizations, clinics, emergency rooms, physicians, etc.).
Realize that human beings are not perfect, and reduce stressors imposed on self.	Teach child that human beings are not perfect.
Determine underlying feelings toward parents and whether child is in collusion with them or is being used by them.	Using puppets, explore for underlying feelings of fear or loss of love by parents (see Behavioral Techniques, Chapter 23).
Explain motivation for the collusion.	Identify motivation for the collusion as love or fear.
Observe how puppets behave and begin to see how new role models react with parents.	Reshape child behavior using puppets. Have puppets discuss their feigned illness and what it means to them (see Resources for Providers, Chapter 33, or Behavioral Techniques, Chapter 23).
Watch how puppets deal with parents' need for child to play the sick role.	Using puppets, role model appropriate reaction to parents.
Learn new ways to handle fears.	Use puppet to role model better ways to deal with parents.
Realize others also feel bad. Relate to puppets in overcoming those feelings.	Investigate for feelings of low self-esteem. Show how puppets talk about how they feel and what they can do about it.
Join discussion with puppets.	Discuss with puppets why they feign sickness and the secondary gains they receive.

Identify irrational beliefs.	Through continued play with puppets, explore irrational beliefs about illness.
Reframe beliefs about love and fear.	Change irrational beliefs by having puppets develop rational alternatives.
Learn from role modeling and shape new behaviors.	Use puppets to shape new behaviors.
Using guided imagery and relaxation techniques, learn to gain control over fears and anxiety.	Teach relaxation techniques and guided imagery to master fears and anxieties (see "Using Guided Imagery to Augment the Play Therapy Process," Behavioral Techniques, Chapter 23).
Communicate life story to therapist.	Use puppets to have child relate the story of his/her life.
Express suppressed feelings in a nonthreatening environment.	Play the *Talking, Feeling, and Doing Game* to understand underlying processes in a nonthreatening way (see Therapeutic Games, Chapter 24).
Understand how trauma may have contributed to existing disorder.	Explore child's background for trauma that may have exacerbated the disorder.
Develop alternative reactions to triggers for factitious behavior.	Investigate with child triggers that create need to feign illness, and discuss alternatives.
Recognize and relate how family impacts the problem.	Explore familial impact on the problem. Who feigns illness and what are the secondary gains?
Learn positive self-talk.	Teach child positive self-talk to interrupt negative patterns.
Learn new techniques to nurture yourself and deal with emotional difficulties.	Use the *Positive Thinking Game, I Can, Bounce Back*, or *The Ungame* to teach how positive self-talk helps control emotional difficulties (see Therapeutic Games, Chapter 24).

Shift focus of attention from problem to accomplishment.	Ask client to describe accomplishments of past week.
Feel more confident as self-esteem improves.	Compliment child whenever possible to provide positive reinforcement.
Communicate problematic feelings to develop new skills or options.	Use technique of "Pounding Away Bad Feelings" and the game *Don't Break the Ice* to help child release frustrations (see Behavioral Techniques, Chapter 23).
Report results to therapist.	Provide positive reinforcement when client reports back that he/she has confronted anxiety-provoking situations. Praise attempt and reward success.
Learn that lying reduces self-esteem, while social skills build self-esteem.	Assign parents to read to child *Don't Tell a Whopper on Friday* or *Don't Worry Dear* (see Bibliotherapy, Chapter 26).
Learn to advocate for yourself.	Instruct client in the technique of self-advocacy.
Resolve separation and dependency issues and develop termination plan.	Develop a termination plan and explain the issues of separation anxiety and dependency.

SHORT-TERM BEHAVIORAL GOALS, **C-FAMILY**	THERAPIST'S INTERVENTIONS
Improve communications among family members to reduce familial anxiety.	Conduct family sessions or refer for family therapy to reduce anger and/or alienation and improve communication skills within the family.
Cooperate in amplifying family genogram.	Amplify family genogram created in first family session to help understand family history.
Discuss genogram openly to fully understand family history as it relates to disorder identified in other family members.	Discuss genogram to reveal family history and possible family secrets dealing with illness. Explore for other members with the disorder.
Demonstrate boundaries, alliances, triangles, and emotional currents that may exacerbate the anxieties.	Explore family boundaries using sculpturing, a useful technique for understanding triangulation, alliances, and emotional currents (see Behavioral Techniques, Chapter 23).
Identify how other members of family deal with the identified patient.	Explore how other siblings deal with "identified patient." Are they angry or jealous of the attention?
Shift focus from problem to possible solutions.	Have family imagine a future without the problem, and suggest actions that can be taken now to make that future possible.
Think about what treatment outcome would look like. Explain what you would like to see change in other family members when treatment is completed.	Ask family members to think about what they might want to say about each other when treatment is completed.
Family members realize they have the power to make important changes, even if these seem small.	Help family members realize they have an opportunity to do some things differently.
Members are empowered. They recognize that they can create positive change.	Ask family members to relate what they have accomplished in the past week.

Realize that major change is the result of small steps taken one at a time.	Help family identify and prioritize achievable goals.
Enhance understanding of condition and see how other families have handled similar problems.	Assign as homework reading *Making Families Work and What to Do When They Don't* or *Do One Thing Different* (see Bibliotherapy, Chapter 26).
Make use of available community resources.	Refer family to available resources in the community. (See Self-Help Groups and On-Line Resources, Chapters 27 and 28.)
Go on family outings to develop new behaviors.	Suggest family outings to develop new behaviors, rather than focusing on illness.
Reduce negative communication.	Develop a system of positive reinforcement with family members to interact better with each other and reduce scapegoating.
Family members work together to develop termination plan.	Discuss termination issues and develop a plan to terminate treatment.

FACTITIOUS DISORDER NOS (300.19)

Factitious Disorder is characterized by physical or psychological symptoms that are intentionally produced or feigned in order to assume the sick role. Although the disorder can appear in childhood, onset is typically in early adulthood, often after a hospitalization for a general medical condition or other mental disorder.

Children are involved in Factitious Disorder by Proxy (Factitious Disorder NOS) as victims rather than perpetrators. Typically, the perpetrator is the mother, or other primary caregiver, who deliberately produces or feigns physical or psychological symptoms in the child. The motivation appears to be a psychological need to assume the sick role by proxy. The mother induces or simulates the symptoms in the victim and then presents the victim for medical treatment, disclaiming knowledge of the etiology of the problem. The victim may be given a diagnosis of 995.5 Physical Abuse of Child, except in the case of voluntary collaboration, which may justify diagnoses of Factitious Disorder for both mother and child.

Behavioral Symptoms
Factitious Disorder NOS
(severity index: 1, mild; 2, moderate; 3, intense)

	Severity
1. Complains of multiple physical or psychological symptoms	_____
2. Symptoms cannot be substantiated medically	_____
3. Feigns illness for mother or other caregiver	_____
4. No apparent incentives for the behavior	_____
5. Produces new symptoms as needed	_____
6. May be in collusion with mother or caregiver	_____
7. Pathological lying	_____
8. Exaggerates illness	_____
9. Excessive worry about self or caregiver	_____
10. Motivated to assume sick or patient role	_____
11. Chronic complaints of illness	_____

TREATMENT PLAN
FACTITIOUS DISORDER—NOS

Client: _____ Date _____

Multiaxial Assessment

Axis I: _____

Axis II: _____

Axis III: _____

Axis IV: _____

Axis V: _____

I. OBJECTIVES OF TREATMENT
(*select one or more*)

   1. Determine parental or caregivers' involvement in the disorder.
   2. Determine family history of the disorder.
   3. Investigate possible acting out for mother or other caregiver.
   4. Explore possible collusion between parent and child.
   5. Review history of past hospitalization and attraction to "sick role."
   6. Rule out or treat substance abuse.
   7. Eliminate need for psychoactive or other drugs.
   8. Restore child and family to optimum level of functioning.
   9. Develop a discharge plan for coping with everyday life without factitious symptoms.

II. SHORT-TERM BEHAVIORAL GOALS AND INTERVENTIONS
(*select goals and interventions appropriate for your client*)

(Note: Separate goals and interventions are provided for treatment of A-Parents, B-Child, and C-Family.)

SHORT-TERM BEHAVIORAL GOALS, **A-PARENTS**	THERAPIST'S INTERVENTIONS
Parents collaborate with therapist in development of a treatment plan.	Attempt to establish therapeutic alliance with parents to enhance outcome of treatment.

Help therapist understand child's development of physical and psychological problems.	Assess problem with parents and record a comprehensive history of the child's development of psychological and physical symptoms.
Cooperate in revealing past patterns of illness.	Explore history of medical and psychiatric treatment (i.e., hospitals, clinics, physicians, etc.).
Sign releases.	Request necessary release to collect child and parent records from all sources.
Cooperate in building a genogram to identify familial history and its relationship to illness.	Construct a genogram to better understand the family history and define how family deals with illness and its impact on the child (see Behavioral Techniques, Chapter 23).
Enter treatment for Factitious Disorder, if appropriate, to enhance outcome of child therapy.	Evaluate parents for pathology related to Factitious Disorder and treat or refer for treatment if appropriate (see *Behavioral Management Guide: Essential Treatment Strategies for Adult Psychotherapy*, in Resources for Providers, Chapter 33).
Become aware of the diagnosis and what to appropriately expect from the child.	Educate parents about the diagnosis.
Develop awareness of how your personal theory influences cognition of the problem in child.	Explore parental theory of the problem.
Identify or deny secondary gains.	Investigate for secondary gains in parents.
Recognize fears and feelings of negative self-blame related to the problem.	Evaluate parents' fears and negative feelings of self-blame for child's problem.
Identify pathological behavior.	Assess parents' understanding of their or other caregivers' pathological behaviors that interfere with child's functioning.

Learn to reach beyond automatic cognitive reactions in viewing the problem.	Expand parental perspective beyond limited cognitive reactions.
Confront your need to have a child in the sick role.	Urge parents to confront and challenge their need to have a sick child.
Identify cognitive distortions.	Weigh reactions against evidence-based reality.
Restructure distortions with evidence-based consequences.	With parents, reframe distortions with reality-based reactions to stressors.
Learn diaphragmatic breathing as a relaxation technique and teach child.	Teach parents diaphragmatic breathing to assist child in relaxation (see Behavioral Techniques, Chapter 23).
Comply with referral for psychological evaluation of child.	Provide referral for psychological testing of child to rule out other diagnostic considerations.
Allow therapist to confer with school to help develop a comprehensive psycho-educational treatment plan for the child.	If appropriate, request and receive parental permission to confer with child's teachers and school administrators.
Comply with referral for medical and psychiatric evaluations.	Provide referral for medical and psychiatric evaluations of child.
Read to child, improving your relationship while teaching new coping skills.	Assign parents to read to child *Cool Cats, Calm Kids; Earth Light;* or *Full Esteem Ahead* (see Bibliotherapy, Chapter 26).
Develop new parenting skills.	Assign parents to read *Making Families Work and What to Do When They Don't* or *Wonderful Ways to Love a Child* (see Bibliotherapy, Chapter 26).
Monitor child's medication schedule and report all reactions or failures to take meds.	If child is on meds, instruct parents on need for a regular schedule and feedback that can indicate need for dosage adjustment.

Meet with other parents who are experiencing similar difficulties and share solutions for coping with your problems.	Refer parents to self-help group or group on parenting skills.
Realize how you can change.	Assign parents to read books on how to change, such as *Do One Thing Different* (see Bibliotherapy, Chapter 26).
Discuss termination plan and resolve related issues.	Develop a termination plan and discuss separation anxiety and dependency.

SHORT-TERM BEHAVIORAL GOALS, **B-CHILD**	THERAPIST'S INTERVENTIONS
Engage in play therapy.	Attempt to engage child in a therapeutic relationship via play therapy.
Learn about diagnosis and develop realistic expectations of self.	Educate child about the diagnosis and discuss symptomatology so he/she can adjust self-expectations.
Determine comprehensive history of treatment.	Explore history of treatment (hospitalizations, clinics, emergency rooms, physicians, etc.).
Realize that human beings are not perfect, and reduce stressors imposed on self.	Teach child that human beings are not perfect.
Determine underlying feelings toward parents and whether child is in collusion with them or is being used by them.	Using puppets, explore for underlying feelings of fear or loss of love by parents (i.e., does child have a love/hate relationship or is he/she afraid of parents? See Resources for Providers, Chapter 33, or Behavioral Techniques, Chapter 23.)
Explain motivation for the collusion.	Identify motivation for the collusion as love or fear.
Observe how puppets behave and begin to see how new role models react with parents.	Reshape child behavior using puppets (see Resources for Providers, Chapter 33, and Behavioral Techniques, Chapter 23).
Watch how puppets deal with parents' need for child to play the sick role.	Using puppets, role model appropriate reaction to parents.
Learn new ways to handle fears.	Use puppet to role model better ways to deal with parents.
Realize others also feel bad. Relate to puppets in overcoming those feelings.	Investigate for feelings of low self-esteem. Show how puppets talk about how they feel and what they can do about it.

Join discussion with puppets.	Discuss with puppets why they feign sickness and the secondary gains they receive.
Identify irrational beliefs.	Through continued play with puppets, explore irrational beliefs about illness.
Reframe beliefs about love and fear.	Change irrational beliefs by having puppets develop rational alternatives.
Learn from role modeling and shape new behaviors.	Use puppets to shape new behaviors.
Using guided imagery and relaxation techniques, learn to gain control over fears and anxiety.	Teach relaxation techniques and guided imagery to master fears and anxieties (see "Using Guided Imagery to Augment the Play Therapy Process," Behavioral Techniques, Chapter 23).
Communicate life story to therapist.	Use puppets to have child relate the story of his/her life.
Express suppressed feelings in a nonthreatening environment.	Play the *Talking, Feeling, and Doing Game* to understand underlying processes in a nonthreatening way (see Therapeutic Games, Chapter 24).
Understand how trauma may have contributed to existing disorder.	Explore child's background for trauma that may have exacerbated the disorder.
Develop alternative reactions to triggers for factitious behavior.	Investigate with child triggers that create need to feign illness and discuss alternatives.
Recognize and relate how family impacts the problem.	Explore familial impact on the problem. Does child feign illness and what are the secondary gains?
Learn positive self-talk.	Teach child positive self-talk to interrupt negative patterns.

Learn new techniques to nurture yourself and deal with emotional difficulties.	Use the *Positive Thinking Game, I Can, Bounce Back,* or *The Ungame* to teach how positive self-talk helps control emotional difficulties (see Therapeutic Games, Chapter 24).
Shift focus of attention from problem to accomplishment.	Ask client to describe accomplishments of past week.
Feel more confident as self-esteem improves.	Compliment child whenever possible to provide positive reinforcement.
Communicate problematic feelings to develop new skills or options.	Use technique of "Pounding Away Bad Feelings" and the game *Don't Break the Ice* to help child release frustrations (see Behavioral Techniques, Chapter 23).
Report results to therapist.	Provide positive reinforcement when client reports back that he/she has confronted anxiety-provoking situations. Praise attempt and reward success.
Increase positive interaction and teach child that lying reduces self-esteem, while social skills build self-esteem.	Assign parents to read to child *Don't Tell a Whopper on Friday,* or *The Self-Control Patrol Workbook* (see Bibliotherapy, Chapter 26).
Learn to advocate for yourself.	Instruct client in the technique of self-advocacy.
Resolve separation and dependency issues and develop termination plan.	Develop a termination plan and explain the issues of separation anxiety and dependency.

SHORT-TERM BEHAVIORAL GOALS, **C-FAMILY**	THERAPIST'S INTERVENTIONS
Improve communications among family members to reduce familial anxiety.	Conduct family sessions or refer for family therapy to reduce anger and/or alienation, and improve communication skills within the family.
Cooperate in amplifying family genogram.	Amplify family genogram created in first family session to help understand family history.
Discuss genogram openly to fully understand family history as it relates to disorder identified in other family members.	Discuss genogram to reveal family history and possible family secrets dealing with illness. Explore for other members with the disorder.
Demonstrate boundaries, alliances, triangles, and emotional currents that may exacerbate stressors in the family.	Explore family boundaries using sculpturing, a useful technique for understanding triangulation, alliances, and emotional currents (see Behavioral Techniques, Chapter 23).
Identify how other members of family deal with the identified patient.	Explore how other siblings deal with "identified patient." Are they angry or jealous of the attention?
Shift focus from problem to possible solutions.	Have family imagine a future without the problem and suggest actions that can be taken now to make that future possible.
Think about what treatment outcome would look like. Explain what you would like to see change in other family members when treatment is completed.	Ask family members to think about what they might want to say about each other when treatment is completed.
Family members realize they have the power to make important changes, even if these seem small.	Help family members realize they have an opportunity to do some things differently.
Members are empowered. They recognize that they can create positive change.	Ask family members to relate what they have accomplished in the past week.

Realize that major change is the result of small steps taken one at a time.	Help family identify and prioritize achievable goals.
Enhance understanding of condition and see how other families have handled similar problems.	Assign as homework reading *Making Families Work and What to Do When They Don't* or *Do One Thing Different* (see Bibliotherapy, Chapter 26).
Make use of available community resources.	Refer family to available resources in the community (see Self-Help Groups, Chapter 27, and On-Line Resources, Chapter 28).
Go on family outings to develop new behaviors.	Suggest family outings to develop new behaviors, rather than focusing on illness.
Reduce negative communication.	Develop a system of positive reinforcement with family members to interact better with each other and reduce scapegoating.
Family members work together to develop termination plan.	Discuss termination issues and develop a plan to terminate treatment.

16

General Medical Conditions

Mental disorders are often associated with comorbid medical conditions and vice versa. *DSM-IV* covers these in three separate chapters entitled: Mental Disorders due to a General Medical Condition, Conditions That May Be the Focus of Clinical Attention, and Psychological Factors Affecting Medical Conditions.

For the purposes of this book, these conditions will be included under a single heading called General Medical Conditions. The medical condition is coded on Axis III of the *DSM-IV* Muliaxial Assessment with an appropriate *ICD*-9 number. However, the name of the medical condition should be included on Axis I. The categories are as follows:

MENTAL DISORDERS DUE TO MEDICAL CONDITION (293.89)

No treatment plan is included in this book for this disorder, since it is not applicable to outpatient treatment. However, the parents and family of a person with this disorder may require outpatient treatment. The plans for parents and family included in this chapter may be used for that purpose.

PERSONALITY CHANGE DUE TO A
GENERAL MEDICAL CONDITION (310.1)

The essential feature of this diagnosis is a persistent personality disturbance that is due to a medical problem. There is a change in the child's previous personality patterns. Common manifestations include instability, aggression out of proportion to the associated stressors, apathy, or paranoid ideations. The child is usually regarded as "not himself or herself." The diagnosis is coded on Axis I and the general medical condition, in *ICD-9* notation, on Axis III.

Behavioral Symptoms
Personality Change due to General Medical Condition
(severity index: 1, mild; 2, moderate; 3, intense)

Specify: Labile, Disinhibited, Aggressive, Apathetic, Paranoid, Other, or Combined

<u>Severity</u>

1. Persistent change in personality not considered normal development and lasting for one year _____
2. Personality disturbance is related to medical condition _____
3. Causes problems or impairments in school and/or in other important areas of functioning _____

MENTAL DISORDER NOT OTHERWISE SPECIFIED
DUE TO A GENERAL MEDICAL CONDITION (293.3)

This category is used when the disturbance does not fully meet the criteria (i.e., dissociative symptoms due to complex partial seizures).

PSYCHOLOGICAL FACTOR AFFECTING MEDICAL CONDITION
(316)

Included here are behavioral or psychological factors that adversely affect a medical condition and constitute a significant risk to health. Such factors may be founded in *DSM-IV* Axis I and II disorders, personality traits that do not fully meet the criteria for these disorders, and social and environmental stressors. This disorder, too, is coded on *DSM-IV* Axis III. (Note: Pain is not diagnosed as a psychological factor causing medical symptoms, but as pain disorder with psychological factors or medical conditions.)

Behavioral Symptoms
Mental Disorder or Personality Change due to Medical Condition
Psychological Factors Affecting Medical Condition
(severity index: 1, mild; 2, moderate; 3, intense)

(Note: A General Medical Condition (Axis III) exists.)

                                                                    Severity

1. Substance use/dependence interferes with medical
   treatment.   _____
2. Mental disorder affects general medical condition.   _____
3. Psychological factor affects, exacerbates, or delays recovery
   from general medical condition.   _____
4. Personality or coping style affects general medical
   condition.   _____
5. Negative health behavior affects general medical
   condition.   _____
6. Stress-related responses exacerbate medical symptoms.   _____
7. Psychological factor increases health risk.   _____
8. There is major impairment in educational, social, or other
   areas of functioning.   _____

Other Diagnostic Considerations

Dysthymia (300.4)
Eating Disorders (307.xx)
Factitious Disorder (300.xx)
Generalized Anxiety Disorder (300.02)
Hypochondriasis (300.7)
Major Depression (296.xx)
Pain Disorders (307.80)
Personality Disorders (301.xx)
Relational Problems (V61.xx)
Substance Use/Dependence (303.xx)

TREATMENT PLAN
MENTAL DISORDER OR PERSONALITY CHANGE DUE TO A GENERAL MEDICAL CONDITION PSYCHOLOGICAL FACTORS AFFECTING GENERAL MEDICAL CONDITION

Client: _____ Date _____

```
Multiaxial Assessment

Axis I:    _____
Axis II:   _____
Axis III:  _____
Axis IV:   _____
Axis V:    _____
```

I. OBJECTIVES OF TREATMENT
    (*select one or more*)

    1. Educate parents about the disorder.
    2. Determine family history of the disorder.
    3. Help family develop better coping skills.
    4. Reduce pervasive anxiety and worry.
    5. Control stressors that affect medical problem.
    6. Identify medical problems that impact psychological problems and refer for treatment.
    7. Increase awareness of medical-psychological interaction.
    8. Replace problem behavior with new coping skills.
    9. Reduce impact of medical and psychological problems on family.
    10. Reduce irrational beliefs.
    11. Promote socialization, reduce alienation.
    12. Optimize treatment and stabilize medical and/or psychological condition.
    13. Restore child/adolescent and family to optimum level of functioning.

II. SHORT-TERM BEHAVIORAL GOALS AND INTERVENTIONS
    (*select goals and interventions appropriate for your client*)

(Note: Separate goals and interventions are provided for A-Parents, B-Child, and C-Family.)

SHORT-TERM BEHAVIORAL GOALS, **A-PARENTS**	THERAPIST'S INTERVENTIONS
Collaborate with therapist in development of a treatment plan.	Establish therapeutic alliance with parents to enhance outcome of treatment.
Help therapist understand child's development of medical and psychological problems.	Assess problem with parents and record a comprehensive history of the child's development and medical/psychological problems.
Become aware of the diagnosis and what to appropriately expect from the child.	Educate parents about the diagnosis.
Cooperate in revealing past patterns of sickness behavior.	Explore history of hospitalizations, treatments, physicians.
Have child evaluated for both medical and psychiatric problems.	After interviewing child, provide with referrals for both medical and psychopharmacological evaluations.
Cooperate in building a genogram to identify familial history and its relationship to medical or psychological problems.	Construct a genogram to better understand the family history and define how family deals with illness and its impact on the child (see Behavioral Techniques, Chapter 23).
Enter treatment for pathology, if appropriate, to enhance outcome of child/adolescent therapy.	Evaluate parents for pathology and refer for treatment, if appropriate (see *Behavioral Management Guide: Essential Treatment Strategies for Adult Psychotherapy*, in Resources for Providers, Chapter 33).
Identify personality or behavioral changes related to illness.	Explore for personality or behavioral changes due to illness.
Develop awareness of how your personal theory influences cognition of the problem in child.	Explore parental theory of the problem.
Confront thoughts of exaggerated and unrealistic consequences— "What ifs?"	Guide parents in confronting distorted reactions to trigger situations.
Parents identify impact of illness on family life.	Explore impact of illness on family life.

Identify cognitive distortions.	Weigh the reactions against evidence-based reality.
Restructure distortions with evidence-based consequences.	With parents, reframe distortions with reality-based reactions to stressors.
Learn diaphragmatic breathing as a relaxation technique and teach child to help in relaxation.	Teach parents diaphragmatic breathing to assist child in relaxation, which may help with medical or psychological problem (see Behavioral Techniques, Chapter 23).
Comply with referral for psychological testing of child.	Provide referral for psychological testing of child to evaluate intellectual capabilities and rule out other diagnostic considerations.
Understand importance of early intervention.	Explain importance of and refer for early intervention for young children (see Early Intervention, Behavioral Techniques, Chapter 23).
Agree to allow therapist to confer with child's school to help in development of a comprehensive psycho-educational treatment plan for the child.	If appropriate, request and receive parental permission to confer with child's teachers and school administrators.
Parents read to child, improving their relationship while learning new coping skills.	Assign parents books they can read to child to enhance the relationship, while increasing their ability to deal with chronic illness, if appropriate (see medical issues in Bibliotherapy, Chapter 26).
Parents develop new parenting skills.	Assign parents to read books on how to deal with their anxiety and increase parenting skills, such as *Making Families Work and What to Do When They Don't* or *Living with Life-Threatening Illness: A Guide for Parents, Their Families, and Caregivers* (see Bibliotherapy, Chapter 26).

Monitor child's medication schedule and report all reactions or failures to take meds.	If child is on meds, instruct parents on need for a regular schedule and feedback that may indicate need for revised dosage.
Meet with other parents who are experiencing similar difficulties, and share solutions for coping with the problem.	Refer parents to self-help group or group on parenting skills.
Discuss termination plan and resolve related issues.	Develop a termination plan and discuss issues of separation anxiety and dependency.

SHORT-TERM BEHAVIORAL GOALS, **B-CHILD**	THERAPIST'S INTERVENTIONS
Engage in play therapy.	Engage child in a therapeutic relationship, via play therapy.
Learn about diagnosis and develop realistic expectations of self.	Educate client about the diagnosis and discuss symptomatology so he/she can adjust self-expectations.
Communicate life story to therapist.	Use puppet to have child relate the story of his/her life.
Undergo treatment for sleep disorder.	Investigate for sleep disorder and treat, if necessary. See appropriate treatment plan.
Understand underlying dynamics that may lead to maladaptive solutions and somatization.	Explore ways in which fears are related to illness and ways they manifest themselves.
Realize that human beings are not perfect, and reduce stressors imposed on self.	Teach child that human beings are not perfect.
Recognize underlying feelings of anger or depression and express appropriately.	Explore for underlying feelings of anger or depression about disability using puppets (see appropriate treatment plan and Behavioral Techniques, Chapter 23).
Learn new ways of dealing with anxieties related to medical condition.	Reinforce adaptive behaviors using puppets. (See Behavioral Techniques, Chapter 23.)
Watch how puppet expresses feelings about anxieties.	Using puppets, promote child's expression of feelings and anxieties about his/her medical condition.
Learn new, more adaptive ways to deal with fears in order to reduce maladaptive functioning.	Use puppets to role model successful ways to deal with fears.
Realize that fears and anxieties are normal.	Display unconditional acceptance of child's fears and anxieties.
Begin to see possible solutions.	Discuss with child, using puppets, how he/she deals with negative feelings.

Identify irrational beliefs.	Through continued play, explore mistaken beliefs about fears and anxieties associated with illness.
Reframe beliefs about fears and anxieties.	Change mistaken beliefs by having the puppets discuss them and develop rational alternatives.
Reduce secondary gains associated with the illness.	Explore for secondary gains associated with the illness.
Learn from role modeling and shape new behaviors.	Use puppets to role model appropriate behavior.
Understand impact that illness may have on thoughts, moods, and feelings.	Investigate for possible personality change from illness.
Using guided imagery and relaxation techniques, learn to gain control over feelings.	Teach relaxation techniques and guided imagery to master anxieties (see Behavioral Techniques, Chapter 23).
Understand anxiety and realize that avoidance does not help.	Teach child the dynamics of anxiety: not dangerous, not permanent, avoidance may increase anxiety. Exposure can promote change.
Express suppressed feelings in a nonthreatening environment.	Play the *Talking, Feeling, and Doing Game* or *Bounce Back* to understand underlying processes in a nonthreatening way (see Therapeutic Games, Chapter 24).
Understand how trauma may have contributed to existing disorder.	Explore client's history of physical or psychological trauma that may have exacerbated the disorder.
Enhance personal coping mechanisms developed to handle the disorder.	Investigate with child possible patterns of withdrawal used to deal with illness.
Determine how family dynamics impact the problems both positively and negatively.	Encourage exploration of family dynamics vis-à-vis the medical and psychological problems.

Understand how positive self-talk interrupts negative patterns and promotes healing.	Teach child positive self-talk to interrupt negative patterns.
Learn new technique for dealing with aggression.	Teach diaphragmatic breathing to control anxiety (see Behavioral Techniques, Chapter 23).
Learn new techniques to nurture yourself and deal with emotional and physical difficulties.	Use the *Positive Thinking Game, Bounce Back*, or *The Stress Less Game* to promote a more positive environment and take care of your body and health (see Therapeutic Games, Chapter 24).
Shift focus of attention from problem to accomplishment.	Ask client to describe accomplishments for the past week.
Feel more confident as self-esteem improves.	Compliment client to provide positive reinforcement whenever appropriate.
Communicate problematic feelings to develop new skills or options.	Use technique of "Pounding Away Bad Feelings" and game *Don't Break the Ice* to help child release frustrations (see Behavioral Techniques, Chapter 23).
Report results to therapist.	Provide positive reinforcement when client reports back that he/she has challenged anxiety-provoking situations. Praise attempt and reward success.
Learn positive problem-solving and how famous people have overcome obstacles.	Assign to read *Anybody Can Bake a Cake* (see Bibliotherapy, Chapter 26).
Learn methods that you can use to advocate for yourself.	Teach client the techniques of self-advocacy.
Understand that you can deal with these issues and bring treatment to an end successfully.	Develop a termination plan and explain issues of separation anxiety and dependency.

SHORT-TERM BEHAVIORAL GOALS, **C-FAMILY**	THERAPIST'S INTERVENTIONS
Improve communications among family members to reduce levels of anger and alienation.	Conduct family sessions or refer for family therapy to reduce anger and/or alienation and improve communication skills within the family.
Cooperate in amplifying family genogram.	Augment genogram created in an early parental session to help understand structure of family and spell out physical and emotional boundaries, including toxic issues.
Discuss genogram openly to fully understand family history as it relates to anxiety over medical issues.	Discuss genogram to reveal family history and possible family secrets and defenses surrounding illness.
Demonstrate boundaries, alliances, triangles, and emotional currents that may exacerbate the anxieties.	Explore family boundaries using sculpturing, a useful technique for understanding triangulation, alliances, and emotional currents (see Behavioral Techniques, Chapter 23).
Negative interactions (i.e., jealousy, competition, enmity) are reduced to establish homeostasis.	Investigate sibling rivalries and reduce negative interactions.
Shift focus from problem to possible solutions.	Have family imagine a future without the problem and suggest actions that can be taken now to best approximate that possibility.
Think about what treatment outcome would look like. Explain what you would like to see change in other family members when treatment is completed.	Ask family members to think about what they might want to say about each other when treatment is completed.
Family members realize they have the power to make important changes, even if these seem small.	Help family members realize they have an opportunity to do some things differently.

Members are empowered. They recognize that they can create positive change.	Ask family members to relate what they have accomplished in the past week.
Realize that major change is the result of small steps taken one at a time.	Help family identify and prioritize achievable goals.
Enhance understanding of condition and see how other families have handled similar problems.	Assign as homework reading *Making Families Work and What to Do When They Don't* or *An Ounce of Prevention: How Parents Can Stop Childhood Behavioral and Emotional Problems before They Start* (see Bibliotherapy, Chapter 26).
Make use of available community resources.	Refer family to available resources in the community. (See Self-Help Groups or 800 Numbers, Chapter 27.)
Reduce negative communication.	Develop a system of positive reinforcement with family members to interact better with each other and reduce scapegoating.
Family members work together to develop termination plan.	Discuss termination issues and develop a plan to terminate treatment.

17

Impulse Control Disorders

TRICHOTILLOMANIA (312.39)

Trichotillomania, or TTM, refers to the habitual and irrepressible pulling out of one's own body hair, frequently resulting in noticeable hair loss and other physical and emotional damage. The most commonly affected body sites are the head, pubic region, legs, and face, including the scalp, eyelashes, and eyebrows. Less common sites are the underarms, ears, nose, and torso. Behaviors associated with this disorder include visual examination of the pulled hair, chewing the hair or dragging the hair between one's teeth, or ingestion of the hair.

This disorder seems to begin around the age of 12 or later, but has been known to start earlier in childhood. More frequent in children and adolescents than in adults, it is also more common in girls than in boys. For some children, the frequency of the behavior and severity of the disorder seem to correlate with stress levels in their lives. The initial hair pulling has been associated by some clinicians with hormonal changes at puberty.

The affected person typically experiences an increasing tension just before pulling out the hair. This is followed by a sense of relief during or just after the act. While it has been argued that affected individuals always experience gratification, pleasure, or tension relief when pulling out their hair, in recent times this has been shown to be untrue for a large percentage of the sufferers. For children, TTM is also the source of significant emotional distress and impairment in their familial and social functioning.

Diagnostically, TTM is not attributable to other mental disorders and is not due to a medical or dermatological condition. It is now suspected that this disorder has both behavioral and biochemical underpinnings. The prevalence of the disorder is roughly estimated to be about 4 percent of the general population at any given time. About 10 percent of the population shows evidence of the disorder at some point in their lives.

Behavioral Symptoms
Trichotillomania
(severity index: 1, mild; 2, moderate; 3, intense)

Severity

1. Recurrent pulling of hair from the body
2. Inspects the hair before and after pulling
3. Chews on the pulled hair
4. Plays with or twirls hair prior to pulling
5. Noticeable bald patches on head
6. Skin irritation or infection
7. Gastrointestinal difficulties due to ingested hair
8. Picks the skin

Other Diagnostic Considerations

Anxiety Disorders (*see Subtypes*)
Depression (296.00)
Mood Disorders (*see Subtypes*)
Obsessive-Compulsive Disorder (300.3)

TREATMENT PLAN
TRICHOTILLOMANIA

Client: _____ Date _____

```
┌─────────────────────────────────────┐
│  Multiaxial Assessment               │
│                                      │
│  Axis I:   _____           │
│  Axis II:  _____           │
│  Axis III: _____           │
│  Axis IV:  _____           │
│  Axis V:   _____           │
└─────────────────────────────────────┘
```

I. OBJECTIVES OF TREATMENT
    (*select one or more*)

    1. Lessen, and eventually ameliorate, hair-pulling behavior.
    2. Determine what initiated the disorder and what maintains it.
    3. Educate family members about TTM.
    4. Explore family history of the disorder to determine possible antecedents.
    5. Diminish anxiety and anger associated with TTM.
    6. Improve self-image and increase levels of self-esteem.
    7. Reduce irrational beliefs about TTM.
    8. Promote socialization in school and at home.
    9. Assure compliance with any needed medical regimen and referrals.

II. SHORT-TERM BEHAVIORAL GOALS AND INTERVENTIONS
     (*select goals and interventions appropriate for your client*)

(Note: Separate goals and interventions are provided for A-Parents, B-Child, and C-Family.)

SHORT-TERM BEHAVIORAL GOALS, **A-PARENTS**	THERAPIST'S INTERVENTIONS
Collaborate with therapist in development of a treatment plan.	Establish therapeutic alliance with parents to promote a positive outcome.

Help the therapist understand the child's development to pinpoint possible origins of the disorder.	Discuss problem with parents and record a complete psychohistory of the child's development to accurately assess problems.
Become aware of the diagnosis and what to reasonably expect from the child.	Inform the parents about the implications of the TTM diagnosis and the prognosis.
Cooperate in building a genogram to identify familial history and its relationship to TTM.	Construct a genogram to better understand the family history with regard to the disorder and its impact on the family (see Behavioral Techniques, Chapter 23).
Become aware of how partial facts and misunderstandings influence your thoughts and actions.	Explore the validity of what the parents think to be true about the disorder and replace with the truth.
Challenge fears and feelings of blame related to the problem.	Evaluate parents' fears and negative perceptions of themselves and each other for child's problem.
Develop a more tempered response repertoire to the manifestations of the disorder.	Help parents to respond calmly and appropriately to the situation, rather than out of strong emotions.
If present, receive treatment for underlying physical and/or emotional problems, which may intensify the child's condition.	Determine if the parents are suffering from some physical and/or emotional disorder that may be affecting the child and treat or refer for therapy (see *Behavioral Management Guide: Essential Treatment Strategies for Adult Psychotherapy* in Resources for Providers, Chapter 33).
Have child evaluated for medical problems that may exacerbate the disorder.	If it has not already occurred, have child evaluated for physical problems related to TTM.
Agree to allow therapist to confer with child's school, extended family members, and others, to help in development of a comprehensive psycho-educational treatment plan.	If absolutely necessary, ask parents' permission to discuss the situation with significant people in the child's life, outside of the family, as a means of furthering support.

Have child evaluated by dermatologist, neurologist, and/or psychiatrist to best determine the most comprehensive treatment.	Provide referral for child to be evaluated by dermatologist, neurologist, and/or psychiatrist for evaluation and possible medication.
Comply with referrals to medical and psychiatric evaluations.	Work through any parental objections to referrals for medical and psychiatric evaluations.
Use games to improve communications with child.	Suggest activities or games to improve communication between parents and child (i.e., *Lifestories*, see Therapeutic Games, Chapter 24).
Become a positive change agent for the child through environmental shaping.	Teach parents how to provide a positive environment for the child that will reinforce his/her healthy and constructive behaviors.
To increase knowledge and lessen impact of false impressions and conclusions, meet with parents of other afflicted children.	Have parents discuss their pain and confusion over the situation. Refer to appropriate self-help group.
Enhance parenting skills.	Assign books on improving parenting skills (see *Good Kids, Difficult Behaviors* or *Parenting Towards Solutions*, in Bibliotherapy, Chapter 26).
Reduce the sense of isolation and "negative specialness" by becoming involved in community organizations that deal with this disorder.	Explain the availability of community resources to provide both concrete and emotional support (see Self-Help Groups or 800 Numbers, Chapter 27).
Parents are educated in ways of reinforcing healthier expressions of feelings in their child.	Teach parents basic behavioral techniques for reinforcing alternative behaviors to hair pulling.
Discuss and approve termination plan. Resolve any unresolved termination issues.	Once the hair pulling has abated, develop a termination plan and discuss issues of separation anxiety and dependency.

SHORT-TERM BEHAVIORAL GOALS, **B-CHILD**	THERAPIST'S INTERVENTIONS
Begin to feel safe and trust the therapist.	Attempt to foster a strong therapeutic relationship.
Learn about the problem and begin to get ideas about how to deal with it.	Educate client about the diagnosis, discuss symptomatology so he/she can better understand what is happening, and begin to develop problem-solving strategies.
See new ways of behaving that may lessen the urge to pull hair.	Modify client behavior through role-playing and other self-expressive techniques (see Behavioral Techniques, Chapter 23).
Learn what your body feels like before hair pulling begins.	Have child recognize somatic indicators that he/she associates with hair pulling.
Continually learn that you can control your behaviors and are not a victim of them.	Teach the child relaxation techniques to lessen the stress associated with resisting the hair-pulling impulse (see Behavioral Techniques, Chapter 23).
Practice positive self-talk with regard to the hair pulling.	Use imagery to guide child while he/she performs self-talk.
Develop internalized guide to help perform self-regulatory tasks.	Instruct child on how to develop an internal, self-monitoring guide or ally to help stop the hair pulling. Initially, the therapist may represent the internalized figure.
Develop and/or discover alternate ways of reducing stress.	Help child develop actions to replace hair-pulling and reduce the stress in his/her life.
Learn to self-monitor and choose behavior at increasing levels.	Teach child that his/her hair pulling behaviors are subject to volition.
Learn that it is healthier to verbally convey feelings than to repress them and have them express themselves through hair pulling.	Reinforce behaviors that the child uses to express feelings other than hair pulling.

Expand vocabulary to express thoughts and feelings that may have gone unexpressed.	When necessary, provide the child with words or phrases that may aid in his/her self-expression.
Underlying feelings of anger or depression are treated to reduce acting-out behaviors.	Explore for underlying feelings of anger or depression and treat (see appropriate treatment plan).
Child puts words to his/her feelings to reduce negative impact on behavior.	Explore for feelings of despair and of low self-esteem related to TTM. Have child talk about how he/she feels and what to do about the situation.
Learn what meaning the hair pulling has taken on. Begin to see possible alternatives.	Discuss with child the meaning of the hair-pullng behaviors.
Identify irrational and negative beliefs about child's self-worth and how TTM may be a way of punishing him- or herself.	Without using punitive or derogatory language, enable the child to see the self-destructive nature of his or her behavior. Explore for underlying self-hatred.
Reframe beliefs about TTM.	Change irrational beliefs by having the child discuss his or her beliefs and develop rational alternatives.
Learn from role modeling and shape new behaviors.	Provide cognitive restructuring and role-model appropriate behavior.
Using guided imagery and other relaxation techniques, learn to gain control over feelings.	Use relaxation techniques or guided imagery to help master troublesome or dangerous feelings (see Behavioral Techniques, Chapter 23).
Understand anxiety and realize that avoidance does not help.	Teach client the dynamics of anxiety: it is not dangerous, not permanent, and avoidance often increases it.
Communicate personal experience of the disorder to the therapist.	Help child to communicate his/her personal experience through the use of *The Storytelling Card Game* (see Therapeutic Games, Chapter 24).

Learn that it is safe to discuss your problems with someone in a nonthreatening environment.	Have client play the *Talking, Feeling, and Doing Game* to understand underlying processes in a nonthreatening way (see Therapeutic Games, Chapter 24).
Understand how trauma may have contributed to the existing disorder.	Explore client's background for trauma that may have exacerbated the disorder.
Discuss how the behaviors associated with TTM may have begun.	Investigate ways the behaviors associated with TTM may have begun as a misguided solution to another issue.
Significantly reduce hair pulling and related behaviors.	Aid client in recognizing that previously uncontrollable behaviors can be controlled through increased awareness.
Make use of a journal or behavioral log to document when and for how long hair pulling was successfully avoided.	Request child to maintain a journal to record success in resisting the urge to pull hair.
Recognize triggers of impulsive behavior and learn to consciously respond rather than react.	Help client to recognize and confront internal and environmental triggers of impulsive behavior.
Attend self-help group to increase understanding and control and get feedback from others who share the problem.	Refer client to self-help group (see Self-Help Groups, Chapter 27).
Through hypnosis, the child is more susceptible to create change and eliminate hair pulling.	Use guided imagery, or with parents permission, hypnosis, to help motivate the child to stop pulling hair (see Behavioral Techniques, Chapter 23).
Recognize the causal relationship between hair pulling and emotional pain.	Help the child to see the connection between his or her hair pulling and the physical and emotional pain he/she feels.
Continue to intensify sense of mastery over the condition.	Help the child to tolerate the impulse to pull for increasingly longer periods.

Determine what factors enable child to successfully resist the hair-pulling urge.	Explore with the patient the ways that he has been able to resist the urge to pull.
Understand that you can effectively deal with TTM and bring treatment to a successful conclusion.	Develop a termination plan and resolve issues of separation anxiety and dependency.

SHORT-TERM BEHAVIORAL GOALS, **C-FAMILY**	THERAPIST'S INTERVENTIONS
Improve communications among all family members.	Conduct family sessions or refer for family therapy to improve communication skills and foster intimacy and cooperation.
Cooperate in understanding the dynamics of the family. Participate in the construction of a family genogram.	Discuss family history to help understand relational dynamics with a focus on how they affect the child. Create family genogram to support this (see Behavioral Techniques, Chapter 23).
Discuss genogram openly to fully understand family history as it relates to TTM.	Discuss genogram to uncover family history and possible prior involvements with TTM.
Understand the roles that the family members may individually and collectively play in the problem.	Recognize and discuss how the family members may influence the problem.
Demonstrate boundaries, alliances, triangles, and emotional currents through family choreography to help understand how the family impacts the problem.	Explore boundaries using family sculpturing to understand triangulation, alliances, and emotional currents (see Behavioral Techniques, Chapter 23).
Emphasize your past success in positive interaction to deal with serious issues in the past. Shift the focus from problems to possible solutions.	Discuss with family members and reinforce the ways that they have successfully dealt with serious issues in the past.
Reduce negative communication.	Develop a system of positive reinforcement with family members to interact better with each other and reduce scapegoating.
Realize you can help each other make important and necessary changes for the benefit of everyone.	Help family members realize that they can do many things differently if they work together.

Family develops a SMART plan.	Develop a SMART action program with family. Small, Measurable, Attainable, Realistic, Timeline goals to help family see they can change (see Change, Behavioral Techniques, Chapter 23).
Recognize you can be effective change agents.	Explore accomplishments they have achieved.
Enhance sense of mastery or competence in the accomplishment of stated goals.	Help family identify and prioritize achievable goals.
Promote understanding of TTM and recognize how other families have handled it in the past.	Assign readings, i.e., *Feelings Are OK, It's What You Do with Them* or *How to Help Children with Common Problems*. (See Bibliotherapy, Chapter 26.)
Make use of available community resources.	Refer family to available resources in the community (see Self-Help Groups or 800 Numbers, Chapter 27).
Family members work together to develop termination plan.	Discuss termination issues and develop a plan to successfully complete treatment.

18

Personality Disorders

Personality disorders pose a separate and distinct problem for most, if not all, major insurance companies. Axis II diagnoses are rooted in childhood development and tend to require long-term treatment, compared with other disorders. In addition, there is no body of evidence to suggest that behavioral management is an effective modality in the treatment of these disorders.

Children with personality disorders usually do not come into treatment complaining of narcissistic, borderline, or other personality disorders. They present with Axis I disturbances, such as anxiety, depression, or social phobia, which represent the tip of the iceberg. They historically respond poorly to medication and are difficult to treat medically, as well as behaviorally. It is not easy to develop a therapeutic alliance or collaborative relationship with these clients. Treating the Axis I behavioral problems of these clients offers a reasonable initial approach to the larger, deep-rooted disorder.

The difference between a personality trait and a personality disorder is a matter of degree. You can be narcissistic without necessarily having a Narcissistic Personality Disorder. The same is true of all personality disorders. A personality trait is a consistent pattern of thinking, viewing, and relating to oneself and the social environment. When the trait is maladaptive, inflexible, and the source of significant impairment in interpersonal or occupational functioning, it becomes a disorder. The behavioral characteristics usually emerge in adolescence or early adulthood and are not the transient response to situational distress. Treatment is often complicated by the fact that the traits are usually ego-systonic.

AVOIDANT PERSONALITY DISORDER (301.82)

Social inhibition, feelings of inadequacy, and sensitivity to criticism characterize Avoidant Personality Disorder. Children with this disorder may avoid activities involving close interpersonal interaction, including school. They fear criticism, disapproval, or rejection and believe themselves to be socially inept and inferior or unappealing to others. The lives of these children are restricted by their low self-esteem. The disorder may coexist with Panic Disorder with Agoraphobia.

This diagnosis must be used cautiously with children, since shyness and avoidance are developmentally appropriate in both younger males and females. The behavioral symptoms must be pervasive and extremely maladaptive to meet the requirements for the diagnosis.

Behavioral Symptoms
Avoidant Personality Disorder
(severity index: 1, mild; 2, moderate; 3, intense)

	Severity
1. Avoids interpersonal activities	_____
2. School phobic	_____
3. Gets involved with others only when assured of being liked	_____
4. Intimate relationships are inhibited by fear of shame or ridicule	_____
5. Preoccupied with being socially criticized or rejected	_____
6. Feelings of inadequacy in social situations	_____
7. Views self as inferior, socially inept, and personally unappealing to others	_____
8. Avoids new activities as potentially embarrassing	_____

Other Diagnostic Considerations

Dependent Personality Disorder (301.6)
Panic Disorder with Agoraphobia (300.21)
Paranoid Personality Disorder (301.0)
Personality Change due to a General Medical Condition (310.1)
Schizoid Personality Disorder (301.20)
Schizotypal Personality Disorder (301.22)
Social Phobia (300.23)

TREATMENT PLAN
AVOIDANT PERSONALITY DISORDER

Client: _____ Date _____

```
┌─────────────────────────────────────┐
│  Multiaxial Assessment              │
│                                     │
│  Axis I:   _____           │
│  Axis II:  _____           │
│  Axis III: _____           │
│  Axis IV:  _____           │
│  Axis V:   _____           │
└─────────────────────────────────────┘
```

I. OBJECTIVES OF TREATMENT
    (*select one or more*)

    1. Educate parents about the disorder.
    2. Determine family history of the disorder.
    3. Help family develop better coping skills using positive reinforcement.
    4. Reduce pervasive anxiety and worry.
    5. Diminish symptoms of anxiety.
    6. Reduce fear of criticism, disapproval, or rejection.
    7. Eliminate interpersonal fears in school.
    8. Control fear of shame or ridicule in close relationships.
    9. End preoccupation with shame or ridicule.
    10. Strengthen self-esteem.
    11. Encourage compliance with educational programs and referrals.
    12. Reduce irrational beliefs.
    13. Promote socialization.
    14. Reduce alienation.
    15. Restore child and family to optimum level of functioning.
    16. Develop a discharge plan for coping with everyday life.

II. SHORT-TERM BEHAVIORAL GOALS AND INTERVENTIONS
     (*select goals and interventions appropriate for your client*)

(Note: Separate goals and interventions are provided for treatment of A-Parents, B-Child, and C-Family.)

SHORT-TERM BEHAVIORAL GOALS, **A-PARENTS**	THERAPIST'S INTERVENTIONS
Parents collaborate with therapist in development of a treatment plan.	Establish therapeutic alliance with parents to enhance outcome of treatment.
Help therapist understand child's development of avoidant behavior.	Assess problem with parents and record a comprehensive history of the child's development and their view of underlying feelings that may lead to avoidant behavior.
Become aware of the diagnosis and what to appropriately expect from the child.	Educate parents about the diagnosis.
Diagnosis is confirmed or rejected.	Explore with parents and confirm that child actually has avoidant behavior and not just developmentally appropriate fears.
Cooperate in building a genogram to identify familial history and its relationship to Avoidant Personality Disorder.	Construct a genogram to better understand the family history and define how family deals with avoidant behavior and its impact on the child (see Behavioral Techniques, Chapter 23).
If appropriate, enter treatment to enhance outcome of child psychotherapy.	Examine parents for avoidant behaviors or anxiety disorder and treat or refer for treatment (see appropriate treatment plan, *Behavioral Management Guide: Essential Strategies for Adult Psychotherapy* in Resources for Providers, Chapter 33).
Develop awareness of how your personal theory influences cognition of the problem in child.	Explore parental theory of the problem.
Recognize fears and feelings of negative self-blame related to the problem.	Evaluate parents' fears and negative feelings of self-blame for child's problem.

Understand how positive reinforcement can raise self-esteem.	Educate parents about positive reinforcement to help encourage child to increase self-esteem.
Learn to reach beyond automatic cognitive reactions in viewing the problem.	Expand parental perspective beyond limited cognitive reactions.
Understand problems related to avoidant behavior.	Identify child's fears of rejection and how avoidant behavior is related to anxiety.
Parents learn how to help their child deal with stressors.	Teach parents the dynamics of anxiety: It is not permanent, is not dangerous, and can be reduced by child confronting the problem. Exposure can produce growth.
Understand how negative feelings exacerbate problems for self and child.	Evaluate parents' negative feelings toward child or themselves and clarify how this impacts child's avoidant behavior.
Confront thoughts of exaggerated and unrealistic consequences— "What ifs?"	Guide parents in confronting distorted reactions to trigger situations.
Understand how child may personalize your responses and be hypercritical of self.	Increase parental awareness of how child may personalize their responses.
Identify cognitive distortions.	Weigh the reactions against evidence-based reality.
Restructure distortions with evidence-based consequences.	With parents, reframe distortions with reality-based reactions to stressors.
Learn diaphragmatic breathing as a relaxation technique and teach child to help in relaxation.	Teach parents diaphragmatic breathing to assist child in relaxation (see Behavioral Techniques, Chapter 23).
Assure compliance with referral for psychological testing of child.	Provide referral for psychological testing of child to evaluate Avoidant Behavior Disorder and rule out other diagnostic considerations.

Understand importance of early intervention.	Explain importance of and refer for early intervention for preschool children (see Chapter 23, Early Intervention).
Agree to allow therapist to confer with child's school to help in development of a comprehensive psycho-educational treatment plan for the child.	Request and receive parental permission to confer with child's teachers and school administrators.
Comply with referral for medical and psychiatric evaluations.	Provide referral for medical and psychiatric evaluations, if appropriate.
Parents read to child, improving their interpersonal relationship with child while learning new coping skills.	Assign parents books they can read to their child to enhance their relationship while increasing their coping skills, such as *Sometimes I'm Afraid* or *Don't Worry Dear* (see Bibliotherapy, Chapter 26).
Parents develop new parenting skills.	Assign parents to read books on how to deal with their anxiety and increase parenting skills, such as *Making Families Work and What to Do When They Don't* or *Feel the Fear and Do It Anyway* (see Bibliotherapy, Chapter 26).
Monitor child's medication schedule and report all reactions or failures to take meds.	If child is on meds, instruct parents on need for a regular schedule and feedback that may indicate need for revised dosage.
Meet with other parents who are experiencing similar difficulties and share solutions for coping with the problem.	Refer parents to self-help group or group on parenting skills.
Read about anxiety disorders to better understand how to cope.	Assign books on anxiety disorders, such as *Your Anxious Child* (see Bibliotherapy, Chapter 26).
Discuss termination plan and resolve related issues.	Develop a termination plan and discuss issues of separation anxiety and dependency.

SHORT-TERM BEHAVIORAL GOALS, **B-CHILD**	THERAPIST'S INTERVENTIONS
Engage in play therapy.	Engage child in a therapeutic relationship, via play therapy. This can be especially difficult, given the essential features of the disorder.
Diagnosis is carefully evaluated to determine that treatment is warranted or should be aborted.	Evaluate and confirm diagnosis. In younger children, therapy may be inappropriate. Symptoms may be consistent with level of development.
Understand underlying dynamics that lead to maladaptive behavior and stress.	Explore ways in which avoidant behaviors manifest themselves and impair functioning.
Realize that human beings are not perfect and reduce stressors imposed on self.	Teach child that human beings are not perfect.
Recognize underlying feelings of anger or depression and express appropriately.	Explore for underlying feelings of anger or depression, using puppet or graphics (see appropriate treatment plan).
Observe puppets and how they behave. Begin to see new role models deal with anxieties.	Shape client behavior by use of puppets (see Behavioral Techniques, Chapter 23).
Watch how puppet expresses feelings about anxieties.	Display socially acceptable expression of feelings about anxieties, using stickers with puppet.
Learn new ways to handle fears.	Use puppet to role model successful ways to deal with fears.
Realize others also feel bad and relate to puppets overcoming the feeling.	Investigate for feelings of low esteem related to avoidant behavior. Have puppets talk about how they feel and what they can do when frightened.

Begin to see possible solutions.	Discuss with puppets how they deal with their fears and solutions they can use when they want to avoid people, places, or things.
Identify irrational beliefs.	Through continued play with puppets, explore irrational beliefs about fears and anxieties.
Reframe beliefs about fears and anxieties.	Change irrational beliefs by having the puppets discuss the beliefs and develop rational alternatives.
Realize there are other ways to respond to your fears.	Have puppets discuss alternative ways of relating to others.
Learn from role modeling and shape new behaviors.	Use puppets to role model appropriate behavior.
Using guided imagery to augment the play therapy process, learn to gain control over feelings.	Teach use of relaxation techniques and guided imagery to master fears and anxieties (see "Using Guided Imagery to Augment the Play Therapy Process," Behavioral Techniques, Chapter 23).
Understand anxiety and realize that avoidance does not help.	Teach child the laws of anxiety: not dangerous, not permanent, avoidance increases anxiety. Exposure can promote change.
Communicate life story to therapist.	Use puppet to have child relate the story of his/her life.
Express suppressed feelings in a nonthreatening environment.	Play the *Talking, Feeling, and Doing Game* to understand underlying processes in a nonthreatening way (see Therapeutic Games, Chapter 24).
Learn new ways to effectively handle emotions.	Play *The Positive Thinking Game* to teach child effective tools to use with stress (see Therapeutic Games, Chapter 24).
Understand how trauma may have contributed to existing disorder.	Explore client's background for trauma that may have exacerbated the disorder.

Discuss personal coping mechanisms developed to handle the disorder.	Investigate with child possible patterns of withdrawal used to avoid anxieties.
Through role-playing, work through fears of interaction.	Conduct role-playing sessions to provide a forum for interactional practice and ease internal pains (see Behavioral Techniques, Chapter 23).
Recognize and relate how family impacts the problem.	Explore familial impact on the problem.
Learn positive self-talk.	Teach child positive self-talk to interrupt negative patterns.
Learn new technique for dealing with fear.	Teach diaphragmatic breathing to control fears (see Behavioral Techniques, Chapter 23).
Learn other techniques to reduce avoidant behavior.	Assign homework from *Forms for Helping the Socially Fearful Child* (see Resources for Providers, Chapter 33).
Learn new techniques to nurture yourself and deal with emotional difficulties.	Use the *Positive Thinking Game*, *Lifestories*, or *The Ungame* to teach ways positive self-talk helps control emotional difficulties (see Therapeutic Games, Chapter 24).
Shift focus of attention from problem to accomplishment.	Ask client to describe accomplishments for the past week.
Feel more confident as self-esteem improves.	Compliment client to provide positive reinforcement whenever possible.
Communicate problematic feelings to develop new skills or options.	Use technique of "Pounding Away Bad Feelings" and game *Don't Break the Ice* to help child release frustrations (see Behavioral Techniques, Chapter 23).
Attempt to use new control skills in school.	Urge child to use new control skills in the classroom setting.

Report results to therapist.	Provide positive reinforcement when client reports back that he/she has challenged anxiety-provoking situations. Praise attempt and reward success.
Learn positive problem solving and how famous people have overcome obstacles.	Assign to read *Don't Be Afraid, Tommy*, or *The Feelings Story Book* (see Bibliotherapy, Chapter 26).
Learn new strategies for dealing with shyness and avoidant behaviors.	Assign to read or have parents read to child *Nobody Likes Me* (see Bibliotherapy, Chapter 26).
Learn methods that you can use to advocate for yourself.	Instruct client in the technique of self-advocacy.
Understand that you can deal with these issues and bring treatment to an end successfully.	Develop a termination plan and explain issues of separation anxiety and dependency.

SHORT-TERM BEHAVIORAL GOALS, **C-FAMILY**	THERAPIST'S INTERVENTIONS
Improve communications among family members to reduce familial anxiety.	Conduct family sessions or refer for family therapy to reduce avoidant behavior and improve communication skills and interpersonal relations within the family.
Cooperate in amplifying family genogram.	Amplify family genogram created in parental session to help understand family history.
Discuss genogram openly to fully understand family history as it relates to anxiety.	Discuss genogram to reveal family history and possible family secrets dealing with anxiety.
Demonstrate boundaries, alliances, triangles, and emotional currents that may exacerbate the anxieties.	Explore family boundaries using sculpturing, a useful technique for understanding triangulation, alliances, and emotional currents (see Behavioral Techniques, Chapter 23).
Experience interpersonal interactions in role-playing sessions with family in a nonthreatening environment.	Conduct role-playing sessions to provide forum for interactive practice (see Behavioral Techniques, Chapter 23).
Shift focus from problem to possible solutions.	Have family imagine a future without the problem and suggest actions that can be taken now to make that future possible.
Think about what the treatment outcome would look like. Explain what you would like to see change in other family members when treatment is completed.	Ask family members to think about what they might want to say about each other when treatment is completed.
Family members realize they have the power to make important changes, even if these seem small.	Help family members realize they have an opportunity to do some things differently.
Members are empowered. They recognize that they can create positive change.	Ask family members to relate what they have accomplished in the past week.

Realize that major change is the result of small steps taken one at a time.	Help family identify and prioritize achievable goals.
Enhance understanding of condition and see how other families have handled similar problems.	Assign as homework reading *Making Families Work and What to Do When They Don't* (see Bibliotherapy, Chapter 26).
Make use of available community resources.	Refer family to available resources in the community (see Self-Help Groups or 800 Numbers, Chapter 27).
Reduce negative communication.	Develop a system of positive reinforcement with family members to interact better with each other and reduce scapegoating.
Family members work together to develop termination plan.	Discuss termination issues and develop a plan to terminate treatment.

BORDERLINE PERSONALITY DISORDER (301.83)

Borderline Personality Disorder is characterized by a pattern of instability in affect, self-image, and interpersonal relationships, including marked impulsivity. Adolescents with this disorder go to great lengths to avoid real or imagined abandonment. The perception of rejection or separation results in significant changes in self-image, affect, behavior, and cognition. They may have an intense fear of being alone and to avoid abandonment may resort to self-mutilation or even attempt suicide. They are known to switch quickly from idealizing others, including caregivers, to devaluing them, sometimes with surprising intensity. Impulsivity may include gambling, irresponsible spending, substance abuse, binge eating, reckless driving, and unsafe sexual activities. They are often bored and may display extreme reactions to interpersonal stress. The disorder usually begins by early adulthood. It may be concurrent with mood disorders. Adolescents with identity problems, especially mixed with substance abuse, may display symptoms of this disorder transiently. See appropriate treatment plans for Substance Abuse, Dissociative Disorder, or Conduct Disorder.

Behavioral Symptoms
Borderline Personality Disorder
(severity index: 1, mild; 2, moderate, 3, intense)

At least five of the following:

	Severity
1. Frantically tries to avoid real or imagined abandonment	_____
2. Unstable and intense interpersonal relationships	_____
3. Switches between extremes of idealization and devaluation	_____
4. Splits between right and wrong	_____
5. Has unstable self-image or sense of self	_____
6. Self-damaging impulsivity in two of the following areas: sex, spending, substance abuse, binge eating, reckless driving	_____
7. Self-mutilating behavior	_____
8. Suicidal ideations, threats, or attempts	_____
9. Short-term affective instability due to marked reactivity of mood: intense dysphoria, irritability, or anxiety	_____
10. Chronic feelings of emptiness, boredom	_____
11. Intense and inappropriate anger, displays of temper, fighting	_____
12. Stress-related paranoid ideations or severe dissociative symptoms	_____

Other Diagnostic Considerations

Dependent Personality Disorder (301.6)
Histrionic Personality Disorder (301.50)
Mood Disorder (296.xx)
Narcissistic Personality Disorder (301.81)
Paranoid Personality Disorder (301.0)
Personality Change due to a General Medical Condition (310.1)
Schizotypal Personality Disorder (301.22)

TREATMENT PLAN
BORDERLINE PERSONALITY DISORDER

Client: _____ Date _____

```
┌─────────────────────────────────────┐
│  Multiaxial Assessment              │
│                                      │
│  Axis I:  _____             │
│  Axis II: _____             │
│  Axis III: _____            │
│  Axis IV: _____             │
│  Axis V:  _____             │
│                                      │
└─────────────────────────────────────┘
```

I. OBJECTIVES OF TREATMENT
    (*select one or more*)

1. Educate parents about disorder.
2. Determine family history of the disorder.
3. Help family develop better coping skills.
4. Realize fears of abandonment are unreal.
5. Control self-damaging impulsivity.
6. Eliminate self-mutilating behavior.
7. Control suicidal ideations, threats.
8. Facilitate self-awareness, stabilize sense of self.
9. Realize that all people are good and bad.
10. Control reactive depression and anxiety.
11. Learn improved reactions to stress.
12. Medicate and/or hospitalize as necessary.
13. Clarify boundaries.
14. Improve communication skills.
15. Encourage compliance with educational programs and referrals.
16. Reduce irrational beliefs.
17. Promote socialization.
18. Reduce alienation.
19. Restore adolescent and family to optimum level of functioning.
20. Develop discharge plan for coping with everyday life.

II. SHORT-TERM BEHAVIORAL GOALS AND INTERVENTIONS
    (*select goals and interventions appropriate for your client*)

(Note: Separate goals and interventions are provided for treatment of A-Parents, B-Child, and C-Family.)

SHORT-TERM BEHAVIORAL GOALS, **A-PARENTS**	THERAPIST'S INTERVENTIONS
Parents collaborate with therapist in development of a treatment plan.	Establish therapeutic alliance with parents to enhance outcome of treatment.
Help therapist understand child's development of borderline problems.	Assess problem with parents and record a comprehensive history of the child's development and borderline symptoms.
Become aware of the diagnosis and what to appropriately expect from the child.	Educate parents about the diagnosis.
Cooperate in building a genogram to identify familial history and its relationship to borderline problems.	Construct a genogram to better understand the family history of borderline problems (see Behavioral Techniques, Chapter 23).
Enter treatment for parental pathology, if appropriate, to enhance outcome of adolescent therapy.	Evaluate parents for pathology that exacerbates problems and refer for treatment, if appropriate (see *Behavioral Management Guide: Essential Strategies for Adult Psychotherapy* in Resources for Providers, Chapter 33).
Develop awareness of how your personal theory influences cognition of the problem in child.	Explore parental theory of the problem.
Recognize fears and feelings of negative self-blame related to the problem.	Evaluate parents' fears and negative feelings of self-blame for child's problem.
Reveal any self-damaging behavior by the child.	Explore for self-damaging behavior by the child.
Learn to reach beyond automatic cognitive reactions in viewing the problem.	Expand parental perspective beyond limited cognitive reactions.
Comply with referral for psychiatric evaluation and possible medication.	Refer for psychiatric evaluation and possible medication if required.

Understand possible need for hospitalization and resolve related fears.	If child is actively suicidal or destructively acting out, discuss possible hospitalization and address related fears.
Accept and cooperate with hospitalization of child.	If necessary, refer child for hospitalization.
Learn how to help child develop appropriate goals and boundaries.	Teach parents the importance of appropriate goals and boundaries for adolescent.
Identify how you deal with adolescent's problem.	Explore how parents deal with adolescent's problem.
Learn new ways to deal with your child.	Acting as a consultant, teach parents new techniques for dealing with their child.
Be evaluated for sexual abuse and, if necessary, enter treatment.	Investigate for possible sexual abuse by parents. If positive, refer for treatment. Explain mandate to notify proper authorities.
Parents, children, or both are treated for substance abuse as appropriate.	Investigate for possible substance abuse in child and parents and treat as required. (For parents, see *Behavioral Management Guide: Essential Strategies for Adult Psychotherapy.* For children, see appropriate treatment plan.)
Confront thoughts of exaggerated and unrealistic consequences—"What ifs?"	Guide parents in confronting distorted reactions to trigger situations.
Identify cognitive distortions.	Weigh the reactions against evidence-based reality.
Restructure distortions with evidence-based consequences.	With parents, reframe distortions with reality-based reactions to stressors.
Comply with referral for psychological testing of child.	Provide referral for psychological testing of child to evaluate intellectual capabilities and rule out other diagnostic considerations.

Understand importance of early intervention.	Explain importance of and refer for early intervention for young children (see Early Intervention in Behavioral Techniques, Chapter 23).
Agree to allow therapist to confer with child's school to help in development of a comprehensive psycho-educational treatment plan for the child.	Request and receive parental permission to confer with child's teachers and school administrators.
Parents develop new parenting skills.	Assign parents to read books on how to deal with their anxiety and increase parenting skills, such as *Making Families Work and What to Do When They Don't* and others (see Bibliotherapy, Chapter 26).
Monitor child's medication schedule and report all reactions or failures to take meds.	If child is on meds, instruct parents on need for a regular schedule and feedback that may indicate need for revised dosage.
Meet witn other parents who are experiencing similar difficulties, and share solutions for coping with the problem.	Refer parents to self-help group or group on parenting skills.
Read about borderline disorders to better understand how to cope.	Assign books on borderline disorders such as *Stop Walking on Egg Shells* or *The Angry Heart* (see Bibliotherapy, Chapter 26).
Discuss termination plan and resolve related issues.	Develop a termination plan and discuss issues of separation anxiety and dependency.

OBSESSIVE-COMPULSIVE PERSONALITY DISORDER
(301.6)

Obsessive-Compulsive Personality Disorder is marked by preoccupation with orderliness and control, both mental and interpersonal, often ignoring the major point of the task or activity. Individuals with this disorder attempt to control through trivial details, painstaking attention to rules and procedures, and repeatedly checking to avoid any and all mistakes. They are oblivious to others who tend to become annoyed at them because of delays and inconvenience. They may be miserly or stingy and often become workaholics, preferring work over play. Although the disorder may begin in childhood, it is more common in adolescence or early adulthood, appearing earlier in males than in females.

Behavioral Symptoms
Obsessive-Compulsive Personality Disorder
(severity index: 1, mild; 2, moderate; 3, intense)

	Severity
1. Preoccupied with rules and order	_____
2. Perfectionism inhibits completion of tasks	_____
3. Excessively devoted to school or work	_____
4. Regards leisure activities and friendships as unimportant	_____
5. Inflexible, overconscientious	_____
6. Unable to discard objects even if worthless	_____
7. Unable to work or play with others	_____
8. Miserly	_____
9. Rigid, stubborn	_____

Other Diagnostic Considerations

Antisocial Personality Disorder (301.7)
Narcissistic Personality Disorder (301.81)
Personality Change due to General Medical Condition (310.1)
Schizoid Personality Disorder (301.20)

THE TREATMENT PLAN
OBSESSIVE-COMPULSIVE PERSONALITY DISORDER

Client: _____ Date _____

```
┌─────────────────────────────────────┐
│  Multiaxial Assessment               │
│                                      │
│  Axis I:  _____            │
│  Axis II: _____            │
│  Axis III: _____           │
│  Axis IV: _____            │
│  Axis V:  _____            │
│                                      │
└─────────────────────────────────────┘
```

I. OBJECTIVES OF TREATMENT
    (*select one or more*)

    1. Educate parents about the disorder.
    2. Determine family history of the disorder.
    3. Help family develop better coping skills.
    4. Reduce anxiety related to the disorder.
    5. Ameliorate preoccupation with order and control.
    6. Encourage compliance with educational programs and referrals.
    7. Reduce or eliminate need to check and recheck details.
    8. Reduce irrational beliefs.
    9. Promote socialization.
    10. Reduce alienation.
    11. Encourage interest in leisure activities.
    12. Develop a normal work schedule.
    13. Restore client to optimal level of functioning.
    14. Develop discharge plan for coping with everyday life.

II. SHORT-TERM BEHAVIORAL GOALS AND INTERVENTIONS
    (*select goals and interventions appropriate for your client*)

(Note: Separate goals and interventions are provided for treatment of A-Parents, B-Child, and C-Family.)

SHORT-TERM BEHAVIORAL GOALS, **A-PARENTS**	THERAPIST'S INTERVENTIONS
Parents collaborate with therapist in development of a treatment plan.	Establish therapeutic alliance with parents to enhance outcome of treatment.
Help therapist understand child's development and accurately assess problem.	Discuss problem with parents and record a comprehensive history of the child's development in order to assess Obsessive-Compulsive Disorder.
Become aware of the diagnosis and what to appropriately expect from the child.	Educate parents about the diagnosis.
Cooperate in building a genogram to identify familial history and its relationship to the disorder.	Construct a genogram to better understand the family history and its impact on the child (see Genograms, Chapter 23).
Develop awareness of how your personal theory influences cognition of the problem.	Explore parental theory of the problem.
Recognize fears and feelings of negative self-blame related to the problem.	Evaluate parents' fears and negative feelings of self-blame for child's problem.
Learn to reach beyond automatic cognitive reactions in viewing the problem.	Expand parental perspective beyond limited cognitive reactions.
Undergo treatment for underlying problems that may exacerbate child's condition.	Explore for underlying problems in parents, (e.g., anxiety, depression) and treat or refer for therapy (see appropriate treatment plan).
Comply with referral.	If appropriate, refer parents for psychological evaluation.
Understand importance of early intervention and follow through with referral.	Refer young children for early intervention (see Early Intervention, Chapter 23).

Agree to allow therapist to confer with child's school to help in development of a comprehensive psycho-educational treatment plan for the child.	Request and receive parental permission to confer with child's teachers and school administrators.
Comply with referral for psychological testing of child.	Provide referral for psychological testing of child to determine intellectual capabilities and rule out other diagnostic considerations.
Agree to psychiatric evaluation, if necessary, after child is interviewed.	Provide referral for psychiatric evaluation and possible medication, if indicated.
Meet with other parents who are experiencing similar difficulties and share solutions for coping with the problem.	Refer parents to self-help group. (See Self-Help Groups and 800 Numbers, Chapter 27.)
Read about parenting skills and Obsessive-Compulsive Disorder to better understand how to cope with the problem.	Assign reading of *The Obsessive-Compulsive Workbook* or alternate book on Obsessive-Compulsive Disorder (see Bibliotherapy, Chapter 26).
Make use of community resources.	Educate parents about available community resources (see Self-Help Groups or 800 Numbers, Chapter 27).
Discuss and approve termination plan. Resolve termination issues.	Develop a termination plan and discuss issues of separation anxiety and dependency.

SHORT-TERM BEHAVIORAL GOALS, **B-CHILD**	THERAPIST'S INTERVENTIONS
Engage in play therapy.	Engage child in a therapeutic relationship, via play therapy.
Learn about diagnosis and develop realistic expectations of self.	Educate client about the diagnosis and discuss symptomatology so he/she can adjust self-expectations.
Undergo treatment for sleep disorder.	Investigate for sleep disorder and treat, if necessary. See appropriate treatment plan.
Understand underlying dynamics that lead to maladaptive behavior and stress.	Explore ways in which Obsessive-Compulsive Personality Disorder manifests itself (e.g., need for perfection, preoccupation with rules and order, overly afraid of making mistakes) and clarify underlying dynamics.
Realize that human beings are not perfect, and reduce stressors imposed on self.	Teach child that human beings are not perfect.
Recognize underlying feelings of anger or depression and express appropriately.	Explore for underlying feelings of anger or depression, using puppet or graphics (see appropriate treatment plan).
Observe puppets and how they behave. Begin to see new role models deal with anxieties.	Shape client behavior by use of puppets (see Behavioral Techniques, Chapter 23).
Watch how puppet expresses feelings about anxieties.	Display socially acceptable expression of feelings about fears using puppets.
Learn new ways to handle fears.	Use puppet to role model successful ways to deal with fears.
Realize others also feel bad and relate to puppets overcoming the feeling.	Investigate for feelings of low esteem related to Obsessive-Compulsive Personality Disorder. . Have puppets talk about how they feel and what they can do about it.

Identify with puppets and recognize that playing is okay.	Have puppets play together, demonstrating that leisure activities are fun.
Begin to see possible solutions.	Discuss with puppets how they deal with negative feelings.
Identify irrational beliefs.	Through continued play with puppets, explore irrational beliefs about fears and anxieties.
Reframe beliefs about fears and anxieties.	Change irrational beliefs by having the puppets discuss the beliefs and develop rational alternatives.
Learn from role modeling and shape new behaviors.	Use puppets to role model appropriate behavior.
Discuss personal coping mechanisms developed to handle the disorder.	Investigate with child possible patterns of withdrawal used to avoid anxieties.
Recognize and relate how family impacts the problem.	Explore familial impact on the problem.
Learn positive self-talk.	Teach child positive self-talk to interrupt negative patterns.
Learn new technique for dealing with aggression.	Teach diaphragmatic breathing to control anxiety (see Behavioral Techniques, Chapter 23).
Learn new techniques to nurture yourself and deal with emotional difficulties.	Use the *Positive Thinking Game, The Anxiety Management Game*, or *The Ungame* to teach ways positive self-talk helps control emotional difficulties (see Therapeutic Games, Chapter 24).
Learn positive problem-solving and how famous people have overcome obstacles.	Assign to read *Don't Be Afraid, Tommy; The Feelings Story Book*; or *Cool Cats* (see Bibliotherapy, Chapter 26).
Learn new strategies for dealing with aggressive behaviors.	Assign to read or have parents read to child *Anybody Can Bake a Cake* (see Bibliotherapy, Chapter 26).

Learn methods that can be used to advocate for yourself.	Instruct client in the technique of self-advocacy.
Understand that you can deal with these issues and bring treatment to an end successfully.	Develop a termination plan and explain issues of separation anxiety and dependency.

SHORT-TERM BEHAVIORAL GOALS, **C-FAMILY**	THERAPIST'S INTERVENTIONS
Improve communications among family members.	Conduct family sessions or refer for family therapy to reduce anger and/or alienation and improve communication skills within the family.
Cooperate in amplifying family genogram.	Amplify family genogram created in first family session to help understand family history.
Discuss genogram openly to fully understand family history as it relates to Obsessive-Compulsive Disorder.	Discuss genogram to reveal family history and possible family secrets dealing with Obsessive-Compulsive Disorder.
Demonstrate boundaries, alliances, triangles, and emotional currents that may exacerbate the problem.	Explore family boundaries using sculpturing, a useful technique for understanding triangulation, alliances, and emotional currents (see Behavioral Techniques, Chapter 23).
Shift focus from problem to possible solutions.	Have family imagine a future without the problem and suggest actions that can be taken now to make that future possible.
Think about what treatment outcome would look like. Explain what you would like to see change in other family members when treatment is completed.	Ask family members to think about what they might want to say about each other when treatment is completed.
Family members realize they have the power to make important changes, even if these seem small.	Help family members realize they have an opportunity to do some things differently.
Members are empowered. They recognize that they can create positive change.	Ask family members to relate what they have accomplished in the past week.
Realize that major change is the result of small steps taken one at a time.	Help family identify and prioritize achievable goals.

Enhance understanding of condition and see how other families have handled similar problems.	Assign homework reading such as *The O.C.D. Workbook* (see Bibliotherapy, Chapter 26).
Make use of available community resources.	Refer family to available resources in the community (see Self-Help Groups or 800 Numbers, Chapter 27).
Reduce negative communication.	Develop a system of positive reinforcement with family members to interact better with each other and reduce scapegoating.
Family members work together to develop termination plan.	Discuss termination issues and develop a plan to terminate treatment.

PARANOID PERSONALITY DISORDER (301.0)

Paranoid Personality Disorder is characterized by a pattern of suspicion and mistrust that perceives the motives of others as malevolent. This disorder may first appear in early childhood with such symptoms as solitariness, underachievement, poor peer relations, and hypersensitivity. These children may appear odd and therefore attract a great deal of teasing. Paranoid Personality Disorder is diagnosed more often in boys than girls. There is some evidence of familial patterns in relatives with delusional disorders or chronic schizophrenia.

Behavioral Symptoms
Paranoid Personality Disorder
(severity index: 1, mild; 2, moderate; 3, intense)

Distrust and suspicion of others, including four of the following:

Severity

1. Unsubstantiated suspicion of exploitation, deception, or harm by others   _____
2. Unjustified preoccupation with the loyalty or trustworthiness of friends and others   _____
3. Unjustified fear that others will maliciously betray confidences   _____
4. Interprets hidden or threatening meanings into benign remarks or events   _____
5. Persistently fails to forgive slights, insults, or injuries by others   _____
6. Imagines attacks on character or reputation not apparent to others, and is quick to react in anger   _____
7. Rigid   _____
8. Critical of others   _____
9. Hypersensitive   _____
10. Has difficulty accepting criticism   _____
11. Solitary; poor peer relations   _____
12. Underachieves academically   _____

Other Diagnostic Considerations

Anxiety Disorders (300.xx)
Mood Disorders (300.xx)
Personality Change due to a General Medical Condition (310.1)
Posttraumatic Stress Disorder (309.81)
Psychotic Disorders (295.xx)
Substance-Related Disorders (*see substance*)

TREATMENT PLAN
PARANOID PERSONALITY DISORDER

Client: _____ Date _____

Multiaxial Assessment

Axis I: _____
Axis II: _____
Axis III: _____
Axis IV: _____
Axis V: _____

I.   OBJECTIVES OF TREATMENT
     (*select one or more*)

     1. Educate parents about the disorder.
     2. Determine family history of the disorder.
     3. Test and resolve unsubstantiated suspicions of exploitation, deception, or harm.
     4. Show that feelings of distrust, disloyalty, or betrayal are unjustified.
     5. Develop understanding that all people are good and bad.
     6. Learn to forgive and forget imagined slights and insults.
     7. Control reactive depression and anxiety.
     8. Improve client's reactions to stress.
     9. Learn to accept and apply constructive criticism.
     10. Ameliorate rigid behavior.
     11. Medicate and/or hospitalize as necessary.
     12. Clarify boundaries.
     13. Control urge to retaliate in anger.
     14. Improve communication skills.
     15. Encourage compliance with educational programs and referrals.
     16. Reframe irrational beliefs.
     17. Promote socialization, reduce alienation.
     18. Restore child and family to optimum level of functioning.
     19. Develop discharge plan for coping with everyday life.

II. SHORT-TERM BEHAVIORAL GOALS AND INTERVENTIONS
(select goals and interventions appropriate for your client)

(Note: Separate goals and interventions are provided for treatment of A-Parents, B-Child, and C-Family.)

SHORT-TERM BEHAVIORAL GOALS, **A-PARENTS**	THERAPIST'S INTERVENTIONS
Parents collaborate with therapist in development of a treatment plan.	Establish therapeutic alliance with parents to enhance outcome of treatment.
Help therapist understand child's development of paranoid problems.	Assess problem with parents and record a comprehensive history of the child's development and paranoid symptoms.
Become aware of the diagnosis and what to appropriately expect from the child.	Educate parents about the diagnosis.
Cooperate in building a genogram to identify familial history and its relationship to personality disorders.	Construct a genogram to better understand the family history of paranoid problems (see Behavioral Techniques, Chapter 23).
Enter treatment for parental pathology, if appropriate, to enhance outcome of therapy.	Evaluate parents for pathology that exacerbates problems and treat or refer for treatment, if appropriate (see *Behavioral Management Guide: Essential Strategies for Adult Psychotherapy*, Resources for Providers, Chapter 33).
Develop awareness of how your personal theory influences cognition of the problem in child.	Explore parental theory of the problem.
Recognize fears and feelings of negative self-blame related to the problem.	Evaluate parents' fears and negative feelings of self-blame for child's problem.
Identify parenting techniques that may exacerbate child's paranoia.	Explore for parenting techniques that may exacerbate paranoia.

Learn to reach beyond automatic cognitive reactions in viewing the problem.	Expand parental perspective beyond limited cognitive reactions.
Comply with referral for psychiatric evaluation and possible medication.	Refer for psychiatric evaluation and possible medication, if required.
Understand possible need for hospitalization and resolve related fears.	If child is actively suicidal or destructively acting out, discuss possible hospitalization and address related fears.
Accept and cooperate with hospitalization of child.	If necessary, refer child for hospitalization.
Learn how to help child develop appropriate goals and boundaries.	Teach parents the importance of appropriate goals and boundaries for child.
Identify how you deal with child's problem.	Explore how parents deal with child's problem.
Learn new ways to deal with your child.	Acting as a consultant, teach parents new techniques for dealing with their child.
Be evaluated for sexual abuse and, if necessary, enter treatment.	Investigate for possible sexual abuse by parents. If positive, refer for treatment. Explain mandate to notify proper authorities.
Parents, child, or both are treated for substance abuse as appropriate.	Investigate for possible substance abuse in child and parents and treat or refer for treatment (for parents, see *Behavioral Management Guide: Essential Strategies for Adult Psychotherapy*, Resources for Providers, Chapter 33. For child, see appropriate treatment plan.)
Confront thoughts of exaggerated and unrealistic consequences—"What ifs?"	Guide parents in confronting distorted reactions to trigger situations.
Identify cognitive distortions.	Weigh the reactions against evidence-based reality.

Restructure distortions with evidence-based consequences.	With parents, reframe distortions with reality-based reactions to stressors.
Meet with other parents who are experiencing similar difficulties, and share solutions for coping with the problem.	Refer parents to self-help group or group on parenting skills.
Have parents read to you about better ways to communicate.	Read to child *The Lovables, In the Kingdom of Self-Esteem, We Can Get Along,* or *Just Because I Am* (see Bibliotherapy, Chapter 26).
Discuss termination plan and resolve related issues.	Develop a termination plan and discuss issues of separation anxiety and dependency.

SHORT-TERM BEHAVIORAL GOALS, **B-CHILD**	THERAPIST'S INTERVENTIONS
Engage in play therapy.	Attempt to engage child in a therapeutic relationship via play therapy.
Learn about diagnosis and develop realistic expectations of self.	Educate client about the diagnosis and discuss symptomatology so he/she can adjust self-expectations.
Understand underlying dynamics that lead to maladaptive behavior and stress.	Explore ways in which anxieties manifest themselves and clarify underlying dynamics.
Realize that human beings are not perfect, and reduce stressors imposed on self.	Teach child that human beings are not perfect.
Recognize underlying feelings of anger or depression and express appropriately.	Explore for underlying feelings of anger or depression, using puppet (see appropriate treatment plan).
Observe puppets and how they behave. Begin to see new role models deal with anxieties.	Shape client behavior by use of puppets (see Behavioral Techniques, Chapter 23).
Watch how puppet expresses feelings about anxieties.	Display socially acceptable expression of feelings about anxieties, using puppet.
Learn new ways to handle paranoid feelings.	Use puppets to role model successful ways to deal with paranoid feelings.
Realize others also feel bad and relate to puppets overcoming their paranoid feelings and hypersensitivity.	Investigate for feelings of low esteem related to paranoia. Have puppets talk about how they feel and what they can do about it.
Begin to see possible solutions.	Discuss with puppets how they deal with negative feelings, especially when others tease them.
Identify irrational beliefs.	Through continued play with puppets, explore irrational beliefs about fears and anxieties.

Reframe beliefs about fears and anxieties.	Change irrational beliefs by having the puppets discuss the beliefs and develop rational alternatives.
Learn from role modeling and shape new behaviors.	Use puppets to role model appropriate behavior.
Using guided imagery to augment the play therapy process, learn to gain control over feelings.	Teach relaxation techniques and guided imagery to master anxieties (see "Using Guided Imagery to Augment the Play Therapy Technique," Behavioral Techniques, Chapter 23).
Understand how trauma may have contributed to existing disorder.	Explore child's background for trauma that may have exacerbated paranoia.
Discuss personal coping mechanisms developed to handle the disorder.	Investigate with child possible patterns of withdrawal used to avoid others.
Recognize and relate how family impacts the problem.	Explore familial impact on the problem.
Learn positive self-talk.	Teach child positive self-talk to interrupt negative patterns.
Learn new technique for dealing with anxiety.	Teach diaphragmatic breathing to control anxiety (see Behavioral Techniques, Chapter 23).
Learn new techniques to nurture yourself and deal with emotional difficulties.	Use the *Positive Thinking Game, Clear Thinking Game*, or *The Ungame* to teach ways positive self-talk helps control emotional difficulties (see Therapeutic Games, Chapter 24).
Shift focus of attention from problem to accomplishment.	Ask client to describe accomplishments for the past week.
Feel more confident as self-esteem improves.	Compliment client to provide positive reinforcement whenever possible.

Communicate problematic feelings to develop new skills or options.	Use technique of "Pounding Away Bad Feelings" and game *Don't Break the Ice* to help child release frustrations (see Behavioral Techniques, Chapter 23).
Attempt to use new control skills in school.	Urge child to use new control skills in the classroom setting.
Report results to therapist.	Provide positive reinforcement when client reports back that he/she has challenged anxiety-provoking situations. Praise attempt and reward success.
Learn positive problem-solving and better ways to get along with others.	Assign to read or read with parent *Why Is Everbody Always Picking on Me?* or *The Self-Control Patrol Workbook* (see Bibliotherapy, Chapter 26).
Learn methods that can be used to advocate for yourself.	Instruct client in the technique of self-advocacy.
Understand that you can deal with these issues and bring treatment to an end successfully.	Develop termination plan and explain issues of separation anxiety and dependency.

SHORT-TERM BEHAVIORAL GOALS, **C-FAMILY**	THERAPIST'S INTERVENTIONS
Improve communications among family members to reduce familial anxiety.	Conduct family sessions or refer for family therapy to reduce anger and/or alienation and improve communication skills within the family.
Cooperate in amplifying family genogram.	Amplify genogram created in early parental session to help understand family history and compare personal views of the problem.
Discuss genogram openly to fully understand family history as it relates to paranoia.	Discuss genogram to reveal family history and possible family secrets dealing with paranoia.
Learn ways to improve communication within the family.	Acting as a consultant, teach family about Paranoid Personality Disorder and discuss ways to improve communications.
Demonstrate boundaries, alliances, triangles, and emotional currents that may exacerbate the anxieties.	Explore family boundaries using sculpturing, a useful technique for understanding triangulation, alliances, and emotional currents (see Behavioral Techniques, Chapter 23).
Experience interpersonal interactions in family role-playing sessions that are worked out psychodramatically in session and can be transferred to everyday life.	Conduct role-playing sessions to provide a forum for family members to interact and practice improved communication skills (see Behavioral Techniques, Chapter 23).
Shift focus from problem to possible solutions.	Have family imagine a future without the problem and suggest actions that can be taken now to make that future possible.
Think about what treatment outcome would look like. Explain what you would like to see change in other family members when treatment is completed.	Ask family members to think about what they might want to say about each other when treatment is completed.

Family members realize they have the power to make important changes, even if these seem small.	Help family members realize they have an opportunity to do some things differently.
Members are empowered. They recognize that they can create positive change.	Ask family members to relate what they have accomplished in the past week.
Realize that major change is the result of small steps taken one at a time.	Help family identify and prioritize achievable goals.
Enhance understanding of condition and see how other families have handled similar problems.	Assign as homework reading *Making Families Work and What to Do When They Don't* (see Bibliotherapy, Chapter 26).
Make use of available community resources.	Refer family to available resources in the community. (See Self-Help Groups or 800 Numbers, Chapter 27.)
Reduce negative communication.	Develop a system of positive reinforcement with family members to interact better with each other and reduce scapegoating.
Family members work together to develop termination plan.	Discuss termination issues and develop a plan to terminate treatment.

19

Problems Related to Abuse or Neglect

PHYSICAL OR SEXUAL ABUSE OF CHILD (995.5x)

The Diagnostic and Statistical Manual of Mental Disorders (*DSM-IV*) addresses child abuse or neglect under Additional Conditions That May Be the Focus of Clinical Attention. This category is a V-code and not reimbursable by insurance companies. However, each abuse or neglect has a code that should be reported on Axis I of the *DSM-IV* Multiaxis Assessment System, with the impairment being treated because of the neglect (i.e, Anxiety, Depression, Posttraumatic Stress Disorder, etc.). Included in this category are:

Physical Abuse of Child (995.54)
Sexual Abuse of Child (995.53)
Neglect of Child (005.52)

Behavioral Symptoms
Child Abuse or Neglect
(severity index: 1, mild; 2, moderate; 3, intense)

	Severity
1. Physical signs of abuse	_____
2. Acts out sexually or aggressively	_____
3. Impaired ability to trust	_____
4. Problems with control and self-mastery	_____
5. Posttraumatic stress disorder	_____
6. Depression or anxiety	_____
7. "Damaged goods" syndrome	_____
8. Low self-esteem	_____
9. Guilt	_____
10. Repressed anger	_____
11. Role confusion/blurred role boundaries	_____
12. Pseudomaturity	_____
13. Failure to accomplish developmental tasks	_____
14. Poor social skills	_____
15. Social withdrawal	_____
16. Nightmares	_____

Other Diagnostic Considerations

Acute Stress Disorder (308.3)
Conduct Disorder (312.81/312.82)
Depersonalization (300.6)
Dissociative Disorder (300.14)
Dysthymia (300.4)
Generalized Anxiety Disorder (300.02)
Major Depressive Disorder (296.xx)
Oppositional Defiant Disorder (313.81)
Personality Disorders (301.xx)
Posttraumatic Stress Disorder (309.81)
Separation Anxiety Disorder (309.21)
Sleep Disorder (307.46)

TREATMENT PLAN
ABUSE OR NEGLECT—VICTIM

Client: _____ Date: _____

```
Multiaxial Assessment

Axis I:    _____
Axis II:   _____
Axis III:  _____
Axis IV:   _____
Axis V:    _____
```

I. OBJECTIVES OF TREATMENT
    (*select one or more*)

    1. Preclude further abuse or neglect.
    2. Prevent recurrence of symptoms.
    3. If parents are perpetrators, relocate child to safe environment.
    4. Educate parents about the problem.
    5. Investigate family history of the problem.
    6. Encourage family to establish rules regarding privacy and boundaries.
    7. Help family develop better coping skills.
    8. Reduce pervasive anxiety and worry.
    9. Eliminate denial and treat perpetrator.
    10. Diminish symptoms of depression.
    11. Reduce guilt.
    12. Eliminate sexual or aggressive acting out.
    13. Build self-esteem.
    14. End nightmares or night terrors.
    15. Reduce role confusion/blurred boundaries.
    16. Treat posttraumatic stress disorder.
    17. Encourage compliance with educational programs and referrals.
    18. Eliminate regressive behaviors.
    19. Reduce irrational beliefs.
    20. Eliminate "damaged goods" syndrome.
    21. Promote socialization, reduce alienation.
    22. Reduce pseudomaturity.
    23. Treat sexual problems, if age-appropriate.
    24. Restore child and family to optimum level of functioning.

II. SHORT-TERM BEHAVIORAL GOALS AND INTERVENTIONS
   (*select goals and interventions appropriate for your client*)

(Note: Separate goals and interventions are provided for A-Parents, B-Child, and C-Family.)

SHORT-TERM BEHAVIORAL GOALS, **A-PARENTS**	THERAPIST'S INTERVENTIONS
Parents collaborate with therapist in development of a treatment plan.	Establish therapeutic alliance with parents to enhance outcome of treatment.
Identify if authorities have been notified and if child has been treated medically or psychiatrically.	Determine if abuse has been reported and if child has been treated medically or psychiatrically.
Help therapist understand child's level of development before and after the abuse.	Assess problem with parents and record a comprehensive history of the abuse, identifying child's level of functioning prior to the abuse, child's current symptomatology and feelings toward the abuse, and parents' reaction.
Become aware of the diagnosis and symptomatology associated with abuse or neglect and learn what to appropriately expect from the child.	Educate parents about the diagnosis and symptomatology associated with abuse.
Become aware of reporting requirements for abusive behavior.	Discuss therapist's obligation to report deviant behavior, if and when mandated.
Cooperate in building a genogram to identify familial history and its relationship to abusive or neglectful behaviors.	Construct a genogram to understand the family history and identify physical and emotional boundaries to get a better idea of the historical "Ghosts of the Past," in order to break pathological cycles (see Behavioral Techniques, Chapter 23).
Enter treatment for abusive or neglectful behavior to enhance child therapy.	If parents are the abusers, child must be removed from the home and moved to a safer environment, while they are referred out for treatment.

Identify level of support child can get from nonoffending parent.	Determine role of nonoffending parents and level of support they can provide for child.
Perpetrator is treated in 12-step program.	If behavior is addictive, refer to 12-step program (see Self-Help Groups, Chapter 27).
Parents are treated for marital discord to reduce tension in the family.	Evaluate for marital discord and, if appropriate, treat or refer for treatment (see *Behavioral Management Guide: Essential Treatment Strategies for Adult Psychotherapy*, Resources for Providers, Chapter 33).
Learn how to deal with child's sleep problems.	Investigate for sleep problems in child and teach parents how to deal with the problem (see appropriate treatment plan).
Identify other symptoms child may be exhibiting.	Explore for other symptoms in child noticed by parents (i.e., depression, anxiety).
Confront thoughts of exaggerated and unrealistic consequences regarding the abuse.	Guide parents in confronting distorted reactions to the child's problems.
Enter treatment for addiction.	Investigate for substance or sexual addictions in parents and treat or refer for treatment (see *Behavioral Management Guide: Essential Treatment Strategies for Adult Psychotherapy*, Resources for Providers, Chapter 33).
Parents feel validated and enter treatment for their own problems related to the child's abuse.	Acknowledge and validate parental problems with the abuse. Determine need for treatment of anxiety, depression, or other reactions (see appropriate treatment plan).
Feel empowered to help child.	Help develop a plan of action for parents to empower them and reduce helplessness.

Recognize abusive nature of certain behaviors.	If abuse is emotional and parents are the perpetrators, address and identify abusive behaviors.
Help develop action plan to avoid abusive behaviors.	Develop an action plan to interrupt pathological behaviors before they get out of control.
Learn better parenting skills.	If abuse is between siblings, help parents develop techniques for interrupting abusive behaviors and restoring appropriate boundaries.
Recognize that change is possible and you can make a difference.	Help parents understand that change is possible.
Read assigned book to understand that there can be recovery.	Assign to read *Trauma and Recovery* (see Bibliotherapy, Chapter 26).
Follow through with referral for psychological testing of the child.	If appropriate, after interviewing the child, provide referral for psychological testing to assess current level of functioning.
Understand importance of early intervention.	If child is young, explain importance and refer for early intervention (see Early Intervention, Treatment Aids, Chapter 23).
Agree to allow therapist to confer with child's school to help in development of a comprehensive psycho-educational treatment plan for the child.	Request and receive parental permission to confer with child's teachers and school officials.
Assign parents to read to child.	Assign parents to read to child to enhance their relationship while helping child share his/her secret feelings, such as *Chilly Stomach, Private Zones, or A Very Touchy Book . . . for Little People and for Big People* (see Bibliotherapy, Chapter 26).

Learn to encourage positive behaviors through respectful parenting.	Explore methods of parenting and, if aversive (i.e., insults, physical punishment, abuse), help parents understand that these methods only suppress negative behavior and teach children aggression. Refer to parenting class.
Parents develop new parenting skills.	Assign parents to read books that increase parenting skills, such as *Making Families Work and What to Do When They Don't* and *Children and Parents Do Make a Difference* (see Bibliotherapy, Chapter 26).
Monitor child's medication schedule and report all reactions or failures to take meds.	If child is on meds, instruct parents on need for a regular schedule and feedback that may indicate need for revised dosage.
Meet with other parents who are experiencing similar difficulties, and share solutions for coping with the problem.	Refer parents to self-help group or group on parenting skills (see Self-Help Groups or 800 Numbers, Chapter 27).
Read about ways in which you and child can deal with sexual abuse.	If appropriate, assign books on molestation, such as *When Your Child Has Been Molested* (see Bibliotherapy, Chapter 26).
Discuss termination plan and resolve related issues.	Develop a termination plan and discuss issues of separation anxiety and dependency.

SHORT-TERM BEHAVIORAL GOALS, **B-CHILD**	THERAPIST'S INTERVENTIONS
Engage in play therapy.	Engage child in a therapeutic relationship, via play therapy.
Realize why you are in treatment.	Discuss with child if he/she knows why he/she comes to treatment.
Take time, if needed, to build trust before discussing the abuse.	Determine how comfortable child may be in discussing the abuse at this time. If advisable, postpone talking about it until the child is more comfortable in treatment and trust has started to build.
Realize you have the power to reshape your bad dreams.	Investigate for sleep disorder and treat, if necessary. Have child draw a picture of nightmare to which the therapist adds a protective figure (see Bad Dreams, Behavioral Techniques, Chapter 23).
Identify with puppets and discuss the abuse openly.	Using puppets or anatomically correct dolls, talk about the abuse directly to bring it out in the open.
Understand the need to report the abuse and need for a safe environment.	If abuse has not been reported or if child is in danger, notify the authorities. Help child understand your concerns for his/her future and that of any siblings.
Other symptoms are identified and treated.	Through the use of puppets, explore for symptoms related to the abuse (i.e., enuresis, encopresis, separation anxiety, sexual acting out) and treat (see appropriate treatment plan).
Reduce anxieties related to pending medical examination.	Even if child has already been medically examined, play doctor with dolls or puppets to reduce anxieties.
Recognize underlying feelings of anger or depression.	Explore for underlying feelings of anger and/or depression using puppets and treat (see appropriate treatment plan).

Realize it is okay to talk about what happened to you.	Have puppets or anatomically correct dolls openly discuss their body parts and explain if they have been hurt in the past and how they feel now (see Real People Dolls or Teach-a-Body Dolls in Therapeutic Games, Chapter 24).
Watch puppets and understand the abuse was not your fault.	Shape client behavior by using puppets. Have puppets discuss two people touching each others' private parts. Ask child whose fault it would be, the big person or the little one?
Learn new ways to deal with abuse or neglect.	Use puppets to role model successful ways to deal with abuse or neglect.
Understand that abuse normally leads to shame and guilt.	Have puppets discuss shame and guilt associated with the abuse.
Realize that others also feel bad and relate to the puppets in overcoming your bad feelings.	Investigate for feelings of low self-esteem related to abuse. Have puppets talk about how they feel and what they can do about it.
Feel less inhibited to talk about the abuse and your feelings indirectly through the use of puppets.	If child is cooperative, have him/her stage a puppet show called "What Goes on in My House," while the therapist interviews the puppets about the facts of the abuse.
Identify how you feel "damaged" as a result of the abuse.	Explore with child his/her negative feelings related to the abuse, the "damaged goods" syndrome.
Identify with puppets and feel acknowledged.	Discuss with puppets what they can do with bad feelings. Acknowledge and validate their points of view about their problems.
Identify irrational beliefs.	Through continued play with puppets, explore irrational beliefs about fears and anxieties.
Reframe beliefs about fears and anxieties.	Change irrational beliefs by having the puppets discuss the beliefs and develop rational alternatives.

Learn from role modeling and shape new behaviors. See new possibilities.	Use puppets to role model appropriate behavior and discuss possibility of change in the future.
Use relaxation technique and guided imagery to gain control over feelings.	Teach relaxation techniques and guided imagery to master anxieties (see Behavioral Techniques, Imagery, Chapter 23).
Create a plan of action for any future incidents of abuse.	Develop with child an action plan to deal with future abusive situations.
Learn what to do if inappropriately touched.	Assign to read or have parents read to child *A Very Touching Book . . . for Little People and Big People* (see Bibliotherapy, Chapter 26).
Read assigned book to child in order to teach him/her how to get help for scary secrets.	Assign parents to read to child *Do You Have a Secret* (see Bibliotherapy, Chapter 26).
Learn methods that you can use to advocate for yourself.	Instruct client in the technique of self-advocacy.
Understand that you can deal with these issues and bring treatment to an end successfully.	Develop a termination plan and explain issues of separation anxiety and dependency.

SHORT-TERM BEHAVIORAL GOALS, **C-FAMILY**	THERAPIST'S INTERVENTIONS
Abuse is identified and acknowledged among family members to reduce anger and alienation.	Conduct family sessions or refer for family therapy in order to address the abuse.
Identify and review the five key cognitions of the problem.	Explore family cognitions of the problem: (1) selective perceptions of what occurred, (2) attributions of blame, (3) expectations of a recurrence, (4) assumptions of the characteristics of family members, and (5) standards each member expects of the others.
Discuss your view of central family problems.	Investigate communication problems, role conflicts, and influence of extended family.
Express your thoughts and emotions regarding aberrant behaviors.	Explore individual thoughts and emotions regarding aberrant behaviors.
Acknowledge actions taken.	Review actions taken to deal with abusive behaviors.
Identify triggers of the abusive event.	Investigate what triggers led to the abusive event.
Family is educated about available resources and creates a safety plan.	Develop with family a plan to assure safety of all members if abuse continues or is possible. Suggest they call an 800 number or the police, etc. (see 800 Numbers, Chapter 27).
Identify substance use in family and urge treatment for addicted member/s.	Investigate possible substance use within family that may contribute to abuse and, if appropriate, treat or refer for treatment (see appropriate treatment plan in *Behavior Management Guide: Essential Treatment Strategies for Adult Psychotherapy* in Resources for Providers, Chapter 33).

Learn better communication skills and conflict resolution.	Explore for communication deficits and discrepancies that may result. Teach new methods of conflict resolution.
Cooperate in amplifying family genogram.	Augment genogram created in an early parental session to help understand family history of abusive behaviors and identify physical and emotional boundaries.
Discuss genogram openly to fully understand family history as it relates to abuse.	Discuss genogram to reveal family history and possible family secrets regarding abusive behavior.
Demonstrate boundaries, alliances, triangles, and emotional currents that may exacerbate the abusive behavior.	Explore family boundaries using sculpturing, a useful technique for understanding triangulation, alliances, and emotional currents (see Behavioral Techniques, Chapter 23).
Work together to reduce denial, anger, and shame.	Develop therapeutic alliance with family to increase understanding of abusive behaviors, break through the denial, and reduce anger and shame.
Shift focus from problem to possible solutions.	Have family imagine a future without the problem and suggest actions that can be taken now to best approximate that possibility.
Think about what treatment outcome would look like. Explain what you would like to see change in other family members when treatment is completed.	Ask family members to think about what they might want to say about each other when treatment is completed.
Become aware of cues that stimulate aberrant behavior.	If parent or family member is the perpetrator, investigate cues that stimulate aberrant behavior.
Family members realize they have the power to make important changes, even if these seem small.	Help family members realize they have an opportunity to do some things differently.
Members are empowered. They recognize that they can create positive change.	Ask family members to relate what they have accomplished in the past week.

Realize that major change is the result of small steps taken one at a time.	Help family identify and prioritize achievable goals.
Enhance understanding of abuse and its behavioral and emotional symptoms.	Assign as homework reading *Making Families Work and What to Do When They Don't* or, if child age 6–10 has been sexually abused, *A Secret: A Child's Story of Sexual Abuse* (see Bibliotherapy, Chapter 26).
Make use of available community resources.	Refer family to available resources in the community. (See Self-Help Resources or 800 Numbers, Chapter 27.)
Reduce negative communication.	Develop a system of positive reinforcement with family members to interact better with each other to reduce scapegoating and abuse.
Family members work together to develop termination plan.	Discuss termination issues and develop a plan to terminate treatment.

20

Relational Problems

SIBLING RELATIONAL PROBLEMS (V61.8)

Sibling rivalry is a normal part of growing up. However, it is pathological when it becomes uncontrollable, tension arises among family members, and recurring arguments get out of hand. Such rivalry may occur when parents have unresolved childhood problems of their own with their siblings. It can also occur because of marital problems (children acting out their parents' problems), role confusion, communication difficulties, or other conflicts with extended family. Other contributing factors may be parental failure to set appropriate boundaries and provide consistent, respectful discipline, or parental overinvolvement in their own lives.

No two children in a family are exactly alike. Some of the major differences include birth order, genetics, and gender. As a result, parents do not act the same with each of them. Siblings often learn to test strong love and hate relations with each other, rather than express their feelings to their parents.

Behavioral Symptoms
Sibling Relational Problems
(severity index: 1, mild; 2, moderate, 3, intense)

<u>Severity</u>

1. Significant impairment in academic and interpersonal functioning   _____
2. Depressed most of the time   _____
3. Persistent anxiety   _____
4. Difficulty falling and staying sleep   _____
5. Displays social phobia   _____
6. Adjustment disorder   _____
7. Personality disorder   _____
8. Developmental delays   _____
9. School or learning problems   _____
10. Somatization   _____
11. Oppositional defiant behavior   _____
12. Acts out   _____
13. Distorted parenting   _____
14. Poor disciplining   _____
15. Physical or sexual abuse   _____
16. Scapegoating   _____
17. Marked inability to empathize with sibling   _____

Other Diagnostic Considerations

Adjustment Disorder (309.xx)
Anxiety Disorders (300.xx)
Attention Deficit/Hyperactivity Disorder (314.xx)
Child Antisocial Behavior (V 61.20)
Conduct Disorder (312.8)
Depressive Disorders (296.xx)
Disruptive Behavior Disorder (312.9)
Dissociative Disorders (300.xx)
Impulse Control Disorder (312.xx)
Obsessive-Compulsive Disorder (301.4)
Oppositional Defiant Disorder (313.81)
Neglect of Child (V61.21/995.5)
Personality Disorders (301.xx)
Physical or Sexual Abuse (V61.21) Axis IV

PARENT–CHILD RELATIONAL PROBLEM (V61.20)

Since V-codes are not usually reimbursable by most insurance companies, it is important to identify a behavioral impairment under treatment on Axis I of the *DSM* Multiaxial Assessment System. Some of the behavioral symptoms that should be coded on Axis I or II include anxiety disorders, conduct disorder, mood disorders, or personality disorders. V-codes are coded on Axis IV. However, the focus of treatment should be on the recurrent patterns of dysfunctional interactions among family members (i.e., inadequate parenting, the "too good" or "not good enough" mother or father syndrome, overprotection, underprotection, or dysfunctional communication).

If indicated by the symptomatology, one or both members of the dyad should be considered candidates for individual or family treatment. If both parents are emotionally impaired, they should be considered for individual or conjoint treatment. Some of the behavioral symptoms that occur are products of unresolved parental conflicts. Since parents are the role models for their children, it is not surprising to find these problems reappearing in the next generation.

Behavioral Symptoms
Parent–Child Relational Problems
(severity index: 1, mild; 2, moderate; 3, intense)

(Note: Behavioral impairment should be coded on Axis I or II and the associated V-code on Axis IV.)

	Severity
1. Parent or child persistently acts out.	_____
2. Parent and child engage in heated quarreling.	_____
3. Parent/child displays significant anxiety and/or stress-related problems.	_____
4. Parent or child is constantly irritable.	_____
5. Parent or child suffers from mood disorder.	_____
6. Neurological disorder of parent or child is exacerbated.	_____
7. Child has serious academic problems.	_____
8. Parent or child has eating disorder.	_____
9. Parent or child has sleep disturbance.	_____
10. Parent or child has personality disorder.	_____
11. Parent exhibits inadequate parenting skills.	_____
12. Parent or child shows marked inability to empathize with each other.	_____
13. Patterns of discipline are irrational, confused, or lacking.	_____

TREATMENT PLAN
PARENT–CHILD RELATIONAL PROBLEMS

Client: _____ Date: _____

```
┌─────────────────────────────────────┐
│ Multiaxial Assessment               │
│                                     │
│ Axis I:   _____           │
│ Axis II:  _____           │
│ Axis III: _____           │
│ Axis IV:  _____           │
│ Axis V:   _____           │
└─────────────────────────────────────┘
```

I. OBJECTIVES OF TREAMENT
    (*select one or more*)

1. Develop better parenting skills.
2. Investigate family history of problem/problems.
3. Reduce overall intensity of quarreling.
4. Ameliorate behavioral symptoms.
5. Improve communication skills.
6. Reduce dysfunctional interactions.
7. Restore rational discipline.
8. Increase ability to empathize with each other.
9. Reduce familial alienation.
10. Restore adolescent and family to optimum level of functioning.

II. SHORT-TERM BEHAVIORAL GOALS AND INTERVENTIONS
    (*select goals and interventions appropriate for your clients*)

SHORT-TERM BEHAVIORAL GOALS, **C-FAMILY**	THERAPIST'S INTERVENTIONS
Improve communications within the family system to reduce anger and alienation.	Conduct family sessions, with focus on reducing anger and/or alienation.
Cooperate with therapist to improve treatment outlook.	Develop therapeutic alliance or collaborative relationship with parents and children to instill trust and enhance treatment outcomes.

Discuss treatment plan and agree on target problems.	Formulate treatment plan and discuss with clients. Agree on target problems.
Cooperate in construction of a family genogram. Begin to understand historical communication patterns and contributions of ancestors to dysfunctional patterns.	Prepare complete genogram to uncover and display family interactions, patterns, roles, and secrets (see Behavioral Techniques, Chapter 23).
Discuss genogram openly to understand pathological patterns of interaction.	Discuss genogram to reveal family history and toxic issues that may have contributed to current pathology.
Identify the things you think have created or contributed to the family problems.	Explore and acknowledge each member's personal view of the problems that have brought him/her into therapy.
Identify behavioral symptoms and enter individual therapy as required.	Explore individual behavioral symptoms and evaluate potential effectiveness of current modality or the need for individual therapy. If required, provide or refer for treatment (see appropriate treatment plan/s or *Behavioral Management Guide: Essential Treatment Strategies for Adult Psychotherapy*, Resources for Providers, Chapter 33).
Identify impact of extended family.	Explore impact of extended family.
Identify crisis that may have created unusual family stress.	Investigate for environmental stressors that may have exacerbated the problem (i.e., death, relocation, loss of employment, financial issues, etc.).
Demonstrate boundaries, alliances, triangulation, and emotional currents that may undermine family functioning.	Explore family boundaries using family sculpting, a useful technique for revealing triangulation, alliances and emotional currents (see Behavioral Techniques, Chapter 23).

Children clearly understand what is expected of them and the consequences for out-of-bounds behavior.	Help parents establish appropriate boundaries, clear rules, and methods of positive reinforcement.
Increase emotional awareness by walking in another family member's shoes and expand your repertoire of behavior.	Conduct role-playing sessions with each member playing the part of another and switching parts as necessary (see Behavioral Techniques, Chapter 23).
Familial homeostasis is established.	Identify and rectify disruptive relational patterns.
Explore impact of rivalry on each child and determine strategy for dealing with it.	Explore sibling rivalry, how it is handled, and the impact on each child. Brainstorm methods of dealing with it.
Help develop family solution and become part of the solution instead of the problem.	Preclude a "search for the guilty" by requiring clients to stay solution-focused.
Realize that anxiety and awkwardness are normal accompaniments to family change.	Instruct clients on barriers and resistance to change.
Learn to listen to one another and ask for clarification when necessary.	Teach active family listening and clarification skills.
Reduce scapegoating of "identified patient."	Determine if there is an "identified patient" within the family system.
All family members assume responsibility for improvement.	Assist family in understanding that current difficulties may be the result of systemic dysfunctions and not the fault of any one individual
Follow up with referrals for evaluation.	If appropriate, refer client/s for medical and psychiatric evaluations.
Maintain a medication log to monitor medication schedule and reactions. Discuss in session with therapist.	If medication is prescribed, assure compliance with regimen. Identify need for dosage adjustment.
Keep journal and discuss during session.	Instruct each client to maintain a thought and feelings log to record events and reactions between visits.

If necessary, enter treatment for substance abuse.	Explore possibility of substance abuse and, if positive, treat or refer to 12-step rational recovery program (see appropriate treatment plan or *Behavioral Management Guide: Essential Treatment Strategies for Adult Psychotherapy*, Resources for Providers, Chapter 33).
Improve parenting skills.	Refer mother and/or father to parenting group to improve parenting skills (see Self-Help Groups, Chapter 27).
Identify and evaluate existing irrational beliefs.	Help clients examine their irrational beliefs.
Reframe your irrational beliefs.	Reframe clients' irrational beliefs with evidence-based reality.
Work toward changing the way you speak to each other.	Educate family about "indoor" (chronic tone) behavior and "outdoor" (social tone) behavior. Encourage family to reduce indoor behavior.
Reduce negative behaviors and interaction.	Explore negative self-talk and familial negative talk and encourage more positive ways to communicate.
Learn new rational perspective.	Further clarify rational distortions in clients' perceptions.
Read assigned book to enhance parenting skills.	Assign parents to read *Making Families Work and What to Do When They Don't* or *Try Me: Simple Strategies That Turn Off the Tantrums and Create Cooperation* (see Bibliotherapy for Parents, Chapter 26).
Read books together that address behavioral problems and how to deal with them.	Assign family members to read together *When Living Hurts* or *An Ounce of Prevention* (see Bibliotherapy, Chapter 26).

Describe your view of what the future should be.	Have each family member describe what he/she would like the future to be like.
Acknowledge your personal barriers and available resources.	Identify barriers and available internal and external resources to overcome them and create change.
Family members work together to create SMART action plan.	Develop a SMART action plan: Small, Measurable, Achievable, Realistic, Timelined Goals (see Change, Behavioral Techniques, Chapter 23).
Learn to abandon old patterns and develop new ways of thinking.	Discuss what actions are going to be taken and encourage family to persist until the goals are reached.
Receive positive reinforcement for success.	Provide positive reinforcement for success.
Imagine what life might be like after treatment and how the lives of all family members will be changed.	Ask family members to verbalize three things they would like to be able to say about each of the others when therapy is completed.
Play and share *Lifestories*.	Have entire family play *Lifestories* to share family tales and bring members closer together. (See Therapeutic Games, Chapter 24.)
Use family outing to practice new knowledge and insights and enhance relationships.	Assign family outings to include all family members.
Discuss termination issues and end treatment.	Develop a termination plan and discuss related issues of dependency and separation anxiety.

CHILDREN OF DIVORCE OR SEPARATION

This is a difficult time for traditional institutions, especially the family. It is estimated (Kurdck 1986; Knell 2000) that almost 40 percent of all children in America will experience parental disruption by their 15th birthday. In divorce or separation, some disturbance is common in the interaction between the child and one or both parents, as well as a period of adjustment that may require therapeutic intervention.

Although there is no category in *DSM-IV* for Children of Divorce or Separation, I believe this growing problem deserves special attention. It is assumed that the diagnosis would be coded as V61.20 on Axis IV of the *DSM-IV* Multiaxis Assessment System, with the associated behavioral impairments coded on Axis I.

Divorce or separation often creates major life changes for all members of the family (i.e., financial problems, new homes or schools, increased mother–child conflict, and others). Adjustment to post-divorce lifestyle changes is challenging for both parent and child.

Behavioral Symptoms
Children of Divorce or Separation
(severity index: 1, mild; 2, moderate; 3, intense)

	Severity
1. Elimination disorders—children 2½–5 years old	_____
2. Depression	_____
3. Aggressive behaviors	_____
4. Withdrawal	_____
5. Decreased frustration tolerance	_____
6. Separation anxiety	_____
7. Fear of interaction with others	_____
8. Difficulty concentrating	_____
9. Self-esteem issues	_____
10. Self-blame, guilt, shame	_____

There may be many more symptoms resulting from divorce as a traumatic event.

Other Diagnostic Considerations

Adjustment Disorder (309.xx)
Conduct Disorder (312.81)
Eating Disorders (301.xx)
Elimination Disorders
General Anxiety Disorder (300.02)
Impulse Control Disorder (312.30)
Oppositional Defiant Behavior (313.81)
Reactive Adjustment Disorder of Early Childhood (313.89)
Separation Anxiety Disorder (309.21)
Social Phobia (300.23)
Somatization Disorder (300.81)
Selective Mutism (313.23)
Sleep Disorders (307.xx)
Stuttering (307.00)
Substance Abuse (*see substance*)
Trichotillomania (312.39)

TREATMENT PLAN
CHILDREN OF DIVORCE OR SEPARATION

Client: _____ Date: _____

```
┌─────────────────────────────────┐
│ Multiaxial Assessment           │
│                                 │
│ Axis I:   _____       │
│ Axis II:  _____       │
│ Axis III: _____       │
│ Axis IV:  _____       │
│ Axis V:   _____       │
│                                 │
└─────────────────────────────────┘
```

I. OBJECTIVES OF TREATMENT
    (*select one or more*)

1. Educate parents about the possible reactions their child/children may have to divorce (i.e., self-blame, magical thinking about reconciliation, fear of abandonment, avoidance behavior, peer ridicule).
2. Teach parents the importance of showing mutual respect in front of children.
3. Determine family history of divorce/separation.
4. Eliminate blame.
5. Help family develop better coping skills.
6. Help parents develop a reasonable visitation schedule.
7. Reduce pervasive anxiety and worry.
8. Treat elimination disorders associated with divorce.
9. Reduce depression.
10. Diminish acting out.
11. Eliminate fears of abandonment.
12. Reduce and eliminate fear of ridicule in social interactions.
13. Increase frustration tolerance.
14. Encourage compliance with educational programs and referrals.
15. Reframe irrational beliefs.
16. Eliminate anxieties.
17. Help child develop a realistic view of the divorce/separation.
18. Reduce "too good" syndrome.
19. Reduce alienation, promote socialization.
20. Treat other disorders related to trauma.
21. Restore child and family to optimum level of functioning.
22. Develop discharge plan for coping with everyday life.

II. SHORT-TERM BEHAVIORAL GOALS AND INTERVENTIONS
(select goals and interventions appropriate for your client)

(Note: Separate goals and interventions are provided for A-Parents, B-Child, and C-Family.)

SHORT-TERM BEHAVIORAL GOALS, **A-PARENTS**	THERAPIST'S INTERVENTIONS
Separately collaborate with therapist in development of a treatment plan.	Establish therapeutic alliance separately with each custodial and noncustodial parent.
If there is any hope of reconciliation, enter couples therapy or marriage counseling.	Identify any hope of reconciliation and, if positive, refer for couples therapy or marriage counseling.
Help therapist understand child's developmental issues and concerns before and after the divorce/separation.	Assess problem separately with both parents and record a comprehensive history of child's development before and after the divorce/separation.
Recognize what to reasonably expect from child.	Educate parents about the possible pitfalls for their child, related to the divorce/separation.
Cooperate in building a genogram.	Construct a genogram to better understand the physical and emotional boundaries, toxic issues, and familial support network (see Behavioral Techniques, Chapter 23).
Enter treatment for individual psychopathology, if appropriate, to support child's treatment and enhance outcome.	Evaluate parents for individual psychopathology and refer for treatment, if appropriate, to reduce negative effects on child (see *Behavioral Management Guide: Essential Treatment Strategies for Adult Psychotherapy*, Resources for Providers, Chapter 33).
Develop awareness of how your personal theory influences cognition of how the child deals with divorce/separation.	Explore parental cognitions of the divorce/separation and identify how they have discussed it with the child. What did they explain and what did they withhold?

Recognize your fears and feelings of responsibility for the separation/divorce.	Evaluate parents' fears and feelings of personal responsibility for the divorce/separation.
Learn to reach beyond automatic cognitive reactions in viewing the problem.	Expand parental perspective beyond limited cognitive reactions.
Identify and explain how well you think your child is coping with the divorce.	Explore parents' understanding of how the child is coping with the divorce. Is child angry with one parent, the other, both, or himself?
Identify conflicts and realize the consequences they can have for the child's recovery.	Explore the dynamics of marital conflict and how its intensity impacts the child.
Confront reactions that can lead to catastrophic outcomes.	Confront parents' distorted reactions that trigger destructive behaviors.
Control the stress to protect the child from the conflict.	Teach parents to reduce the stress during the marital breakup and ultimate family separation in order to protect the child from their hostilities and conflict.
Feel acknowledged instead of blamed.	Acknowledge each parent's point of view (see Change, Behavioral Techniques, Chapter 23).
Identify cognitive distortions and correct them.	Have parents weigh their reactions against evidence-based reality.
Collaborate in development of a direction-based plan.	Develop a direction-based plan for a controlled, nonhostile separation and divorce.
Parents become aware of the possibility of change.	Explore possibilities of change (i.e., internal barriers, old patterns) and identify resources for making modifications.
Identify financial concerns and actions to limit the impact on the child.	Explore financial situation and identify actions to reduce negative impact.

Understand importance of early intervention and follow up on referral.	If appropriate, stress importance of and refer child for early intervention (see Behavioral Techniques, Chapter 23).
Cooperate with therapist's efforts to enlist the school's assistance in developing a psycho-educational treatment plan for the child.	When indicated, request and receive parental permission to confer with child's teachers and school officials.
Comply with referral for evaluations.	If necessary, after interviewing the child, provide referral for medical and psychiatric evaluations.
Read assigned book/s to child to help understand and deal with feelings triggered by the divorce or separation.	Assign books for parents to read with the child: *The Divorce Workbook* or *Surviving Divorce* (see Bibliotherapy, Chapter 26).
Learn new skills and strategies for managing child's anxieties related to the divorce/separation.	Assign parents to read on their own *Helping Your Kids Cope with Divorce* (see Bibliotherapy, Chapter 26).
Understand common behavioral pitfalls to help child cope, if it becomes necessary.	Educate parents about problematic reactions by the child (i.e., peer avoidance or ridicule, interfamilial blame, personal blame, abandonment issues, unfounded hopes of reconciliation).
Meet with other parents who are going through the same difficulties and share solutions for dealing with the problems.	Refer parents to appropriate self-help group.
Expand your repertoire of strategies to help your child cope with divorce/separation.	Assign parents to read: *Growing Up with Divorce, Helping Children Cope with Divorce*, or *Caught in the Middle* (see Bibliotherapy, Chapter 26).
Discuss termination plan and resolve related issues.	Develop a termination plan and discuss issues of separation and dependency.

SHORT-TERM BEHAVIORAL GOALS, **B-CHILD**	THERAPIST'S INTERVENTIONS
Engage in play therapy.	Engage child in a therapeutic relationship via play therapy.
Child reveals symptoms through play.	Identify child's symptoms and determine most appropriate course of treatment.
Recognize and explain your reactions to the divorce or separation.	Explain the common reactions to divorce or separation (i.e., self-blame, parental blame, abandonment issues, separation anxiety, social ostracism, and unfounded hopes of reconciliation).
Understand underlying dynamics that lead to maladaptive behavior and stress.	Explore ways in which anxieties manifest themselves.
Undergo treatment for sleep disorder.	Investigate for sleep disorder and treat, if necessary (see appropriate treatment plan).
Ease the blame and increase self-acceptance.	Teach child that human beings are less than perfect.
Listen to the puppets and talk with them about the divorce or separation. Feel understood.	Use puppets to share their feelings with child over the divorce/separation (see Behavioral Techniques, Chapter 23).
Learn new ways to handle visitations.	Use puppets to role-model ways to deal with visitations.
Identify feelings about stepparent and siblings.	If parent/s are remarried after divorce, have puppets discuss with the child how they feel about their new stepparent and stepsiblings.
Realize you are not alone. Others also feel bad. Talk to puppets about how they overcome those feelings.	Investigate for low self-esteem related to the divorce/separation. Have child discuss these feelings with the puppets.
Begin to see possible solutions.	Discuss through puppets how negative feelings are dealt with and develop a plan of action.

Identify beliefs related to marital dissolution.	Through continued play with the puppets, explore relevant attitudes, fears, and anxieties regarding marital dissolution.
Increase repertoire of adaptive responses.	Develop effective alternatives to reduce negative emotions and behaviors triggered by stressors.
Learn from role-modeling and shape new behaviors.	Use puppets to role-model appropriate behavior.
Identify with puppets and realize that parents' problems were not caused by you.	Have puppets discuss how they might feel that the divorce/separation was their fault because they were "bad."
Use relaxation techniques and guided imagery to handle anxieties.	Teach relaxation techniques and guided imagery to master anxieties (see Behavioral Techniques, Chapter 23).
Understand anxiety and realize that avoidance does not help.	Teach child the dynamics of anxiety: not dangerous, not permanent, avoidance increases it. Exposure can promote change.
Lessen impact of socioeconomic change.	Discuss how changes in family's financial status have affected the child.
Relate life story to therapist or play *Lifestories*.	Use puppets to have child relate his/her life story, or play *Lifestories* (see Therapeutic Games, Chapter 24).
Develop better coping skills to lessen the impact on painful emotions.	Play *Bounce Back* or *My Two Homes* to help child adjust to parents' divorce/separation (see Therapeutic Games, Chapter 24).
Discuss personal coping mechanisms used to handle the divorce/separation.	Investigate with child possible patterns of withdrawal used to avoid shame of divorce/separation.

Identify magical thinking and replace it with rational expectations.	Explore for magical thinking (e.g., mommy and daddy will reconcile, if I am exceptionally good, we will all be together again). Replace with rational expectations.
Discuss how extended family impacts the problem.	Explore impact of extended family (grandparents, aunts, uncles, etc.) on the divorce/separation.
Recognize that violence is wrong; that it happens in other families, too, and that it is okay to talk about it.	Investigate for physical or emotional abuse before separation.
Learn positive self-talk.	Teach child positive self-talk to interrupt negative patterns.
Admit fear of abandonment and clarify rational responses.	Facilitate child's admission of fears of abandonment and clarify reality.
Learn new technique for dealing with anxiety.	Teach child diaphragmatic breathing to control anxiety (see Behavioral Techniques, Chapter 23).
Learn new ways to nurture yourself and deal with emotional difficulties.	Use the *Positive Thinking Game*, *Clear Thinking*, *Attitude Adjustment in a Box*, or *The Ungame* to practice positive self-talk and control negative emotions (see Therapeutic Games, Chapter 24).
Shift focus of attention from the problem to accomplishment.	Ask child to describe accomplishments of the past week.
Feel more confident as self-esteem improves.	Compliment client to provide positive reinforcement whenever possible.
Communicate problematic feelings to develop new skills or options.	Use technique of "Pounding Away Bad Feelings" and game *Don't Break the Ice* to help child release frustrations (see Behavioral Techniques, Chapter 23).

Report results to therapist.	Provide positive reinforcement when client reports back that he/she has challenged anxiety-provoking situations. Praise attempt and reward success.
Learn positive problem-solving and how famous people have overcome obstacles.	Assign to read *Dinosaurs' Divorce* or *How It Feels When Parents Divorce* (see Bibliotherapy, Chapter 26).
Learn methods that you can use to advocate for yourself.	Instruct client in the technique of self-advocacy.
Understand that you can deal with these issues and bring treatment to an end successfully.	Develop a termination plan and explain issues of separation anxiety and dependency.

SHORT-TERM BEHAVIORAL GOALS, **C-FAMILY**	THERAPIST'S INTERVENTIONS
Improve communications among family members to reduce levels of anger and alienation.	Conduct family sessions with either one or both parents present or refer for family therapy to reduce anger and/or alienation and improve communication skills within the family.
Cooperate in amplifying family genogram.	Expand genogram created in earlier parental session to help understand family history.
Discuss genogram openly to develop consensus.	Discuss genogram to reveal possible family secrets dealing with divorce/separation.
Family works out conflicts psychodramatically and attempts to share and understand.	Role-play family dynamics, having family members switch roles to clarify dynamics and improve communications (see Behavioral Techniques, Chapter 23).
Demonstrate boundaries, alliances, triangles, and emotional currents that may exacerbate divorce/separation difficulties.	Explore boundaries using family sculpturing (see Behavioral Techniques, Chapter 23).
Family members share how divorce has affected their lives.	Discuss symptoms of divorce/separation, i.e., self-blame, ridicule, avoidance behavior, fear of abandonment, magical thinking of reconciliation.
Each family member feels acknowledged and blame is reduced.	Acknowledge and validate each family member's point of view about the problem/s.
Identify internal and external barriers (i.e., fears, irrational beliefs, old habits, finances, lack of information) that lead to maladaptive behaviors.	Investigate internal and external barriers to development of a better future.

Identify resources that will help each other and reduce the stress of divorce/separation.	Investigate possible available resources to help make change possible (i.e., support systems, other extended family members who might be helpful, tasks older children might assume).
Create a SMART action plan.	Create a SMART action plan: Small, Measurable, Achievable, Realistic, Timed Goals (see Change, Behavioral Techniques, Chapter 23).
Shift focus from problem to possible solutions.	Have family imagine a future without these problems and suggest actions that can be taken now to best approximate that possibility.
Family members realize they have the power to make important changes, even if these seem small.	Help family members realize they have an opportunity to do some things differently.
Members are empowered. They recognize that they can create positive change.	Ask family members to relate what they have accomplished in the past week.
Enhance understanding of parenting and divorce and see how other families have handled similar problems.	Assign homework reading and discuss: *Making Families Work and What to Do When They Don't* or *Does Wednesday Mean Mom's House or Dad's?* (see Bibliotherapy, Chapter 26).
Make use of available community resources.	Refer family to available resources in the community. (See Self-Help Groups, Chapter 27.)
Reduce negative communication.	Develop a system of positive reinforcement with family members to interact better with each other and reduce scapegoating.
Family members work together to develop termination plan.	Discuss termination issues and develop a plan to terminate treatment.

21

Sleep Disorders

There are two principal types of sleep disorder: Dyssomnias and Parasomnias. Dyssomnias include disturbances in the amount of sleep, falling asleep, and staying asleep. In Primary Insomnia, the problem is maintaining sleep, compared with Primary Hypersomnia, which is marked by excessive sleepiness. In the recurrent form of Primary Hypersomnia, known as Kleine-Levin syndrome, individuals may spend 18–20 hours in bed or asleep. Primary Insomnia usually appears in early adulthood and is rare in childhood or adolescence, while Primary Hypersomnia and Kleine-Levin syndrome may begin in early adolescence.

Narcolepsy includes the presence of cataplexy or daily, uncomfortable attacks of sleep. Breathing-related disorders feature excessive sleep or insomnia, sleep apnea, or Circadian Rhythm Sleep Disorder, caused by an environmentally imposed sleep-wake schedule.

Parasomnias include nightmares, sleep terror, and sleepwalking, in which abnormal events occur during sleep. These may be characterized by repeated or sudden awakenings, frightening dreams, or sleepwalking, which usually occurs during the first third of major sleep episodes. Parasomnias cause inappropriate activation of cognitive processes in the nervous and motor systems.

All Dyssomnias and Parasomnias can cause significant distress or impairment in school and other major areas of functioning. Sleep disorders can be related to other Axis I and Axis II mental disorders. Characteristically, children have trouble falling asleep and problems with bad dreams. Sleep disorder in young children is usually associated with separation anxiety and fear of being alone. Systematic assessment of sleep disorders includes evaluation of other comorbid mental disorders, general medical conditions, and substance abuse, including prescribed medications.

Although there are no formal studies, there appears to be a familial disposition associated with sleep problems.

Dyssomnias include Breathing-Related Sleep Disorder (780.59); Circadian Rhythm Sleep Disorder (307.45); Narcolepsy (347); Primary Hyposomnia (307.44); Primary Insomnia (307.42); and Dyssomnia NOS (307.47).

Parasomnias include Nightmare Disorder (307.47); Sleep Terror Disorder (307.46); Sleep-Walking Disorder (307.46); and Parasomnia NOS (307.47).

Behavioral Symptoms
Sleep Disorder
(severity index: 1, mild; 2, moderate; 3, intense)

Severity

Dyssomnias:

    1. Difficulty falling asleep   _____

    2. Difficulty staying asleep   _____

    3. Irresistible attacks of refreshing sleep (Narcolepsy)   _____

    4. Daytime fatigue   _____

    5. Excessive sleepiness   _____

    6. Uncontrollable attacks of sleep   _____

    7. Sudden loss of muscle tone (Cataplexy)   _____

    8. Intrusions in REM sleep   _____

    9. Breathing-related sleep problems (Apnea)   _____

    10. Restless leg syndrome   _____

Parasomnias:

    11. Nightmares   _____

    12. Recurrent, abrupt awakenings due to night terrors   _____

    13. Signs of autonomic arousal   _____

    14. Terror related to unrecalled dream   _____

    15. Sleepwalking   _____

    16. Sleepwalking with blank staring face, difficult to awaken   _____

    17. Amnesia of sleepwalking event   _____

Other Diagnostic Considerations

Adjustment Disorder with Anxiety (309.24)
Adjustment Disorder with Depressed Mood (309.0)
Adjustment Disorder Mixed (309.28)
Bipolar Disorders (301.xx)
Dysthymic Disorder (300.4)
Eating Disorders (307.xx)
Generalized Anxiety Disorder (300.02)
Major Depressive Disorder (296.31)
Personality Disorders (301.xx)
Posttraumatic Stress Disorder (309.81)
Schizophrenia (295.xx)
Separation Anxiety Disorder (309.21)

TREATMENT PLAN
SLEEP DISORDER

Client: _____   Date: _____

```
┌─────────────────────────────────────────┐
│  Multiaxial Assessment                   │
│                                          │
│  Axis I:    _____              │
│  Axis II:   _____              │
│  Axis III:  _____              │
│  Axis IV:   _____              │
│  Axis V:    _____              │
│                                          │
└─────────────────────────────────────────┘
```

I.   I. OBJECTIVES OF TREATMENT
     (*select one or more*)

1. Educate parents about the disorder.
2. Determine family history of the disorder.
3. Help family develop better coping skills.
4. Reduce pervasive anxiety and worry.
5. Reduce symptoms of separation anxiety.
6. Identify any medical disorders and treat or refer for treatment.
7. Identify any psychological problems and treat or refer for treatment.
8. Reduce nightmares or sleep terrors.
9. Establish healthy sleep patterns, regular sleep schedule.
10. Reduce irrational beliefs.
11. Rule out other mental disorders, general medical conditions, and substance abuse, including prescribed medications.
12. Restore adolescent and family to optimum level of functioning.
13. Develop a discharge plan for coping with everyday life.

II. SHORT-TERM BEHAVIORAL GOALS AND INTERVENTIONS
     (*select the goals and interventions appropriate for your client*)

(Note: Separate goals and interventions are provided for the treatment of A-Parents, B-Child, and C-Family.)

SHORT-TERM BEHAVIORAL GOALS, **A-PARENTS**	THERAPIST'S INTERVENTIONS
Collaborate with therapist in development of a treatment plan.	Establish a therapeutic alliance with parents to enhance outcome of child's treatment.
Help therapist understand child's development of sleep problems.	Assess problem with parents and record a comprehensive history of the child's development of sleep-related problems.
Identify specific nature of the problem.	Does child have problems falling asleep or staying asleep? (i.e., dyssomnias or parasomnias)?
Become aware of the diagnosis and what to expect from the child.	Educate parents about the disorder.
Help identify origin of problem and predominant sleep patterns of the child.	Determine origin of sleep problem and the sleep stage in which it occurs.
Identify if child has sleep terrors or is sleepwalking.	Determine if child has sleep terrors or is sleepwalking.
Disclose possible problems with separation anxiety.	Explore for separation anxiety and treat (see appropriate treatment plan).
Assist in building a family genogram.	Construct a genogram to better understand the family history of sleep problems and how the family deals with them (see Behavioral Techniques, Chapter 23).
Undergo evaluation for sleep disorder and enter treatment as indicated.	Examine parents for sleep disorders and treat or refer for treatment (see *Behavioral Management Guide: Essential Treatment Strategies for Adult Psychotherapy*, Resources for Providers, Chapter 33).
Develop awareness of how your personal theory of the problem influences cognition of the problem in the child.	Explore parental theory of the problem.

Recognize fears and feelings of self-blame for child's sleep disorder.	Evaluate parents' fears and negative feelings of self-blame for child's problems.
Realize that sleep is a habit, and develop a more appropriate sleep schedule.	Teach parents that sleep is a habit, and help them establish an appropriate sleep schedule.
Learn to reach beyond automatic cognitive reactions in viewing the problem.	Expand parental perspective of the problem beyond limited cognitive reactions.
Become aware of family tensions that may exacerbate sleep disorder in child.	Assess family tensions that may contribute to the problem.
Teach child that napping to make up for lost sleep is ineffective.	Teach parents of older children that napping to compensate for lost sleep does not work.
Understand need to restrict use of certain stimulants that may impair sleep.	Advise parents about the effects of certain stimulants (i.e., sugar, chocolate, caffeine, Coca-Cola) on sleep patterns.
Confront thoughts of exaggerated reactions and unrealistic consequences—"what ifs?"	Guide parents in confronting distorted reactions that can trigger sleep problems.
Identify cognitive distortions and weigh against reality.	Evaluate cognitive distortions against evidence-based reality.
Restructure distortions with evidence-based consequences.	With parents, reframe distortions with reality-based reactions to stressors.
Understand the importance of REM sleep.	Educate parents about the importance of REM sleep in healing the body physically and psychologically.
Restrict use of bed to sleep only.	Educate parents about limiting child's use of bed only for sleep (i.e., no TV, reading, or doing homework in or on bed).
Help develop awareness of other problems that may cause or contribute to sleep problems.	Identify other problems that may exacerbate sleep disorder (i.e., trauma, troubled relationships).

Learn diaphragmatic breathing as a relaxation technique and teach child to use it.	Teach parents diaphragmatic breathing to assist child in relaxation and sleep (see Behavioral Techniques, Chapter 23).
Sexual abuse uncovered. Child removed to safe environment. Undergo treatment as appropriate.	Investigate for sexual abuse and, if necessary, revise diagnosis (see appropriate treatment plan). Refer parents (if they are the perpetrators) for treatment and advise of need to notify proper authorities (see *Behavioral Management Guide: Essential Treatment Strategies for Adult Psychotherapy*).
Comply with referral for psychological testing of the child.	Provide referral for psychological testing of the child.
Cooperate in protecting child from accidental injury during sleepwalking episodes.	Explore sleepwalking episodes and assess potential physical danger to client.
Develop new parenting skills.	Assign parents to read *How to Make Families Work and What to Do When They Don't* (see Bibliotherapy, Chapter 26).
Read assigned book.	Assign parents to read *Your Anxious Child* to better understand how to deal with problem.
Monitor child's medical schedule and report all reactions or failures to comply.	If child is on medication, instruct parents on importance of a regular schedule and feedback that may indicate need for dosage adjustment.
Meet with other parents who experience similar problems and share coping strategies.	Refer parents to self-help group or group on parenting skills.
Discuss termination plan and resolve related issues.	Develop a termination plan and discuss issues of separation anxiety and dependence.

SHORT-TERM BEHAVIORAL GOALS, **B-CHILD**	THERAPIST'S INTERVENTIONS
Engage in play therapy.	Engage child in a therapeutic relationship via play therapy.
Understand how underlying tensions may create sleep problems.	Investigate tensions that may cause sleep problems.
Identify nature of sleep disorder.	Determine whether child has problems falling asleep or staying asleep.
Recognize underlying feelings of anger or depression.	Using puppets, explore for underlying feelings of anger or depression (see Behavioral Techniques, Puppetry, Chapter 23).
Observe puppets and begin to see new solutions for dealing with sleep problems.	Shape client behavior using puppets to act out a typical nighttime scenario. What they do to fall asleep and stay asleep.
Learn new ways to handle fears.	Use puppets to role model successful ways to deal with night terrors or nightmares.
Realize that others also feel bad and relate to puppets overcoming that feeling.	Investigate for feelings of low self-esteem related to sleep problems and associated anxieties. Have puppets discuss their feelings and what they can do about them.
Identify triggers for nightmares and understand the underlying dynamics of your sleep problems.	Explore nightmares and determine trigger for night terrors.
Identify irrational beliefs.	Through continued play with puppets, explore irrational beliefs about fears and anxieties.
Reframe beliefs about fears and anxieties.	Change irrational beliefs by having puppets discuss them and develop rational alternatives based on evidence-based reality.

Understand importance of sleep routines.	Have puppets discuss sleep routines (i.e., routine bedtime, use bed only for sleep, not for homework, play, or watching TV).
Learn to gain control over anxieties and encourage sleep.	Teach child guided imagery and relaxation technique to master anxieties and promote sleep (see Behavioral Techniques, Chapter 23).
Understand dynamics of anxiety and understand that avoidance does not help.	Teach child the dynamics of anxiety: not dangerous, not permanent. Avoidance increases anxiety.
Realize that dreams are creations of the mind and can be changed.	Play the game *Bad Dreams* to teach child that dreams are created in their heads and can be changed (see Behavioral Techniques, Chapter 23). Note: Do not play this game with severely disturbed or sexually abused children.
Communicate life story to therapist.	Use puppets to have child relate the story of his/her life or play *Life-stories* (see Therapeutic Games, Chapter 24).
Learn to find and use new solutions for handling stressors.	Play *Stress Strategies* or *Stop, Relax, and Think* to teach better ways to handle stress (see Therapeutic Games, Chapter 24).
Use creative visualization or hypnosis to help fall sleep and stay asleep.	With parental permission, use creative visualization or hypnosis to help child sleep. Provide audiotape for child to use at home (see Behavioral Techniques, Chapter 23).
Understand how trauma may have contributed to existing disorder.	Explore child's background for trauma that may have exacerbated the disorder.
Discuss personal coping mechanisms developed to handle the disorder.	Investigate with child patterns of behavior used to avoid sleep anxieties.

Recognize and relate how family impacts the problem.	Explore familial impact on the disorder.
Learn positive self-talk.	Teach child positive self-talk to interrupt negative patterns.
Learn new technique for dealing with anxiety.	Teach client diaphragmatic breathing to control anxiety (see Behavioral Techniques, Chapter 23).
Learn to nurture yourself and overcome emotional difficulties.	Play the *Positive Thinking Game*, *Stress Strategies*, *Personal Power Pow!*, or *The Ungame* to teach how positive self-talk helps control emotional difficulties (see Therapeutic Games, Chapter 24).
Shift focus of attention from problem to accomplishment.	Ask child to describe accomplishments of the past week.
Child sees how parents can help him/her go to sleep.	Assign parents to read to child *Can't You Sleep, Little Bear?* (see Bibliotherapy, Chapter 26).
Feel more confident as self-esteem improves.	Compliment child to provide positive reinforcement whenever possible.
Use games to release frustrations.	Use technique of "Pounding Away Bad Feelings" and game *Don't Break the Ice* to help child release frustrations (see Therapeutic Games, Chapter 24).
Acquire new tools for dealing with anxieties.	Assign parents to read to child *Don't Be Afraid, Tommy*, *The Feeling Storybook*, or *Ready, Set, Relax* (see Bibliotherapy, Chapter 26).
Understand you can deal with these issues and bring treatment to an end successfully.	Develop a termination plan and address issues of separation anxiety and dependency.

SHORT-TERM BEHAVIORAL GOALS, **C-FAMILY**	THERAPIST'S INTERVENTIONS
Improve communication among family members to reduce familial anxiety and sleep problems.	Conduct family sessions or refer for family therapy to reduce sleep problems and improve communication skills within the family.
Cooperate in building a family genogram.	Create a family genogram to help understand family history of the disorder (see Behavioral Techniques, Chapter 23).
Help compare parental and family genograms.	Compare with parental genogram to reveal family history and secrets dealing with sleep.
Demonstrate boundaries, alliances, triangles, and emotional currents that may exacerbate sleep problem.	Explore family boundaries using family sculpturing to understand triangulation, alliances, and emotional currents (see Behavioral Techniques, Chapter 23).
Learn how to establish healthy sleep routines.	Teach family that sleep is a habit and how to develop a regular bedtime routine.
Shift focus from problem to possible solutions.	Have family imagine a future without the sleep problem and suggest actions that can be taken now to make that future possible.
Think about what treatment the outcome would look like. Explain what you would like to see change in other family members when treatment is completed.	Ask family members to think about what they might want to say about each other when treatment is completed.
Family members realize they have the power to make important changes, even if these seem small at first.	Discuss the technique of "Bad Dreams" (see Behavioral Techniques, Chapter 23). Show family members they have an opportunity to do some things differently.

Recognize that major change is the result of small steps taken one at a time.	Help family identify and prioritize achievable goals.
Enhance understanding of the disorder and see how other families have handled similar problems. See how the parents helped Little Bear to sleep.	Assign as family homework reading *Making Families Work and What to Do When They Don't* and *Can't You Sleep, Little Bear?* (see Bibliotherapy, Chapter 26).
Make use of available community resources.	Refer family to available resources in the community (see Self-Help Groups, Chapter 27).
Reduce negative communication.	Develop a system of positive reinforcement with family members to interact better with each other and reduce scapegoating.
Family members work together to develop termination plan.	Discuss termination issues and develop a plan to end treatment.

22

Additional Conditions That May Be the Focus of Clinical Attention

BEREAVEMENT (V62.82)

Bereavement is a reaction to the death of a loved one. Some grieving people react with symptoms typical of Major Depressive Disorder (e.g., sadness, insomnia, poor appetite, weight loss). Typically, they regard the depressed mood as normal. The duration of the bereavement and how it is expressed may vary widely among different cultural groups. However, the diagnosis of Major Depressive Disorder is not usually given unless the symptoms persist for more than two months. Certain symptoms may be helpful in differentiating major depression and bereavement. Bereavement may include guilt about actions or lack of action at the time of death; thinking he/she, too, should have died; and auditory and visual hallucinations of the deceased. Depression may include other unrelated guilt and thoughts of death, preoccupation with feelings of worthlessness, marked psychomotor retardation, prolonged functional impairment, and other hallucinatory experiences.

V-codes, such as that for Bereavement, should be entered on Axis IV of the *DSM-IV* Multiaxial Assessment System, with the associated impairment coded on Axis I.

Behavioral Symptoms
Bereavement
(severity index: 1, mild; 2, moderate; 3, intense)

Severity

1. Major persistent depression   _____
2. Inability to fall asleep or stay asleep   _____
3. Nightmares or night terrors   _____
4. Loss of appetite   _____
5. Adjustment disorders   _____
6. Serious impairment of school activities   _____
7. Hyperactivity   _____
8. Persistent anger   _____
9. Guilt over being a survivor   _____
10. Constant anxiety or panic attacks   _____
11. Hears voice of or sees transitory images of deceased   _____
12. Difficulties in interpersonal relationships   _____
13. Somatization   _____

Other Diagnostic Considerations

Acute Stress Disorder (308.3)
Adjustment Disorder (*see Subtypes*)
Anxiety Disorder due to a General Medical Condition (293.84)
Hypocondriasis (300.7)
Mood Disorders (*see Subtypes*)
Major Depressive Disorder (296.xx)
Obsessive-Compulsive Disorder (300.31)
Panic Disorder (not codable)
Posttraumatic Stress Disorder (309.81)
Psychotic Disorders (*see Subtypes*)
Separation Anxiety (309.21)
Sibling Relational Problems (V61.2)
Sleep Disorders (*see Subtypes*)
Social Phobia (300.23)

TREATMENT PLAN
BEREAVEMENT

Client: _____ Date: _____

```
┌─────────────────────────────────────┐
│  Multiaxial Assessment               │
│                                      │
│  Axis I:    _____          │
│  Axis II:   _____          │
│  Axis III: _____           │
│  Axis IV: _____            │
│  Axis V:   _____           │
│                                      │
└─────────────────────────────────────┘
```

I. OBJECTIVES OF TREATMENT
   (*select one or more*)

      1. Educate parent, parents, or caretakers about the stages of death.
      2. Determine whether the death was sudden or after a long illness.
      3. Help family develop better coping skills.
      4. Help the mourners through the grieving process.
      5. Reduce pervasive anxiety and worry.
      6. Diminish symptoms of anxiety and guilt.
      7. Resolve feelings of despair and hopelessness.
      8. Eliminate sleep disturbances and nightmares.
      9. Restore appetite, stop weight loss.
     10. Encourage compliance with educational programs and referrals.
     11. Reframe irrational beliefs.
     12. Promote socialization, reduce alienation.
     13. Develop discharge plan for coping with everyday life.

II. SHORT-TERM BEHAVIORAL GOALS AND INTERVENTIONS
   (*select goals and interventions appropriate for your client*)

(Note: Separate goals and interventions are provided for treatment of A-Parents, B-Child, and C-Family.)

SHORT-TERM BEHAVIORAL GOALS, **A-PARENTS**	THERAPIST'S INTERVENTIONS
Parent, parents, or caretaker collaborate with therapist in development of a treatment plan.	Attempt to establish a therapeutic alliance with parent, parents, or caretaker to enhance outcome of treatment.
Identify the circumstances of the death and the child's reactions to it.	Explore nature of the death and how the child has reacted.
Become aware of the diagnosis and what to generally expect from the child.	Educate parents about the diagnosis.
Parent(s) is treated for grief reactions to death in order for him or her to be more available.	If parent(s) exhibit posttraumatic symptoms or separation anxiety, treat individually (see appropriate treatment plan in *Behavioral Management Guide: Essential Treatment Strategies for Adult Psychotherapy*, Resources for Providers, Chapter 33).
Parents identify their style of dealing with death.	Explore how parents(s) dealt with the death. Did they respond overtly to the loss and talk about it, or did they go underground emotionally, acting as if it never happened?
Parents are treated to help them through the process of mourning.	If death was of a sibling, investigate the parent's reaction and treat or refer for treatment (see *Behavioral Management Guide: Essential Treatment Strategies for Adult Psychotherapy*, Resources for Providers, Chapter 33).
Cooperate in building a genogram to identify familial history and typical cultural and emotional responses to death.	Construct a genogram to better understand the family history and define how they historically deal with death (i.e., culturally, religiously, and emotionally). What familial support systems are available? (See Behavioral Techniques, Chapter 23.)

Parent states whether children have been included or excluded in the mourning process.	Investigate how the funeral was handled. Were the children excluded to avoid upsetting them or included to realistically involve them in mourning the death?
Parent/s identifies underlying death anxieties.	Explore parent/parents' underlying death anxieties.
Identify religious beliefs and what the parents have said to the child about death.	Explore parent/s' religious beliefs about death and what they have told the child.
Learn the stages of death and understand that mourning is a normal and important act.	Educate the family members about the stages of death (denial, anger, bargaining, depression, and accommodation) to help them understand normal grieving.
Family is treated as a single unit in order to help each member work through the grieving process together.	Investigate if other children in the family are reacting to the death. It may be more effective to treat the family as a unit rather than individually (see family plan or refer for family treatment).
Parents understand that it is okay to express their reactions and encourage their children to talk about it.	Encourage parent/s to express pain and grief reactions to their loss in order to help them act as role models for their children.
Parent/parents realize that death anxiety is a universal problem and that its denial can lead to other problems.	Educate the parent/s to realize that death anxiety is universal and if we deny death or don't talk with our children, it can cause further problems.
Develop awareness of how your personal theory influences cognition of the problem in child.	Explore parental theory of the problem.
Recognize fears and feelings of negative self-blame.	Evaluate parent/s' fears and negative feelings of self-blame related to the death.
Learn to reach beyond automatic cognitive reactions in dealing with death.	Expand parental perspective beyond limited cognitive reactions.

Parent/s learn how to help themselves and their children deal with anxiety.	Teach parent/s the dynamics of anxiety: It is not permanent, is not dangerous, is time limited, and can produce growth.
Family members understand that certain tasks need to be accomplished so they can continue to live.	Teach parent/s to understand that the experience of grief is not a passive state. To move beyond it involves adaptation to be in the world without the dead person.
Parent/s learn to deal with child's sleep disorder.	Investigate for sleep problems or nightmares in child, and teach parents how to deal with them.
Parent/s read book with child to improve their relationship and help the child cope with grief.	Have parent/s read with young child *Don't Despair on Thursday* in order to increase bonding and help the child cope with his/her grief (see Bibliotherapy, Chapter 26).
Confront thoughts of exaggerated and unrealistic consequences—"What ifs?"	Guide parent/s in confronting distorted reactions to trigger situations.
Identify cognitive distortions.	Weigh the actions against evidence-based reality.
Parent/s understand that going through a transitional period of grief can lead to greater development.	Educate parents to understand the Phoenix Model, which consists of five phases: (1) Impact; (2) Chaos; (3) Adaptation; (4) Equilibrium; and (5) Transition (see *The Phoenix Phenomenon: Rising from the Ashes of Grief*, in Resources for Providers and in Bibliotherapy, Chapters 33 and 26).
Parents attend bereavement groups, get support from others, and share coping solutions.	Refer parent/s to a bereavement group in order to help them connect with others who are also experiencing grief (see Self-Help Groups, Chapter 27).

Parent/s develop new parenting skills and learn how to help their children cope with death.	Assign parent/s books to read on how to deal with death and increase parenting skills, such as *Making Families Work and What to Do When They Don't* (see Bibliotherapy, Chapter 26).
Discuss termination plan and resolve related issues.	Develop a termination plan and discuss issues of separation anxiety and dependency.

SHORT-TERM BEHAVIORAL GOALS, **B-CHILD**	THERAPIST'S INTERVENTIONS
Child develops a therapeutic relationship in order to help him/her through the loss of a loved one.	Engage child in a therapeutic relationship in order to enhance the outcome of treatment.
Child identifies the way he/she is attempting to deal with the death.	Investigate how the child is dealing with the death.
Child expresses the way the loss has affected him/her.	Explore the crisis. What effect has the loss had on the family and ultimately on the child?
Child realizes that he/she can look to others for support.	Identify and explore the availability of support systems. Are there aunts, uncles, or friends available to help the family adjust to the "emotional shock wave"?
Child understands the necessary stages of grief and is reassured that he or she will be able to go through the grieving process.	Educate the child about the stages of grief: (1) Shock or denial and disbelief. (2) Anger about the loss, a yearning for the lost person, or "Why did it happen to me?" (3) Chaos and despair: "How can it ever get better?" (4) Bargaining: "If I behave better or if I am a better person, things will improve." Help child to see new ways to reorganize and create a new life, while reassuring the child that he/she will be able to get through the grieving process.
Child identifies feelings about the death of the sibling.	If it was a sibling who died, explore how the surviving child is dealing with the loss. Does survivor blame self or feel guilty?
Child identifies his/her feelings about the death in order to work through the pain of grief.	Determine which stage of grief the survivor is experiencing.

Child understands that there can also be physical responses to loss.	Investigate for any physical responses such as hyperactivity, or somatization (i.e., tightness in the chest, stomach pains, fatigue, etc.).
Undergo treatment for sleep disorder.	Investigate for symptoms of a sleep disorder, nightmares, insomnia, etc. (see appropriate treatment plan).
Realize that human beings are not perfect, and reduce stressors imposed on the self.	Teach the child that human beings are not perfect.
Identify the impact of the loss on schoolwork.	Explore for any manifestations of academic problems related to the death and treat accordingly (see appropriate treatment plan).
Through play therapy, the child learns new skills for dealing with death.	Engage the child in play therapy in order to help him/her develop coping skills to deal with the death.
Realize that others also feel bad when a loved one dies and that talking about it helps.	Through the use of puppets, investigate for feelings of low self-esteem related to the loss. Have puppets talk about how they feel and what they can do about it (see Behavioral Techniques, Chapter 23).
Begin to see possible solution.	Have puppets discuss how they deal with negative feelings.
Identify irrational beliefs.	Through continued play with puppets, explore irrational beliefs about death.
Reframe beliefs about fears and anxieties.	Change irrational beliefs by having the puppets discuss the beliefs and develop rational alternatives.
Learn from role modeling and shape new behaviors in order to let go and live in the world without the deceased person.	Use puppets to role model appropriate behavior and talk about letting go and being in the world without their loved one.

Using guided imagery to augment the play therapy process, learn to gain control over feelings.	Teach relaxation techniques and guided imagery to master anxieties (see Behavioral Techniques, Chapter 23).
Understand anxiety and realize that avoidance does not help.	Teach child the dynamics of anxiety: It is not dangerous, it is not permanent, and confrontation can promote change.
Communicate life story to the therapist.	Use puppets to have the child relate the story of his/her life.
Express suppressed feelings about saying goodbye to a loved one.	Play *The Goodbye Game* to help further educate the child and dispel myths and false ideas regarding death (see Therapeutic Games, Chapter 24).
Discuss personal coping mechanisms developed to handle death.	Investigate with child possible patterns of social withdrawal or becoming overly active as a way of dealing with feelings about the deceased.
Recognize and discuss how the family affects the problem.	Explore the family's impact on the problem Are family members supportive; do they talk about the death or pretend that it never happened? Remind the child that anxiety and uncertainty are a normal part of grief.
Learn positive self-talk.	Teach child positive self-talk to interrupt negative patterns.
Learn new techniques for relaxing and dealing with anxieties.	Teach diaphragmatic breathing to help the child relax and reduce stress (see Behavioral Techniques, Chapter 23).
Child identifies ways that he/she has changed.	Investigate ways that the child has changed in an attempt to create meaning for what he/she has gone through.
Shift focus of attention from problem to accomplishments.	Ask client to describe accomplishments for the past week.

Feel more confident as self-esteem improves.	Compliment client to provide positive reinforcement whenever possible.
Communicate problematic feelings to develop new skills or options.	Use technique of "Pounding Away Bad Feelings" and game *Don't Break the Ice* to help the child release frustrations (see Behavioral Techniques, Chapter 23).
Report results to therapist.	Provide positive reinforcement when client reports that he/she has challenged anxiety-provoking situations. Praise attempts and reward success.
Learn that grieving is a natural process and learn skills to cope.	Assign to read or have parents read to child, *What on Earth Do You Do When Someone Dies?* or *The Hyena Who Lost Her Laugh* (see Bibliotherapy, Chapter 26).
Learn positive problem solving and how famous people have overcome obstacles.	Assign to read or have parents read to child *Anybody Can Bake a Cake* or *Don't Despair on Thursdays* (see Bibliotherapy, Chapter 26).
Learn methods that you can use to advocate for yourself.	Instruct client in the technique of self-advocacy.
Understand that you can deal with these issues and bring treatment to a successful end.	Develop a termination plan and explain issues of separation anxiety and dependency.

SHORT-TERM BEHAVIORAL GOALS, **C-FAMILY**	THERAPIST'S INTERVENTIONS
Improve communications among family members to reduce familial anxiety.	Conduct family sessions or refer for family therapy to reduce alienation, improve communication skills, and enhance understanding of the impact of the loss on the family.
Drawings offer help in communicating alliances and feelings and may also allow members to express toxic issues.	Ask family members (especially the young children) to draw a picture of the family before and after the death.
Cooperate in amplifying family genogram.	Amplify genogram created in first parental session to help understand how the family has historically dealt with death culturally, religiously, and emotionally.
Discuss genogram openly to fully understand family history as it relates to the issue of death.	Discuss genogram to reveal family history and possible family secrets about death.
Demonstrate boundaries, alliances, triangles, and emotional currents that may exacerbate the problem.	Explore boundaries using family sculpturing, a useful technique for understanding triangulation, alliances, and emotional currents (see Behavioral Techniques, Chapter 23).
Identify outside sources that can lend support and help the grieving process.	Determine if there are members of the extended family (aunts, uncles, cousins) who can provide additional support.
Each family member identifies his/her reaction to the loss.	Explore individual reactions to the death. See how each member felt before and after the loss.

Family members understand the normal stages of grieving and what to expect from each other.	If the rest of the family doesn't know about the stages of grief, explain it, using both the Elizabeth Kubler-Ross model: Denial, Anger, Bargaining, Depression and Acceptance and the Phoenix Model: Impact, Chaos, Adaptation, Equilibrium, and Transformation (see Bibliotherapy or Resources for Providers, Chapters 26 and 33).
Each member shares his or her view, which helps bonding and reduces stress.	Have each member explore his/her individual feelings about the person and the death in order to give his or her sorrow words, which can be cathartic. Discuss each member's adaptations.
Identify methods of coping.	Discuss methods of coping.
Identify ways family can grow out of loss.	Have family members imagine a future without their loved one and suggest actions that can be taken now that can help them grow, even in the middle of a loss.
Identify irrational thoughts related to the death.	Explore irrational methods of coping in both parents and children. Do they feel guilty for the death, blame each other, etc.?
Each member identifies his or her unfinished business with regard to the deceased and works through psychodynamically relevant issues that have been unresolved.	Use role-playing with an empty chair (the chair representing the person who died). Ask members to express what they would like to relate to the dead person. Include any unfinished business they would like to complete (see Behavioral Techniques, Chapter 23).
Identify hidden blame in order to work it out.	Explore for hidden blame among family members.
Each member identifies if and how he or she experiences survivor's guilt.	Investigate for survivor's guilt and educate family that it is a normal part of the grieving process.

Family identifies the impact and changes created by the loss.	Explore the crisis the loss has produced in the family (i.e., financial, housing, single parenting, etc.).
Family members realize that through growth and adaptation they can find hope.	Educate family members about the phases of adaptation, helping them realize that their old life has ended. Helping them to let go and see that this process can be the birthplace for hope.
Family members become empowered by realizing, through trial and error, that they can take on new roles and grow.	Assist family to establish equilibrium, by taking on new roles and by planning a life without the deceased person.
Each member strengthens himself or herself by developing new and productive roles.	Help each member build self-confidence through realistic, actual achievements.
Each member individually develops a SMART plan.	Develop a SMART action plan: Small, Measurable, Achievable, Realistic, Timeline goals (see Change, in Behavioral Techniques, Chapter 23).
Family members realize they have the power to make important changes, even if these seem small.	Help family members realize they have an opportunity to do some things differently.
Members are empowered. They recognize that they can create positive change.	Ask family members to relate what they have accomplished in the past week
Realize that major change is the result of small changes taken one at a time	Help family identify and prioritize achievable goals.
Identify individual transformation.	Have each member identify ways he or she has transformed since the death of his or her loved one.
Enhance understanding of grief work. Parents discuss the books that are too difficult for the younger children to read and thus enhance the relationship.	Assign homework reading, i.e., *The Phoenix Phenomenon: Rising from the Ashes of Grief.* Also recommend *Grief's Courageous Journey* (see Bibliotherapy, Chapter 26).

Make use of available community resources.	Refer family to available bereavement groups in the community (see Self-Help Groups, Chapter 27).
Reduce negative communication.	Develop a system of positive reinforcement with family members to help them interact better with each other and reduce scapegoating.
Family members work together to develop a termination plan.	Discuss termination issues and develop a plan to terminate treatment.

PART IV

TREATMENT AIDS

23

Behavioral Techniques

ANGER

"Pounding Away Bad Feelings" by Donna Cangelosi

(From *101 Favorite Play Therapy Techniques*, edited by H. Kaduson and C. Schaefer. Copyright © 1999 by Jason Aronson and reprinted with permission.)

Introduction

This technique was designed to help children communicate about problematic feelings and situations and to help them develop options and skills for approaching similar situations in the future.

Rationale

The mechanisms through which play serves as a modality for therapeutic change have been outlined by Schaefer (1993). This play technique provides the therapist with a tool to promote several of these mechanisms or curative powers. Among these are: overcoming resistance, communication, creative thinking, catharsis, abreaction, relationship enhancement, enjoyment, understanding and empathy, mastery, and game play.

The game *Don't Break the Ice* is very appealing to youngsters and is seen as fun, challenging, and exciting. As such, it is a helpful addition in the playroom. The game has set rules, such as taking turns and tolerating the frustration of losing, and therefore promotes socialization. Used as a therapeutic tool, *Don't Break the Ice* can provide a vehicle for communication, catharsis, and abreaction, as well as an opportunity for the therapist to promote creative thinking and mastery (i.e., through direct statements, metaphorical teaching, or modeling).

Description

Materials Needed:
Don't Break the Ice™ by the Milton Bradley Company.

Directions

The child is asked to discuss a situation that caused him or her to feel angry, frustrated, hurt, bad, sad, or mad. She or he then taps out a block of ice with the plastic mallet (provided in the game) to "get rid of the feeling." The therapist then prompts the child to think about ways to effectively handle the situation in the future. Options and ideas are offered for anticipating similar situations, preventing them, and/or dealing with them when they arise. The therapist then takes a turn and builds upon the child's example, in order to highlight certain points and to role model effective coping and problem solving. The child and therapist continue taking turns in this manner until all of the ice pieces have been tapped away. When the game is used for group or family therapy, individuals can ask each other how they would handle the situation, or each person can offer options. (In some cases it may be helpful to start the game talking about less-threatening feelings to ease the child into the game and to gather information about his or her pleasures, coping, etc.)

Applications

This technique can be used in individual, group, or family therapy. When used with a group of children or with family members, ideas for effective coping are solicited from all participants. The exercise promotes open communication, cooperative efforts toward problem resolution, catharsis of negative or other overwhelming feelings, and understanding of self and others. It is therefore useful for a wide variety of clinical populations.

References

Milton Bradley Company. *Don't Break the Ice*.
Schaefer, C. E. (1993). *The Therapeutic Powers of Play*. Northvale, NJ: Jason Aronson.

BAD DREAMS

"Bad Dreams" by L. G. Agre

(From *101 Favorite Play Therapy Techniques*, edited by H. Kaduson and C. Schaefer. Copyright © 1999 by Jason Aronson and reprinted with permission.)

Introduction

Bad dreams sometimes come up in the play situation. This technique was derived from reading about dream work in *The Centering Book* by Gay Hendricks and Russell Wills (1975) and about neuro-linguistic programming (NLP) in books by Grinder and Bandler (1982, 1985).

Rationale

Using this technique allows a child to understand that each of us creates our dreams and that we can choose to change our dreams if we so desire. A child is empowered by this technique, and this technique is open-ended.

Depending on the child's intellectual capacity, a child can go on to use NLP principles to develop goals and visualize himself performing tasks the way he would like to perform tasks. When a child brings up nightmares, I talk about how we make up our dreams in our own heads and about how we can change our dreams. We can pretend to have our own remote control to squeeze to change our dreams.

Description

First the child is asked to describe his dream. Then we talk about how he would like his dream to end, how he could change his dream. Then I have the child draw a picture of how he wants his dream to end. Next, I have the child close his eyes and tell me about the dream. When the child gets to the scary part of the dream, I have him squeeze his hand as if it held a remote control, and then the child finishes the dream the way he wants it to end.

When the child tells me he can see the new ending, I touch him lightly on the wrist or arm to anchor the new ending. The child is then told to open his eyes. We repeat this process at least three times. I have the child take home his picture of the new ending to put under his pillow. I check with the child the next two or three days to see if we were successful. If not, we repeat the process.

Applications

I use this technique with a child whose nightmare appears to be the result of scary movies or tall tales told by older siblings. The dreamer and dream cue me in to whether or not the dream is of benign origin. This technique seems to work with almost all children. However, it did not work with a severely emotionally disturbed child (as defined by special education guidelines) or with one other child.

I rarely use this technique with children I know or suspect of having been sexually abused.

References

Bandler, R. (1985). *Using Your Brain—For a Change*. Moab, UT: Real People Press.

Bandler, R., and Grinder, J. (1982). *Reframing—Neuro-Linguistic Programming and the Transformation of Meaning*. Moab, UT: Real People Press.

Hendricks, G., and Wills, R. (1975). *The Centering Book*. Englewood Cliffs, NJ: Prentice-Hall.

CHANGE

"How to Change 101" by Bill O'Hanlon, MS.

(From *Possibilities E-Mail*, April 2001, by B. O'Hanlon, reprinted with permission.)

Step 1: Acknowledge

- Acknowledge people and validate their points of view.
- Don't blame or make them wrong.
- Get specific: Use action talk (videotalk[+]) to avoid labeling or generalizing.
- Acknowledge concerns (yours and others).
- Acknowledge problems.
- Acknowledge what has worked: no need to throw the baby out with the bathwater.

Step 2: Find and Agree on a Direction/Mission/Vision

- If you don't know where you're going, you'll probably end up somewhere else.

[+] *Videotalk* means to describe something only in terms of what one could see or hear if watching and listening to a videotape.

- If possible, paint a vivid picture of the future, again in action talk (videotalk).
- Get a consensus or at least mutual understanding of that future.
- Use possibility talk (expect change, open up possibilities for change, etc.).

Step 3: Acknowledge Barriers and Identify Resources to Achieving That Future

- What has stopped you or tripped you up in moving toward that future?
- What are internal barriers (fears, old habits, outdated or unhelpful beliefs) to moving on?
- What are real-world barriers (money, lack of consensus, lack of information, actions that haven't been taken) to moving on?
- What or who are resources available to overcome or resolve the barriers?
- What has worked well in the past?
- Identify patterns of thinking, focus, and action that do not help the situation change.

Step 4: Make an Action Plan

- Start small.
- SMART (small, measurable, achievable, realistic, timeline) goals and directions are more likely to succeed.

Step 5: Act (Just Do It!)

- Take action, notice results, adjust action if needed.
- Break patterns of thinking, focus, and action.
- Decide who is going to take what action by when.
- Get a promise and arrange to follow up.
- Persist until goal is achieved.

Step 6: Acknowledge and Celebrate Progress and Success

- Give lots of credit.
- Use rituals/awards/celebrations to acknowledge milestones achieved and goals met.

DIAPHRAGMATIC BREATHING AND RELAXATION EXERCISE

Commonly known as stomach or body breathing, diaphragmatic breathing can be used as an effective coping skill for anxiety. This exercise should be practiced at least once a day because the first step in developing a coping skill is getting your body acquainted with and used to it. After you feel comfortable with this exercise, your therapist can show you how a briefer version can be used to cope during public encounters.

Let's take a moment to think about breathing. Our lungs sit in our chest in a space that is surrounded on the top and sides by our rib cage and on the bottom, by our diaphragm. The diaphragm is a sheet of muscle that bows upward like a dome beneath our lungs and separates the lung space from the abdominal cavity. As we breathe in, we must increase this lung space. Yet when we are anxious, the muscles of our shoulders and chest tighten and can make us feel that our breathing is labored, which in turn increases our feelings of anxiety. While there are several ways of increasing our lung space, diaphragmatic or stomach breathing requires the least effort and therefore can serve as the most effective coping skill for managing anxious situations.

While some people achieve diaphragmatic breathing naturally and with ease, others may need to practice for a while before they feel comfortable with the exercise. But don't worry, practicing can be very relaxing and enjoyable! To see what it feels like to breathe diaphragmatically, lie with your stomach down on a bed or on the floor and cross your arms beneath your head. You might even imagine that you are lying on the beach sunning your back as you look at the waves swell and crash at the shore. Now relax your stomach muscles and breathe normally, inhaling through your nose. In this position, you are most likely to breathe diaphragmatically. If you feel pressure from the floor or bed on your stomach as you inhale, you are breathing diaphragmatically. Try this for a few moments until you feel comfortable doing it without having to think about what you are doing so intensely. Now practice it as follows: sit in a comfortable chair with both feet on the floor. If you like, you can place one hand lightly on your chest and the other on your stomach just above your navel. Now breathe slowly through your nose, relaxing your stomach and using only your diaphragm. You might even feel as if you are inhaling with your stomach. Inhale as deeply as is comfortable and then exhale through pursed lips as if you were blowing through a straw. When you are breathing correctly, your stomach will rise as you breathe in, and slowly fall when you exhale. Now try to exhale for as long as it took you to inhale. This is called paced breathing.

When you feel comfortable with the paced diaphragmatic breathing, you can add one more component to this exercise. After you have taken a few breaths, mildly contract the muscles of your face and neck and then relax them again during the most convenient exhale. When you feel comfortable with this coordination component, try it with your neck and then back. This can be a great way to stretch and relax all of your major muscle groups! You may have to do some of the more tense muscle groups a few times before they fully unwind.

You should do this exercise at least once and preferably twice a day. Begin with 5 minutes of paced diaphragmatic breathing and then spend approximately 10-20 minutes combining it with the muscle stretching and relaxing followed by five more minutes of breathing. During those last five minutes allow your breathing to slow considerably and your muscles to feel heavy. Now indulge yourself in this quiet and calm place; you are finally fully relaxed!

A shorter version of this exercise can be used as a practical coping skill to manage anxiety before or during exposure. If you find yourself in such a situation, don't panic! You have all of the tools necessary to cope with your anxiety. Just take a deep diaphragmatic breath through your nose. Hold it for a second or so, then exhale slowly through pursed lips. Then pace your diaphragmatic breathing with the goal of slowing your rate of breathing. This may not seem so easy at first but just begin by extending your exhale and taking a deep breath when you can. You can even try holding your breath for a moment.

Eventually, you will be able to slow your breathing. As you are slowing your breathing rate, begin stretching and relaxing your major muscle groups; this will help you overcome the natural inclination to "freeze" when anxious. This will help you to regroup and feel as if you can cope at your own pace. Remember that the goal is not to stop your feeling of anxiety, but rather to cope with the feelings that anxiety induces. Back at the beach, it would be like riding out an ocean wave, allowing it to pick you up, and then set you back down. Your goal is not to stop it, but rather to flow with it and cope with it. You may also find it helpful to focus on your thoughts while you cope with your anxiety. Talk to your therapist about how to create coping self-statements and other strategies for this exercise.

Reference

Bruce, T.J. and Sanderson, W.C. (1998). *Specific Phobias: Clinical Applications of Evidence-Based Psychotherapy.* Northvale, NJ: Jason Aronson.

EARLY INTERVENTION

Individual differences in intelligence appear to depend on diverse elements such as genetic inheritance, prenatal environment, sociocultural practices, behavioral interactions, and others (Ramey, Campbell, and Ramey 1998). Early intervention describes corrective actions and programs for use with young children at risk for poor intellectual development. Those risk factors may include psychological, social, and biological components, such as intergenerational poverty, low levels of parental intelligence and education, nonstimulating parent–child interactions, poor nutrition, low birthweight, and premature birth.

A number of key studies on the effects of early intervention were conducted around the country and, in general, indicate a significant increase in IQ for participating children. Notable among these were three randomized controlled trials (RCTs): the Abecedarian Project, Project CARE, and the Infant Health and Development Program. These programs were multidisciplinary, intergenerational, individualized for children and their families, coordinated with local service delivery systems, and organized around common key concepts.

In summary, these concepts involved:

- Preschool treatment
- Family supports, social services, and counseling
- Pediatric care and referral
- Early childhood education at a center
- Good teacher–child ratios
- Developmentally appropriate practices
- Nursing and nutritional services
- "Occupational" therapy
- A Partners in Learning curriculum, emphasizing language development
- Nutritional supplements
- Daily transportation

A supplementary K-2 education program emphasized individualized supplementary educational activities at home and at school; a focus on reading and mathematics; master home/school resource teachers for twelve children and families per year, with a high frequency of home and school visits; extra attention to relevant family circumstances; and specialized summer camps.

The results of these programs indicate that early intervention significantly benefits socially and biologically defined high-risk children. The gains in IQs are sustained in high-resource school environments and diminish in low-resource facilities. Research is continuing.

Programs such as those described are state controlled. For example, the New York State Education Department's Office of Vocational and Educational Services for Individuals with Disabilities (VESID) oversees a statewide preschool special education program with school districts, municipalities, approved providers, and parents. Evaluations and specially designed individual or group instruction services and programs are provided to eligible children with a disability that affects learning. Funding is provided by the state and municipalities. The programs start with a referral to the Committee on Preschool Special Education (CPSE). Upon evaluation and approval, an Individualized Education Program (IEP) will be forwarded to your local school board.

Additional information may be available by contacting your local school-board or school district office, principal, or the chairperson of the Committee on Preschool Special Education (CPSE), or Director of Special Education in your particular state.

FAMILY SCULPTURING

(From *Behavioral Management Guide: Essential Treatment Strategies for Adult Psychotherapy* by M. P. Warren. Copyright © by Jason Aronson and reprinted with permission.)

Family sculpturing is a technique that emerged from attempts to translate systems theory into physical form through special arrangements. It uses space as a metaphor for understanding human relationships.

Sometimes called family choreography, sculpturing depicts emotional relationships that are always in motion. In a sense it choreographs important transactional patterns such as alliances, triangles, and shifting emotional currents. The technique can be used with any theoretical modality and modified to implement a variety of goals. Virginia Satir used family sculpturing to demonstrate what she called the four most common stances of family members: the accuser, the placatory one, the rational one, and the irrelevant one. The technique is also used to realign family relationships, create new patterns, and change the family system.

In practice, after defining or describing the family problem, each family member is asked to arrange family members as the individual experiences them or show a visual picture of the way he or she experiences the problem, to arrange the family members according to their emotional relationship with each member, and to identify their characteristic way of coping with this relationship. The technique can also be used to show how major stressors (death, illness) have altered the relationships over time. To help move the process along, the therapist might ask questions aimed at shedding light on the traditional patterns. Each member is asked to arrange the other family members, as he or she would like to interact with them. In this way, family sculpturing or family choreography can be used to reveal human relationships within a social, psychological, and physical system and to realign those relationships when necessary. It is a silent motion picture of the family that removes the linguistic traps and cuts through the barrage of attack and counterattack that often characterizes family sessions.

GENOGRAMS

(From *Behavioral Management Guide: Essential Treatment Strategies for Adult Psychotherapy* by M. P. Warren. Copyright © by Jason Aronson and reprinted with permission.)

A genogram is a diagram that depicts the relationships between family members over three generations. The genogram uses symbols to illustrate the relationships with the units and major stressors in chronological order. The diagram is used to help understand the family dynamics over time. The symbols include:

Genogram symbols:

□	Male	|	Offspring
O	Female	- - - -	Marriage
Δ	Child	D/	Divorce
∅	Abortion/Stillbirth	X	Death

Construction of a genogram begins with the collection of facts about each member, his or her position in the family, and his or her relationships to other family members. Physical location is important for tracking distance and boundaries. Analysis of the genogram provides information about how conflicts are resolved, as well as family secrets such as abortion. It is also helpful in identifying whether the family is cohesive or explosive. The genogram is used to spell out physical and emotional boundaries, characteristics of the membership, modal events, toxic issues, emotional cut-offs, a general openness/closedness index, and the available relationship options within the family.

The resulting diagram allows one to see at a glance the basic structural framework of the family, including triangulation and repetitive family issues. Such information might otherwise require a lengthy document to record. General questions that should be explored include cultural, ethnic, and religious affiliations; socioeconomic level; the way the family relates to the community socially and economically; and whether the family is cohesive or isolated.

Once the basic information is collected, including names, ages, births, deaths, and divorces, the structure is expanded to include other significant data that points up critical nodal points. As patterns of interaction emerge, other universal issues are exposed, such as money, sex, power, control, parenting, children, and others. Does the family discuss problems or is there a conspiracy of silence? What events in the lifecycle will shape the future? The genogram has proved to be an important tool for family therapists.

HYPNOSIS

(From *Behavioral Management Guide: Essential Treatment Strategies for Adult Psychotherapy* by M. P. Warren. Copyright © by Jason Aronson and reprinted with permission.)

Hypnosis is an induced altered state of consciousness or trance state in which the individual is more susceptible to suggestion. People are imprinted

Figure 22–1. Example of a Genogram

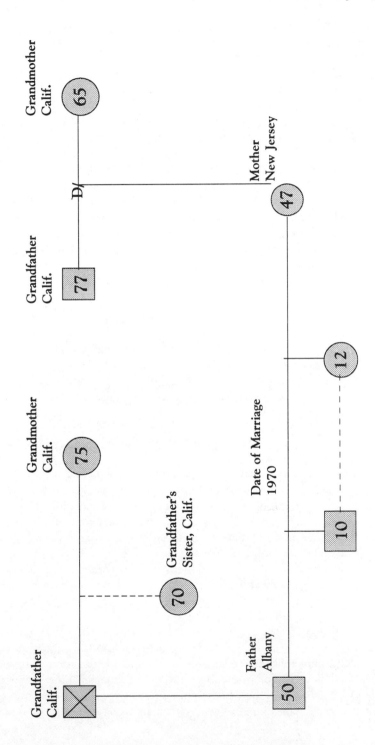

with mindsets that originate in their families of origin and are incorporated into the unconscious. People organize their personalities and act around these imprints. We do not operate directly on the world, but through a map or model of the world, a created representation of what we believe. In hypnosis, the therapist aims at changing or otherwise influencing the maps we hold in our minds.

Hypnosis can be a highly effective therapeutic tool. When the client has slipped into trance after induced relaxation, the client may be instructed to imagine himself or herself the way he or she would like to be. For example, in hypnosis, a shy child may be asked to imagine himself or herself as confident and through visualization begin to change his or her belief systems.

Hypnosis appears to work well with the cognitive-behavioral modality. However, insurance company reaction to the technique is mixed. Although many find it an acceptable psychotherapeutic technique, some prefer to call it relaxation technique rather than hypnosis. It is best to find out where the insurance company stands on the issue.

GUIDED IMAGERY

"Using Guided Imagery to Augment the Play Therapy Process" by Kevin O'Connor

(From *101 Favorite Play Therapy Techniques*, edited by H. Kaduson and C. Schaefer. Copyright © 1999 by Jason Aronson and reprinted with permission.)

Introduction and Rationale

Within Ecosystemic Play Therapy, the modality practiced by the author, the primary goal of treatment is to help a child learn new and effective strategies for getting his or her needs met in ways that do not interfere with others getting their needs met. Children who exhibit problem behavior or emotional distress are seen as unable to get their needs met, either effectively or in ways that are both effective and socially acceptable.

To resolve this problem, the child and the play therapist must identify the child's needs, identify current factors that prevent those needs from being met, and then identify and master effective new strategies that the child can use to get those needs met. Guided imagery can be used to augment many aspects of this process.

Guided imagery is similar both to many relaxation strategies and to hypnosis. One can envision a continuum with standard relaxation techniques on one end and hypnosis on the other and guided imagery somewhere in the middle. As used by the author, guided imagery involves having the child engage in some focused relaxation exercise and then using visual imagery for the purpose of either direct or indirect problem solving with respect to getting the child's needs met. Guided imagery brings two advantages to the play therapy process. One advantage is that it can be used to help children gain a sense of mastery over their bodies and their feelings. The other advantage is that it can be used to augment generalization of other gains made in the play therapy, by allowing children to use their imaginations to create hypothetical life situations in the playroom so as to practice their newly acquired skills with the support of the therapist. In other words, guided imagery can be used to create an elaborate form of role-playing. While the latter use can be very effective, it is the use of guided imagery to augment mastery that is the focus of this discussion.

Description

Guided imagery can be introduced at any point in the play therapy process. The child must be able to follow simple sequential directions and must be willing to relax in session. Although the ultimate goal is to provide the child with an increased sense of mastery, the initial process requires that the child relinquish some control to the therapist, as the therapist will need to teach the child the technique. There are a number of ways the therapist may introduce the process to the child. Younger children often respond to the idea of taking an imaginary trip, while older children often like the idea of personal mastery, including the concept of self-hypnosis.

However guided imagery is introduced, the therapist begins by teaching the child a basic relaxation strategy. If the child is willing, it is useful to have him or her lie down or sit in a recliner for the early training. Alternatively, sitting in a beanbag chair works well. Progressive deep muscle relaxation (Jacobson 1938) is probably the most effective way of preparing the child for guided imagery. In this approach to relaxation the child is asked to focus on one muscle group at a time, while working to achieve maximum relaxation of that group. Groups of muscles are added in sequence, with the goal of achieving total body relaxation. Younger children may have difficulty with progressive deep muscle relaxation because it is such a passive process. For them, a sequence of contract-relax instructions that takes them through all of the major muscle groups is usually more effective (O'Connor 1991). For example, the child might be told to curl his toes, then relax them; push his knees together, then relax; tighten his stomach muscles and relax; and so on. Each muscle group is contracted and relaxed several times in a slow, sequential progression. While deep relaxation facilitates the guided imagery process, it is not necessary; simply getting the child to focus and follow directions is sufficient. Note that the child should be encouraged to achieve relaxation with her eyes open. This will make it easier for the child to access the effects of the imagery later, in situations where full relaxation is not possible.

Once even minimal relaxation has occurred, guided imagery can be introduced. The imagery used needs to be tailored to the child's needs, experiences, and developmental level. This is best illustrated through a case example.

Applications

Michael was 8 years old when he was brought to play therapy for many anxiety-related behaviors. There had been many changes in his life, and neither of his parents had been particularly able to address his needs because of their own distress. While play therapy focused on helping to identify Michael's basic needs and those factors that were preventing him from getting his needs met, guided imagery was introduced to help him achieve symptom mastery, thereby reducing some portion of his anxiety. Specifically, Michael found his nightmares to be so distressing that they were interfering with his getting a full night's sleep.

Because of his age, a contract-relax procedure was used to initiate relaxation. Although the therapist wanted Michael to practice his guided imagery while lying on the floor, using a pillow and a blanket, Michael found this set-up too anxiety-provoking, since he was afraid he would fall asleep and actually have a nightmare. For this reason Michael was initially trained while he sat in a beanbag chair and later moved to a pretend bed.

In an interview with Michael it was determined that one of the images he found very relaxing was swimming in a lake (so long as the water was clear enough that he could see the bottom and make sure there were no creatures about to get him). Once he was relaxed, the therapist guided him through imagining lying in very shallow water by the side of a lake. The image was strengthened by making it multisensory. Michael was asked to imagine that the sand he was lying on was warm and very soft and that it felt and sounded like the shifting of the beans in the beanbag chair. Then he was asked to imagine the water as being quite warm as it flowed over his body. He was told to picture a bright blue sky with puffy white clouds and to hear the sound of very gentle waves as they moved past his ears. The ebb and flow of the waves were then synchronized to his breathing, so that the waves came up as he breathed in and flowed out as he exhaled. Michael enjoyed the image very much and was more than willing to practice it at home. The therapist instructed Michael to begin by practicing in the morning after he woke up, so as to reduce the chance that Michael would be so anxious about the possibility of falling asleep that he would avoid the task.

In session the therapist helped Michael learn to use the image as a way of regaining control when anxious material was discussed. If Michael became anxious in session, the therapist would cue him to begin "breathing with the waves" in a slow and measured pace. As Michael reported achieving a more relaxed state, he and the therapist began to introduce images from his nightmares into the process. At first, Michael was told to remain lying in the lake and to practice seeing some of the monsters from his dreams in the clouds overhead. Since these were clouds, not monsters, they were not particularly threatening. Later the monsters were brought to life and Michael engaged in many mastery fantasies. He would have his own monsters rise up out of the lake to protect him. He would become a knight with magic powers. Or he would tell a joke and the monsters would laugh until they literally broke into pieces. At this time the therapist began having Michael use the imagery when he woke up from a nightmare during the night as a way of soothing himself. As Michael reported more success, he was encouraged to use the imagery prior to going to sleep at night to create dreams that would not be frightening. In essence Michael scripted his dreams and took control over the expression of his anxiety.

As can be seen in the previous description, it is important for the relaxation process and the imagery to come under the child's control. The therapist moves from the role of instructor to one where he or she is simply cuing the start of the process, to one where he or she is simply reinforcing and helping to focus the use of the process outside of the session. If the children do not gain control of the process, it is unlikely that they will be able to use it outside of session, as they will remain dependent on the therapist. It should also be apparent that the process, at least in this case, also contained elements of cognitive-behavioral therapy and systematic desensitization. As stated in the introduction, guided imagery effectively enhances the therapeutic process.

In this case, as intense as his nightmares were, it took Michael only a few weeks to reduce them by 80 percent and then a few more days to virtually eliminate them. Once he experienced mastery, rapid gains and generalization followed. This same process was used to help him master some other anxiety-related symptoms and to enhance his school performance.

References

Jacobson, E. (1938). *Progressive Relaxation—A Physiological and Clinical Investi-gation of Muscular States and Their Significance in Psychology and Medical Practice*, 2nd ed. Chicago: University of Chicago Press.

O'Connor, K. (1991). *The Play Therapy Primer*. New York: Wiley.

LEARNING-CHECKLIST

Identifying Modality Strengths

Understanding one's preferred modalities helps children discover their strengths. Using the following chart, review the styles with the child and help him/her identify his/her modality strengths and improve his/her learning styles.

Observable Characteristics
Indicative of Modality Strength

(From *Teaching through Modality Strengths: Concepts and Practices*, by W. B. Barbe, R. H. Swassing, and W. B. Milove. Copyright © 1979 by Zanner-Blosser. Reprinted with permission.)

	Visual	Auditory	Kinesthetic
Learning Style	Learns by seeing; watching demonstrations	Learns through verbal instructions from others or self	Learns by doing; direct involvement
Reading	Likes description; sometimes stops reading to stare into space and imagine scene; intense concentration	Enjoys dialogue, plays; avoids lengthy description, unaware of illustrations; moves lips or subvocalizes	Prefers stories where action occurs early, fidgets when reading, handles books, not an avid reader
Spelling	Recognizes words by sight; relies on configuration of words	Uses a phonics approach; has auditory word skills	Often is a poor speller, writes words to determine if they "feel" right
Handwriting	Tends to be good, particularly when young; spacing and size are good; appearance is important	Has more difficulty teaming in initial stages; tends to write lightly; says strokes when writing	Good initially, deteriorates when space becomes smaller; pushes harder on writing instrument
Memory	Remembers faces, forgets names; writes things down, takes notes	Remembers names, forgets faces; remembers by auditory repetition	Remembers best what was done, not what was seen or talked about
Imagery	Vivid imagination; thinks in pictures, visualizes in detail	Subvocalizes, thinks in sounds; details less important	Imagery not important; images that do occur are accompanied by movement
Distractibility	Generally unaware of sounds; distracted by visual disorder or movement	Easily distracted by sounds	Not attentive to visual, auditory presentation so seems distractible
Problem Solving	Deliberate; plans in advance; organizes thoughts by writing them; lists problems	Talks problems out, tries solutions verbally, subvocally; talks self through problem	Attacks problems physically; impulsive; often selects solution involving greatest activity

LIFE MAPS

"Life Maps" by Glenda F. Short

(From *101 Favorite Play Therapy Techniques*, edited by H. Kaduson and C. Schaefer. Copyright © 1999 by Jason Aronson and reprinted with permission.)

Introduction

The Life Map is a simple art technique where children draw four (or more) specific important life events they have experienced.

Rationale

This technique is used to allow children to comprehend a past, present, and future and to be able to identify, express, and own their feelings regarding their life events.

Description

The therapist can provide the child with a piece of paper with four circles on it, or the child can draw the four circles. Children are to draw in the circles four events they deem important in their lives. This can be discussed beforehand with the child, allowing the child to tell stories of his life events prior to drawing them. The drawings are then talked about in detail, giving feelings to each picture. Often parents are given a chance to listen to the children. Sometimes the child changes his story for the parents. It then becomes important for the therapist to explore with the child what his fears are if he tells his "true feelings." Pictures often give important information to the therapist about the family and the child's relationship with others.

Applications

This activity is used with children beginning at age 4 years. It is used with all types of cases, as it helps children tell stories, identify feelings, and express those feelings. It helps children begin to see the process of life events and how there is a past, present, and future.

In Example A on page 444, circle number one: Shows his mother cuddling him and loving him. He tells that "I was the best baby. I was better than my baby sister."

Circle number two: Shows him scratching his father's back and with his swimming tube. He tells that if he scratches his dad's back, they will go

Example A: Loss of father in the home and adjusting to a new baby sister and to school.

swimming. He talks with the therapist about how much he misses his dad and that he doesn't see him enough. (When telling his mother about the second circle, he glosses over his missing his dad and does not elaborate about him and his dad swimming.)

Circle number three: Shows the child in school his kindergarten year. He tells, "I was scared. I didn't know much what to do and the teacher yelled." When telling his mother about the picture, the child states, "There I am in kindergarten doing everything I was supposed to do." His original words to the therapist are congruent with the look on his face.

Circle number four: Shows the child in school once again. He states, "This is me in first grade and I feel better about knowing what to do in school. Sometimes I like school." A general rule is that children who are older will often have more elaborate life maps and give more description of the events. It is important to write a story with each circle so the child can understand that he has a story. One step further to the life maps is to have the child talk about his control in the situations and what could the story have been if he or she made a different choice about the event. If the child has no control, talking about that is important, as the child will begin to understand that he sometimes does not have a choice about the event, but does have a choice about what he will do about how the event impinges on his life.

Explained to therapist:

1. "This is my mom. She loves me and helps me."
2. "This is me and my dad. When he was home, we scratched each others' back in the morning." (Explained to mom: "You know how I had to scratch dad's back—glad that's over.")
3. "This is me in kindergarten. I was scared and didn't understand what to do. My dad left when I was in kindergarten." (Explained to mom: "This is me in kindergarten doing everything I was supposed to do.")
4. "This is me in first grade. I wasn't so scared." (Explained to mom: "This is me in first grade doing everything I was supposed to do.")

PUPPETRY

"Battaro and the Puppet House" by Martha J. Harkin

(From *101 Favorite Play Therapy Techniques*, edited by H. Kaduson and C. Schaefer. Copyright © 1999 by Jason Aronson and reprinted with permission.)

Introduction

A creative therapy technique is often born from necessity and/or desperation. Battaro and the Puppet House emerged initially to meet the expressive needs of children and evolved as powerful catalysts to communication between child and therapist. In response to children often wishing to be on television, the Puppet House was created as a decorative canvas theater that hung from a wide shelf. After a 7-year-old boy in treatment for terrorizing adults and children destroyed three inflatable punching bags in three sessions, Battaro was created: a 54″ durable fabric bag filled with shredded polyfoam, sewn and hand-painted with a nonaggressive human figure.

Rationale

The therapeutic value of these tools became immediately apparent. First, they needed no introduction. Children (and adults) responded to them as unique features of the office, an instant attraction that provided client-initiated activity. The 7-year-old exhausted himself on Battaro during the fourth session.

By the fifth and sixth sessions his aggressive response weakened. He began to demonstrate issues through play in the Puppet House, revealing his fear of, and concern for, the imprisoned father who had abused him. Parent and teachers immediately noted positive behavior changes.

More important, the Puppet House offers a safe retreat during an intense session. The child can regroup his or her energies while observing the therapist through peepholes in the doorknob and flower prints in the canvas. (Adults have also used the screen while discussing painful material.) Children often participate more actively in the initial interview process when they take refuge in the Puppet House. This enables them to add their reactions and comments through puppets. In observation situations, parents can be seated behind the screen, while therapist and child pretend that no one else is present. This is a very useful avenue when working with small children where a one-way mirror is not available, or when the child is having difficulty separating from the parent.

Description

Technique within the framework of these useful tools evolves from the therapist's ability to allow the child to lead self-initiated activity in a safe place with unpressured time. The therapist adheres to Virginia Axline's (1969) guidelines that the child leads the action or conversation and that the therapist maintains the relationship through acceptance and permission for the child to express feelings completely and reflects the child's words or behavior in ways that help the child understand the feelings expressed. As the child interacts with the therapist through Battaro and the Puppet House, he or she has the opportunity to develop a feelings vocabulary and to experiment with ways of solving problems. The therapist can role-play a bumbler and ask, "What do I say (or do) now?" If the child's directions are something the therapist cannot or will not do, then the two can negotiate what will be acceptable. This kind of interchange provides the child with a feeling of empowerment.

Applications

Since work with Battaro and the Puppet House is initiated by the client, they are useful tools with a variety of problems. In addition to use with the aggressive child, the withdrawn and/or neglected child is also served. He or she seeks the comfort of hugging Battaro, often taking Battaro into the Puppet House, where he or she talks with him, observes the therapist through peepholes, and can move outward at a self-selected place. Usually, the withdrawn child is eventually able to express suppressed anger through Battaro.

The most common sequence in interactions with Battaro begins with expressions of aggression and anger that move toward demonstrations of frustration and need for power; Battaro is battered, knocked down, trampled, and bounced against the wall. This phase may end after one or two sessions, or the child may develop a ritual around his or her interaction with Battaro, as illustrated in the case study to follow. The second phase often reflects client insight into his or her feelings and a move to incorporate Battaro as an ally. As the child heals, he or she begins to separate from Battaro, using it less and turning to developmental games and talks with the therapist as a way to develop adequate coping skills. As therapy progresses through its ups and downs, the client can always return to Battaro and/or the Puppet House to dramatize a current stress and work through the problem.

Battaro and the Puppet House are useful for helping the therapist assess the child's progress through the content and affect of the material presented. During the termination phase of therapy, often difficult for many children, Battaro and the Puppet House can be incorporated into termination ceremonies, allowing the child to express him- or herself through a familiar medium.

Example

The following example demonstrates some of the possibilities these tools offer. All names are fictitious and identifying detail has been omitted.

Peter is a 5-year-old boy who had been in therapy for one year and was transferred to me when his therapist left the agency. When Peter was 4 years old, he climbed onto a bed where his father had laid a loaded gun after leaving the room for a few moments. The gun discharged and killed the younger brother, a toddler. Peter has been a difficult child from early childhood and the younger brother, an easy child, was clearly the favorite. The parents had also been in therapy for a year but had not yet cleared the toddler's room or let go of their grief and anger. Marital tensions present before death were also exacerbated.

Peter uses the first two sessions to explore the therapy room, test the therapist, and spend a great deal of time venting his feelings on Battaro. At the opening of the third session, Peter throws Battaro head first into the Puppet House again and again.

Peter: [shouts] Arrest that man.
Therapist: You want me to arrest that man?
Peter: Yeah! He's a robber! He drives fast—and one bad thing—he shot someone.
Therapist: He shot someone.

Peter devises a scenario where I am a sheriff asleep in the office. He takes Battaro into the Puppet House and hides himself behind Battaro. He then shoots a rubber dart out into the office.

Therapist: (awakens] What did I hear?
Peter: [shoots gun again]

Therapist: Fee Fi Fo Fum—I smell a robber with a gun. [Looks into Puppet House] Who are you?
Peter: I'm the landlord.
Therapist: I'm looking for a robber with a gun.
Peter: He's not here.
Therapist: [aside] What should I do?
Peter: Keep looking for the robber.
Therapist: [Searches high and low around the office, pretending the file and bookcases are buildings. Returns to Puppet House door and pretends to knock.]
Peter: (falsetto) Who's there?
Therapist: It's the sheriff. I'm looking for a robber with a gun.
Peter: (falsetto) He's not here, keep looking.

I search, all over the office, returning to the Puppet House, bumbling, unable to see behind Battaro, much to Peter's glee. This scenario is repeated week after week, with Peter developing a gentler affect as we work on the idea that maybe the robber isn't really a robber and maybe he isn't bad. The funeral anniversary stirs up a strong aggressive reaction, and Peter comes to the next session threatening to hit me and giving me orders that I shoot the robber. I set limits, diverting aggressive demonstration to Battaro and assuring Peter that I do not shoot robbers. In the next few sessions he continues the scenario, introducing a lion and a tiger mask. Peter wears the lion (a symbol of power), I wear the tiger. Soon after, he announces at school that he had shot his brother. This is reported to the parents who, in turn, discuss the event with the therapy team. After two more sessions of ritual play, Peter comes to the next session looking very quiet. He initiates our Fee Fi Fo Fum ritual and I am sent high and low in the office, looking for the origin of the "shots." On the third return to the Puppet House:

Therapist: [knocks on door] Hello. Is anyone here?
Peter: [normal voice] Yes.
Therapist: [opens Puppet Theater, speaks to Battaro] Who are you?
Peter: [normal voice] Peter. (Peter is hiding behind Battaro.)
Therapist: May I come in?
Peter: [normal voice] Yes.
Therapist: [putting arms around Battaro, holding tenderly] Oh Peter, I've been wanting to talk with you about your brother. How sad that there was such a terrible accident. I have wanted to hug you. [hugs Battaro] I've wanted to tell you that you couldn't know the gun would shoot. You were a little boy, 4 years old, who wasn't protected from a gun. [Then holds Battaro, tenderly patting head and back while Peter watches intently. I invite Battaro out into the office and carry him to stand near my chair where I quietly sit. In a few moments Peter

emerges, lays his hand on Battaro for a few seconds. He then brings out the *Don't Break the Ice* game, which he has used often after our weekly sessions. Usually, he has dashed the blocks out of the frame before the game is finished, but this time he carefully and skillfully takes out blocks so that the final block to drop the "ice" is mine, and he wins.]

After this session, his use of Battaro and the Puppet House diminished, and as Peter moved into first grade, he initiated play with sand and clay. He was eventually able to tolerate board games with rules, play on a T-ball team, and manage his behavior more productively at school.

A year later we were able to use Battaro and the Puppet House in a difficult termination experience. When I told Peter that I was leaving the agency to work in a treatment center, he struck Battaro viciously several times, then entered the Puppet House and snapped the thick dowel in the lower edge of the theater opening over his knee. We were able to talk about his anger over my leaving and the feelings each of us was having. The broken dowel symbolized the break in our relationship, so we talked about making change without breaking the meaning of our relationship. We planned how we would spend our final session the following week, which included his helping me install a new dowel in the Puppet House and planning which games we would play before meeting his new therapist.

(Note: Battaro and the Puppet House are made and sold by Harkin & David Designs, Inc., 5601 Mapleleaf Dr., Austin, TX 78723 (512) 929-8611.)

Reference

Axline, V. (1969). *Play Therapy*. New York: Ballantine.

"Puppetry" by Marie Boultinghouse

(From *101 Favorite Play Therapy Techniques*, edited by H. Kaduson and C. Schaefer. Copyright © 1999 by Jason Aronson and reprinted with permission.)

Introduction

Play is a natural activity of childhood and possibly the most effective means of learning. Play is really practice for real life and provides sufficient elasticity for accommodating any number of events, people, and situations. Although the child knows that play isn't real, in some ways it assumes real-life proportions. It provides for the safe practice of behaviors with possible built-in consequences by which the child learns. It provides for the development of empathy through role playing and behavior rehearsal. The many shades and colors of play provide an infinite number of possibilities for practice and learning that would be unlikely through other modalities.

Puppetry is a potent form of play and one that readily adapts to an endless variety of combinations and possibilities. The child is readily able to identify with animal or people puppets and their problems and is thus able to suggest and think through appropriate problem-solving strategies. Puppetry lends itself naturally to storytelling, with its own endless variety of possibilities. The child is able to "act" through the puppets and is able to vicariously try out different behaviors and problem-solving strategies and then to consider resulting consequences to himself or herself and to others in his or her environment.

Rationale

I have become interested in the use of puppetry due to the lasting consequences of its use. Although I have rarely had a child remember very long what was said through discussion, I have discovered that children remember many months later the lessons that Fritz, the firehouse dog puppet, learned. These are always real-life lessons, such as the consequences of violating family rules by running in the doghouse or climbing on the doghouse roof. After the puppet has finished its story, the child is readily able to apply it to his or her own life circumstances. Puppetry can also be effectively used to help the child deal with anxiety and what the puppet has learned about facing the source of fears, coping with anxiety, and ultimately reducing anxiety to a manageable level. Fritz, of course, has had some school experiences of early life, so he is able to identify with the child's fears and problems pertaining to getting along with his or her teacher and peers, coping with academic demands, and cultivating the ability to delay gratification. The use of puppetry is readily adaptable to empathizing with the child who has inattentional/hyperactivity/impulsive characteristics; this provides for the introduction of procedures that Fritz has found effective and that provide for teachers and parents therapeutic procedures for their own use.

Description

It is helpful to have a variety of puppets and allow the child to choose which one he or she wishes to use. The writer has Fritz, the firehouse dog (red fireman's hat, white and black spots, and long pink tongue), a yellow "banana" kangaroo with baby in its pouch, and an orange monkey. Although children like all of them, they seem to prefer puppets that open their mouths, whether or not they have teeth. Children find it pleasant to have Fritz bite their ears or give them a kiss (sometimes as a reward). The kangaroo with a baby in its pouch lends itself to the subject of siblings, as well as single-parent families. In one instance, the orange monkey's mother left the jungle to work in a people-making factory, while the yellow kangaroo baby's father left home because he often drank too much "rotted coconut juice" (alcohol). Children, as well as their parents, have to learn to cope with changed circumstances.

One use of puppets is the creation of stories similar to those of the child but slightly removed in time, place, or circumstances. The therapist begins the story by introducing characters with their own contexts (parents were fighting, parent left home, parent became unemployed), each child adds to the story spontaneously without coaching, and the therapist adds a component that gives the children something to think about or suggestions for problem solving (similar procedures were described by Richard A. Gardner). Children are asked to draw a picture about what might happen next or to use clay to make something pertaining to the story theme. At the next session, the drawings or clay activities are reviewed; the story is then reviewed briefly (the therapist having previously recorded the main ideas and events of the story) and the session begins with a new story segment with use of the puppets. When appropriate, allowing the parent to remain in the session is often quite fruitful. Careful observation of puppet choice and the role played in developing the story is quite productive.

Another wrinkle in the use of puppetry is to have each of the puppets share its own story and the impact of events beyond its ability to control, following the setting created by the therapist. Each puppet may be encouraged to share what came before, what is happening now, and what may happen in the future (as is used in projective storytelling strategies). Ask the child specifically what the puppet can do about the situation, regardless of what parental or caretaker figures do.

It is both easy and fun to create a group story drawn on flipchart-sized paper, with all children sharing in the story and drawing what is happening. It is important to see that each child contributes through the use of the puppet drawing.

Another possibility is to have children write the puppet's journal through use of the puppet or the memory of the puppet. From nonhardening clay, create something the puppet may have created to represent the events of the puppet's day; store the clay in zipper plastic bags for use in another session. Bring journals and drawings or what was created to the next session; discuss what each child thought and felt about the journal writing, clay creation, and drawing.

Another very productive possibility includes the use of Fritz or a similar puppet to address racial issues. Fritz, a Dalmatian by inheritance, can readily identify with children who are faced with biracial issues. It is very simple for him to talk about his grandfather, a dog who had more black spots than white spots, and unkind remarks with which he had to cope. He can also help, through role playing, to teach the child how to remove fun from name-calling (such as smiling, shrugging his dog shoulders, talking about how the remark thrilled him, etc.). Beyond that, it is very easy to provide homework assignments that the child "research" (through imagination) other figures on his family tree to the grandfather's grandfather. This is great fun, but it also provides for considering issues of loss, family changes, and many kinds of unexpected (perhaps undesirable) events.

Applications

Many applications were referred to previously and others are possible. I find it helpful to use puppetry with other compatible strategies in dealing with phobias, aggression, family problems, bullying, biracial issues, peer problems, anxiety (including fear of the dark), taking the fun out of name-calling, and sibling rivalry. Doubtless, there are many other applications. Puppetry and associated procedures can be used successfully with children at least through the fourth grade.

A recent new wrinkle that the writer has used dealt with biracial issues. The biracial child (whose Caucasian mother and African-American father were college students) was adopted at birth by an African-American couple whose own child was born a few months later. Parents attempted to share the adoption realities with the child. After being told that he was adopted, he went to school and told his teacher that he was a doctor. He referred to his adoptive mother and himself as orange and his adoptive father and sister as black. He decided that he didn't want to be black; he is a most attractive child with light brown skin and curly brown hair. It was very easy to have Fritz talk about his own wise grandfather dog's experiences, since he had more black than white spots. It was easy to turn this into drawings and ultimately a family tree. The family tree was very timely and provided for a discussion of losses, since his own adoptive grandfather died only a few months previously. His adoptive sister and his mother were included in the session; sister contributed and mother observed. Mother also read and discussed with children at home stories related to the main theme. The children both loved the activities. When the child hadn't been seen for a few months, his first question at next contact was "Where is Fritz?" At other times, there was practice in conflict resolution, removing the fun of name-calling, and dealing with bullying by others. According to the mother's report, the child has become much more self-confident, his crying has almost disappeared, and he does extremely well in school.

References

Gardner, R. (1971). *Therapeutic Communication with Children: The Mutual Storytelling Technique.* New York: Science House.

Irwin, E. (1993). "Using Puppets for Assessment." In *Play Therapy Techniques*, ed. C. E. Schaefer and D. Cangelosi, pp. 69–81. Northvale, NJ: Jason Aronson.

"Using a Puppet to Create a Symbolic Client" by Carolyn J. Narcavage

(From *101 Favorite Play Therapy Techniques*, edited by H. Kaduson and C. Schaefer. Copyright © 1999 by Jason Aronson and reprinted with permission.)

Rationale

The use of puppets in therapeutic work with children was introduced by Woltmann (1940). Woltmann found puppets to be useful because they provide opportunities for spontaneity, are easily manipulated, and lend themselves naturally to a symbolic process of self-expression. Puppet play creates an atmosphere of fantasy that is absorbing to the child, while at the same time being nonthreatening (Haworth 1968). Children tend to identify with the characters involved in puppet play and to project their feelings and interpersonal conflicts onto them. In this way, children are able to communicate their distress without having to directly claim traumatic experiences and painful emotions as their own (Webb 1991). The therapist, in turn, can use puppets to reflect understanding and provide corrective emotional experiences in response to the child's play.

Description

Although many children naturally gravitate toward puppets and begin the process of projective expression on their own, some children are so withdrawn, fearful, and self-conscious in the beginning stages of therapy that they strongly resist expression and interaction. These children often sit stiffly in the playroom, avoid eye contact with the therapist, and become increasingly reticent with every direct, yet reassuring, comment the therapist makes. Severely withdrawn children often avoid joining the therapist, even when she models play behavior and invites the child to participate. Bow (1993) describes one means of overcoming child resistance with the use of puppets, called the "hidden puppet technique." In this technique, the therapist hides a puppet in a sack and encourages the child to help coax the "resistant" puppet out.

Another way that the therapist can remove the focus from a withdrawn child and stimulate productive work in therapy is to *facilitate* projection of the child's feelings onto a puppet. For instance, if the therapist experiences the child as being frightened, she might take out a puppet, present it as being scared, acknowledge its fear, and reassure it of its safety. The next step is to enlist the child's help in attending to the puppet's needs. For example, the therapist might ask the child to hold and comfort the "frightened" puppet. By facilitating projection and enlisting the child's help in caring for the puppet, the therapist is able to achieve three important goals: (1) she is able to respond to the child's feelings in a nonthreatening manner; (2) she is able to mobilize the child's participation in therapy; and (3) she is able to begin fostering a positive, collaborative relationship with the child. As therapy proceeds, the puppet often becomes a safety object and is used by the child as a primary means of affective expression and interaction with the therapist.

Applications

Puppets are useful in therapy with children because these play materials tend to naturally elicit affective projection. In work with extremely withdrawn children, however, the therapist may need to facilitate this projective process by creating a "symbolic client" out of a puppet. Creating a symbolic client removes the focus from the withdrawn child, increases her comfort level, and enables her to explore feelings from a safe distance. The therapist engages the child in helping to care for the symbolic client. This initiates the process of relationship building between the child and the therapist and allows them to metaphorically attend to the child's needs.

Puppet Play Techniques

Bethany was a 4-year-old, selectively mute child who presented as withdrawn, depressed, and fearful. At the time of her referral to play therapy, Bethany had been in preschool for several months and had not made even the slightest utterance in that setting. Her teachers described her as "emotionally dead" because she never smiled or registered typically expected affect in response to circumstances in her environment. In contrast to her behavior at school, Bethany reportedly talked with great fervor at home.

Bethany was the third of four children. When she was 3, her parents, Rick and Kelly, divorced. Kelly had a long history of severe alcoholism and mental illness. She would drink continuously throughout most mornings and afternoons and would fly into rages in the evenings—screaming at the family, smashing furniture and dishes, and physically attacking Rick. The children frequently overheard Kelly threaten to kill Rick. Kelly was arrested a half-dozen times for public drunkenness and disorderly conduct and for physically attacking her siblings and her husband. Rick was awarded custody of the children after the divorce. Although supervised visitation was initially granted to Kelly, it was suspended after she showed up intoxicated to several visits with Bethany and her siblings.

Bethany began play therapy early in her second year of preschool. During our first session, she refused to explore the toys, resisted eye contact with me, hid her eyes when I spoke to her, sat motionless in the middle of the floor, and said nothing. My attempts to reassure her of my safety and to give her permission to play anything she wished only prompted her to become increasingly self-conscious and withdrawn.

During the second session, I decided to approach Bethany's fear in a less threatening manner. I took a cuddly bear puppet off the shelf and made him cover his eyes fearfully. I talked gently to Mr. Bear, acknowledging how scary it is to come to a new place and play with a grown-up he didn't know. I reassured Mr. Bear that we were in a safe place, that I was a safe person, and that I would not let anything bad happen to him or to Bethany while we played together.

Next, I used the bear puppet to convey a sense of unconditional acceptance toward Bethany and to give her permission to do whatever she wanted in therapy, including remaining silent. I made Mr. Bear say in a frightened voice, "I don't feel like talking. Talking seems scary sometimes." I responded to Mr. Bear by validating this feeling and telling him that it was all right with me if he chose not to talk when he didn't feel like it. I told him that I enjoyed being with him and that he didn't have to do anything in the playroom he didn't want to do. I gave Mr. Bear permission to communicate with me in other ways, such as pointing to the toys he wanted.

In the third session, Bethany appeared less frightened but remained inhibited. I repeated the interaction with Mr. Bear, in which I responded to his fear. I invited Mr. Bear and/or Bethany to choose what we would play that day. Bethany sat motionless, so I made Mr. Bear point to some dishes. Bethany watched as Mr. Bear made some food. Toward the end of the session, I talked to Bethany about how scared Mr. Bear was and invited her to help comfort him, a symbolic way of helping her to begin accepting comfort. Mr. Bear indicated that he wanted to hear a story. I framed this to Bethany as "helping Mr. Bear to feel better and less scared" and invited her to hold him while I read. She held the puppet and gave it several gentle hugs during the story. I commented on how good Bethany was at helping Mr. Bear to feel safe.

In the fourth session, Bethany entered the room and went immediately to Mr. Bear, giving him an affectionate look and a hug. I told Bethany that Mr. Bear was glad to see her and that he liked the things she did to make him feel safe, like holding him gently and hugging him. The puppet had become Bethany's safety object, and for several weeks after this point she incorporated it into every activity we did together. At the end of session four, Bethany placed Mr. Bear on her own hand. I said, "Mr. Bear, you felt really scared when you first started to come here and play. Are you starting to feel better inside?" Bethany made the puppet nod his head affirmatively.

Bethany's early life experiences prevented her from accepting any type of physical nurturance from me in the early stages of therapy. She would not allow me to make even simple nurturing gestures, like helping her put on her shoes or caring for her when she played baby. However, Mr. Bear became our means of showing affection toward one another. Bethany allowed Mr. Bear to hug her and care for her during "baby play." She began to use the bear puppet to give me hugs.

As therapy continued, I used the bear puppet to explore Bethany's past traumatic experiences. During session eleven, Bethany presented Mr. Bear with a variety of new puppets to meet. I made him cover his eyes and shake with fear.

After several repetitions of this, I said gently, "A long time ago, someone used to be very mean to Mr. Bear. Now he gets scared of people sometimes and doesn't know who is safe and who isn't."

Bethany demonstrated that the new puppets were safe by having them display gentle behavior, like hugging Mr. Bear. Also in this session, I used the puppet to demonstrate a way Bethany could practice communicating with people while feeling "in control" (e.g., without people she didn't want to hear her, being privy to what she was saying). I had the puppet whisper to me and to Bethany throughout the session. To my amazement, Bethany began whispering to her preschool teachers the following week and to me several weeks later.

The bear puppet became less central as therapy progressed and as Bethany began using other puppets and dolls as a means of symbolic communication. However, before therapy ended, Bethany and I had spent a great deal of time doctoring Mr. Bear and fixing his wounds so that he was strong and felt good inside. Mr. Bear, the symbolic client, was an invaluable tool in Bethany's process of healing.

References

Bow, J. N. (1993). "Overcoming Resistance." In *The Therapeutic Powers of Play*, ed. C. E. Schaefer, pp. 17–40. Northvale, NJ: Jason Aronson.

Haworth, M. R. (1968). "Doll Play and Puppetry." In *Projective Techniques in Personality Assessment*, ed. A. L. Rabin, pp. 327–365. New York: Springer.

Webb, N. B. (1991). *Playing for Their Lives: Helping Troubled Children through Play Therapy*. New York: Free Press.

Woltmann, A. G. (1940). "The Use of Puppetry in Understanding Children." *Mental Hygiene* 24: 445–458.

RELAXATION

"Relaxation Training for Children" by Arlene S. Koeppen

(From *Play Therapy Techniques* by C. E. Schaefer and D. M. Congelosi. Copyright © 1993 by Jason Aronson and reprinted with permission.)

Children experience some degree of tension at one time or another in the elementary grades. This tension can range from an "uptight" feeling right before an unprepared-for oral book report to a generalized tension and worry throughout the day. Some children experience discomfort during specific subject matter periods, others when beginning a new task, while others become upset after a correction from the teacher. Pressure to succeed, to always be right, to be liked, to have approval, or to cope with family problems can produce tension in a child.

School counselors are often called on to work with children whose academic or social development is hampered by similar kinds of pressures, and they deal with these problems in a variety of ways. Some provide individual or group counseling to improve poor self-concept or poor peer relations or to reduce acting-out behavior. Some consult with a child's teacher to bring about change in the educational setting or provide remedial instruction for diagnosed learning disabilities Some counselors seek the parents' help in alleviating the problem. Others use various methods and combinations of methods to involve the home and school, as well as the child, in bringing about positive change.

A potentially significant contribution to the counselor's repertoire of skills in this area is the use of relaxation techniques. These techniques are often used as one method of preparing an individual for dealing with anxiety-producing material, but they can be an end in themselves. Lazarus (1971) and Carkhuff (1969) have published guides for conducting relaxation sessions. Woody (1971) has provided a review of literature, citing studies using systematic desensitization, with relaxation as the first step. Further cases are cited by Krumholtz and Thoresen (1969) and Lazarus (1971). Lazarus has also recorded his relaxation material on tape. Most of the published materials on relaxation seem most applicable to adolescents and adults, and no intentions are stated regarding the application of these models to children. While the use of these models with children is not proscribed, such an extension is not readily apparent. A script written just for children could conceivably enhance the process of helping children learn to relax.

Relaxation exercises designed especially for children can help them to become aware of the feelings of body tension and provide skills to reduce it. Children can be taught how to reduce their muscle tension, and this seems to reduce anxiety as well. There was one boy whose arms and legs seemed like perpetual motion machines, yet he showed no awareness of this manifest tension. He mentioned that his parents were considering "putting me on some kind of pills to help me pay attention better." Though he denied any feelings of tension, he agreed to try a few relaxation exercises. He worked hard on the exercises, but said he didn't feel any different afterward. Five minutes later his puzzled expression became a grin as he said, "It worked!"

Relaxation training can take place during individual or group counseling sessions, in physical education classes, or in a regular classroom setting. Once children develop the skills, they can relax without instructions from a trainer and thereby implement a higher degree of self-control. If successful mastery of relaxation skills works like successful mastery of academic tasks, then perhaps a case could be made for improved self-concept as well.

In training children to relax various muscle groups, it is not necessary that they be able to identify and locate them. The use of the child's fantasy can be incorporated into the instructions in such a manner that the appropriate muscle groups will automatically be used. Some precedent for the use of fantasy in a similar context was set by Lazarus and Abramovitz (1962). The use of fantasy also serves to attract and maintain a child's interest. One child told his counselor that the exercises stopped the butterflies in his stomach. The butterfly imagery expressed a real feeling for him; it has been replaced by the feelings connoted by a lazy cat.

It has been noted that although children will agree that they want to learn how to relax, they don't want to practice their newly acquired skills under the watchful eyes of their classmates. Fortunately, several muscle groups can be relaxed without much gross motor activity, and practice can go unnoticed. It pleases some children to perform these exercises in class and relax themselves without drawing the attention of those around them. It seemed important to one little girl that the exercises were "our secret that we won't tell the other kids." The effects of this type of training can extend beyond the classroom. A fourth-grade boy said that he used the exercises to help him get to sleep at night.

Below is a relaxation script designed for and used successfully with children in the intermediate grades. This script is similar in design with those used with adults (Carkhuff 1969, Lazarus 1971), but is intended to be more appealing to children. It is likely that the script is equally appropriate for children in the primary grades. Counselors are encouraged to experiment with it and to revise and extend it to include specific interests of children and incorporate other muscle groups. Eight muscle groups are included here. Other exercises can be developed to work with the upper thighs, upper arms, and different muscles around the face and neck, as well as the flexing muscles in the feet and extending muscles in the hands.

In working with this script, it is recommended that no more than fifteen minutes be devoted to the exercises at any one time and that no more than three muscle groups be introduced at one time. In the initial training sessions, the children are learning a new concept and new material. Two or three short sessions per week will help to establish these new behaviors. Aside from theoretical considerations, it is just too hard for some children to keep their eyes closed for more than fifteen minutes. Later sessions serve more to maintain the skills and provide a foundation for work in other areas. This type of session can follow a weekly pattern, with ten or fifteen minutes devoted to relaxation and the remainder of the time spent on other things.

It should be noted that many of the instructions should be repeated many more times than are indicated in the script and that such repetitions have been intentionally deleted. Each child or group of children is unique. Timing and pacing must follow the individual pattern created in the specific situation. One word of caution requires consideration. Children tend to get into this type of experience as much or more than adults and they are likely to be a bit disoriented if the session ends abruptly. Preparing children to leave the relaxed state is just as important as proper introduction and timing.

A Relaxation Training Script

Introduction

Today we're going to do some special kinds of exercises called *relaxation exercises*. These exercises help you learn how to relax when you're feeling uptight and help you get rid of those butterflies-in-your-stomach kinds of feelings. They're also kind of neat, because you can do some of them in the classroom without anybody noticing.

In order for you to get the best feelings from these exercises, there are some rules you must follow. First, you must do exactly what I say, even if it seems kind of silly. Second, you must try hard to do what I say. Third, you must pay attention to your body. Throughout these exercises, pay attention to how your muscles feel when they are tight and when they are loose and relaxed. And, fourth, you must practice. The more you practice, the more relaxed you can get. Does anyone have any questions?

Are you ready to begin? Okay. First, get as comfortable as you can in your chair. Sit back, get both feet on the floor, and just let your arms hang loose. That's fine. Now close your eyes and don't open them until I say to. Remember to follow my instructions very carefully, try hard, and pay attention to your body, Here we go.

Hands and Arms

Pretend you have a whole lemon in your left hand. Now squeeze it hard. Try to squeeze all the juice out. Feel the tightness in your hand and arm as you squeeze. Now drop the lemon. Notice how your muscles feel when they are relaxed. Take another lemon and squeeze it. Try to squeeze this one harder than you did the first one. That's right. Real hard. Now drop your lemon and relax. See how much better your hand and arm feel when they are relaxed. Once again, take a lemon in your left hand and squeeze all the juice out. Don't leave a single drop. Squeeze hard. Good. Now relax and let the lemon fall from your hand. (Repeat the process for the right hand and arm.)

Arms and Shoulders

Pretend you are a furry, lazy cat. You want to stretch. Stretch your arms out in front of you. Raise them up high over your head. Way back. Feel the pull in your shoulders. Stretch higher. Now just let your arms drop back to your sides. Okay, kittens, let's stretch again. Stretch your arms out in front of you. Raise them over your head. Pull them back, way back. Pull hard. Now let them drop quickly. Good. Notice how your shoulders feel more relaxed. This time let's have a great big stretch. Try to touch the ceiling. Stretch your arms way out in front of you. Raise them way up high over your head. Push them way, way back. Notice the tension and pull in your arms and shoulders. Hold tight, now. Great. Let them drop very quickly and feel how good it is to be relaxed. It feels good and warm and lazy.

Shoulder and Neck

Now pretend you are a turtle. You're sitting out on a rock by a nice peaceful pond, just relaxing in the warm sun. It feels nice and warm and safe here. Oh-oh! You sense danger. Pull your head into your house. Try to pull your shoulders up to your ears and push your head down into your shoulders. Hold in tight. It isn't easy to be a turtle in a shell. The danger is past now. You can come out into the warm sunshine, and, once again, you can relax and feel the warm sunshine. Watch out now! More danger. Hurry, pull your head back into your house and hold it tight. You have to be closed in tight to protect yourself. Okay, you can relax now. Bring your head out and let your shoulders relax. Notice how much better it feels to be relaxed than to be all tight. One more time, now. Danger! Pull your head in. Push your shoulders way up to your ears and hold tight. Don't let even a tiny piece of your head show outside your shell. Hold it. Feel the tenseness in your neck and shoulders. Okay. You can come out now. It's safe again. Relax and feel comfortable in your safety. There's no more danger. Nothing to worry about. Nothing to be afraid of. You feel good.

Jaw

You have a giant jawbreaker bubble gum in your mouth. It's very hard to chew. Bite down on it. Hard! Let your neck muscles help you. Now relax. Just let your jaw hang loose. Notice how good it feels to let your jaw drop. Okay, let's tackle that jawbreaker again now. Bite down hard. Try to squeeze it out between your teeth. That's good. You're really tearing that gum up. Now relax again. Just let your jaw drop off your face. It feels so good just to let go and not have to fight that bubble gum, Okay, one more time. We're really going to tear it up this time. Bite down. Hard as you can. Harder. Oh, you're really working hard. Good. Now relax. Try to relax your whole body. You've beaten the bubble gum. Let yourself go as loose as you can.

Face and Nose

Here comes a pesky old fly. He has landed on your nose. Try to get him off without using your hands. That's right, wrinkle up your nose. Make as many wrinkles in your nose as you can. Scrunch your nose up real hard. Good. You've chased him away. Now you can relax Oops, here he comes back again. Right back in the middle of your nose. Wrinkle up your nose again. Shoo him off. Wrinkle it up hard. Hold it just as tight as you can. Okay, he flew away. You can relax your face. Notice that when you scrunch up your nose, your cheeks and your mouth and your forehead and your eyes all help you, and they get tight, too. So when you relax your nose, your whole face relaxes, too, and that feels good. Oh-oh! This time that old fly has come back, but this time he's on your forehead. Make lots of wrinkles. Try to catch him between all those wrinkles. Hold it tight, now. Okay, you can let go. He's gone for good. Now you can just relax. Let your face go smooth, no wrinkles anywhere. Your face feels nice and smooth and relaxed.

Stomach

Hey! Here comes a cute baby elephant. But he's not watching where he's going. He doesn't see you lying there in the grass, and he's about to step on your stomach. Don't move. You don't have time to get out of the way. Just get ready for him. Make your stomach very hard. Tighten up your stomach muscles real tight. Hold it. It looks like he is going the other way. You can relax now. Let your stomach go soft. Let it be as relaxed as you can. That feels so much better. Oops, he's coming this way again. Get ready. Tighten up your stomach. Real hard. If he steps on you when your stomach is hard, it won't hurt. Make your stomach into a rock. Okay, he's moving away again, You can relax now. Kind of settle down, get comfortable, and relax. Notice the difference between a tight stomach and a relaxed one. That's how we want it to feel, nice and loose and relaxed. You won't believe this, but this time he's really coming your way and no turning around. He's headed straight for you. Tighten up. Tighten hard. Here he comes. This is really it. You've got to hold on tight. He's stepping on you. He's stepped over you. Now he's gone for good. You can relax completely. You're safe. Everything is okay, and you can feel nice and relaxed.

This time imagine that you want to squeeze through a narrow fence and the boards have splinters on them. You'll have to make yourself very skinny if you're going to make it through. Suck your stomach in. Try to squeeze it up against your backbone. Try to be as skinny as you can. You've got to get through. Now relax. You don't have to be skinny now. Just relax and feel your stomach being warm and loose. Okay, let's try to get through that fence now. Squeeze up your stomach. Make it touch your backbone. Get it real small and tight. Get as skinny as you can. Hold tight, now. You've got to squeeze through. You got through that skinny little fence and no splinters. You can relax now. Settle back and let your stomach come back out where it belongs. You can feel really good now. You've done fine.

Legs and Feet

Now pretend that you are standing barefoot in a big, fat mud puddle. Squish your toes down deep into the mud. Try to get your feet down to the bottom of the mud puddle. You'll probably need your legs to help you push. Push down, spread your toes apart, and feel the mud squish up between your toes. Now step out of the mud puddle. Relax your feet. Let your toes go loose and feel how nice that is. It feels good to be relaxed. Back into the mud puddle. Squish your toes down. Let your leg help push your feet down. Push your feet. Hard. Try to squeeze that mud puddle dry. Okay. Come back out now. Relax your feet, relax your legs, relax your toes, It feels so good to be relaxed. No tenseness anywhere. You feel kind of warm and tingly.

Conclusion

Stay as relaxed as you can. Let your whole body go limp and feel all your muscles relax. In a few minutes I will ask you to open your eyes, and that will be the end of this session. As you go through the day, remember how good it feels to be relaxed. Sometimes you have to make yourself tighter before you can be relaxed, just as we did in these exercises. Practice these exercises every day to get more and more relaxed. A good time to practice is at night, after you have gone to bed and the lights are out and you won't be disturbed. It will help you get to sleep. Then, when you are a really good relaxer, you can help yourself relax here at school. Just remember the elephant, or the jawbreaker, or the mud puddle and you can do our exercises and nobody will know. Today is a good day and you are ready to go back to class feeling very relaxed. You've worked hard in here, and it feels good to work hard. Very slowly, now, open your eyes and wiggle your muscles around a little. Very good. You've done a good job. You're going to be a super relaxer.

References

Carkhuff, R. R. (1969). *Helping and Human Relations*, vol. 1. New York: Holt, Rinehart, and Winston.

Krumholtz, J. D., and Thoresen, C. E. (1969). *Behavioral Counseling: Cases and Techniques*. New York: Holt, Rinehart & Winston.

Lazarus, A. A. (1971). *Behavior Therapy and Beyond*. New York: McGraw-Hill.

Lazarus, A. A., and Abramovitz, A. (1962). "The Use of Emotive Imagery in the Treatment of Children's Phobias." *Journal of Afentat Science* 108:191–195.

Woody, R. H. (1971). *Psychobehavioral Counseling and Therapy. Integrating Behavioral and Insight Techniques*. New York: Appleton-Century-Crofts.

ROLE PLAYING

"Role Playing" by Richard L. Levinson, Jr., and Jack Herman

(From *Play Therapy Techniques* by C. E. Schaefer and D. M. Congelosi. Copyright © 1993 by Jason Aronson and reprinted with permission.)

The goal of child psychotherapy is to help alleviate a child's difficulty in affective, cognitive, or behavioral areas that impede developmental adaptations. According to Dodds (1985), child psychotherapy "is designed to change the child in some way either to ease internal pain, change undesirable behavior or improve relationships between the child and other people who are important in the child's life" (p. 15). Interventions typically have ranged from the direct type, for example, analytic, behavioral, client-centered, and family therapies, to the indirect type, which include consultation and "parent counseling" (Dodds 1985), as well as other methods.

As in adult psychotherapy, the relationship between therapist and child is crucial in order to set the stage for the intervention to have a successful outcome. There must be a working alliance and the establishment of a supportive, nonjudgmental atmosphere with empathic understanding, in which the child can feel respected, nonthreatened, and free to think, act (within limits), and say what he or she feels. There must be regularly scheduled sessions, ranging from one to three sessions per week. Yet psychotherapy with children differs from adult psychotherapy, in that children do not possess the cognitive abilities to assimilate that which is heavily language oriented. Harter (1977) noted that within Piaget's (1952) concept, the child is in the midst of a developmental shift from prelogical to logical thought. As Harter (1977) stated: "for it is this particular transition, and the gradual development and solidification of logical operations during the concrete operational period, that seem intimately related to the child's comprehension and construction of a logical system of emotional concepts that define the affective spheres of his/her life" (p. 421).

For this reason, play therapy techniques, as well as numerous other primarily nonlanguage-oriented methods, were developed (e.g., A. Freud 1965, Klein 1975). The therapeutic playing out of inner experience, ideas, affects, and fantasies associated with life events seems to aid the child in becoming more aware of the feelings and thoughts, conflicts, and ego dysfunctions that may underlie problematic or disturbed behaviors and affects, and this provides an opportunity for the child to revise and resolve psychological and psychosocial problems.

Reisman (1973) provided a brief, but excellent, theoretical history of play therapy. Allen (1942) believed that play therapy served to help the child become aware of his or her identity as an individual in relation to the therapist and the nature of their relationship. Moustakas (1953) reported that play therapy was "a progression [of] the child's expression of feelings" (p. 111). Anna

Freud (1965) saw a similarity between play therapy and psychoanalysis and theorized that "there is movement from surface to depth, from the interpretation of unconscious impulses, wishes, and fears or id content" (in Reisman 1973, p. III). Anna Freud believed that play therapy reduced anxiety and emotional (neurotic) disturbance by helping the child become more aware of unconscious conflicts and hidden material.

Waelder (1933) wrote an interesting and early paper on psychoanalytic play therapy, with a special emphasis on the repetition theme. Of course, Sigmund Freud (1920) was the first to posit that some forms of play are repetitious acts, possibly to gain mastery over some particular event that was anxiety producing or frustrating, by reversal of roles from passive to active. Erikson (1950) described play as a form of hallucinatory mastery over life experiences that induced feelings of anxiety and helplessness. When children use repetition or repeat an act or game, they are, in a sense, working through, possibly undoing or redoing via displacement and symbolization, and thereby articulating, assimilating, and integrating that which is unconscious and connected to a special set of circumstances. These circumstances might range from separation anxiety to protection against unconscious wishes or feelings of dread or hostility, for example, in relation to a parent.

Some children have imaginary playmates or friends; others may act out roles or take the part of a significant person in their environment. Repetition or role reversal, however, does not seem to be a pathological set of behaviors or solutions to anxiety or conflictual issues, but rather is curative, in that it serves to repair hurts and losses. It helps the child separate and individuate by inculcating a sense of mastery and competence, by giving an "illusion of accomplishment" (J. L. Herman, personal communication, February 23, 1987), and by contributing to the healthy adaptation and resolution of the normally stressful or anxiety-producing events that must occur during childhood.

It seems logical, then, that some forms of child psychotherapy incorporate techniques involving repetition. An indirect example is Gardner's Mutual Storytelling Techniques (1971). Gardner's method involves encouraging the child to tell a story into a tape recorder. According to Schaefer and Milliman (1977), "the child is asked to be guest of honor on a make-believe television program in which stories [are] to be told" (p. 38). The therapist then tells a parallel story, but after a psychoanalytic fashion, "healthier adaptations and resolutions of conflicts are introduced" (p. 38). Gardner's method is essentially a projective technique in which, with a minimum of structure, the child is asked to make up a story that is apprehended psychodynamically by the therapist and then relayed back to the child with more adaptive solutions. We know that in the process, the child is going to construct a story based on her construction of herself in relation to the world and her characteristic adaptive or maladaptive ways of emotional problem solving. The issue of Gardner's technique is that, while it may be a useful diagnostic device, it may be questionable (from a psychoanalytic standpoint) as a therapeutic technique. The psychoanalytic concept of therapy relies on creating a therapeutic climate that promotes natural, evolving, moment-to-moment spontaneous self-expression through play and verbalization, with a *minimum* of structuring and interference by the therapist. The therapist aims to enable the patient to express himself *in his own way*, in a stream-of-consciousness fashion, whether via verbalization, play, or both. The therapist's job is to help the patient expand on whatever the patient initiated, not to introduce anything new. Introducing an artificial task for the child patient, extraneous to what might be on the child's mind at the moment, is to distract the child from whatever he or she might be immediately experiencing and expressing. It is important to stay within the immediate experience and not disrupt an ongoing experiential process that might bear fruit if followed.

The therapist attempts to follow and expand on whatever the child has introduced, rather than distract the child by suggesting a game make-believe television show, even when a child may be resisting. In the latter case, the therapist attempts to follow the resistance and verbalize what it might mean, rather than to introduce a device to try to bypass it. The therapist acknowledges, clarifies, and interprets his or her understanding of the defensive reasons for the resistance, rather than trying to distract the child by introducing a new activity. The child's attention must be in the realm of everyday experience or occurrences so that there will be some connection between therapeutic interpretations and the child's incorporation of a corrective emotional experience.

The technique of role-playing has had a long history in various psychotherapeutic approaches. Traditionally, role-playing has been used by gestalt psychotherapists and in behavioral methodologies for reasons ranging from increasing emotional awareness to expanding repertoires of behaviors. Social psychological theorists such as McGuire (1961) and his "inoculation theory" have sought methods of cognitive-behavioral rehearsal to increase the individual's ability to deal with new and unfamiliar situations. Moreno (1969) utilized psychodrama, a psychotherapeutic technique of structuring, or partially structuring a real or hypothetical life situation, that the patient, along with assistants, is encouraged to dramatize in an improvisational manner while the therapist directs and comments upon the action. Perhaps the most important effort to utilize role-playing in psychotherapy was put forth by George Kelly within his Psychology of Personal Constructs. Kelly (1955) defined fixed-role therapy as "a sheer creative process in which therapist and client conjoin their talents" (p. 380). Rychlak (1973) reported that prior to fixed-role therapy, the client is asked to write a self-descriptive sketch of his own character, which the therapist then rewrites in a role "based upon what the client has said of himself," but in contrasting themes, a role that the client knows he or she can act within as "experimental fantasy" (p. 496). Fixed-role therapy is then carried out for as many as eight sessions, during which the client gains insight into the way he or she normally construes events and others, and thereafter he or she may decide to incorporate new behaviors and/or affective changes.

Within a social learning paradigm, Gottman, Gonso, and Shuler (1976) used modeling, role-playing, and behavioral rehearsal to improve social interactions among "isolated children." LaGreca (1983) discussed the efficacy of "role-play assessments" that serve to give the clinician insight into a child's repertoire of behaviors in contrived versus "structured observation formats." The contrived format is of particular interest here, in that the patient is "asked to respond to a 'pretend' situation as if the situation were really occurring" (p. 121). Kendall and Braswell (1985), in their work with impulsive children, stated that "one reason for even including role-play tasks is to heighten the child's level of emotional involvement and arousal" (p. 135). Kendall and Braswell (1985), like LaGreca (1983), also reported that "hypothetical problem situations" that are role-played should be practiced prior to real problem situations (p. 136).

Gresham (1986) routinely uses role-playing when remediating social skills deficits in children. He reported that "behavioral role play tests or performances in analogue situations have essentially become the mark of assessment in social skills research" (p. 161). Among the advantages of using role-playing is that the technique depicts "actual behavioral enactment of a skill rather than a rating or perception of that skill" (p. 161). Irwin (1983) reported that role-playing and pretending may be used as a diagnostic technique in order to discern "the child's ability to present and solve a problem, tolerance for frustration, capacity for language . . . the ability to talk about and reflect on the experience including a discussion of feelings about the product which has just been created" (p. 164).

Irwin also highlighted that role-playing gives insight into the quality of the child's ability to relate with his or her therapist.

More recently, research has focused on using role-play as a direct therapeutic intervention. Goldstein and Glick (1987) reported that successful interventions occurred from the use of role-play within their program for "anger control" for adolescents who are "chronically delinquent" (p. 13). Goldstein and Glick's intervention is based in part on the premise that these youngsters often demonstrate "impulsiveness and overreliance on aggressive means for goal attainment . . . and characteristically reason at more egocentric, concrete, and in a sense, more primitive levels of moral reasoning" (p. 13). The program for anger control includes the role-playing of situations that have led previously to inappropriate expressions of anger. Role-plays focus upon achieving insight into underlying cognitive and affective issues that are triggered either internally or externally. Trainers use modeling, clear descriptions of conflict situations, and behavioral rehearsal with repetitive demonstrations of appropriate behaviors that lead to nonaggressive, positive outcomes.

In child psychotherapy, we are not so much interested in using role-play for the traditional uses of learning and rehearsal per se, but rather for its experiential value in promoting an internal corrective emotional experience, in which repressed affects can be integrated with cognitions of the self. We contend that what has been called *catharsis* is really a form of integration and mastery since, in apparently discharging pent-up affects, the child patient is undoing via reversal of roles or identities situations that created feelings of helplessness, but now serve to create a sense of completeness and control. It is suggested that children may not be especially insightful, but are willing to directly examine problematic areas in their emotional life. As noted, the necessary cognitive, language-based structures may not be sufficiently mature to allow for direct verbal intervention. Children, especially troubled children, lack the capacity for psychosynthesis—that is, the integration of intellectual and affective data. For these reasons, the technique of role-playing in child psychotherapy is seen as a valuable aid in reducing psychopathology and increasing awareness, understanding, and mastery in children and adolescents.

Preliminary reasons for the positive potential of this method are straightforward. First, it is simple to employ and involves the child in direct, everyday experiences in which he or she has interacted. Second, although it is a verbal technique and requires some sophistication in language use and comprehension, it taps the stream of consciousness and underlying conflictual material by allowing the child to use repetition as a tool toward mastery over an event that stimulated unresolved issues or conflicts. Unlike Gardner's (1971) Storytelling Technique, role-playing with children allows for direct participation and discussion in an area of conflict, and, through controlled therapeutic guidance, an implicit insightful experience might be achieved.

Role-playing in child psychotherapy may be utilized in any number of ways. Simply, it may be of use to help the angry child, for example, become aware of possible dysphoric feelings. The child may be enlisted in a role in which one can reexperience an upsetting conversation or event, one that centers around significant relationships or strong, disturbing affects or thoughts that perhaps are related to referral questions as to why the child was initially brought to therapy. Here is a typical example:

Brief Background: This child, S., a 9.6-year-old boy, was referred for outpatient psychodiagnostic evaluation, after which an interview was conducted for about thirty minutes. He was referred for evaluation as he had expressed suicidal ideation, but would not discuss this. The following are verbatim excerpts of parts of a session, about ten minutes into the interview.

Therapist:	The previous doctor, who talked with you, S., let me know you have had thoughts of hurting yourself. Have you had thoughts like that lately?
Child:	(removing eye contact) No, not for over a year. Now I feel better because I can talk to my mommy more.
Therapist:	S., when you have had these thoughts, what are you doing at the time. I mean, where are you when you think like that?
Child:	They happen when I go to the store for my mommy.

Therapist:	What happens when you go to the store—do other boys, girls, or people bother you? Does something happen to make you afraid?
Child:	No. (becoming anxious, restless, and distracted)
Therapist:	S., let's try something here. I'm going to play, with you. I'll be your mommy and you be you.
Child:	Okay.
Therapist:	(playing the role of the mother) S., I'm sending you down to the store again.
Child:	I don't want to go.
Therapist:	You have to. Get me a quart of milk, some eggs, and a loaf of bread.
Child:	But mommy, I don't want to go again. That makes six times today—I won't go again.

(Note: At this time, the therapist is struck by S's revelations of the "sixth" time and stops the role play.)

Therapist:	Okay, let's stop here S. You said six times? Why does your mommy send you to the store so many times? Does this happen a lot?
Child:	It happens when I'm home, on weekends and nights. I don't like it.
Therapist:	When do you have thoughts of hurting yourself?
Child:	Sometimes when I'm outside or when I'm walking down those stairs. We live on the fourth floor. I just say that I'm going to jump in front of a car or off a roof.
Therapist:	You know, it must make you feel very upset to go up and down those stairs so many times a day. I wonder if you ever feel angry about having to do that?
Child:	I feel upset, but I'm not angry. I just don't want to go to the store so many times.

This information clearly demonstrates that valuable information may be obtained by both the therapist and child patient. The therapist has gained awareness of the typical situations in which these disturbing thoughts occurred, and the child has begun the process of catharsis. The child has also been given an opportunity to indirectly express his true feelings and knows consciously what is happening, but feels less threatened because he is acting within a role.

After this information is obtained, another role-play takes place, but this time the therapist may use role reversal and play the child, while the child models the therapist role character. It is within this second role-play that the therapist must reformulate, interpret, and provide clear and simple language so that the child may incorporate what he is hearing into the beginning of a corrective emotional experience. Here the therapist clearly models what he perceives the child to be feeling. Such an example follows:

Therapist:	S., let's play another game. This time I'll be you, and you play your mother.
Child:	Okay, I'll do it.
Therapist:	Okay, you tell me to go to the store, and we'll play act again.
Child:	S., go to the store and get me some cupcakes, some soda, some cigarettes, and some pie.
Therapist:	But, mommy, please, I don't want to go to the store again. You made me go five times already today.
Child:	You go or else!
Therapist:	Please, mommy, sometimes when I go, I feel awful, like sad. I don't ever get to do what I want to do.
Child:	You better go!
Therapist:	Mommy, just listen. When I go to the store, I feel upset and sad. Sometimes, I might feel angry, too, but I also feel tired, because I'm little and I have to carry those big bags up to the fourth floor. Couldn't you go? Why do I always have to go?
Child:	Well, I guess I could go sometimes.
Therapist:	Maybe if I told you sometimes I'm very angry, you'd know I don't want to go.
Child:	Yes, from now on, you and I will both go, but I'll go more.
Therapist:	Good, but I also want you to know that I sometimes feel sad or angry at other times, too—maybe we could talk about that, too.
Child:	Okay.
Therapist:	(concluding role play) Okay, S., let us stop here. Do you think you let me know how you feel?
Child:	I guess so, but I never talked about that before. I'm nervous. (starts to move around the room)
Therapist:	S., let's see if maybe we could just play now. What would you like to do?

(Session continues.)

There is precedent within the literature for using role-play as a psycho-therapeutic technique with children. Smith (1977) found that role-playing had a significant impact upon the behavior of children. Aggressive children exposed to counterattitudinal measures became less aggressive after role-playing than those children who were "adult informed" (p. 400b). Sarnoff (1976) reports of a case in which, during displaced fantasy play, the therapist acted out the role of a slave boy and used this opportunity to help make the child more aware of his anger. Although displaced fantasy play utilizes imaginary characters, role-playing relies on the child's real experience with significant others, such as parents, siblings, friends, and teachers. Even if the child cannot say "I, " role-play may be created in which children play the parts of others with whom they interact. Sarnoff (1976) stated that

> Once fantasy play has been established, it can be used as a means for working through conflicts and complexes. It is frequently wise for a therapist to approach a fantasy in terms of its affects. Often a child who cannot otherwise express his feelings can talk of them when speaking for a third person. There is an organizing and focusing effect that results from the experience of talking about a fantasy and affect in organized fashion with the therapist. (p. 1991)

Harter (1977) employed role-playing in the cognitive-behaviorally oriented psychotherapy of a 6-year-old girl. Harter believed that, following a Piagetian model, a child whose cognitive skills are a function of the concrete operations stage "cannot yet think about his/her own thinking" (p. 425). Even if logical thought is present, it is probable that

> the conceptualization of an emotional network of concepts may lag considerably behind the application of logical principle. . . . thus it is not surprising that children in the seven to ten year old range are still struggling with emotional concepts and are still subject to the kind of unidimensional all-or-none thinking that has been the focus (work). (p. 425)

Harter believed that children of the latency stage have extreme difficulty expressing contradictory emotions or "polarized feelings that seem incompatible" (p. 425). In her case study, Harter utilized role-playing to model feelings for a girl who was depressed and exhibiting lack of success in school, but would not express herself through standard play materials. Harter reported that her attempts to deal indirectly with the child's feelings were consistently hampered, especially during a game in which the child role-played her teacher, while Harter played the role of the child. Harter, in this role, had typically remained passive, modeling the child's behaviors and feelings, until one session when she spoke up and told the child what it felt like to be frustrated in school and to feel upset. Within several sessions, the child began to assimilate this type of communication of feelings through discussion, as well as blackboard drawings. Harter (1977) interpreted her success to the child's being able to concretize her "powerful but conflictual feelings," and the drawings they did "provide a concrete visualizable symbol to which we could attach real experiences" (p. 428).

Perhaps the most interesting and detailed description of the technique of role-playing within child psychotherapy was provided by Halberstadt-Freud (1975). Halberstadt-Freud conducted psychoanalytic psychotherapy with a 4-year-old girl, Lara, for a period of four years. Lara's traumatic history included the divorce of her parents, two hospitalizations for eye surgery, and suicide attempts by her mother. Her verbal expressiveness was meager and limited to one- or two-word responses; her level of play was extremely limited, in that "she assembles the play-material and piles it in a big heap without taking pleasure in this activity" and gives no expression of affect, neither "pleasure or of pain" (pp. 164–165).

As Lara's ability to interact with standard play materials was inadequate, Halberstadt-Freud employed two types of role-play as a therapeutic technique. First, standard role-play, with the child and therapist alternating roles, was used. During this type of role-play, Halberstadt-Freud took note of the actions of Lara as indicators of what she was feeling. Then, these actions were discussed and further developed within role-playing, but they were not interpreted directly. According to Halberstadt-Freud, "interpretation follows only later when reconstruction has taken place. . . . besides voicing the thoughts and feelings of the [therapist's] part he also accompanies it with clarification and interpretation wherever he sees fit" (p. 167). Second, role-playing can be further removed if it is played out through dolls. Halberstadt-Freud stated that "feelings most defended against and defenses hardest to point out can thus be visualized and verbalized in an unobtrusive way" (p. 168).

In the case of Lara, Halberstadt-Freud reported that her depression improved in three months as she "gradually expressed more feelings, both positive and negative," and, at the end of treatment, Lara was doing well in school, able to form relationships, and work through her difficult, early stages to be able to develop a "good and stable sense of self" (p. 175). Halberstadt-Freud further stated that employing role-play as a technique was valuable because, in the case of Lara, "direct interpretation of defense and content would lead to shame, withdrawal, and denial. . . . though very direct in dealing with feelings, this technique is indirect as regards ego participation or conscious awareness of the hitherto unconscious" (p. 175).

In summary, it has been shown that role-playing, a psychotherapeutic technique used with adult patients in numerous psychotherapy models, may be a useful technique in the psychotherapy of children and adolescents. Role-playing may be used in psychodynamic psychotherapy as a prerequisite to clarification and interpretation, and by cognitive-behaviorally oriented psychotherapists who may need an action-oriented method of increasing the power of a talking, reality-oriented intervention. Role-playing may be used with children whose emotional difficulties may manifest themselves in depression, hyperkinesis, or phobic reactions, for example, to dealing verbally with affects or feelings behind conditions of enuresis, aggressiveness, impulsiveness, and interpersonal difficulties. It is a significant and powerful technique for the child and adolescent psychotherapist.

Yet role-playing is not only a valuable technique within the therapist's repertoire; it provides much information that can enlighten the therapist as to the background of the child. First, role-playing gives the therapist an opportunity to view how the child construes his or her world; what impact the world has had on the child; and how the child moves toward, against, or away from it (after Horney 1945). Second, insight into how the child is treated by significant others (parents, siblings, peers, etc.) and the quality of those interactions may be noted. Finally, role-playing is a nonthreatening technique in which most any child will become engaged, even those who may be guarded, suspicious, phobic, or dysphoric. Perhaps the most vital function role-playing may serve is to immediately and unequivocally provide a direct, child-centered view of the feelings and/or affects one may be experiencing. Dramatic improvement may be seen in the matter of weeks, or months, when role-playing is employed, as the psychotherapist may quickly focus on specific issues or affective domains in which the child is experiencing some difficulty or conflict.

We have used role-playing with children and have found it to be a valuable technique and an exciting experience, in that it increases rapport and gives the child a sense of being understood, cared for, and respected. Role-playing may be employed in a variety of settings, for example, during child psychotherapy, or prior to or after a diagnostic evaluation. Future clinical research should assess the efficacy of role-playing within the psychotherapy or with difficult children, such as the silent child. Perhaps these children need to be shown, indeed, that they are waiting to be helped into helping themselves.

References

Allen, F. H. (1942). *Psychotherapy with Children*. New York: Norton.

Dodds, J. B. (1985). *A Child Psychotherapy Primer*. New York: Human Sciences.

Erickson, E. H. (1950). *Childhood and Society*. New York: Norton.

Freud, A. (1965). *Normality and Pathology in Childhood*. New York: International Universities Press.

Freud, S. (1920). *Beyond the Pleasure Principle*. New York: Norton, 1961.

Gardner, R. A. (1971). "The Mutual Storytelling Technique in the Treatment of Anger Inhibition Problems." *International Journal of Child Psychoanalysis* 1:34–64.

Goldstein, A. P., and Glick, B. (1987). *Aggression Replacement Training. A Comprehensive Intervention for Aggressive Youth*. Champaign, IL: Research Press.

Gottman, J. M., Gonso, J., and Shuler, P. (1976). "Teaching Social Skills to Isolated Children." *Journal of Abnormal Psychology* 4:179–197.

Gresham, F. M. (1986). "Conceptual Issues in the Assessment of Social Competence in Children." In *Children's Social Behavior. Developmental,*

Assessment, and Modification, ed. P. S. Strain, M. J. Gurainick, and H. M. Walker. Orlando, FL: Academic.

Halberstadt-Freud, L. (1975). "Technical Variations in the Psychoanalytic Treatment of a Pre-School Child." *Israel Annals of Psychiatry and Related Disciplines* 13:162–176.

Harter, S. (1977). "A Cognitive-Developmental Approach to Children's Expression of Conflicting Feelings and a Technique to Facilitate Such Expression in Play Therapy." *Journal of Consulting and Clinical Psychology* 45:417–432.

Horney, K. (1945). *Our Inner Conflicts*. New York: Norton.

Irwin, E. C. (1983). "The Diagnostic and Therapeutic Use of Pretend Play." In *Handbook of Play Therapy*, ed. C. E. Schaefer and K. J. O'Connor. New York: Wiley.

Kelly, G. A. (1955). *The Psychology of Personal Constructs*. Vol. 2: *Clinical Diagnosis and Psychotherapy*. New York: Norton.

Kendall, P. C., and Braswell, L. (1985). *Cognitive Behavioral Therapy for Impulsive Children*. New York: Guilford.

Klein, M. (1975). *The Psycho-Analysis of Children*. New York: Free Press.

La Greca, A. M. (1983). "Interviewing and Behavioral Observations." In *Handbook of Clinical Child Psychology*, ed. C. E. Walker and M. C. Roberts. New York: Wiley.

McGuire, W. J. (1961). "The Effectiveness of Supportive and Refutational Defenses in Immunizing and Restoring Beliefs against Persuasion." *Sociometry* 24:184–197.

Moreno, J. (1969). *Psychodrama*. New York: Beacon House.

Moustakas, C. E. (1953). *Children in Play Therapy*. New York: McGraw Hill.

Piaget, J. (1952). *The Origins of Intelligence*. New York: Norton.

Reisman, J. M. (1973). *Principles of Psychotherapy with Children*. New York: Wiley.

Rychlak, J. F. (1973). *Introduction to Personality and Psychotherapy. A Theory-Construction Approach*. Boston: Houghton Mifflin.

Sarnoff, C. (1976). *Latency*. New York: Jason Aronson.

Schaefer, C. E., and Millman, H. L. (1977). *Therapies for Children*. San Francisco: Jossey-Bass.

Smith, C. D. (1977). "Counter Attitudinal Role-Playing and Attitude Change in Children." *Dissertation Abstracts International* 39:400–B.

Waelder, R. (1933). "The Psychoanalytic Theory of Play." *Psychoanalytic Quarterly* 2:208–224.

24

Therapeutic Games

ANGER

Battaro, Harkin & David Designs, Inc.
Don't Break the Ice, Milton Bradley Company.
Exploring My Anger, Western Psychological Services.
The Anger Control Game, Childswork/Childsplay.
Breaking the Chains of Anger, Western Psychological Services.
Furious Fred, Western Psychological Services.
The Angry Monster Machine, Childswork/Childsplay.

ANXIETY

The Anxiety Management Game, Childswork/Childsplay.

BEHAVIOR

The Good Behavior Game, Childswork/Childsplay.
The Helping, Sharing, and Caring Game, Western Psychological Services.
The Talking, Feeling, Doing Game, Western Psychological Services.

CHARACTER/MORALS

The Odyssey Islands Game, Childswork/Childsplay.

COGNITIVE SKILLS

Bop It, Parker Bros., Beverly, MA.
Captain's Log, BrainTrain, Richmond, VA.
Personal Trainer, BrainTrain, Richmond, VA.
Simon, Milton Bradley, Springfield, MA.
Smart Driver, BrainTrain, Richmond, VA.
Sound Smart, BrainTrain, Richmond, VA.

COMMUNICATION

Communicate, Western Psychological Services.
Lifestories, Western Psychological Services.
The Ungame, Western Psychological Services.
The Storytelling Card Game, Western Psychological Services.
The Parent Report Card for Children, Western Psychological Services.
The Talking, Feeling and Doing Game, Childsworth/Childsplay.

DEATH

The Goodbye Game, Childswork/Childsplay.

DEPRESSION

Bounce-Back, ChildsworkChildsplay.
Chicken Soup for the Kid's Soul, Childswork Childsplay

DIVORCE

My 2 Homes, Childswork/Childsplay.

FAMILY ISSUES

DUPLO HOME, Western Psychological Services.

LIFE SKILLS

Attitude Adjustment in a Box, Childswork/Childsplay.
Clear Thinking, Childswork/Childsplay.
Bounce Back, Childswork/Childsplay.
The Coping Skills Game, Childswork/Childsplay.

MOTIVATION

Bounce Back, Childswork/Childsplay.
Never Say Never, Childswork/Childsplay.

RELAXATION

Stop, Relax, and Think, Childswork/Childsplay.

ROLE-PLAYING

Social Skills Role-Playing Masks, Childswork/Childsplay.

SELF-CONTROL

The Self-Control Game, Western Psychological Services.
Teaching Self Control, Childswork/Childsplay.
The Stop, Think, and Go Bears Self-Control Game, Childswork/Childsplay.

SELF-CONFIDENCE

The Bridge of Self-Confidence Game, Western Psychological Services.

SELF-ESTEEM

Self-Esteem Game, Childswork/Childsplay.
The Dinosaur's Journey to High Self-Esteem, Childswork/Childsplay.
Turn Low Self-Esteem into Positive Self-Image, Childswork/Childsplay.

SEXUAL ABUSE

Teach-A-Bodies Dolls, Mission, TX.
Real People Dolls, Western Psychological Services.

SOCIAL SKILLS

The Social Skills Game, Western Psychological Services.
Personal Power! Pow! Childswork/Childsplay.

STRESS

Stress Attack, Childswork/Childsplay.
Stress Strategies, Childswork/Childsplay.
The Stress Less Game, Childswork/Childsplay.

THINKING AND FEELING

Positive Thinking Game, Childswork/Childsplay.
Futurestories, Childswork/Childsplay.
Stop Being So Mean, Childswork/Childsplay.
Clear Thinking, Childswork/Childsplay.

TOILET TRAINING

Talking Potty Dotty, Playmate Toys, Costa Mesa, CA.

CATALOGS

There are many therapeutic games designed by professionals for use in child psychotherapy. A few are listed here. For a catalog or more information, contact the following distributors:

Childswork/Childsplay
135 Dupont Street
PO Box 760
Plainview, NY 11803-0760
1-800-962-1141; Fax 1-800-262-1886

Creative Therapy Store
Western Psychological Services
12031 Wilshire Blvd.
Los Angeles, CA 90025-1251
1-800-648-8857; Fax 1-310-478-7838

Teach-A-Body Dolls
7 Doris Drive
Mission, TX 78572
1-888-228-1314, Fax 1-956-585-3089

BrainTrain
727 Twin Ridge Lane
Richmond, VA 23235
1-800-822-0538, Fax 1-804-320-0242

25

Homework Assignments

Homework Assignments grew out of managed care's strategy that patients take a more active role in their treatment to provide a quicker outcome. Homework is a technique that facilitates change outside of sessions and encourages clients to explore changes on their own.

The provider recertification form distributed by Merit Behavioral Care specifies that "patients are expected to take an active part in their own therapy, often completing assignments between sessions."

In order to help providers deal more effectively with that request, this chapter offers some suggestions for homework, as well as a list of available books that contain homework assignments.

CHALLENGING COGNITIONS

This exercise involves identifying existing patterns of cognitive distortion and replacing them with rational thinking. Clients are given the Challenging Distortions Worksheet (Table 1) and a list of Common Cognitive Distortions (Table 2). They are asked to identify their distortions and then to use the worksheet to get immediate feedback and discover their own ways to change their thinking, based on evidence-based reality. They are then asked bring the completed worksheet to the next session to discuss it with the therapist.

Table 1
Challenging Cognitions Worksheet

Initial Thought (Belief Rating 1–100):

Associated Behavior (or Behavioral Urge):

Cognitive Distortion:

Weigh the Evidence:

Challenge: (What are other possible ways of looking at this?):

From *Marital Distress* by J. H. Rathus and W. C. Sanderson. Copyright © 1999 by Jason Aronson Inc. and used with permission.

Table 2
Common Cognitive Distortions

Can you identify those cognitive distortions that apply to you?

- *All or Nothing Thinking:* Either your behavior is perfect or it is awful. Things are either black or white.

- *Emotional Reasoning:* You imagine that negative emotions are real (i.e., John just doesn't like me).

- *Ignoring the Positive:* You disqualify positive experiences as if they don't count, yet hold on to negative beliefs (i.e., I am just unlucky. The fact that my boss gave me a raise is a quirk).

- *Magical Thinking:* Thinking that if you do something or don't do something, it will cause some problem in someone else's life (i.e., if I step on this crack in the sidewalk, so and so will get sick).

- *Maximization or Catastrophizing:* Making a mountain out of a mole hill.

- *Minimization:* Making a mole hill out of a mountain.

Table 2
Common Cognitive Distortions (*continued*)

- *Negative Interpretation*: You assume that someone is acting negatively toward you without checking it out.

- *Negative Labeling*: Attaching names to errors rather than describing the event. "I am stupid because I forgot to lock the door."

- *Overgeneralization*: Taking one event and viewing it as a pattern that never ends.

- *Personalization*: Giving yourself credit for being the cause of a negative or positive event for which you are not really responsible (i.e., I didn't remind her, so she left the car unlocked).

- *Personification*: A form of projection in which the desirable or undesirable properties of reality are attributed to some other person, even if they are unrelated to what happened (i.e., you send a letter to someone, which is not delivered, and you accuse someone else of intercepting the letter).

- *Shoulds*: Using the word *should* to motivate yourself and others. Using *should* directed at yourself creates guilt. When directed at others, it results in anger and frustration.

From *Marital Distress* by J. H. Rathus and W. C. Sanderson. Copyright © 1999 by Jason Aronson Inc. and used with permission.

DEPRESSION

Clients are given a list of Suggested Pleasurable Activities (Table 3) and requested to engage at least one activity for the week in order to expand the client's interests. Clients are also given a Pleasurable Activities Self-Monitoring Form (Table 4) to record their feelings before and after the event, as well as their sense of self-mastery and pleasure.

The client may also be asked to keep a Thought Record (Table 5) of automatic thoughts during an upsetting event and a list of Common Cognitive Distortions of Depression (Table 6). The Thought Record is used to identify and rate the upsetting event, the associated emotions, and automatic thoughts, then to replace them with rational responses. Instructions are provided for identifying the distortions and building a rational response.

Homework may incorporate use of an integrated therapist-client package on *Overcoming Depression* by Gary Emery, New Harbinger Publications, Oakland, CA, which includes a therapist treatment protocol and client manual of exercises and worksheets.

Table 3
Suggested Pleasurable Activities

1. Tend the garden.	41. Pray.
2. Listen to music.	42. Have a pleasant daydream.
3. Read a book.	43. Take a bath.
4. Go for a walk in a natural setting, such as the woods or a park.	44. Contemplate your career path.
5. Watch a movie.	45. Start a collection (of books, coins, dolls, etc.).
6. Help someone.	46. Go camping.
7. Watch sports.	47. Arrange flowers.
8. Exercise.	48. Chop wood.
9. Play a board game.	49. Go to a concert.
10. Watch children play.	50. Redecorate a part of your home.
11. Play cards.	51. Educate yourself in some aspect of a profession you like.
12. Ride a bicycle.	52. Write a poem.
13. Go for a run.	53. Play with an animal.
14. Visit a friend.	54. Go to a party.
15. Call someone on the phone.	55. Go scuba diving.
16. Sing a song.	56. Do volunteer work.
17. Play a musical instrument.	57. Go bowling.
18. Play a computer game.	58. Go to the theater.
19. Surf the Internet.	59. Get dressed up.
20. Watch the sun rise or set.	60. Play chess.
21. Draw or paint outdoors.	61. Go skating.
22. Take photographs.	62. Go sailing.
23. Write a letter.	63. Plan a trip.
24. Visit a new place.	64. Join a club.
25. Go to an amusement park.	65. Play a musical instrument.
26. Dance.	66. Go sightseeing.
27. Go for a car ride.	67. Join a discussion group.
28. Build a model.	68. Write in your journal.
29. Fix something that is broken.	69. Go on a picnic.
30. Go to a museum.	70. Do a crossword puzzle.
31. Learn a new craft.	71. Read the Bible.
32. Walk on the beach.	72. Go to a religious service.
33. Solve a brainteaser.	73. Go horseback riding.
34. Make a videotape.	74. Put together a jigsaw puzzle.
35. Go to the library.	75. Study your schoolwork.
36. Meditate.	76. Bird-watch.
37. Listen to a relaxation tape.	77. Repair something.
38. Go hiking.	78. Participate in a discussion.
39. Go fishing.	79. Read the newspaper.
40. Go swimming.	

Table 23–3.
Suggested Pleasurable Activities (*continued*)

80. Do an activity with other children.
81. Play a game of pool.
82. Perform a community service.
83. Look at the night sky.
84. Go out for ice cream.
85. Figure out how something works.
86. Go skiing.
87. Play golf.
88. Walk around the city.
89. Go to the zoo.
90. Go to the aquarium.
91. Go to a mall.
92. Invite a friend to visit.
93. Go to the mountains.
94. Tell a joke.
95. Do yardwork.
96. Play a word game.
97. Play Frisbee.
98. Tell a story.
99. Compliment someone.
100. Sew.
101. Give to charity.
102. Do woodworking.
103. Watch television.
104. Listen to talk radio.
105. Look at the stars through a telescope.
106. Have your fortune told.
107. Brush your hair.
108. Practice yoga.
109. Go to a martial arts class.
110. Rake the leaves.
111. Go to a bookstore.
112. Go window shopping.
113. Finish some task you have been putting off.
114. Observe animals in the wild.
115. Go to the ballet.
116. Fly a kite.
117. Have a conversation.
118. Learn a new song.
119. Sit on the porch and watch the world.
120. Organize something (your closet, books, music, tools, etc.).
121. Send someone a fax or e-mail.
122. Go to sleep on clean sheets.
123. Invent a healthful drink.
124. Visit a planetarium.
125. Play tennis.
126. Play a lawn game (croquet, badminton).
127. Experience your five senses, one by one.
128. Dress up in a disguise.
129. Smile.
130. Prepare a lovely table for a meal.
131. Look at beautiful pictures in a book.
132. Hug someone.
133. Listen to the rain.
134. Walk in the rain, stepping in puddles.
135. Skip.
136. Go on the swings.
137. Eat something sweet.
138. Buy or make someone a present.
139. Throw a party.
140. Buy or make yourself a present.
141. Get a pet (with your parent's permission).
142. Go for a long walk with your dog.
143. Learn how to work an electronic device (cellular phone, VCR, computer, answering machine, etc.).
144. Install a new computer program.
145. Read interesting entries in the encyclopedia.
146. Refinish a piece of furniture.
147. Play baseball.

148. Act.
149. Play football.
150. Put lotion on your body.
151. Take a shower.
152. Go to a video arcade.
153. Play volleyball.
154. Get a good night's sleep.
155. Carry out an assertiveness exercise.

156. Go for a train ride along a scenic route.
157. Visit a relative.
158. Talk politics.
159. Conduct an experiment.
160. Play soccer.
161. Practice listening well to another person.
162. Make someone laugh.

Table 4
Pleasurable Activities Self-Monitoring Form

Date:

Time:

Activity: _____

_____

Intensity of Emotion Ratings

0 ------------- 25 ------------- 50 ------------- 75 ------------- 100
None   Mild   Moderate   Intense   Very Intense

	Before		After	
	Feeling	Rating	Feeling	Rating
Feelings	_____	_____	_____	_____
	_____	_____	_____	_____
	_____	_____	_____	_____
	_____	_____	_____	_____

Sense of Mastery: _____

Sense of Pleasure: _____

Table 5
Automatic Thought Log
Fill out when you have a negative feeling or if a negative feeling becomes worse.

1. Feeling
   How do you feel now? Check ✔ and rate how much on a scale of 0 (usual) to 100 (worst I can imagine).

   Anxious – (   )
   Sad   – (   )
   Guilty   – (   )
   Angry   – (   )
   Other   – (   )   Specify which one _____

2. Situation
   What were you doing when you felt this way?

3. Automatic Thought
   What went through your mind that could have made you feel this way? List all thoughts here and rate each thought on how much you believe it — 0 (not at all) to 100 (completely).

4. Behavior
   What did you do? How did you cope with the situation?

Table 6
Common Cognitive Distortions of Depression

1. Black or White Thinking: Seeing things as either black or white, rather than in shades of gray.

Examples of black and white thinking when depressed: Feeling that if you are not perfect, then you are a complete failure; believing that if you do not have total control over a situation, then you are helpless; feeling that your relationships are either "all good" or "all bad."

2. Overgeneralizing: Erroneously assuming that the specifics of one case are true of other cases.

Examples of overgeneralizing when depressed: Because you perform poorly in one situation, you erroneously view yourself as incompetent in other situations. Because a partner rejects you, you feel that no one will ever love you. Because your parent was critical of you, you feel that all authority figures are critical of you. Because something bad happened in one situation, you decide that all similar situations are hopeless.

3. Focusing on the Negative: Focusing on the negative aspects of a situation and ignoring the positive aspects, so that you see the situation as more negative than it is realistically.

Examples of focusing on the negative when depressed: You focus only on the bad aspects of yourself, the world, or the people around you, ignoring the good aspects. You focus only on the ways you lack control in a situation, rather than on the ways you could (and should) exert control. You focus on the ways you failed to cope with a challenge, rather than acknowledging the ways you succeeded in coping.

4. Jumping to Conclusions: Jumping to a conclusion without enough evidence to do so, when other conclusions are also possible.

Examples of jumping to conclusions when depressed: You notice a physical symptom and assume you have a serious illness. You hear a noise in the house, and assume that a criminal has broken in. A friend breaks a date, and you assume that the person no longer wants to be your friend. Your girlfriend is late coming home, and you assume that she has gotten into a car accident.

5. Catastrophizing: Thinking "what if" bad things happen—usually at great length and in imaginative detail.

Examples of catastrophizing: You vividly imagine something bad happening. You experience a manageable event as catastrophic. You imagine the worst possible outcome, and then you play it out again and again in your mind.

From *Cognitive-Behavioral Treatment of Depression* by J. S. Klosko and W. C. Sanderson. Copyright © 1999 by Jason Aronson Inc. and used with permission.

ANGER

Children can be given examples of Positive and Negative Aspects of Anger Expression (Table 7) to think about during the week and discuss at the next session. The Anger Worksheet (Table 8) can be given to clients to fill out at home and bring back, to address further issues rather than blame each other.

Table 7
The Steps to Constructing a Rational Response

Automatic Thoughts

_____

_____

Rate belief in automatic thoughts (0–100):

What evidence do you have to support your automatic thoughts?

What evidence do you have against your automatic thoughts?

What are some alternative explanations?

Have you made any cognitive distortions?

Can you design a test of your automatic thoughts?

Have you identified a realistic problem? If so, go through the steps of the problem-solving exercise, and write the results here. What solution have you chosen? What steps can you take to carry out this solution?

Has one of your schemas been triggered? Which one? What do you need to do to battle the schema in this case?

Summarized rational response: _____

_____

_____

Rerate belief in automatic thoughts (0–100) _____

From *Cognitive-Behavioral Treatment of Depression* by J. S. Klosko and W. C. Sanderson. Copyright © 1999 by Jason Aronson Inc. and used with permission.

Table 8
Potential Positive and Negative Aspects of Anger Expression

Positive Aspects of Anger Expression
- Signaling to oneself that a right or standard has been violated.
- Motivating oneself for action toward protecting rights or values.
- Maintaining self-respect.
- Getting one's way.
- Gaining a friend's attention.
- Punishing a partner.
- Quieting a partner or avoiding an uncomfortable topic.
- Communicating strong feelings.
- Providing a sense of empowerment.
- Releasing tension.

Negative Aspects of Anger Expression (short term)
- Hurting a person's feelings.
- Frightening a friend.
- Saying something one later regrets.
- Provoking an escalation of conflict.
- Driving a friend away.
- Failing to resolve a problem.
- Causing an embarrassing situation (e.g., if in public).
- Sabotaging pleasant occasions or important events.
- Feeling *dis*empowered or out of control.
- Exacerbating one's own negative mood state.

Negative Aspects of Anger Expression (long term)
- Being a partner who is viewed as unapproachable or who causes others to "walk on eggshells."
- Creating distance in the relationship.
- Emotionally scarring one's partner.
- Accumulating a roster of unresolved marital conflicts.
- Creating a poor environment for your family.
- Frightening other children.
- Causing difficulty at school.
- Alienating outside relationships.
- Increasing stress.
- Creating health problems.

From *Marital Distress* by J. H. Rathus and W. C. Sanderson. Copyright © 1999 by Jason Aronson Inc. and used with permission.

Table 9
Anger Worksheet

Situation: Date:

Warning Signs of Increasing Anger:

Physical:

Cognitive:

Behavioral:

Environmental:

Behavior (or behavioral urges):

From *Marital Distress* by J. H. Rathus and W. C. Sanderson. Copyright © 1999 by Jason Aronson Inc. and used with permission.

OBSESSIVE-COMPULSIVE DISORDER

This exercise also uses the Challenging Cognitions Worksheet (Table 1), combined with a list of Common Misconceptions Observed in Obsessive-Compulsive Disorder (Table 10). Clients can identify their irrational thoughts and behaviors and reframe them with more rational responses.

Homework may incorporate use of an integrated therapist-client package on *Overcoming Obsessive-Compulsive Disorder* by Gail Sketekee, New Harbinger Publications, Oakland, CA, which includes a therapist treatment protocol and client manual of exercises and worksheets.

Table 10
Common Misconceptions Observed in Obsessive-Compulsive Disorder

1. **Catastrophizing**

   I will have a nervous breakdown if the anxiety continues any longer.

   My family will die in a fire unless I unplug all the electrical appliances in the house.

   If Michael didn't call to say he will be late, it means that he is dead.

2. **Overestimating the risk of harm or danger**

   I will become ill if I use the public restroom.

   I'd better wash my hands over and over again; otherwise, I am liable to fall sick.

   Planes crash, so Michael shouldn't fly.

3. **Underestimating ability to cope**

   I am no good at handling my anxiety.

   I am not sure I remembered to check, so let me check again.

   I don't trust myself to decide one way or the other. What if I am wrong?

4. **Personalization/self-blame**

   If Mom dies, it will be my fault.

   I had better call and check to see if he is alive, or else I will be responsible for his death.

   If I don't check the gas stove to see that it is off, it is as good as saying that I want him dead.

5. **Negative labeling**

   I am a sinner because I imagine my husband dying.

   I am wicked, evil, wretched, a degenerate.

   I am weak.

6. **All-or-nothing thinking**

   If I make even one mistake, it means I am no good.

   Even the slightest anxiety is intolerable.

   Everything must be in perfect order; even the slightest disorder is not okay.

7. **Magical reasoning**

   My brother will die if I touch the knife.

   If I say "safe Mike," I will prevent his death.

Table 10
Common Misconceptions Observed in Obsessive-Compulsive Disorder
(*continued*)

8. **Should and must statements**

I should be able to control my obsessions.

I should never make a mistake.

I should not feel anxious.

From L. K. McGinn and W. C. Sanderson, *Treatment of Obsessive-Compulsive Disorder.* Copyright © 1999 by Jason Aronson Inc.; adapted with permission.

PHOBIAS

There are multiple parts to this assignment. First ask the child to read or read to him/her "Things You Should Know about Social Phobia" (Table 11) and then ask him/her to complete the "Phobic Types Questionnaire" (Table 12), and next, "Phobic Objects, Situations, and Activities Questionnaire" (Table 13). Then complete the following questionnaires (Tables 14–17) in order.

Homework may incorporate use of an integrated therapist-client package on *Overcoming Agoraphobia and Panic Disorder* by Elke Zuercher-White, *Overcoming Generalized Anxiety Disorder* by John White, or *Overcoming Specific Phobias* by Edmund J. Bourne, New Harbinger Publications, Oakland, CA, which includes a therapist treatment protocol and client manual of exercises and worksheets.

Table 11
Things You Should Know about Social Phobia

1. It is a way of relating to the world.

2. At certain times, we all feel shy, and people who do not feel shy can often be inappropriate.

3. The reason people feel shy is not completely known.

4. People with social phobias are afraid of what other people will think about them.

5. Self-monitoring can provide information about your life to help overcome the problem.

From *Social Phobia* by R. C. Rapee and W. C. Sanderson. Copyright © 1998 by Jason Aronson Inc. and used with permission.

Table 12
Phobic Types Questionnaire

Check	Rank	Type of phobia
_____	_____	Animals: _____
_____	_____	Insects: _____
_____	_____	Heights: _____
_____	_____	Storms: _____
_____	_____	Water: _____
_____	_____	Blood: _____
_____	_____	Needles: _____
_____	_____	Dental work: _____
_____	_____	Seeing a doctor: _____
_____	_____	Bridges: _____
_____	_____	Driving: _____
_____	_____	Enclosed places: _____
_____	_____	Flying: _____
_____	_____	Elevators: _____
_____	_____	Choking: _____
_____	_____	Vomiting: _____
_____	_____	Getting a disease: _____
_____	_____	Other: _____

Table 13
Phobic Objects, Situations, and Activities Questionnaire

Type of Phobia: _____

Please use this scale to rate your *fear*.

0-----1-----2-----3-----4-----5-----6-----7-----8-----9-----
No fear   Mild fear   Moderate   Strong   Severe

Please use the following scale to make your rating of *avoidance*:

0-----1-----2-----3-----4-----5-----6-----7-----8-----9-----

| No | Some | Often | Mostly | Always |
| Avoidance | Avoidance | Avoid | Avoid | Avoid |

Objects, Situations, or Activities	Fear (0–10)	Avoidance (0–10)
_____	_____	_____
_____	_____	_____
_____	_____	_____
_____	_____	_____
_____	_____	_____
_____	_____	_____
_____	_____	_____
_____	_____	_____
_____	_____	_____

Table 14
Methods of Coping Questionnaire

Type of Phobia: _____

Check	Method of Coping:

_____ Avoid it _____

_____ Escape _____

_____ Keep my distance when in its presence _____

_____ Avert my attention _____

_____ Wear protective garments _____

_____ Have a safe person with me (who?) _____

_____ Have a safe object with me (what?) _____

_____ Talk to myself (what?) _____

_____ Pray _____

_____ Prepare for encounters (how?) _____

_____ Freeze or stand still _____

_____ Take medicine/alcohol/drugs (specify) _____

_____ Try to be informed/read/learn about object or situation _____

_____ Fight off feelings _____

_____ Try to relax _____

_____ Other _____

Table 15
Fearful Thoughts Questionnaire

Type of Phobia _____

Please use this scale to rate how often the feared thought has occurred:

0-----1-----2-----3-----4-----5-----6-----7-----8-----9-----10

Never   Seldom   Half the time   Often   Always

Please use this scale to rate *how believable* the thought has been:

0-----1-----2-----3-----4-----5-----6-----7-----8-----9-----10
No Belief   Mildly   Moderately   Strongly   Completely

Fearful Thought	How Often (0–10)	Belief (0–10)
_____	_____	_____
_____	_____	_____
_____	_____	_____
_____	_____	_____
_____	_____	_____
_____	_____	_____
_____	_____	_____
_____	_____	_____

From *Social Phobia* by R. C. Rapee and W. C. Sanderson. Copyright © 1998 by Jason Aronson Inc., and used with permission.

Table 16
Phobic Sensations Questionnaire

Type of Phobia _____

Use this scale to rate the *intensity* (*strength*) and your *fear* of each sensation marked:

0- - - - -1- - - - -2- - - - -3- - - - -4- - - - -5- - - - -6- - - - -7- - - - -8- - - - -9- - - - -10

| None | Mild | Moderate | Strong | Severe |

Check	Feelings (Sensations)	Intensity (0–10)	Fear (0–10)
_____	Heart beats faster.	_____	_____
_____	Heart pounds harder.	_____	_____
_____	Breathing is faster.	_____	_____
_____	Breathing is difficult.	_____	_____
_____	Chest feels tight.	_____	_____
_____	Feel faint, dizzy, unsteady. Have you ever fainted? yes ____ no ____	_____	_____
_____	Vision changes. (How? _____)	_____	_____
_____	Weakness. Have you ever collapsed? yes ____ no ____	_____	_____
_____	Shaky or trembling.	_____	_____
_____	Numbness/tingling.	_____	_____
_____	Chills or hot flashes.	_____	_____
_____	Feeling of choking.	_____	_____
_____	Feeling detached from oneself.	_____	_____
_____	Other things seem unreal.	_____	_____
_____	Nauseous or other stomach distress. Have you ever vomited? yes ____ no ____	_____	_____
_____	Other (specify)	_____	_____

Table 17
Exposure Record Form

Immediately before the Exposure Phase, complete this page:

1. Date/Time: _____

2. Briefly describe the exposure task and whether this is the first or second, etc., time you have done it. _____

3. Please rate your anxiety level right now. (0–10) _____

4. How confident are you that you can manage this exposure? (0–10) _____

5. Before doing the exposure, imagine doing it. As you do that, briefly list (one or two words) what you fear could happen during the encounter. List each and all fears that come to mind. Then rate how believable each fear *feels* on the following scale.

0-----1-----2-----3-----4-----5-----6-----7-----8-----9-----10
No belief   Mildly   Moderately   Strongly   Completely

Predicted fears and rated beliefs (0–10)

_____

_____

_____

_____

6. Now re-imagine the encounter. However, this time, instead of listing the feared events, list the most likely challenges you will face (be objective) and how you intend to cope with these. Remember to include that you might feel fear or doubt, if that is most likely; indicate also how you plan to manage these feelings. Briefly describe the alternative prediction below. Finally, rate how believable it feels, using the 0–10 scale. Immediately after the encounter, complete these questions:

   1. Did any of the things you feared happen?
   2. Did any other fears come up during the encounter?
   3. What physical sensations did you experience during the encounter?
   4. Did any of the sensations frighten you?
   5. How did you try to cope with the encounter? (List all ways.)
   6. Why did you stop the exercise?

Other comments?

26

Bibliotherapy

BIBLIOTHERAPY FOR CHILDREN

Self-Help Books

Anger

Aborn, A. (1994). *Everything I Do You Blame on Me!* Plainview, NY: Childswork/ Childsplay. (A sensitive approach to anger issues in children.)

Crary, E. (1992). *I'm Mad.* Seattle, WA: Parenting Press. (How to handle anger constructively.)

———. (1994). *I'm Furious.* Seattle, WA: Parenting Press. (Ways to express and eliminate anger.)

———. (1992). *I'm Frustrated.* Seattle, WA: Parenting Press. (Dealing with frustration.)

Eastman, M., and Rozen, S. C. (1994). *Taming the Dragon in Your Child.* New York: Wiley. (Solutions for breaking the anger cycle.)

Namka, L. (1995). *The Mad Family Gets Their Mads Out.* Tucson, AZ: Talk, Trust and Feel Therapeutics. (Helpful ways for getting rid of anger without hurting others.)

Shapiro, L. E. (1995). *Sometimes I Like to Fight, but I Don't Do It Much Anymore.* Plainview, NY: Childswork/Childsplay. (How children can control anger and fighting.)

———. (1994). *The Very Angry Day That Amy Didn't Have.* Plainview, NY: Childswork/Childsplay. (Learn alternatives to getting angry.)

Shore, H. (1995). *Angry Monster Workbook.* Plainview, NY: Childswork/ Childsplay. (Taming the angry monster within.)

Sobel, M. (2000). *The Penguin Who Lost Her Cool.* Plainview, NY: Childswork/ Childsplay. (How to control your temper.)

Tower, T. (1995). *The Self-Control Patrol Workbook.* Plainview, NY: Childswork/ Childsplay. (Learn to think before you act.)

Anxiety

Balter, L. (1989). *Linda Saves the Day.* New York: Barron's. (Confronting your feelings.)

Baumgart, K. (1998). *Don't Be Afraid, Tommy.* Waukesha, WI: Little Tiger. (Overcoming your fears.)

Lamb-Shapiro, J. (2000). *The Bear Who Lost His Sleep.* Plainview, NY: Childswork/Childsplay. (Reduce anxiety by reasoning things out.)

Moser, A. (1991). *Don't Feed the Monster on Tuesdays!* Kansas City, MO: Landmark Editions. (Develop a stronger self-esteem with positive self-talk.)

Nash, M. S. (2000). *The Lion Who Lost His Roar.* Plainview, NY: Childswork/ Childsplay. (Techniques to overcome common fears.)

Werner-Watson, J. (1971). *Sometimes I'm Afraid.* New York: Golden. (Fear lessens when it is discussed and not hidden inside.)

Attention Deficit/Hyperactivity Disorder

Moss, D. H. (1989). *Shelley, the Hyperactive Turtle.* Kensington, MD: Woodbine House. (Understanding ADHD.)

Quinn, P. O., and Stern, J. M. (1991). *Putting on the Brakes.* New York: Magination. (The causes of AD/HD and how to cope with them.)

Shapiro, L. E. (1993). *Sometimes I Drive My Mom Crazy, but I Know She's Crazy about Me.* Plainview, NY: Childswork/Childsplay. (Everyday issues of children with AD/HD.)

Shapiro, L. E., and Shore, H. M. (1994). *Jumpin' Jake Settles Down.* Plainview, NY: Childswork/Childsplay. (Activities to help you think before you act.)

Behavior Problems

Lamb-Shapiro, J. (2000). *The Hyena Who Lost Her Laugh.* Plainview, NY: Childswork/Childsplay. (Optimistic thinking can change your attitude.)

Shapiro, L. E. (1997). *Don't Be Difficult Workbook.* Plainview, NY: Childswork/ Childsplay. (Workbook for oppositional children.)

Tower, T., and Van Patter, B. (1995). *Self-Control Patrol Workbook.* Plainview, NY: Childswork/Childsplay. (Teaches children to cope with problems.)

Bereavement

Brown, L . (1996). *When Dinosaurs Die*. Boston, MA: Little, Brown. (Coping with death.)

Hipp, E. (1995). *Help for the Hard Times*. Center City, MN: Hazelden. (Getting over the death of a loved one.)

Moser, A. (1996). *Don't Despair on Thursdays!* Kansas City, MO: Landmark. (Tackles issues of loss and death.)

Romain, T. (1999). *What on Earth Do You Do When Someone Dies?* Minneapolis, MN: Free Spirit. (Answers to questions about the death of a loved one.)

Communication

Delis-Abrams, A. (1991). *The Feelings Storybook: ABC Feelings*. Idaho: Adage. (Demonstrates how to express feelings.)

Conduct

Brown, M., and Krensky, S. (1983). *Perfect Pigs: An Introduction to Manners*. Boston, MA: Little Brown & Co. (Learning about manners can be fun.)

Moser, A. (1994). *Don't Rant and Rave on Wednesdays!* Kansas City, MO: Landmark. (Reduce anger and control your actions.)

———. (1999). *Don't Tell a Whopper on Fridays!* Kansas City, MO: Landmark. (The importance of honesty.)

Conflict Resolution

Doyle, T. (1991). *Why Is Everybody Always Picking on Me? A Guide to Handling Bullies*. Middlebury, VT: Atrium. (How to handle bullies and resolve conflicts without violence.)

Petty, K. (1991). *Being Bullied*. New York: Barron's. (How to handle a bully.)

Romain, T. (1997). *Bullies Are a Pain in the Brain*. Minneapolis, MN: Free Spirit. (What to do about bullies.).

Divorce

Blakslee-Ives, S., Fassler, D., and Lash, M. (1988). *The Divorce Workbook*. Burlington, VT: Waterfront Books. (Understand and express emotions triggered by divorce.)

Brown, L. K., and Brown, M. (1986). *Dinosaurs Divorce*. Boston, MA: Atlantic Monthly. (Picture book to help children cope with divorce.)

Cook, J. T. (1995). *Room for a Stepdaddy*. Morton Grove, IL: A. Whitman. (Adapting to a stepparent.)

Field, M. B. (1992). *All about Divorce*. King of Prussia, PA: Center for Applied Psychology. (Importance of parent–child communication during a divorce.)

Ford, M. (1997). *My Parents Are Divorced, Too*. Washington, DC: Magination. (Shows children that divorce is quite common.)

Krementz, J. (1984). *How It Feels When Parents Divorce*. New York: Random House. (Your feelings toward divorce are normal.)

Lansky, V. (1998). *It's Not Your Fault, KoKo Bear*. Minnetonka, MN: Book Peddlers. (Don't blame yourself for your parents' divorce.)

Moser, A. (2000). *Don't Fall Apart on Saturdays!* Kansas City, MO: Landmark. (Ways to help yourself when parents divorce.)

Shore, H. (1994). *My Life Turned Upside Down, but I Turned It Rightside Up*. Plainview, NY: Childswork/Childsplay. (Meeting the challenges of divorce.)

Sinberg, J. (1978). *Divorce Is a Grown Up Problem*. New York: Avon. (Helpful information about divorce.)

Stern, Z., and Stern, E. (1997). *Divorce Is Not the End of the World; Zoe and Evan's Coping Guide for Kids*. Berkeley, CA: Tricycle. (A practical guide to divorce, written by children for children.)

Weninger, B., and Marks, A. (1995). *Good-Bye, Daddy!* New York: North-South Books. (Help in expressing feelings about separation of parents.)

Whitmore-Hickman, M. (1995). *Robert Lives with His Grandparents*. Morton Grove, IL: Albert Whitman. (A reassuring story of children being raised by their grandparents.)

Eating Disorders

Apple, R. F., and Agras, W. S. (1987). *Overcoming Eating Disorders: A Cognitive-Behavioral Treatment for Bulimia Nervosa and Binge-Eating Disorders*. San Antonio, TX: Harcourt Brace. (A guided plan to healthy eating patterns.)

Berg, F. M. (1997). *Afraid to Eat: Children and Teens in Weight Crisis*. Hettinger, ND: Healthy Weight Journal. (Break those unhealthy eating patterns.)

Ebbett, J. (1994). *The Eating Illness Workbook*. Center City, MN: Hazelden. (A blueprint of exercises for recovery.)

Elimination Disorders

Allison, A. (1984). *A Toddler's Potty Book*. Los Angeles, CA: Price Stern Sloan. (Helps teach children that using the toilet is positive.)

Galvin, M. (1989). *Clouds and Clocks: A Story for Children Who Soil*. New York: Magination. (Helps encopretic children realize they are not alone.)

Lansky, L. (1986). *Koho Bear's New Potty*. New York: Bantam. (Positive approach to helping children realize that using the toilet is a step toward independence.)

Family Issues

Davol, M. W. (1993). *Black, White, Just Right*. Morton Grove, IL: Albert Whitman & Co. (Appreciate your racial background.)

Joosse, B. M. (1982). *Nugget and Darling.* New York: Clarion Books. (Exploring jealousy and the parent–child relationship.)

Simon, N. (1976). *All Kinds of Families.* Chicago, IL: Albert Whitman. (Families are defined as people who belong together.)

Stanek, M. (1985). *All Alone after School.* Niles, IL: Albert Whitman. (Hold on until your parents get home.)

Walvoord-Girard, L. (1989). *We Adopted You, Benjamin Koo.* Niles, IL: Albert Whitman. (The difficulties of interracial adoptions.)

———. (1987). *At Daddy's on Saturday's.* Niles, IL: Albert Whitman. (A realistic story of divorce from a child's viewpoint.)

Fears

Balter, L. (1989). *Linda Saves the Day.* New York: Barrons. (Helps children learn to overcome fear.)

Fassler, J. (1971). *Don't Worry, Dear.* New York: Human Sciences. (Teaches children how to deal with fear at their own pace.)

Watson, J. W., Switzer, R. E., and Hirchberg, J. C. (1971). *Sometimes I'm Afraid.* New York: Golden. (Everybody's afraid sometimes.)

Feelings

Shapiro, L. E. (1993). *All Feelings Are Okay; It's What You Do with Them That Counts.* Plainview, NY: Childswork/Childsplay. (It's okay to express how you feel.)

Friendship

Krasilovsky, P, (1970). *The Shy Little Girl.* Boston, MA: Houghton Mifflin. (Overcome shyness and take the first step in making friends.)

Krischanitz, R. (1999). *Nobody Likes Me!* New York: North-South Books. (How to make friends.)

Marcozzi, B. A. (1995). *My Best Friend Is Me!* Plainview, NY: Childswork/Childsplay. (When you feel good about yourself, others want to be your friend.)

Zolotow, C. (1963). *A Tiger Called Thomas.* New York: Lothrup, Lee & Shepard. (Others like you for who you are.)

Hypnosis, Relaxation, and Visualization

Allen, J. S., and Klein, R. J. (1996). *Ready . . . Set . . . R.E.L.A.X.* Watertown, WI: Inner Coaching. (Tools to handle stress.)

Williams, M. (1996). *Cool Cats, Calm Kids.* California: Impact. (Guide to relaxation and stress management.)

Learning

Hernes-Silverman, S. (1998). *13 Steps to Better Grades*. Plainview, NY: Childswork/Childsplay. (Comprehensive guide to many school-related issues.)

Mosatche, H. S., and Unger, K. (2000). *Too Old for This, Too Young for That!* Minneapolis, MN: Free Spirit. (Overcoming the confusion of the middle-school years.)

Medical Issues

Anderson, M. E. (2000). *Taking Cerebral Palsy to School*. Valley Park, MO: JayJo. (Learn the facts about cerebral palsy.)

Aseltine, L., and Mueller, E. (1986). *I'm Deaf and It's Okay*. Niles, IL: Albert Whitman. (Teaches deaf children it's okay even if they live in a world without sound.)

Henry, C. S. (2000). *Taking Cystic Fibrosis to School*. Valley Park, MO: JayJo. (Understanding cystic fibrosis.)

London, J. (1992). *The Lion Who Had Asthma*. Morton Grove, IL: Albert Whitman. (Coping with breathing problems.)

Walvoord-Girard, L. (1991). *Alex, the Kid with AIDS*. Morton Grove, IL: Albert Whitman. (A school's reaction to a child with AIDS.)

Weiner, E. (1999). *Taking Food Allergies to School*. Valley Park, MO: JayJo. (Suggestions for coping with food allergies.)

White-Pirner, C. (1991). *Even Little Kids Get Diabetes*. Morton Grove, IL: Albert Whitman. (Learning to live with diabetes.)

Obsessive-Compulsive Disorder

Moritz, E. K. (1998). *Blink, Blink, Clop, Clop: Why Do We Do Things We Can't Stop?* Plainview, NY: Childswork/Childsplay. (Animal storybook describes the disorder and its symptoms.)

Parenting

Crary, E. (1993). *Without Spanking or Spoiling*. Seattle, WA: Parenting Press. (Investigating less extreme options for raising children.)

Schaefer, C. E. (1994). *How to Help Children with Common Problems*. Northvale, NJ: Jason Aronson. (A parenting guide that covers early childhood through the teen years.)

Physical Abuse

Davis, D. (1985). *Something Is Wrong at My House*. Seattle, WA: Parenting Press. (Help break the pattern of violence.)

Problem Solving

Fassler, J. (1971). *The Boy with a Problem.* New York: Human Sciences. (Seek advice from someone who cares and will listen.)

Shapiro, L. (1996). *The Kid's Solutions Workbook.* Plainview, NY: Childswork/Childsplay. (New ways to think about problems.)

Zimmerman, T. (1995). *The Problem-Solving Workbook.* Plainview, NY: Childswork/Childsplay. (A new approach to problems.)

———. (1995). *The Cooperation Workbook.* Plainview, NY: Childswork/Childsplay. (You don't have to do it alone.)

Selective Mutism

Bafrry, S. (1992). *The Boy Who Wouldn't Speak.* Toronto: Annick. (Insights into mutism.)

Self-Esteem

Carlson, N. (1988). *I Like Me!* New York: Penguin. (Feel good about yourself.)

Loomans, D. (1991) *The Lovable: In the Kingdom of Self-Esteem.* Tiburon, CA: H. J. Kramer, Starseed. (Helping children feel confident and loved.)

Loomans, D., and Loomans, J. (1994). *Full Esteem Ahead: 100 Ways to Build Self-Esteem in Children & Adults.* Tiburon, CA: H. J. Kramer. (A practical guide to increasing your self-esteem.)

Mather, A., and Weldon, L. (1991). *The Cat at the Door.* Center City, MN: Hazelden. (Short stories that promote healthy values and sense of self.)

Shapiro, L., and Shore, H. (1995). *Anybody Can Bake a Cake.* Plainview, NY: Childswork/Childsplay. (Short stories of entertainers, sports figures, and scientists who overcame obstacles and achieved success.)

Zack, L. R. (1995). *Building Self-Esteem through the Museum of I: 25 Original Projects That Explore and Celebrate the Self.* Minneapolis, MN: Free Spirit. (Twenty-five open-ended projects that build self-esteem.)

Sexual Abuse

Bean, B., and Bennett, S. (1997). *The Me Nobody Knows.* San Francisco, CA: Jossey-Bass. (How to begin to cope with sexual abuse.)

Caines, J. (1986). *Chilly Stomach.* New York: Harper & Row. (Sharing your secret feelings.)

Davis, N. (1988). *Once upon a Time: Therapeutic Stories.* MD: Oxon Hill. (Stories of physical, sexual, and emotional abuse.)

Freeman, L. (1984). *It's MY Body.* Seattle, WA: Parenting Press. (You control your own body.)

Gil, E. (1987). *I Told My Secret.* Walnut Creek, CA: Launch Press. (Answers to questions in the aftermath of abuse.)

Girard, L. W. (1984). *My Body Is Private*. Niles, IL: A. Whitman. (Your privacy rights.)

Hindman, J. (1985). *A Very Touching Book . . . for Little People and Big People*. Durkes, OR: McClure-Hindman. (What's okay and what's not okay.)

Hoke, S., and Van Patter, B. (1995). *My Body Is Mine, My Feelings Are Mine*. Plainview, NY: Childswork/Childsplay. (How to identify inappropriate touching.)

Kehoe, P. (1987). *Something Happened and I'm Scared to Tell*. Seattle, WA: Parenting Press. (Disclosure and recovery from abuse.)

Lee, I., and Sylvester, K. (1997). *When Mommy Got Hurt*. Indianapolis, IN: Kidsrights. (A story for young children about divorce.)

Loiselle, M. B., and Wright, L. (1997). *Shining Through*. Brandon, VT: Safer Society. (A guide to the healing process for girls after sexual abuse.)

McCoy, D. L. (1986). *The Secret: A Child's Story of Sex Abuse for Children Ages 7 through 12*. Knoxville, TN: Magic Lantern. (A story of father–daughter incest.)

Rape Crisis Center. (1980). *Red Flag, Green Flag People*. Fargo, ND: Rape and Abuse Crisis Center. (Different kinds of people and different kinds of touches.)

Russell, B., and Stone, B. (1986). *Do You Have a Secret?* Minneapolis, MN: CompCare. (How to get help for scary secrets.)

Spelman, C. (1997). *Your Body Belongs to You*. Morton Grove, IL: Albert Whitman. (How to say "no" to unwanted attention.)

Stowell, J., and Dietzel, M. (1987). *My Very Own Book about Me*. Spokane, WA: Lutheran Social Services. (A comprehensive book about abuse for children and parents.)

Sweet, P. E. (1981). *Something Happened to Me*. Racine, WI: Mother Courage. (Reduce the fear, shame, and confusion of abuse.)

Watcher, O. (1982). *No More Secrets for Me*. Boston: Little Brown and Company. (Stories of male and female abuse victims.)

White, L. A., and Spencer, S. L. (1998). *Take Care with Yourself*. Indianapolis, IN: Kidsrights. (Understanding, preventing, and healing from abuse.)

Wright, L., and Loiselle, M. B. (1997). *Back on Track*. Brandon, VT: Safer Society. (Help for boys dealing with sexual abuse.)

Sexuality

Dayes, F. S. (1982). *Private Zones*. New York: Warner. (Defines private body parts.)

Madras, L. (1993). *My Body, Myself for Girls*. New York: Free Market. (Explore your feelings about the changes your body is going through.)

———. (1995). *My Body, My Self for Boys*. New York: Free Market. (Address issues of puberty, body image, and sexuality.)

Spellman, C. (1997). *Your Body Belongs to You*. Morton Grove, IL: Albert Whitman. (Being hugged or kissed is your choice.)

Sleep Problems

Masurel, C., and Henry, M. H. (1994). *Good Night!* San Francisco, CA: Chronicle. (Enticing reluctant sleepyheads to bed.)

Stress Management

Gurth, M. (1991). *Earthlight*. San Francisco, CA: Harper. (Visualization for stress management.)

Moser, A. (1988). *Don't Pop Your Cork on Mondays!* Kansas City, MO: Landmark. (Explains the causes and effects of stress.)

Romain, T., and Verdick, E. (2000). *Stress Can Really Get on Your Nerves*. Minneapolis, MN: Free Spirit. (Learn how to lessen worry and stress.)

Scott-Cameron, N. (2000). *Bad Hair Day?* New York: HarperCollins. (The road to inner calm.)

Slap-Shelton, L. (1999). *Everytime I Blow My Top I Lose My Head!* Plainview, NY: Childswork/Childsplay. (Learning to relax.)

Williams, M. (1996). *Cool Cats, Calm Kids*. San Luis Obispo, CA: Impact. (Cats demonstrate their secrets to staying calm.)

School Problems

McCutcheon, R. (1998). *Get Off My Brain*. Minneapolis, MN: Free Spirit. (Help for the bored, frustrated, sick-of-school child.)

Suicide

Goldman, L. (1998). *Bart Speaks Out: Breaking the Silence on Suicide*. Los Angeles, CA: Western Psychological Services. (Develop skills for coping with suicide.)

BIBLIOTHERAPY FOR PARENTS

Self-Help Books

Abuse

Hagan, K., and Case, T. (1988). *When Your Child Has Been Molested*. New York: Harper & Row. (How to deal with problems of molestation without blaming yourself.)

Herman, J. L. (1992). *Trauma and Recovery*. New York: Basic Books. (Hope for recovery from trauma.)

Alcohol

Althauser, D. (1998). *You Can Free Yourself from Alcohol and Drugs.* Oakland, CA: New Harbinger. (A 12-step approach to recovery.)

Fanning, P., and O'Neill, J. (1996). *The Addiction Workbook.* Oakland, CA: New Harbinger. (A guide for quitting alcohol and drugs.)

Tanner, L. (1996). *The Mother's Survival Guide to Recovery.* Oakland, CA: New Harbinger. (Alcohol, drugs, and babies.)

O'Neill, J., and O'Neill, P. (1992). *Concerned Intervention.* Oakland, CA: New Harbinger. (What to do when your loved one won't quit alcohol or drugs.)

Anger

Eastman, M. (1994). *Taming the Dragon in Your Child.* New York: Wiley. (Teaching book for parents on how to diffuse a child's anger.)

McKay, M., and Fanning, P. (1996). *When Anger Hurts Your Kids.* Oakland, CA: New Harbinger. (Explores how anger expressed by parents affects children.)

Namka, L. (1995). *The Mad Family Gets Their Mads Out.* Tucson, AZ: Talk, Trust and Feel Therapeutics. (Supplies helpful ways for getting rid of anger without hurting others; includes helpful hints for managing anger.)

Anxiety

Bassete, L. (1995). *From Panic to Power.* New York: HarperCollins. (Techniques to calm your anxieties.)

Bodger, C. (1999). *Smart Guide to Relieving Stress.* New York: Wiley. (Customized plans for overcoming stress.)

Bourne, E. J. (1997). *The Anxiety and Phobia Workbook,* 2nd Ed. Oakland, CA: New Harbinger. (A comprehensive and practical guide.)

———. (1998). *Healing Fear.* Oakland, CA: New Harbinger. (Offers a range of strategies for dealing with anxiety.)

Copeland, M. E. (1998). *The Worry Control Workshop.* Oakland, CA: New Harbinger. (Exercises and self-tests for worriers.)

Dacey, J. S., and Fiore, L. B. (2000). *Your Anxious Child: How Parents and Teachers Can Relieve Anxiety in Children.* San Francisco, CA: Jossey-Bass. (Teaches anxious children coping skills; helps them build courage.)

Ellis, A. (1998). *How to Control Your Anxiety before It Controls You.* Secaucus, NJ: Carol. (Demonstrates how to control thoughts that contribute to unhealthy anxiety.)

Gerzon, R. (1997). *Finding Serenity in the Age of Anxiety.* New York: Bantam. (New insights into anxiety.)

Jacobson, E. (1978). *You Must Relax.* New York: McGraw-Hill. (Practical suggestions for reducing tension and stress.)

Jeffers, S. (1988). *Feel the Fear and Do It Anyway.* New York: Fawcett Columbine. (A humorous ten-step plan to stop negative self-talk.)

Johnson, S. (1998). *Who Moved My Cheese?* New York: Putnam. (New ways to handle changes in your work and life.)

Kopp, S. (1988). *Raise Your Right Hand Against Fear, Extend the Other One in Comparison.* Minneapolis, MN: CompCare. (How to manage your fears.)

Wetherill, M. J. (2000). *The Eye of the Storm: Discovering Inner Calm amidst Inner Pressure.* Holbrook, MA: Adams Media. (Using your inner strength to cope with pressure and anxiety.)

Wilson, R. R. (1996). *Don't Panic: Taking Control of Anxiety Attacks.* New York: HarperCollins. (A straightforward self-help program.)

Ziegler, R. G., and Ziegler, P. (1992). *Homemade Books to Help Kids Cope.* New York: Magination. (Shows how to help children write stories to participate in solutions to problems.)

Attention Deficit Disorder

Barkley, R. A. (2000). *Taking Charge of ADHD.* New York: Guilford. (Gives parents of children with ADHD information, advice, and guidance.)

Christ, J. J. (1997). *ADHD—A Teenager's Guide.* Plainview, NY: Childswork/Childsplay. (Comprehensive guide features everything teens want to know about ADHD.)

Hartman, T. (1995). *Success Stories: A Guide to Fulfillment with Attention Deficit Disorder.* Grass Valley, CA: Underwood. (Practical knowledge for dealing with all areas of life.)

———. (1995). *Healing ADD: Simple Exercises That Will Change Your Daily Life.* Grass Valley, CA: Underwood. (Visualizations and positive thinking.)

Parker, H. C. (1999). *The ADD Hyperactivity Workbook.* Plantation, FL: Specialty Press. (Highly informative workbook to help lessen frustration with common problems.)

Quinn, P. O., and Stern, J. M. (1991). *Putting on the Brakes: Young People's Guide to Understanding ADHD.* New York: Magination. (Tells kids all they need to know about ADHD.)

———. (2000). *The Best of "Brakes": An Activity Book for Kids with ADD.* Washington, D.C.: Magination. (Activity book containing games and puzzles for kids with ADD.)

Rief, S. (1998). *The ADD/ADHD Checklist.* Paramus, NJ: Prentice Hall. (Help for ADD/ADHD patients.)

Roberts, S., and Jansen, G. J. (1997). *Living with ADD.* Oakland, CA: New Harbinger. (A workbook of interactive exercises.)

Sears, W., and Thompson, L. (1998). *The ADD Book.* Boston, MA: Little Brown. (Shows a nondrug approach to ADD.)

Weiner, E. (1999). *Taking ADD to School.* Valley Park, MO: JayJo. (Tips for parents of children with ADD.)

Behavioral Disorders

Bloomquist, M. L. (1996). *Skills Training for Children with Behavior Disorders.* New York: Guilford. (Teaches new skills to address behavior problems.)

Divinyi, J. (1997). *Good Kids, Difficult Behavior*. Peachtree, CA: Wellness Connection. (Effective and straightforward techniques for parenting a difficult child.)

Greene, R. W. (1998). *The Explosive Child*. New York: HarperCollins. (Suggestions on how to calm explosive behavior.)

Haag, K., Kasper, K., Dziak-Kryst, E., and Young, E. (1982). *Common Solutions for the Uncommon Child*. Danville, IL: Interstate Printers & Publishers. (Displays 25 types of behavioral or learning problems.)

Levy, R., and O'Hanlon, B., with Goode, T. N. (2000). *Try and Make Me: Simple Strategies That Turn Off the Tantrums and Create Cooperation*. New York: Rodale. (Simple strategies to deal with defiant children behaviors.)

Manson, P. T., and Kreger, R. (1998). *Stop Walking on Eggshells*. Oakland, CA: Harbinger. (A family guide when someone you care about has Borderline Personality Disorder.)

Bereavement

Caplan, S., and Lang, G. (1998). *Grief's Courageous Journey*. Oakland, CA: New Harbinger. (A workbook to help cope with the loss of a loved one.)

Fitzgerald, H. (1994). *The Mourning Handbook*. New York: Simon & Schuster. (Learning to grieve.)

Jarrat, C. (1994). *Helping Children Cope with Separation and Loss*. Boston, MA: Harvard Common. (Coping with death.)

Jozefowski, J. (1996). *The Phoenix Phenonemon: Rising from the Ashes of Grief*. Northvale, NJ: Jason Aronson.

———. (1999). *The Phoenix Phenonemon: Rising from the Ashes of Grief*. Northvale, NJ: Jason Aronson. (Advice and inspiration for those who are suffering from a loss.)

Viorst, J. (1986). *Necessary Losses*. New York: Simon & Schuster. (Coping with death and loss.)

Bipolar Disorders

Lynn, G. T. (2000). *Survival Strategies for Parenting Children with Bipolar Disorder*. Grass Valley, CA: Underwood. (Teaches parents how to live with boarderline children.)

Borderline Personality Disorder

Manson, P. T., and Kreger, R. (1998). *Stop Walking on Eggshells*. Oakland, CA: New Harbinger. (A guide for family and friends on how to take your life back when someone you love is borderline.)

Santoro, J., and Cohen, R. (1997). *The Angry Heart*. Oakland, CA: New Harbinger. (Exercises and techniques for overcoming borderline and addictive behaviors.)

Change

O'Hanlon, W. H. (2000). *Do One Thing Different: Ten Simple Ways to Change Your Life*. New York: HarperCollins.

Communication

Brinkman, R., and Kirschner, R. (1994). *Dealing with People You Can't Stand: How to Bring out the Best in People at Their Worst*. New York: McGraw-Hill. (Learn how to improve relationships with others by understanding why they act like they do.)

Clarke, J. I., and Dawson, C. (1998). *Growing Up Again*. Center City, MN: Hazelden. (Encouraging adult children to talk about childhood experiences.)

Nichols, M. P. (1995). *The Lost Art of Listening*. New York: Guilford. (Simple exercises help revive listening skills to improve and repair relationships.)

Conflict Resolution

Hernes-Silverman, S. (1998). *13 Steps to Help Families Stop Fighting and Solve Problems Peacefully*. Plainview, NY: Childswork/Childsplay. (Step-by-step method for helping families practice conflict resolution.)

O'Hanlon, W. H., and Hudson, P. (2000). *Stop Blaming, Start Loving*. Dunmore, PA: Norton. (A solution-oriented approach to improving relationships.)

Schmidt, F., and Friedman, A. (1989). *Fighting Fair for Families*. Miami Beach, FL: Peace Education. (New ground rules for family arguments.)

Defiant Child

Barkley, R. A. (1997). *Managing the Defiant Child: A Guide to Parent Training*. New York: Guilford. (Help with the defiant child.)

Levy, R., and O'Hanlon, W. H. (2001). *Try and Make Me: A Revolutionary Program for Raising Your Defiant Child Without Losing Your Cool*. Emmaus, PA: Rodale. (Strategies that turn off tantrums and create cooperation.)

Depression/Suicide

Burns, D. (1999). *Feeling Good*. New York: Avon. (How to eliminate depression, anxiety, and guilt without drugs.)

Copeland, M. E. (1992). *The Depression Workbook; A Guide for Living with Depression and Manic Depression*. Oakland, CA: New Harbinger. (Offers causes of depression and manic depression and guides adolescents in dealing with it.)

Williams, K. (1995). *A Parent's Guide to Suicidal and Depressed Teens*. Center City, MN: Hazelden. (Help for recognizing when a child is in crisis and what to do about it.)

Developmental Disorders

Brill, M. (1994). *Keys to Parenting the Child with Autism*. NY: Barrons. (How to parent a child with autism).

Simons, J., and Oishi. (1997). *The Hidden Child*. Bethesda, MD: Woodbine House. (Strategies for dealing with developmental disorders.)

Difficult Child

Greene, R. W. (1998). *The Explosive Child*. New York: HarperCollins. (How to handle chronically inflexibile children.)

Greenspan, S. I. (1995). *The Challenging Child*. Reading, MA: Addison-Wesley. (Discusses five types of difficult children and how to adapt your parenting style to them.)

Divorce

Ahrons, C. (1995). *The Good Divorce: Keeping Your Family Together When Your Marriage Comes Apart*. New York: HarperCollins. (Provides tools for parents to help their children feel a sense of belonging to a family after a divorce.)

Garrity, C. B., and Baris, M. A. (1997). *Caught in the Middle*. San Francisco, CA: Jossey-Bass. (How emotional damage occurs to children during a divorce.)

Hickey, E., and Dalton, E. (1994). *Healing Hearts; Helping Children and Adults Recover from Divorce*. Carson City, NV: Gold Leaf Press. (Words of advice from divorce's most vulnerable individuals, children.)

Johnson, J. R., Breunig, K., Garrity, C., and Baris, M. (1997). *Through the Eyes of Children: Healing Stories for Children of Divorce*. New York: Free Press. (Stories provide children a way to understand and cope with divorce.)

Neuman, M. G., and Romanowski, P. (1998). *Helping Your Kids Cope with Divorce*. New York: Ballantine. (How children think and feel about divorce and how to talk about it constructively.)

Prokop, M. (1986). *Divorce Happens to the Nicest Kids*. Warren, OH: Alegra House. (Divorce is ubiquitous.)

Domestic Violence

Fall, K. A., Howard, S., and Ford, J. E. (1999). *Alternative to Domestic Violence*. Philadelphia, PA: Accelerated Development. (Homework manual for battering intervention groups that addresses many individual issues.)

Eating Disorders

Apple, R. F., and Agras, W. S. (1977). *Overcoming Eating Disorders: A Cognitive-Behavioral Treatment for Bulimia Nervosa and Binge-Eating Disorders*. San Antonio, TX: Harcourt Brace. (A guided plan for healthy eating habits.)

Danowski, D., and Lazaro, P. (2000). *Why Can't I Stop Eating?* Center City, MN: Hazelden. (Recognizing, understanding, and overcoming food addiction.)

Ebbett, J. (1994). *The Eating Illness Workbook.* Center City, MN: Hazelden. (A blueprint of exercises for recovery.)

Edell, D. (1999). *Eat, Drink, and Be Merry.* New York: HarperCollins. (You can be fatter than you think.)

Nash, J. D. (1999). *Binge No More.* Oakland, CA: New Harbinger. (How to overcome eating disorders.)

Sandbek, T. (1993). *The Deadly Diet.* Oakland, CA: New Harbinger. (Proven cognitive techniques to overcome eating problems.)

Schroder, C. R. (1992). *Fat is Not a Four-Letter Word.* New York: Chronemed. (You don't have to be ashamed if you don't look like a fashion model.)

Sherman, R. T., and Thompson, R. T. (1996). *Bulimia: A Guide for Family and Friends.* San Francisco, CA: Jossey-Bass. (A step-by-step guide for family and friends to help with the disorder.)

Zerbe, K. J. (1993). *The Body Betrayed: Eating Disorders and Their Treatment.* Washington, DC: American Psychiatric. (Eating disorders that affect women and other factors associated with them.)

Elimination Disorders

Arnold, S. J. (1997). *No More Bedwetting; How to Help Your Child Stay Dry.* New York: Wiley. (Offers strategies for staying dry and dispels myths about bedwetting.)

Fassler, J. (1971). *Don't Worry, Dear.* New York: Human Sciences. (Helps children solve problems by allowing them to set their own pace.)

Mack, A. (1989). *Dry All Night.* Boston, MA: Little Brown. (Children are encouraged to be an active part in overcoming bedwetting.)

Gambling

Heineman, M. (1988). *When Someone You Love Gambles.* Center City, MN: Hazelden. (Support for family members.)

Horvath, A. T. (2000). *Sex, Drugs, Gambling, and Chocolate.* Atascadaro, CA: Impact. (An easy-to-follow workbook to deal with cravings.)

Lesieur, H. R. (1986). *Understanding Compulsive Gambling.* Center City, MN: Hazelden. (A resource for clients and their families.)

Lorenz, V. (1988). *Releasing Guilt about Gambling.* Center City, MN: Hazelden. (Explains how guilt is often accompanied by other destructive emotions.)

Learning Skills

Hernes-Silverman, S. (1998). *13 Steps to Better Grades.* Plainview, NY: Childswork/Childsplay. (Comprehensive guide to assisting children in many school-related issues.)

Radencich, M. C. (1988). *How to Help Your Child with Homework.* Minneapolis, MN: Free Spirit. (Children become more responsible about homework with these proven techniques.)

Medical

Caufield, J., Hansen, M. V., Aubry, P., and Mitchell, N. M. (1996). *Chicken Soup for the Surviving Soul.* Deerfield, FL: Health Communications. (Inspiring stories for the soul.)

Doka, K. J. (1998). *Living with Life-Threatening Illness: A Guide for Patients, Their Families, and Caregivers.* (Practical suggestions from personal experience.)

Kabat-Zinn, J. (1990). *Full Catastrophe Living: Using the Wisdom of your Body and Mind to Face Stress, Pain, and Illness.* New York: Dell. (Learn to live your life more fully.)

Pitzele, S. K. (2000). *Finding the Joy in Today.* Center City, MN: Hazelden. (Living with chronic illness.)

Register, C. (2000). *Living with Chronic Illness.* Center City, MN: Hazelden. (Living the imperfect life.)

Wilens, T. E. (1999). *Straight Talk about Psychiatric Medications for Kids.* New York: Guilford. (Guidelines for parents of children recommended for medication.)

Motivation

O'Hanlon, W. H. (2000). *Do One Thing Different: Ten Simple Ways to Change Your Life.* New York: Harper Collins. (Solutions for creating change in your life.)

Rathvon, N. (1996). *The Unmotivated Child.* New York: Simon & Schuster. (Pinpoints warning signs to watch for in students in grades K–12.)

Nurturing

Bradshaw, J. (1990). *Homecoming: Reclaiming and Championing Your Inner Child.* New York: Bantam. (Teaches parents how to comfort their inner child so they can become more adept at comforting their own children.)

Domar, A., and Dreher, H. (2000). *Self-Nurture: Learning to Care for Yourself as Effectively as You Care for Everyone Else.* New York: Viking-Penguin. (Caring for yourself is important, too.)

Ford, A. (1994). *Wonderful Ways to Love a Child.* Berkeley, CA: Conari. (Teaches you to accept yourself and comfort your feelings of hidden hurt.)

Obsessive-Compulsive Disorder

Roy, C. (2000). *Obsessive-Compulsive Disorder.* Center City, MN: Hazelden. (A survival guide for family and friends.)

Hyman, B. M., and White, K. (1990). *The OCD Workbook.* Oakland, CA: New Harbinger. (A self-directed program for breaking free of the disorder.)

Parenting

Borba, M. (1999). *Parents Do Make a Difference*. San Francisco, CA: Jossey-Bass. (Creative suggestions for raising successful human beings.)

Borcherdt, B. (1996). *Making Families Work and What to Do When They Don't*. New York: Haworth. (Practical ideas for getting back on track.)

Briesmeister, J. M., and Schaefer, C. E. (1998). *Handbook of Parent Training*. New York: Wiley. (Identifying and assessing family problems through parent training.)

Butler, B., and Sussman, M. B. (1989). *Museum Visits and Activities for Family Life Enrichment*. New York: Haworth. (Some good ideas for building positive family relations.)

Clarke, J. I. (1999). *Time-In*. Seattle, WA: Parenting Press. (Help offered to those who feel frustrated over parenting issues.)

Covey, S. R. (1997). *The 7 Habits of Highly Effective Families*. New York: Golden. (Offers practical guidance to build and balance a strong family.)

Crary, E. (1993). *Without Spanking or Spoiling*. Seattle, WA: Parenting Press. (A middle-road solution to child rearing.)

Crites-Price, S. (1996). *The Working Parents Help Book*. Princeton, NJ: Peterson's. (Challenges of working parents are discussed in this self-help book.)

Edwards, C. D. (1999). *How to Handle a Hard-to-Handle Kid*. Minneapolis, MN: Free Spirit. (How to identify and address problem behaviors.)

Faber, A. (1999). *How to Talk So Kids Will Listen, and Listen So Kids Will Talk*. New York: Avon. (Improving your communications with children.)

Forehand, R. L. (1996). *Parenting the Strong-Willed Child*. Chicago, IL: Contemporary Books. (Step-by-step instructional book to effective parenting.)

Glennon, Will. (1995). *Fathering*. Berkeley, CA: Conari. (100 fathers share personal experiences to assist in deepening the bond with their children.)

Greenspan, S. I. (1995). *The Challenging Child*. Reading, MA: Addison-Wesley. (Discusses five different types of children and how to adapt parenting skills to them.)

Haag, F. L., Bates-Ames, L., and Baker, S. M. (1955). *Child Behavior*. New York: Harper. (Helps parents understand children's different stages and problems that accompany those stages.)

Koplewicz, H. S. (1996). *It's Nobody's Fault*. New York: Times Books. (Reduce parents' blame and guilt relating to common disorders in children.)

Levy, R., and O'Hanlon, with Goode, N. (2001). *Try and Make Me*. New York: Rodale. (A revolutionary program for raising defiant children.)

Metcalf, L. (1997). *Parenting toward Solutions; How Parents Can Use Skills They Already Have to Raise Responsible, Loving Kids*. Englewood Cliffs, NJ: Prentice Hall. (Solution-focus approach to help parents solve difficult problems.)

Nelson, J. (1993). *Positive Discipline A–Z*. Rocklin, CA: Prima. (Offers solutions to child-raising problems.)

Newman, S. (1993). *Little Things Long Remembered*. New York: Crown. (Provides suggestions for making your child feel special.)

Renshaw-Joslin, K. (1994). *Positive Parenting from A to Z*. New York: Fawcett Columbine, Ballentine. (Provides alphabetically arranged, age-specific solutions to behavior problems.)

Schaefer, C. E. (1994). *How to Help Children with Common Problems*. Northvale, NJ: Jason Aronson. (Everyday solutions for everyday problems.)

Shapiro, L. E. (2000). *An Ounce of Prevention: How Parents Can Stop Childhood Behavioral and Emotional Problems before They Start*. New York: HarperCollins. (How to reduce the risk of emotional problems before the start.)

Tobin, L. (2000). *Parenting on the Go*. Duluth, MN: Whole Person Associates. (Help for busy parents.)

Whitham, C. (1994). *"The Answer Is No."* Los Angeles, CA: Perspective. (Parents learn to set appropriate limits and be firm with their children.)

Willens, T. (1999). *Straight Talk about Psychiatric Medications for Kids*. New York: Guilford. (A parents' guide to psychiatric medications.)

Wilmes, D. L. (1995). *Parenting for Prevention*. Center City, MN: Hazelden/Johnson Institute. (Practical advice on raising balanced kids.)

Windell, J. (1994). *8 Weeks to a Well-Behaved Child*. New York: Macmillan. (Parents provided with information on how to modify children's behavior.)

Personality Disorders

Basco, M. R. (1999). *Never Good Enough: How to Use Perfectionism to Your Advantage without Letting It Ruin Your Life*. New York: Simon & Schuster. (How to make perfectionism positive.)

Kreisman, J. J., and Straus, H. (1999). *I Hate You, Don't Leave Me*. New York: HarperCollins. (How to deal with the issues of Borderline Personality Disorder.)

Linehan, M. M. (1993). *Skills Training Manual for Treating Borderline Personality Disorders*. New York: Guilford. (A guide for teaching mindfulness, interpersonal effectiveness, emotional regulation, and frustration tolerance.)

Masterson, J. F. (1988). *The Search for the Real Self: Unmasking the Personality Disorder of Our Age*. New York: Free Press. (Practical suggestions on gaining the power to alter your life.)

Phobias

Anthony, M. M., Craske, M. G., and Barlow, D. H. (1995). *Mastering Your Special Phobia*. San Antonio, TX: Harcourt Brace. (Exploring phobias and the strategies to overcome them.)

Colas, E. (1988). *Scenes from the Life of an Obsessive-Compulsive*. New York: Pocket Books. (A world where kitchen utensils become instruments of contamination.)

Foa, E. B., and Kozak, M. J. (1997). *Mastery of Obsessive-Compulsive Disorder: A*

Cognitive-Behavioral Approach. San Antonio, TX: Harcourt Brace. (How to control ritualistic behavior.)

Gravitz, H. L. (1998). *New Help for the Family*. Santa Barbara, CA: New Visions. (Help for the family of an obsessive-compulsive.)

Robinson, B. E. (2000). *Don't Let Your Mind Stunt Your Growth*. Oakland, CA: New Harbinger. (Stories, fables, and techniques to change the way you think.)

Schwartz, J. M., and Bigette, B. (1996). *Brain Lock*. New York: HarperCollins. (A four-step approach to gaining control of your life.)

Zuercher-White, E. (1997). *Taming Panic Disorder and Agoraphobia*. Oakland, CA: New Harbinger. (A step-by-step cognitive-behavioral guide.)

Posttraumatic Stress Disorder

Matsakis, A. (1998). *Trust after Trauma*. Oakland, CA: New Harbinger. (A guide to relationships for survivors and those who love them.)

———. (1999). *I Can't Get Over It*. Oakland, CA: New Harbinger. (Handbook for trauma survivors.)

———. (1999). *Survivor Guilt*. Oakland, CA: New Harbinger. (A self-help guide for coming to terms with guilt.)

Rothblum, B. O., and Foa, E. B. (2000). *Reclaiming Your Life after Rape*. San Antonio, TX: Harcourt Brace. (Cognitive-behavioral threapy for Posttraumatic Stress Disorder.)

Relational Problems

Davis, D. (1985). *Something Is Wrong at My House*. Seattle, WA: Parenting Press. (Encourages children to deal with feelings of violence at home.)

Nowicki, S., and Duke, M. P. (1992). *Helping the Child Who Doesn't Fit In*. Atlanta, GA: Peachtree. (Concrete methods for assisting children who are socially rejected.)

Schizophrenia

Muesler, K., and Gingerich, L. (1994). *Coping with Schizophrenia*. Oakland, CA: New Harbinger. (A strategy guide for families.)

School Problems

Kindlon, D., and Thompson, M. (1999). *Raising Cain: Protecting the Emotional Life of Boys*. New York: Ballantine. (Helps parents understand the difficulties boys have in school.)

Martin, M., and Waltman-Greenwork, C. (1995). *Solve Your Child's School Related Problems*. New York: Harper Perennial. (Assists parents to effectively deal with children's problems in school.)

Self-Esteem

Caissy, G. A. (1994). *Early Adolescence.* New York: Insight. (Help in understanding the 10–15-year-old.)

Clarke, J. I. (1978). *Self-Esteem: A Family Affair.* Center City, MN: Hazelden. (Creative options for parents in building child self-esteem.)

Fraiberg, S. H. (1996). *The Magic Years: Understanding and Healing the Problems of Early Childhood.* New York: IDG. (Development theory from birth through age 6.)

Gookin, S. H. (1995). *Parenting for Dummies.* New York: IDG. (A simple parenting book.)

Loomans, D., and Loomans, J. (1994). *Full Esteem Ahead: 100 Ways to Build Self-Esteem in Children & Adults.* Tiburon, CA: H. J. Kramer. (Offers parents practical ways to help increase their child's self-esteem.)

McKay, M., and Fanning. P. (1987). *Self-Esteem.* New York: MJF. (Cognitive techniques for improving self-esteem.)

Ramirez-Basco, M. (1999). *Never Good Enough.* New York: Free Press. (Learn to overcome perfectionist tendencies.)

Sorensen, M. J. (1998). *Breaking the Chain of Low Self-Esteem.* Sherwood, OR: Wolf. (Suggests ways to face life with new courage and enthusiasm.)

Sensory Integration

Ayres, A. J. (1979). *Sensory Integration and the Child.* Los Angeles, CA: Western Psychological Services. (Explains sensory integrative dysfunction; question and answer section included.)

Stock-Kranowitz, C. (1998). *The Out-of-Sync Child.* New York: Perigee. (Advice for parents dealing with children with sensory integration dysfunction.)

Sleep

Ancoli, I. S. (1996). *All I Want Is a Good Night's Sleep.* St. Louis, MO: Mosby Year Book. (Suggested ways to help you sleep better.)

Huntley, R. (1991). *The Sleep Book for Tired Parents.* Seattle, WA: Parenting Press. (Covers common sleep problems in children.)

Masurel, C., and Henry, M. H. (1994). *Good Night!* San Francisco, CA: Chronicle. (Helps reluctant children go to bed through a role-reversal story.)

Waddell, M., and Firth, B. (1988). *Can't You Sleep, Little Bear?* Cambridge, MA: Candlewick. (Shows parents how to relax a child when he or she is afraid of falling asleep.)

Substance Abuse

Schaefer, D. (1987). *Choices and Consequences.* Center City, MN: Hazelden/ Johnson Institute. (What to do when a teenager uses alcohol or drugs.)

Washton, A. (1990). *Cocaine Recovery Workbooks*. Center City, MN: Hazelden. (Three-book collection: *Quitting Cocaine, Staying Off Cocaine,* and *Maintaining Recovery.*)

Violence

Deaton, W. (1994). *I Saw It Happen*. Los Angeles, CA: Western Psychological Services. (A workbook for children who witnessed a crime.)

Videos

Clark, L. (1996). *SOS! Help for Parents*. Bowling Green, KY. (A video to help parents handle everyday behavior problems.)
Hazelden Video. (1998). *Alcohol*. Center City, MN: Hazelden. (The substance, the addiction, the solution.)
Hazelden Video. (1999). *Cross-Addiction*. Center City, MN: Hazelden. (The impact of multiple drugs.)
Hazelden Video. (1998). *Methamphetamine*. Center City, MN: Hazelden. (Facts about use, addiction, and recovery.)
Hickey, E. *Children: The Experts on Divorce*. Livingston, TX: Pale Horse. (Video is geared toward separating parents and features candid interviews with children of divorced parents.)
Washton, A. (1993). *Quitting Cocaine and Staying Quit*. Center City, MN: Hazelden Video. (A deeper understanding of the recovery process.)
Zelby, P. (2000). *The Voice of Addiction*. Center City, MN: Hazelden. (Package includes one 30-min. video, a 30-min. audiotape, and 15 workbooks.

Self-Help Audiotapes

The following audiotapes are available from New Harbinger Publications, Oakland, CA.

Anxiety and Stress

Time Out from Stress: Vol. 1: *Lakeside* and *The Path to Lookout Mountain*. Vol. 2: *Five Finger Exercise* and *Country Inn*.
Body Relaxed, Mind at Ease. 1993. (Harriett Sanders).
Peaceful Body, Relaxed Mind. 1995. (Harriett Sanders).

Cognition

Combating Distorted Thinking
Thought Stopping
Systematic Desensitization and Visual Goals
Covert Modeling and Covert Reinforcement
Pain Control and Healing

Communication Skills

Assertiveness Training
Effective Self-Expression
Becoming a Good Listener
Making Contact
Sexual Communication
Fair Fighting

Couples

Conflict Resolution for Couples (Susan Heitler).

The following series is based on McKay and colleagues (1994):

Exchanging Favors
Constructive Conflict Resolution
Listening
Expressing Feelings
Clean Communication
Negotiation
Time Out from Anger
Coping with an Angry Partner

Depression

Depression and Anxiety Management (John Preston)
Living with Depression and Manic Depression (M. E. Copeland)

General

Visualizations for Change (Patrick Fanning)
Stress Reduction
Allergies and Asthma
Healing Injuries
Curing Infectious Disease
Shyness
Transforming Your Chronic Pain

Hypnosis

Hypnosis for Sleep
Hypnosis for Self-Esteem
Hypnosis for Improved Learning
Hypnosis for Motivatng Change and Problem Solving
Hypnosis to End Anxiety and Panic Attacks
Hypnosis for Overcoming Depression
Hypnosis for Coping before and after Surgery

Phobias

By E. J. Bourne:

Flying
Shopping in a Supermarket
Driving Freeways
Giving a Talk
Speaking in Public
Fear of Illness
Driving Far from Home
Heights

27

Self-Help Groups
and 800 Numbers

ALCOHOL

Al-Anon & Alateen: 1-898-425-2666
American Council on Alcohol Addiction: 1-800-527-5344
National Council on Alcohol Addiction: 1-800-622-2255
National Clearinghouse for Alcohol and Drug Information:
    1-800-729-6686
Alcohol and Drug Abuse Testing Center: 1-900-942-3784
National Council on Alcoholism and Drug Dependence: 1-800-475-HOPE

CHILD ABUSE

If a child is in immediate danger or risk, call: 1-800-THE-LOST
National Child Abuse Hotline: 1-800-25-ABUSE

DEPRESSION

National Depressive and Manic Depressive Association: 1-800-826-2632
DAD (Depression after Delivery): 1-800-944-4773
National Foundation for Depressive Illness: 1-800-926-3632

DIVORCE

Association for Children for Enforcement of Support (ACES):
    1-800-537-7072

Children's Rights Council: 202-547-6227
Joint Custody Association: 310-475-6962
North American Conference of Separated and Divorced Catholics:
    401-943-7903
Rainbows: 708-310-1880

DRUG ABUSE

Narcotics Anonymous: 1-888-994-9484
National Council on Alcoholism and Drug Dependence Inc.:
    1-800-622-2255
Schick Shadel Hospital: 1-800-CRAVING (1-800-272-9464)
National Parents Resource Institute for Drug Education (PRIDE):
    1-800-241-794
National COCAINE Hotline: 1-800-COCAINE
Office of Substance Abuse Prevention: 1-900-638-2045, Marijuana Anonymous: 1-800-766-6779
Teen Help Adolescent Resources: 1-800-637-0701
National Substance Abuse Hotline: 1-800-DRUG-HELP or
    1-900-HELP-III

MENTAL HEALTH

National Alliance for the Mentally Ill: 1-800-950-NANG (6264)

SEXUAL ADDICTION:

Sex Addicts Anonymous (SAA): 713-869-4902
Sex and Love Addicts Anonymous (SLAA): 617-332-1845
Sexaholics Anonymous (SA): 615-331-6230
Sexual Compulsives Anonymous (SCA):
        West Coast: 310-85-5585
        East Coast: 212-439-1123
S-Anon Family Groups: 818-990-6910

28

Online Resources

GENERAL

Internet Mental Health
  http://www.openmarket.com/

Pharmaceutical Information Network Home Page
  http://pharminfo.com/

Psychology Organizations on the Web
  http://www.wesleyan.edu/spn/psych.htm

Search Page for articles in Psychology and Social Science Journals
  http://www.shef.ac.uk/~psych/journals/jsearch.html

Social Work and Social Services Web Sites
  http://www.gwbweb.wustl.edu/websites.html

The Social Statistics Briefing Room
  http://www.whitehouse.gov/fsbr/ssbr.html

Child Welfare Home Page
  http://www.childwelfare.com/

Internet Mental Health
  http://www.mentalhealth.com/

Mental Health Net
   http://www.cmhc.com/

NIMH Home Page
   http://www.nimh.nih.gov/

Psyjourn, Inc.
   http://www.psyjourn.com

Psychscapes Worldwide
   http://www.mental-health.com

The Shrink Tank BBS Web Site
   http://www.shrinktank.com/testing.htm

PROFESSIONAL ORGANIZATIONS

American Academy of Child and Adolescent Psychiatry Home Page
   http://www.aacap.org/web/aacap/

American Psychiatric Association Online
   http://www.paych.org

American Psychoanalytic Association Online
   http://apsa.org/

American Psychological Association Psych Net
   http://www.apa.org

California Coalition for Ethical Mental Health Care
   http://www.pw1.netcom/~mastery/coalitionMain.html

Clinical Social Work Federation
   http://www.cswf.org

NASW Online
   http://www.socialworkers.org/main.htm

SELF-HELP AND SUPPORT GROUP RESOURCES

Adult Children of Alcoholics
   http://www.adultchildren.org

Alateen and Alanon Family Groups
   http://www.al-anon.org or http://www.alateen.org

Alcoholics Anonymous
   http://www.alcoholics-anonymous.org

Emotional Support on the Internet
http://www.cix.co.uk/~net-sercvices/care

Mental Health Net-Self-Help Questionnaires
http://www.cmhc.com/guide/quizes.htm

Mental Health Net-Self-Help Resources Index
http://www.cmhc.com/selfhelp.htm

Support-Group.com
http://support-group.com

SPECIFIC DISORDERS

ADHD

Children and Adults with Attention Deficit Disorders (C.H.A.D.D.)
http://chadd.org/

Anxiety

Anxiety-Panic
http://www.algy.com/anxiety/

Alcoholism

Adult Children of Alcoholics
http://www.couns.uiuc.edu/adukt.htm

Al-Anon and Alateen
http://www.Al-Anon-Alateen.org

Alcohol Dependence
http://www.mentalhealth.com/dx/fdx-sb01.html

Alcohol—An Interactive Assessment
http://www.mayohealth.org//mayo/9707/htm/alcohol.htm

Alcoholics Anonymous
http://www.alcoholics-anonymous.org/

Another Empty Bottle
http://www.alcoholismhelp.com

Concerned about Your Drinking?
http://www.carebetter.com

Habitsmart (Alcohol)
http://www.cts.com/crash/habitsmart

JACS—Jewish Alcoholics, Chemically Dependent Persons, and Significant Others
http://www.jacsweb.org

Mothers Against Drunk Driving
http://www.madd.org

National Institute on Alcohol Abuse and Alcoholism
http://www.niaaa.gov

Secular Organization for Sobriety/Save Our Selves
http://www.unhooked.com/toolbox/index.html

Bipolar Disorder

Bipolar and other mood disorders: Pendulum Resources
http://www.pendulum.org

Co-Dependency

The Issues of Co-Dependency
http://www.soulselfhelp.on.ca/coda.hml

Critical Incident Stress Management

American Red Cross
www.crossnet.org

Department of Veterans Administration Disaster Mental Health Manual
www.wramc.amedd.army.mil/departments/socialwork/provider/dmhs.htm

National Center for Post-Traumatic Stress Disorder
www.Dartmouth.edu/dms/ptsd

International Critical Incident Stress Foundation
www.icisf.org

Traumatology Institute, Florida State University
www.fsu.edu/~gcp

Davis Baldwin's Trauma Pages
www.trauma-pages.com

Death

Death, Dying, and Grief Resources: The WEBster
http://www.cyberspy.com/@7Ewebster/death.html

Depression

Depression Central
http://www.psycom.net/depression.central.html

Dissociation

International Society for the Study of Dissociation
http://www.issd.org/

Drugs

Addiction Resource Guide
http://www.addictionresourcegguide.com

Cocaine Abuse and Addiction
http://www.nida.nih.gov/researchreports/cocaine/cocaine.html

Cocaine Anonymous
http.//www.ca.org

COLA-Center for Online Addiction
http://netaddiction.com/

Commonly Abused Drugs
http://nida.nih.gov/drugs of anuse.html

Drug/Alcohol brochures
http://www.uiuc.edu/departments/mckinley/health-info/drug-alc/drug-alc.html

National Inhalant Coalition
http://inhalants.org

National Institute on Drug Abuse
http://www.nida.nih.gov

Web of Addictions
http://www.well.com/user/woa

Eating Disorders

Cyber-Psych: Eating Disorders
http://www.cyber-psych.com/eat.html

Gambling

Debtors Anonymous
http://www.gamblersanonymous.org

Compulsive Gambling
http://drkoop.com/wellness/mental_health/compulsive_gambling

Pathological Gambling
http://www.cme-reviews.com/pathologicalgambling.html

General Medical

Quick Docs
http//www.health.org/pubs/qdocs/index.htmex.html

Obsessive-Compulsive Disorder

Obsessive Compulsive Disorders
http://www.cmhc.com/guide/ocd.htm

Psychosis

Futur.com (Schizophrenia and other psychoses)
http://www.futur.com/

Recovery

Moderation Management
http://moderation.org

Rational Recovery
http://www.rational.org/recovery

Recovery Online
http://www.recovery.alano.org

SMART: Self-Management and Recovery Training
http://www.smartrecovery.org

Software for Recovering People
http://Christians-in-recovery.org/software

Suicide

The Samaritans (Suicide)
http://www.samaritans.org.uk/

PART V

APPENDIX

29

Insurance Forms

OUTPATIENT TREATMENT REPORT (OTR)

The outpatient treatment report (OTR), sometimes called a treatment authorization request (TAR), is required for continuing patient certification and authorization of additional treatment sessions. Most insurance companies supply their own OTR forms for provider use. What you write in these reports, and how you write it, will often determine how many sessions the insurance company will allocate for treatment. The following completed form is provided to give you a better idea of the information usually required.

SAMPLE OUTPATIENT TREATMENT REPORT

Check One:	X Initial OTR	☐ Continuing OTR

DEMOGRAPHICS

Patient: John Doe   ID: xxxxxxxxx   Group #: 0000
Date of Birth: XX/XX/XXXX First Date of Service XX/XX/XXXX Gender: ☐M ☐F

DSM-IV DIAGNOSIS

Axis I: 314.01/300.02
Axis II: V71.09
Axis III: None
Axis IV: Problems with primary support group, peers, and school.
Axis V: (GAF) - Current: 50   Highest Last Year: ?
          Expected GAF at Discharge: 71

Global Assessment of Functioning (GAF)

91–100	Superior functioning	81–90	Good functioning, minimal symptoms
71–80	Transient symptoms, slight impairment	61–70	Minor symptoms, functions fairly well
51–60	Moderate symptoms, functioning	41–50	Serious symptoms, impairments
31–40	Impairments in reality testing or communication	21–30	Major impairment or delusions/ hallucinations
11–20	Risk of harm to self/others, poor hygiene	1–10	Serious danger to self/others, or actively suicidal
0	Not enough information		

Practitioner's Name: Dr. James Morton, DSW, CSW
Practitioner's Address: xxx East xth Street
City: New York   State: NY   Zip: xxxxx
Telephone Number: 212-xxx-xxxx
Discipline, State License, and Number: DSW, CSW, PR0XXXX-XX
Federal Tax ID Number: SS# 000-00-0000

Name: John Doe   SS#: XXX-XX-XXXX

ASSESSMENT
Previous Treatment (*Please check all that apply.*)

Psychiatric	Substance Abuse	Treatment Outcomes
X None	☐ None	_____
☐ Outpatient	☐ Outpatient	_____
☐ Inpatient	☐ Inpatient	_____
☐ within last 12 months	☐ within last 12 months	_____
☐ one prior admission	☐ one prior admission	_____
☐ 2 or more prior admissions	☐ 2 or more prior admissions	_____

Symptoms (*Please check symptoms that apply.*)

					Substance Use (check if applicable)
X	Anxiousness	X	Hyperactivity		
	Concomitant Medical Condition	X	Irritability		Active Substance Abuse
X	Lack of Energy	X	Impulsiveness		Early Full Remission
	Delusions		Obsessions/ Compulsions		Early Partial Remission
	Depressed Mood		Oppositionalism		Sustained Full Remission
	Dissociative State		Panic Attacks		Sustained Partial Remission
	Elevated Mood		Paranoia		Other—specify:
	Grief		Somatic Complaints		Other—specify:
	Guilt	X	Thought Disruption		
	Hallucinations		Trauma Victim		
	Hopelessness	X	Worthlessness		

Duration of symptoms:
☐ Less than one month   ☐ 1–6 months   ☐ 7–11 months   X more than a year

page 2

Name: John Doe   **OTR**   SS#: XXX-XX-XXXX

Functioning (*Please assess the current level of impairment and anticipated level at discharge.*)

Impairment Level
(*Please circle appropriate level.*)

Categories	None	Mild	Moderate	Marked	Extreme	Discharge
Activities of daily living (hygiene)	1	②	3	4	5	1
Ability to concentrate	1	2	3	④	5	2
Ability to control temper	1	2	3	④	5	2
Eating habits	1	②	3	4	5	1

☐ Weight loss/gain _____ lbs.   ☐ Current weight _____ lbs.   ☐ Height _____

Categories	None	Mild	Moderate	Marked	Extreme	Discharge
Financial Situation	1	2	3	4	5	NA
Friendship/peer relationship	1	2	3	④	5	2
Hobbies/interests/play activities	1	2	③	4	5	2
Job/school/performance	1	2	3	④	5	2
Marriage/relationship/ family	1	2	3	④	5	2
Physical health	①	2	3	4	5	NA
Sexual functioning	1	2	3	4	5	NA
Sleeping habits	1	2	3	④	5	2

Ⓧ Difficulty falling asleep   X Difficulty staying asleep   X Early awakening

NA = Not Applicable

RISK ASSESSMENT (*Check all that apply.*)

Suicide: ☑ None   ☐ Ideation   ☐ Plan   ☐ Means
                ☐ Prior attempt Date:
Homicide: ☑ None   ☐ Ideation   ☐ Plan   ☐ Means
                ☐ Prior attempt Date:
Other risk behaviors:
(If Yes to any risk issues, provide plan: Patient has suicidal ideations and has agreed to inform me or her psychiatrist of her intentions before taking any action.)

TREATMENT PLAN

Primary Treatment Approach (*Check one.*)
☐ Problem focused   X Symptom focused   ☐ Complex case
☐ Therapeutic stabilization   ☐ Medication management only

Progress in treatment (*Check one.*)
X Continues with/or recurrence of acute presenting problems
☐ Somewhat improved
☐ Much improved
☐ Needs support/maintenance only
☐ Near completion of treatment
☐ Other:

Expected treatment outcomes (*Check all that apply.*)
☐ Reduction in symptoms and discharge from active treatment
☒ Return to highest GAF and discharge from active treatment
☐ Transfer to self-help/other supports and discharge from active treatment
☐ Provide ongoing supportive counseling and maintain stabilization of
   symptoms
☐ Provide ongoing medication management

Did patient concur with goals and strategies of treatment plan? X Yes ☐ No

Medication (*List all psychotropic and other medications*)

Has patient been evaluated for medication?   X Yes ☐ No
Current Medication: ☐ None X Psychotropic ☐ Medical
                          ☐ Other:
Does patient follow medication regime?   X Yes ☐ No
Prescribing physician (indicate if PCP
   or psychiatrist):   Dr. Mary Smith, MD (Psychiatrist)

Name of Medication	Current Dosage /Frequency	Start Date	Side Effects
Concerta	54 mg/day	5/30/2001	☐ Yes ☒ No

Name: John Doe   SS#: XXX-XX-XXXX

Care Planning:

Problem: Inattention, hyperactivity, impulsivity
Goal: Increase frustration tolerance   **Est. Time:** 3 mos.
Intervention: Educate child about the diagnosis and discuss symptoms in order to develop alternate problem-solving strategies.
Progress since start of tx: _25%_ **of goal as evidenced by:** Child understands diagnosis and is cooperating in development of alternate strategies.

Problem: Generalized Anxiety Disorder
Goal: Reduce anxiety and worry.   **Est. Time:** 2 mos.
Intervention: Determine ways in which anxieites manifest themselves.
Progress since start of tx: _10%_ **of goal as evidenced by:** Child understands dynamics that lead to maladaptive behaviors and stress.

Problem: Poor communication with family and school.
Goal: Improve communication among family members and develop a psycho-educational program with child and school. **Est. Time:** 4 mos.
Intervention: Conduct family sessions to reduce pathological communication and reduce anger and alienation.
Progress since start of tx: _10%_ **of goal as evidenced by:** Family has agreed to come to therapy and has given permission for collaboration with school to help develop psycho-educational program.

Name: John Doe   SS#: XXX-XX-XXXX

Clinical Summary:

> Child is a 10-year-old boy who is having difficulties getting along with family, with peers, and in school. He is restless, has difficulty concentrating, and is irritable. Although highly intelligent, he is doing poorly at school. Parents blame themselves for poor discipline, but are eager to help their son. They claim he was born hyperactive. Child appears to be an active participant in treatment.

Clinical Coordination: What arrangements have been made to refer client to psychiatrist or PCP?

> Patient was referred to Dr. Mary Smith, MD, for psychiatric evaluation and medication.

Treatment Frequency and Duration

Date first seen: XX/XX/XXXX   Date last seen: XX/XX/XXXX

Total number of visits used to date for this course of treatment: (9) Nine

Estimated total visits for entire course of treatment: (20) Twenty, 1x/week

☐ Medication Management 90862

☐ Initial Diagnostic Interview 90801

☐ Psychotherapy (20–30 min.) 90804 90805

☐ Psychotherapy (45–50 min.) 90806

☐ Family Psychotherapy (45–50 min.) 90847

☐ Group Psychotherapy (60–90 min.) 90853

☐ Other:

What other treatment or community service is the patient receiving?

☐ None	☐ Individual	☐ Group	☐ EAP
☐ Medication Management	X Family	☐ AA/NA	☐ Structured Program
☐ Other			

Medical treatment (date of last physical examination?)   XX/XX/XXXX

Last date of contact to coordinate treatment: Behavioral: XX/XX/XXXX
                                                 Medical: XX/XX/XXXX

Are other family members in treatment?   X Yes   ☐ No
                            With you?   X Yes   ☐ No

Treating Provider's Signature: *Dr. James Morton, DSW, CSW*
Date: XX/XX/XXXX

OUTPATIENT MEDICAL MANAGEMENT OTR—
Psychiatrist's Report

[To be completed by psychiatrist and submitted to the insurance company. The referring therapist, if any, should receive a copy.]

Client Information:	Provider Information:
Name: John Doe **DOB:** xx-xx-xxxx	**Name:** Dr. Mary Smith, MD
Case #: xxxxxx	**Title:** Psychiatrist
Treatment Start Date: xx/xx/xxxx	**Address:** xxx East xxth
Treatment End Date: xx/xx/xxxx	**State:** New York **Zip:** xxxxx
SS#: xxx-xx-xxxx	**Telephone:** xxx/xxx-xxxx
Employer: NA	**Tax ID: SS#** xxx-xx-xxxx

DSM-IV Multiaxial Diagnosis: Based on current symptoms.
Axis I: 314.01/300.02
Axis II: V71.09
Axis III: None
Axis IV: Problems with primary support, school, and peers.
Axis V: GAF: Current: _50_   At treatment start: _50_   Highest last year: _?_

Current Medication:

Medication	Dosage/Freq.	Start Date	Reaction
Concerta	54 mg./day	xx/xx/xxxx	None

Substance Abuse:
Current problem: ☐ Yes   X No   Past problem: ☐ Yes   ☒ No

Clinical Synopsis:
Parents brought child for an evaluation. Claim he has had Attention Deficit/Hyperactivity Disorder since birth. They indicate he is acting out in school and fighting with siblings and peers, who no longer want to play with him. Child is irritable and has difficulty sitting still or concentrating. Parents also seem extemely anxious.

page 1

Risk:
☐ Suicidal   ☐ Violent   X None
☐ Homicidal   ☐ Other

Safety plan in place? If so, please describe:

Medication Management CPT Code: 90862   Frequency: 1x/Month
Start date: XX/XX/XXXX   End date: XX/XX/XXXX

I certify that I personally direct treatment to this client and that the above information is accurate to the best of my knowledge.
Signature: *Dr. Mary Smith,* MD   Date: XX-XX-XXXX

page 2

BILLING

Despite some inroads in electronic billing, notably by Medicare, GHI, and others, the HCFA 1500 (12-90) is now the universal form for billing, and all insurance companies require that it be filled out accurately (see Chapter 29). If not, the form may simply be discarded. It is rare that an insurance company will return a form to you, indicating why it has been rejected. For that reason, providers must keep detailed records and be prepared to follow up by telephone or rebilling if the claim has not been paid for sixty days. Insurance companies frequently misplace forms, pay incorrect fees, or ignore some billed sessions. Benefit statements should be reviewed as they are received and all discrepancies followed up promptly.

CPT CODES

Current procedural terminology (CPT) codes represent the procedure and services performed by providers. They are followed by modifiers that indicate the provider's specialty, AH for licensed psychologist, and AJ for clinical social worker. The current codes for psychiatric treatment procedures include:

Description of Services	CPT Code
Initial diagnostic interview	90801
Individual psychotherapy, 23–30 minutes	90804
Individual psychotherapy, 35–50 minutes	90806
Individual psychotherapy, 75–80 minutes	90808
Family psychotherapy—without patient present	90846
Family/conjoint psychotherapy therapy—with patient present	90847
Group psychotherapy (other than multiple family group)	90853
Interactive group psychotherapy	90857
Pharmacological management	90862

HCFA-1500

HEALTH INSURANCE CLAIM FORM

NONAME INSURANCE CO. (201) 477-6868
1 MAPLE STREET
HAWTHORNE, NY 07075

PICA

PATIENT AND INSURED INFORMATION

1. MEDICARE MEDICAID CHAMPUS CHAMPVA GROUP HEALTH PLAN FECA BLK LUNG OTHER
1a. INSURED'S I.D. NUMBER 100010111-002

2. PATIENT'S NAME (Last Name, First Name, Middle Initial) JONES JESSICA J
4. INSURED'S NAME (Last Name, First Name, Middle Initial) JONES JESSICA J

5. PATIENT'S ADDRESS (No., Street) 120 EAST 70TH STREET
7. INSURED'S ADDRESS (No., Street) SAME

CITY NEW YORK STATE NY
ZIP CODE 10022 TELEPHONE (Include Area Code) (212) 8828888

3. PATIENT'S BIRTH DATE 01 01 1948 M
a. INSURED'S DATE OF BIRTH 02 04 1946 M X

6. PATIENT RELATIONSHIP TO INSURED Self X Spouse Child Other

8. PATIENT STATUS Single Married X Other
Employed X Full-Time Student Part-Time Student

9. OTHER INSURED'S NAME (Last Name, First Name, Middle Initial)

10. IS PATIENT'S CONDITION RELATED TO:
a. EMPLOYMENT? (CURRENT OR PREVIOUS) YES NO X
b. AUTO ACCIDENT? YES NO X PLACE (State)
c. OTHER ACCIDENT? YES NO X

11. INSURED'S POLICY GROUP OR FECA NUMBER 173990216
b. EMPLOYER'S NAME OR SCHOOL NAME ABC CONSTRUCTION
c. INSURANCE PLAN NAME OR PROGRAM NAME LIBERTY PLAN
d. IS THERE ANOTHER HEALTH BENEFIT PLAN? YES NO X

10d. RESERVED FOR LOCAL USE

READ BACK OF FORM BEFORE COMPLETING & SIGNING THIS FORM.
12. PATIENT'S OR AUTHORIZED PERSON'S SIGNATURE I authorize the release of any medical or other information necessary to process this claim. I also request payment of government benefits either to myself or to the party who accepts assignment below.
SIGNED SIGNATURE ON FILE DATE 07 01 2000

13. INSURED'S OR AUTHORIZED PERSON'S SIGNATURE I authorize payment of medical benefits to the undersigned physician or supplier for services described below.
SIGNED SIGNATURE ON FILE

If yes, return to and complete item 9 a-d.

SECOND FOLD

NV-SS

Health Care Financing Administration, Baltimore, MD.

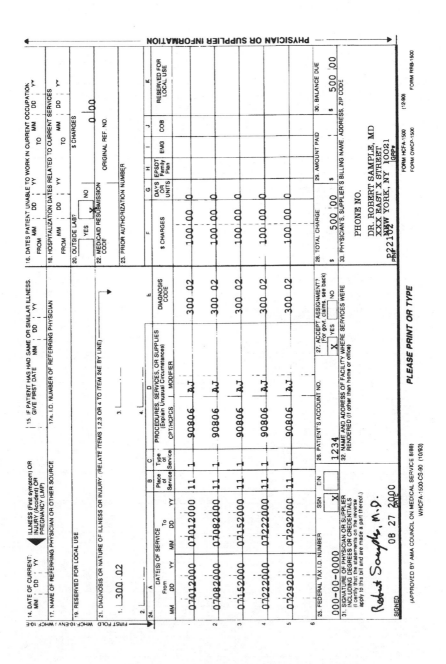

PSYCHOSOCIAL INTAKE REPORT

[To be completed at intake and retained for the therapist's records]

Date: _____

First name:			Last name:		
Address:					
SS#:			Birth date:		
Presenting problem:					
Assessment of mental status:					
Affect: (*Check*)	☐ Poor		☐ Okay		☐ Good
Explain:					
Mood:	☐ Poor		☐ Okay		☐ Good
Explain:					
If suicidal:	☐ With plan		☐ Ideation		
Speech	☐ Poor		☐ Okay		☐ Good
Explain:					
Thought content:	☐ Poor		☐ Okay		☐ Good
Explain:					
Judgment:	☐ Poor		☐ Okay		☐ Good
Explain:					
Insight	☐ Poor		☐ Okay		☐ Good
Explain:					
Concentration:	☐ Poor		☐ Okay		☐ Good
Explain:					
Memory:	☐ Poor		☐ Okay		☐ Good
Explain:					
Relevant medical conditions:					

Provider: Name: _____

Signed: _____ Date:_____

DISCHARGE SUMMARY

Some, but not all, insurance companies require a discharge summary. Since many companies are tracking your success rate and duration of treatment, it is a good idea to submit a discharge summary even if you suspect the client may return to treatment and you have authorized sessions left. You can always open the case again.

DISCHARGE SUMMARY

CLIENT:	DATE:
SS#:	INSURER:
DATE OF FINAL VISIT:	
REASONS FOR DISCHARGE: (Check)	
☐ Treatment Objective Achieved	☐ Client Relocated
☐ Treatment Regarded as Ineffectual by Therapist	☐ Referred to New Therapist
☐ Treatment Regarded as Ineffectual by Client	☐ Quit Treatment
☐ Substantial Progress Made and Client Satisfied	☐ Other:
☐ Client No Longer Eligible for Service	

Describe Situation at Discharge:

Diagnosis at Discharge:

Axis 1:

Axis 2:

Axis 3:

Axis 4:

Axis 5:

GAF (at Discharge):

GAF (at Start of Treatment):

Client Attitude toward Treatment:

☐ Well Motivated ☐ Somewhat Motivated ☐ Unmotivated ☐ Uncooperative

Prognosis:

Provider: _____ Date: _____

Signature: _____

30

Practice Management Reports

PAYMENT AND SESSION MONITOR*

It is well worth your time and effort to use the Basic Session Monitor for all managed care patients. It is designed to organize all critical information in one place and advises you when future outpatient treatment reports (OTRs) are due. In addition to client data, it provides space to track client sessions and payments. The form should be started right from the initial telephone referral from an insurance company. It can be entered into your computer or kept in a notebook for manual notation.

The form also provides space to enter the telephone numbers and contacts for the client's insurance company. This eliminates the need to pore through a lengthy provider manual every time you must contact the insurer to confirm coverage, co-pay amounts, and treatment authorizations. It is recommended that the completed form be checked weekly.

Record keeping can be a nightmare, and the requirements are a lot more extensive than many providers realize. However, the more complete your documentation and the more behavioral it is, the better your chances of getting the authorized sessions your client needs.

---

*This section, including the form that follows, is from *The Psychotherapists' Guide to Managed Care in the 21st Century* by S. Tuckfelt, J. Fink, and M. P. Warren. Copyright © 1997 by Jason Aronson Inc. and used with permission.

PAYMENT AND SESSION MONITOR

CLIENT NAME:	PRIMARY INSURANCE CO.:
Address:	Billling Address:
City, State, Zip:	City, State, Zip:
Tel. Home: Work:	Telephone: Fax:
SS#: DOB:	Contact:
Ins. Member #:	Your Provider #:
Date of First Visit:	SECONDARY INSURANCE CO.:
CPT 1st Visit—90801	Billing Address:
90806 Individual; 90847 Couples/Family	City, State, Zip:
90846—Parents without Patient	Telephone: Fax:
MANAGED CARE PROTOCOL:	Contact:
	Your Provider #:
	PCP:
	Address:
	City, State, Zip:
AUTHORIZATIONS:	Telephone: Fax:
No. # of Visits Date:	PSYCHIATRIST:
	Address:
	City, State, Zip:
	Telephone: Fax:

(PAYMENT AND SESSION MONITOR—continued)

OTR Alert #	Auth. Start	Auth. End	Visit #	Date of Visit	Date OTR Filed	Ins. Amt.	Date Paid	Co-Pay Amt.	Date Paid:	Ins. Bal.	Pt. Bal.
			1								
			2								
			3								
			4								
			5								
			6								
			7								
			8								
			9								
			10								
			11								
			12								
			13								
			14								
			15								

PROGRESS NOTES

These guidelines for progress notes have been recommended by the National Committee on Quality Assurance (NCQA) and are required by many insurance companies, including Magellan.

Progress notes must be kept for each session. The notes must include the name of the client; the date; a summary of what transpired in the session, including your intervention; and an evaluation of progress toward a treatment goal. The progress notes for each session must be signed by the provider. Dictated notes are considered preliminary until the transcription is reviewed and signed.

The treatment plans contained in this book make the creation of progress notes simple and easy. At the end of each intervention, we have included space to summarize what transpired in the session. A space for the provider's signature is included at the end of every page. If you download the treatment plan, record your session summaries, and sign off the page, your note-keeping requirements have been met. It's that easy.

However, if you still prefer to keep separate notes, you can use the form below.

PROGRESS NOTES

Client:	Date:
Address:	Insurance co.:
City, State, Zip:	
SS#:	ID#:

Session summary:
Intervention:
Behavioral goals:

Provider: _____ Date: _____

Signed: _____

31

State Insurance Departments

Alabama	201 Monroe St. (Suite 1700) Montgomery, AL 36104 334/269-3550; Fax: 241-4192
Alaska	3601 C St. (Suite 1324) Anchorage, AK 99503-5948 907/269-7912; Fax: 269-7900
American Samoa	American Samoa Govt. Pago Pago, American Samoa 96799 011/684/633-4116; Fax: 633-2269
Arizona	2910 North 44th St. (Suite 210) Phoenix, AZ 85018-7256 602/912-8400; Fax: 912-8452
Arkansas	1200 West Third Street Little Rock, AR 72201-1904 501/371-2600; Fax: 371-2629
California	300 Capitol Mall (Suite 1500) Sacramento, CA 95814 916/492-3500; Fax: 445-5280

445 Fremont St. (23rd Floor)
San Francisco, CA 94102
415/538-4040; Fax: 904-5889

300 South Spring St.
Los Angeles, CA 90013
213/346-6400; Fax: 897-6771

Colorado

1560 Broadway (Suite 850)
Denver, CO 80202
303/894-7499; Fax: 894-7455

Connecticut

PO Box 816
Hartford, CT 06142-0816
860/297-3800; Fax: 566-7410

District of Columbia

810 First St. NE (Suite 701)
Washington, DC 20002
202/727-8000; Fax: 535-1196

Delaware

841 Silver Lake Blvd.
Dover, DE 19904
300/739-4251; Fax: 739-5280

Florida

State Capital—Plaza Level Eleven
Tallahassee, FL 32399-0300
850/922-3101; Fax: 488-3334

Georgia

2 Martin Luther King Jr. Drive
Floyd Memorial Bldg.
Atlanta, GA 30334
404/656-2056; Fax: 657-7493

Guam

Building 113-3, First Floor
Mariner Avenue
Tiyan Barrigada, Guam 96913
671/475-1843; 472-2643

Hawaii

250 South King St., Fifth Floor
Honolulu, Hawaii 96813
808/586-2790; Fax: 586-2806

Idaho

700 West State St., Third Floor
Boise, ID 83720-0043
208/334-4250; Fax: 334-4398

Illinois

320 West Washington St., Fourth Floor
Springfield, IL 62767-0001
217/785-0116; Fax: 524-6500

100 West Randolph St. (Suite 15-100)
Chicago, IL 60601-3251
312/814-2420; Fax: 814-5435

Indiana

311 West Washington St. (Suite 300)
Indianapolis, IN 46204-2787
317/232-2385; Fax: 232-5251

Iowa

330 East Maple Street
Des Moines, IA 50319
515/281-5705; Fax: 281-3059

Kansas

420 S.W. Ninth Street
Topeka, KS 66612-1678
785/296-7801; Fax: 296-2283

Kentucky

PO Box 517
215 West Main St.
Frankfort, KY 40602-0517
502/564-6027; Fax: 564-1453

Louisiana

950 North Fifth St.
Baton Rouge, LA 70802
225/342-5423; Fax: 342-8622

Maine

State Office Bldg., Station 34
Augusta, ME 04333-0034
207/624-8475; Fax: 924-8599

Massachusetts

One South Station, Fourth Floor
Boston, MA 021110
617/621-7301; Fax: 521-7758

Maryland

525 St. Paul Place
Baltimore, MD 21202-2272
410/468-2090; Fax: 468-2020

Michigan

611 West Ottawa St., 2nd Floor North
Lansing, MI 48933-1020
517/373-9273; Fax: 335-4978

Minnesota	121 Seventh Place East (Suite 200) St. Paul, MN 55101-2145 651/296-6025; Fax: 282-2568
Mississippi	1804 Walter Sillers 550 High Street Jackson, MS 39201 601/359-3569; Fax: 359-2474
Missouri	301 West High St. (6 North) Jefferson City, MO 65102-0690 573/751-4126; Fax: 751-1165
Montana	840 Helena Avenue Helena, MT 59601 406/444-2040; Fax: 444-3497
Nebraska	Terminal Bldg. (Suite 40) 941 'O' Street Lincoln, NE 68508 702/471-2201; Fax: 471-4610
Nevada	788 Fairview Drive Carson City, NV 89701-5753 775/687-4270; Fax: 687-3937
New Hampshire	56 Old Suncook Road Concord, NH 03301 603/271-2261; Fax: 271-1406
New Jersey	20 West State St. (CN325) Trenton, NJ 08625 609/292-5360; Fax: 984-5273
New Mexico	PO Drawer 1269 Santa Fe, NM 87504-1269 505/827-4601; Fax: 476-0326
New York	25 Beaver Street New York, NY 10004-2319 212/480-22899; Fax: 480-2310 Agency Bldg. One Empire State Plaza Albany, NY 12257 518/474-6600; Fax: 473-6814

North Carolina   PO Box 26387
                               Raleigh, NC 27611
                               919/733-3058; Fax: 733-6495

North Dakota   600 E. Blvd.
                               Bismark, ND 58505-0320
                               701/328-2440; Fax: 328-4880

Ohio   2100 Stella Court
                               Columbus, OH 43215-1067
                               614/644-2658; Fax: 644-3743

Oklahoma   2401 N.W. 23rd St. (Suite 28)
                               Oklahoma City, OK 73107
                               405/521-2828; Fax: 521-6635

Oregon   350 Winter St. N.E. (Room 200)
                               Salem, OR 97310-0700
                               503/947-7980; Fax: 378-4351

Pennsylvania   1326 Strawberry Square (13th Floor)
                               Harrisburg, PA 17120
                               717/783-0442; Fax: 772-1969

Puerto Rico   Cohan's Plaza Bldg.
                               1607 Ponce de Leon Ave.
                               Santuree, Puerto Rico 00909
                               787/722-8686; Fax: 722-4400

Rhode Island   233 Richmond St. (Suite 233)
                               Providence, RI 02903-4233
                               401/222-2223; Fax: 222-5475

South Carolina   1612 Marion St.
                               Columbia, SC 29201
                               803/737-6100; Fax: 727-6229

South Dakota   118 West Capitol Avenue
                               Pierre, SD 57501-2000
                               605/773-3563; Fax: 773-5369

Tennessee   500 James Robertson Parkway
                               Nashville, TN 37243-0565
                               615/741-2241; Fax: 532-6934

Texas	333 Guadalupe Street Austin, TX 78701 512/463-6464; Fax: 475-2005
Utah	3110 State Office Building Salt Lake City, UT 84114-1201 801/538-3800; Fax: 538-3829
Vermont	89 Main Street, Drawer 20 Montpelier, VT 05620-3101 802/828-3301; Fax: 828-3306
Virginia	PO Box 1157 Richmond, VA 23218 804/371-9694; Fax: 371-9873
Virgin Islands	18 Konders Gade, Charlotte Amalie St. Thomas, Virgin Islands 00/802 340/773-6449; Fax: 773-4052
Washington	PO Box 40255 Olympia, WA 98504-0255 360/753-7301; Fax: 586-3535
West Virginia	PO Box 50540 Charleston, WV 25305-0540 304/558-3354; Fax: 558-0412
Wisconsin	121 East Wilson Madison, WI 53702 208/267-1233; Fax: 267-8570
Wyoming	122 West 25th Street (Third Floor East) Cheyenne, WY 82002-0440 307/777-7401

32

Glossary of Managed Care Terms

Allowable: A fee decided by the third-party payer that the provider is paid or allowed to charge. It's usually lower than the therapist's normal fee.

Appeal: A request to an insurance company for reconsideration of sessions that have been denied as unauthorized. It may be written or oral, depending on the requirements of a particular insurance company. Many companies have multiple levels of appeal, from telephone review to consideration by an external committee of experts.

Assignment: The client designates or assigns the third-party payer or insurance company to pay the therapist or provider directly.

Authorization: The process by which insurance companies approve a number of therapeutic sessions within a specific amount of time, based on medical necessity. Precertification is usually required before the first session.

Biofeedback: A technique similar to hypnosis, in which monitoring equipment is used to teach clients relaxation control. The monitor can display whether the client is in a trance state and how deep.

Capitation: A system developed by insurance companies to pay a group or organization of providers a set fee over time to provide services to a designated population. The population is usually confined to a state, city, or community. In practice, the capitation company is responsible for treatment decisions. The system has been criticized as creating a conflict of interest for capitation providers, since the more treatment is denied or withheld, the higher the profits.

Case manager: A clinician who monitors client sessions for medical necessity at the least intensive level that is appropriate.

Certification: The number of treatment sessions approved by the insurance company as medically necessary.

Coding: Communications shorthand used by insurance companies and providers to describe the diagnosis *(DSM-IV)* and services performed in Current Procedural Terminology (CPT).

Cognitive-behavioral therapy: Systematic use of behavioral strategies to help clients gain mastery over unwanted behaviors. Procedures include (1) identification of dysfunctional or distorted cognitions and the realization that they result in negative feelings and behaviors; (2) self-monitoring of negative thoughts (self-talk); (3) identification of the relationship of thoughts to underlying beliefs and feelings; (4) identification of alternative thinking patterns based on reality; and (5) hypothesis testing of the validity of the client's basic assumptions about self, the world, and the future.

Concurrent review: The process of assessing justification of treatment authorizations from initial session to discharge. The review focuses on the appropriateness of treatment, measurable goals, and progress to termination.

Consent form: A standard form signed by a client, authorizing the provider to release confidential information about the client to his/her insurance company.

Coordination of benefits: A procedure of coordinating payments by more than one insurance company to assure that no more than 100 percent of costs are reimbursed to the client or paid to the provider. When two insurance companies are involved, the primary plan pays a portion of the allowable amount, and an explanation of benefits from the primary plan is then sent to the secondary insurance company, which may pay some of the remaining portion of the allowable amount.

Copayment: The portion of the total fee for which an insured client is responsible. The amount is usually fixed by the insurance company.

Current Procedural Terminology (CPT): A systematic listing of coded procedures and services performed. The codes are changed periodically. The CPT codes in the year 2001 for psychotherapy include:

Individual psychotherapy, 90806
Families/couples without patient present, 90846
Families/couples with patient present, 90847
Group psychotherapy, 90849
Pharmacological management, 90802
Biofeedback training, 96100
Electroconvulsive therapy, 90870

Deductible: The amount payable by the client before insurance benefits become payable.

Diagnosis: The *Diagnostic and Statistical Manual of Mental Disorders*, fourth edition (*DSM-IV*), and the *International Classification of Diseases*, ninth revision (*ICD-9*), provide classification codes of clients' conditions.

Drug utilization review: The goal of this insurance company review is to reduce the cost of drug therapy by substituting generic drugs for name brands or using a formulary to limit drugs physicians are permitted to prescribe. Since some drug companies own or are owned by insurance companies, use of a formulary has been criticized as a possible conflict of interest.

Dual diagnosis: Comorbid Axis I mental disorders.

Emergency: A medical or behavioral condition that is sudden and severe and places the client's life or health in jeopardy.

Employment Retirement Income Security Act (ERISA): Regulates employee benefit plans, including health insurance. ERISA regulations supersede state regulations.

Explanation of Benefits (EOB): A statement that accompanies insurance company payment and describes the session dates and amounts per session covered by the enclosed check.

Fee for service: Payment on a session-by-session basis.

Focal therapy: A treatment modality focused on restoring a client to his/her level of functioning prior to the onset of an acute or chronic disorder. Focal therapy uses a brief intervention designed to bring about a specific outcome. It structures the treatment by asking, "Why now?" which reveals the client's expectations and develops an alliance toward change. Much of the work is performed outside the therapy sessions as homework assignments. Focal therapy and "Why now?" are service marks of Merit Behavioral Care.

Formulary: A list of select medications and approved dosages. In some managed care plans, providers can prescribe only from the formulary.

Gatekeeper: A clinician or case manager who controls access to health-care services to keep costs in check.

Global assessment of functioning (GAF): A scale that indicates the overall functioning of a client on Axis V of the *DSM-IV* multiaxial assessment system.

Grievance: A formal complaint to an insurance company by either a client or a provider regarding dissatisfaction with access to, administration of, or reimbursement for services.

Group practice: A number of providers who come together as a single practice and bill insurance companies under a single tax identification number.

Health Care Financing Administration (HCFA): Overseer of Medicare and Medicaid, which thus has a major impact on health insurance policies and procedures. The HCFA-1500 is the standard form for submission of claims to insurance companies.

Health Maintenance Organization (HMO): Provider of health-care services to enrolled members, usually using primary care physicians as gatekeepers to keep costs down.

Hypnosis: An induced altered state of consciousness or trance state in which the individual is more susceptible to suggestion. People are imprinted with mindsets that originate in their families of origin and are incorporated into the unconscious. People organize their personalities and act around these imprints. We don't operate directly on the world, but through a map or model of the world, a created representation of what we believe. In hypnosis, the therapist aims at changing or otherwise influencing the maps we hold in our minds.

Hypnosis can be a highly effective therapeutic tool. When the clients have slipped into trance after induced relaxation, they may be instructed to imagine themselves the way they would like to be. For example, in hypnosis, smokers may be asked to imagine themselves as nonsmokers and through visualization begin to change their belief systems.

Hypnosis appears to work well with the cognitive-behavioral modality. However, insurance company reaction to the technique is mixed. Although many companies find it an acceptable psychotherapeutic technique, some prefer to call it a relaxation technique rather than hypnosis. It is best to find out where the insurance company stands on the issue.

Impairments: Objective, observable reasons why a client seeks treatment. Impairments are not the disorder, but rather behavioral expressions of *DSM-IV* codes.

Individual practice association (IPA): An HMO that provides services through an association of self-employed providers in their own offices under a contract negotiated with the group.

Individual practitioner: An individual clinician who provides behavioral case services to managed care companies. These clinicians must meet specific insurance company credentialing criteria.

Inpatient treatment: A program that provides twenty-four-hour care, usually in a hospital or similar health-care facility, with multiple treatment disciplines licensed by the Joint Commission on Accreditation of Healthcare Organizations (JCAHO).

Intensive outpatient care: A structured treatment program outside of a health-care facility, consisting of multiple sessions accessing various treatment modalities.

Joint Commission on Accreditation of Healthcare Organizations (JCAHO): An accrediting organization for health-care companies.

Level of care: Specific structural and staffing components that support the designated level of treatment required. Level of care may evolve during an episode of treatment.

Managed behavioral health organization (MBHO): Manager of benefits under a special arrangement with a managed behavioral health program. This may include everything from provision of services to organizing a provider network.

Managed health care: A system created to control health-care costs. It uses management techniques and financial incentives to direct clients to providers who will provide appropriate care in the most cost-effective manner.

Medical necessity: The criterion used by insurance carriers to approve treatment services. Medical necessity may vary from company to company.

Member: A subscriber, or eligible dependent, who participates in an insurance plan.

National Committee for Quality Assurance (NCQA): An accrediting agency for managed behavioral health care or HMOs that sets standards and reviews and reports on performance.

Peer review: Evaluation by a therapist of the quality of care given. Also used to determine the number of treatment sessions required before termination.

Place of Service Code: Standardized codes used by providers to report the location where the billed services were performed.

Point of service (POS): A benefit plan in which the subscriber can elect to use a nonparticipating provider, usually at a level of reduced coverage and higher out-of-pocket costs.

Practice guidelines: Standardized clinical specifications for specific *DSM-IV* diagnoses to assist provider and client in making appropriate health-care decisions.

Precertification: Treatment approval by insurance company, following review to determine medical necessity.

Preferred provider organization (PPO): A group of practitioners that contracts with a health-care payer to provide services at competitive rates.

Primary care physician (PCP): A doctor who assumes responsibility for the mental care of a patient. A PCP provides patient referrals to medical specialists as needed.

Primary insurance: An insurance company that provides reimbursement of medical costs, regardless of any other insurance coverage.

Problem-focused: A treatment modality, usually limited to one to ten sessions, that has a high probability of solving a concrete problem in daily living. This approach is typically educative and identifies and directs the client to use available resources.

Psychoanalysis: Treatment modality that analyzes past and present emotional experiences to determine sources of pathology and reduce unconscious conflicts by making clients aware of their existence and origins. This modality is not usually acceptable to insurance companies, which regard it as unfocused, lengthy, and costly compared to behavioral modalities.

Psychodynamic: Aspect of psychoanalytic theory that explains thoughts, feelings, and behaviors as the result of opposing goal-directed or motivational forces.

Quality management: A program designed by the insurance company to provide systematic quality control and risk management.

Rehabilitation Accreditation Commission (CARF): An accreditation authority for the disabled that accredits programs and services, not organizations.

Relaxation technique: A treatment technique used in hypnosis, in which clients are taught how to progressively relax their muscles and thus calm themselves. Breathing and pulse slow down and blood pressure is lowered. Relaxation itself is thought to be healing. When completely relaxed, it is impossible to feel negative emotions (*see* Hypnosis).

Site visits: As part of the insurance companies' agreement with NCQA, they conduct site visits to provider offices to review treatment records and have developed criteria as part of the credentialing and recredentialing processes.

Symptom-focused: Treatment modality, usually brief, that targets maladaptive thoughts and feelings and interpersonal problems. Interventions are focused on the symptom or problem that has caused a decline in the client's level of functioning.

Utilization Management (UM): Process of determining and evaluating treatment. UM oversees preauthorization reviews and discharge planning.

Visualization: Use of creative imagery for the purpose of change. Through visualization, clients are taught how to cancel out negative thinking and acting. Used in hypnosis.

33

Resources for Providers

BOOKS

Art Therapy

Selekman, M. (1997). *Solution-Focused Therapy with Children*. New York: Guilford. (A solution-focused model that combines family and art therapy.)

Asperger's Syndrome

Klin, A., Volkmar, F., and Sparrow, S., eds. (2000). *Asperger Syndrome*. New York: Guilford. (Definitive diagnostic and conceptual information.)

Attention Deficit/Hyperactivity Disorder

Barkley, R., and Benton, C. (1995). *Taking Charge of ADHD*. New York: Guilford. (Empowering parents to take control of ADHD.)

Parker, H. (1999). *Put Yourself in Their Shoes*. Plantation, FL: Specialty. (Understanding your teen's struggle with ADHD.)

Rief, S. (1998). *The ADD/ADHD Checklist*. Paramus, NJ: Prentice Hall. (A resource for teachers and parents.)

Robin, A. (1998). *ADHD in Adolescents*. New York: Guilford Press. (Understanding, diagnosing, and treating ADHD in adolescents.)

Communications

Faber, A., and Mazlish, E. (1995). *How to Talk So Kids Can Learn*. New York: Rawson. (Assists parents to become more effective and happier in their relationships with their children.)

Taffel, R. (2000). *Getting through to Difficult Kids and Parents: Unommon Sense for Professionals*. New York: Guilford Press. (Provides effective techniques for connecting with children and their families.)

Conduct

Barkley, R., and Benton, C. (1998). *Your Defiant Child*. New York: Guilford. (An eight-step program to resolve a strained relationship.)

Barkley, R., Edwards, G., and Robin, A. (1999). *Defiant Youth*. New York: Guilford. (A manual for assessment and family intervention.)

———. (1999). *Defiant Teens*. New York: Guilford. (A manual for assessment and family intervention.)

Greene, R. (1998). *The Explosive Child*. New York: HarperCollins. (A practical approach to helping children prone to explosive tantrums.)

Magid, K., and McKelvey, C. (1987). *High Risk: Children without a Conscience*. New York: Bantam. (How to avoid raising children with this problem.)

Price, J. (1996). *Power and Compassion*. New York: Guilford. (Strategies for working with out-of-control teens and their families.)

Sommers-Flanagan, J., and Sommers-Flanagan, R. (1997). *Tough Kids, Cool Counseling*. Alexandria, VA: American Counseling Association. (Treatment strategies.)

Taffel, R. (2000). *Getting through to Difficult Kids and Parents*. New York: Guilford. (A handbook for therapists working with challenging children.)

Wexler, D. (1991). *The Adolescent Self*. New York: Norton. (PRISM [Program for Innovative Self-Management].)

Critical Incident Stress Management

Figley, C. R. (1989). *Helping Traumatized Families*. San Francisco, CA: Jossey-Boss. (Strategies for working with traumatized families.)

———. (1995). *Compassion Fatigue*. New York: Brunner-Mazel.

Figley, C. R., Bride, B., and Mazza, N., eds. *Death and Trauma*. London: Taylor and Francis. (Helps mental health workers understand their own fatigue in helping clients deal with their trauma.)

FEMA Home Study Program. (1993). *A Citizen's Guide to Disaster Assistance.* Emergency Management Institute: Emmitsburg, MD. *www.fema.gov*

Center for Mental Health Services (1994). *Disaster Response and Recovery: A Handbook for Mental Health Professionals. U.S. Department of Health and Human Services. www.mentalhealth.org/CMHS/EmergencyServices/.index.htm*

Death

Fitzgerald, H. (1994). *Grieving Child.* New York: Simon & Schuster. (Practical advice for coping with loss.)

———. (1994). *Mourning Handbook,* New York: Simon & Schuster. (A compassionate approach to a difficult subject.)

Grollman, E., ed. (1995). *Bereaved Children and Teens.* Boston, MA: Beacon. (A complete resource on death for children by fourteen experts.)

Grollman, E., and Malikow, M. (1999). *Living When a Young Friend Commits Suicide.* Boston, MA: Beacon. (Resolving the pain of survivors.)

Goldman, L. (1994). *Life and Loss.* Muncie, IN: Accelerated Development. (How to recognize and understand different types of loss.)

———. (1994). *Breaking the Silence.* Muncie, IN: Accelerated Development. (Untangling the complex and confusing emotions of children dealing with loss.)

Jarratt, C. (1994). *Helping Children Cope with Separation and Loss.* Boston, MA: Harvard Common. (A guide to recovering from a significant loss.)

Jozefowski, J. T. (1999). *The Phoenix Phenomenon: Rising from the Ashes of Grief.* Northvale, NJ: Jason Aronson. (Provides a developmental model of the phases of grief.)

Perschey, M. (1997). *Helping Teens Work through Grief.* Washington, DC: Accelerated Development. (Activities to promote reflecting and talking about loss and concerns.)

Webb, N. (1993). *Helping Bereaved Children.* New York: Guilford. (Intervention approaches for healing bereaved children.)

Wolfelt, A. (1996). *Healing the Bereaved Child.* Fort Collins, CO: Companion. (A view of grief as a natural healing process.)

Worden, J. W. (1996). *Children and Grief.* New York: Guilford. (Help for a mourning child.)

Development

Greenspan, S., and Wieder, S. (1998). *The Child with Special Needs.* Reading, MA: Adison-Wesley. (Helping the special child reach important developmental milestones.)

Divorce

Garrity, C., and Baris, M. (1997). *Caught in the Middle*. San Francisco, CA: Jossey-Bass. (Protecting the children of high-conflict divorce.)

Johnson, J. and Roseby, V. (1997). *In the Name of the Child*. New York: Free Press. (Developmental problems of children of high conflict divorce.)

Johnson, J., Breuing, K., Garrity, C., and Baris, M. (1997). *Through the Eyes of Childen*. New York: Free Press. (Healing stories for children of divorce.)

Prokop, M. (1986). *Divorce Happens to the Nicest Kids*. Warren, OH: Alegra House. (Disproving myths children have about divorce.)

Diagnosis

Samuels, S., and Sikorsky, S. (1998). *Clinical Evaluations of School-Aged Children*. Sarasota, FL: Professional Resource Press. (A structured approach to the diagnosis of child and adolescent mental disorders.)

Ziegler, R. G., and Ziegler, P. (1992). *Homemade Books to Help Kids Cope*. New York: Magination Press. (How to create personalized stories to help kids cope.)

Managed Care and Treatment Plans

Berghuis, D. J., and Jongsma, A. E., Jr. (2000). *The Severe and Persistent Mental Illness Treatment Planner*. New York: Wiley. (Use in in-patient and out-patient settings.)

Bjorck, J. P., Brown, J.A., and Goodman, M. (2000). *Casebook for Managing Managed Care: A Self-Study Guide for Treatment Planning, Documentation, and Communication*. Washington, DC: American Psychiatric. (Guide for managing managed care.)

Blount, L., Mendoza, E. M., Udello, C. J., and Walters, J. M. (2000). *Mastering the Reimbursement Process*, 2nd ed. Chicago, IL: American Medical Association. (Help in getting reimbursed.)

Dattilio, F. M., and Jongsma, A. E., Jr. (2000). *The Family Therapy Treatment Planner*. New York: Wiley. (Family treatment plans organized around presenting problem.)

De Piano, F. A. (1999). *Critical Strategies: Psychotherapy in Managed Care*. Binghamton, NY: Haworth. (Psychotherapy and managed care.)

Frager, S. (2000). *Managing Managed Care: Secrets from a Former Case Manager*, New York: Wiley. (How to get what you need from managed care.)

Frazer, D. W., and Jongsma, A. E., Jr. (1998). *The Older Adult Psychotherapy Treatment Planner*. New York: Wiley. (Treatment plans for older adults.)

Goodman, M., Brown, J. A., and Dietz, P. M. (1996). *Managing Managed Care II:*

A *Handbook for Mental Health*, 2nd ed. Washington, DC: American Psychiatric.

Jongsma, A. E., Jr. (2000). *The Child and Adolescent Psychotherapy Treatment Planner*. New York: Wiley. (Effective treatment plans for children and adolescents.)

Jongsma, A. E., Jr., and Perkinson, L. M. (1999). *The Complete Adult Psychotherapy Planner*, 2nd ed. New York: Wiley. (Treatment plans that deal with multiple adult issues.)

O'Leary, K. D., Heymon, R. E., and Jongsma, A. E., Jr. (1998). *The Couples Therapy Treatment Planner*. (An array of treatment plans for couples and marital problems.)

Perkinson, R. R., and Jongsma, A. E., Jr. (1997). *The Chemical Dependence Treatment Planner*. New York: Wiley. (Comprehensive planner for substance abuse and related issues.)

Tuckfelt, S., Fink, J., and Warren, M. P. (1997). *The Psychotherapist's Guide to Managed Care in the 21st Century*. Northvale, NJ: Jason Aronson. (Surviving Big Brother while providing quality mental health services.)

Warren, M. P. (2001). *Behavioral Management Guide: Essential Treatment Strategies for Adult Psychotherapy*. Northvale, NJ: Jason Aronson. (Resource to help develop and write treatment plans.)

Wiger, D. (1999). *The Clinical Documentation Sourcebook*, 2nd ed. New York: Wiley. (A complete reference book for clinical documentation.)

———. (1999). *The Psychotherapy Documentation Primer*. New York: Wiley. (The basics of clinical documentation.)

Winegar, N., and Hayter, L. M. (1998). *Guidebook to Managed Care and Practice Management Terminology*. Binghamton, NY: Haworth. (The language of managed care.)

Parenting

Dinkmeyer, D., Sr., McKay, G., and Dinkmeyer, D., Jr. (1989). *STEP: Systematic Training for Effective Parenting*. Circle Pines, MN: American Guidance Service. (Training in parenting.)

———. (1989). *STEP: Systematic Training for Effective Parenting-Parents' Handbook*. Circle Pines, MN: American Guidance Service. (Parenting handbook.)

Guerney, L. (1978). *Parents: A Skill Training Manual*. State College, PA: Ideals. (Five essential parental skills for child rearing.)

Kraft, A., and Landreth, G. (1998). *Parents as Therapeutic Partners*. Northvale, NJ: Jason Aronson. (How to conduct a play therapy session.)

Schaefer, C., and Briesmeister, J. (1989). *Handbook of Parent Training*. New York: Wiley. (An update on the latest intervention strategies.)

Play Therapy

Axline, V. M. (1969). *Play Therapy*. New York: Ballantine. (Growing through play.)

Ciottone, R., and Madonna, J. (1996). *Play Therapy with Sexually Abused Children*. New York: Jason Aronson. (Principles and techniques of synergistic play therapy.)

Gil, E. (1901). *The Healing Power of Play*. New York: Guilford. (Healing abused children through play.)

―――. (1994). *Play in Family Therapy*. New York: Guilford. (Making family therapy more interesting for children.)

Kaduson, H., and Schaefer, C. E. (1997). *101 Favorite Play Therapy Techniques*. Northvale, NJ: Jason Aronson. (Easy-to-use play therapy techniques.)

―――. (2000). *Short-Term Play Therapy for Children*. New York: Guilford. (Play therapy techniques for short-term treatment.)

Kaduson, K., Cangelosi, D., and Schaefer, C. (1997). *The Playing Cure*. Northvale, NJ: Jason Aronson. (Play therapy techniques for specific childhood problems.)

Knell, S. (1993). *Cognitive Behavioral Play Therapy*. Northvale, NJ: Jason Aronson. (Applying cognitive behavioral theory to play therapy.)

Kottman, T., and Schaefer, C. (1993). *Play Therapy in Action*. Northvale, NJ: Jason Aronson. (Various play therapy theories in action.)

Moustakis, C. (1997). *Relationship Play Therapy*. Northvale, NJ: Jason Aronson. (Unlocking childhood potential.)

Norton, C., and Norton, B. (1997). *Reaching Children through Play Therapy*. Denver, CO: The Publishing Cooperative. (An experiential model of children's play.)

O'Connor, K., and Braverman, L. (1997). *Play Therapy: Theory and Practice*. New York: Wiley. (The why and how of play therapy.)

Schaefer, C. E. (1993). *The Therapeutic Powers of Play*. Northvale, NJ: Jason Aronson. (The therapeutic benefits of play.)

Schaefer, C., and Carey, L. (1994). *Family Play Therapy*. Northvale, NJ: Jason Aronson. (Integrating play and family therapies.)

Schaefer, C., Gitlin, K., and Sandgrund, A. (1991). *Play Diagnosis and Assessment*. Muncie, IN: Accelerated Development. (The quantitative measurement of play therapy results.)

Singer, D. (1993). *Playing for Their Lives*. New York: Free Press. (The stories of six children with major contemporary problems.)

Straus, M. (1999). *No-Talk Therapy*. New York: W.W. Norton. (Overcoming the barrier of silence in child therapy.)

Sweeney, D. (1997). *Counseling Children through the World of Play*. Wheaton, IL: Tyndale House. (Therapy in a child's world.)

Van Fleet, R. (1994). *Filial Therapy: Strengthening Parent–Child Relationships through Play.* Sarasota, FL: Professional Resource. (Techniques for building a stronger parent–child relationship.)

Webb, N. B. (1991). *Play Therapy with Children in Crisis.* New York: Guilford. (Case studies of play therapy.)

Posttraumatic Stress Disorder

Brohl, K. (1996). *Working with Traumatized Children.* Washington, DC: CWLA. (Ideas for enhancing the healing process.)

James, B. (1989). *Treating Traumatized Children.* Lexington, MA: Lexington. (New insights in the treatment of childhood trauma.)

———. (1994). *Handbook for Treatment of Attachment-Trauma Problems in Children.* New York: Maxwell Macmillan International. (Treating trauma in children.)

Levy, T., and Orlans, M. (1998). *Attachment, Trauma, and Healing.* Washington, DC: CWLA. (Treatment of childhood trauma.)

Self-Help Resources

Norcross, J. C., Santrock, J. W., Campbell, L. F., Smith, A. T. P., Sommer, R., and Zuckerman, E. L. (2000). *Authoritative Guide to Self-Help Resources in Mental Health.* New York: Guilford. (A comprehensive range of resources, including books, films, Internet sites, and groups.)

Madura, E. J., and White, B. J. (1998). *The Self-Help Sourcebook: Your Guide to Community and Online Support Groups, 6th Edition.* Nutley, NJ: Hoffman La Roche.

Sexual Abuse

Hewitt, S. (1999). *Assessing Allegations of Sexual Abuses in Preschool Children.* Newbury, CT: Sage. (Interviewing pre-verbal children about sex.)

O'Hanlon, W. H., and Bertolino, B. (2000). *Even from a Broken Web: Brief, Respectful, Solution-Oriented Therapy for Sexual Abuse and Trauma.* New York: Wiley.

Social Phobia

Shore, H. M. (1996). *Forms for Helping the Socially Fearful Child.* Plainview, New York: Childswork/Childsplay. (Forms designed to help the entire treatment process.)

Social Skills

Begun, R. W. (1995). *Social Skills: Lesson and Activities for Pre-K and K.* West Nyack, NY: Center for Applied Research in Education. (Lessons in social skills.)

————. (1995). *Social Skills: Lesson and Activities for Grades 1–3.* West Nyack, NY: Center for Applied Research in Education. (Lessons in social skills.)

————. (1995). *Social Skills: Lesson and Activities for Grades 4–6.* West Nyack, NY: Center for Applied Research in Education. (Lessons in social skills.)

————. (1995). *Social Skills: Lesson and Activities for Grades 7–12.* West Nyack, NY: Center for Applied Research in Education. (Lessons in social skills.)

Stress

Hipp, E. (1995). *Fighting Invisible Tigers.* Minneapolis, MN: Free Spirit. (A stress management guide for teenagers.)

Copeland, M. E. (1998). *The Worry Control Workbook.* Oakland, CA: New Harbinger. (Help for teens in relieving worry.)

Story-Telling

Brett, D. (1992). *More Annie Stories.* New York: Magination. (Using story-telling to tackle different issues.)

Mills, J., and Crowley, R. (1986). *Therapeutic Metaphors for Children and the Child within.* New York: Brunner/Mazel. (A multi-faceted therapeutic story-telling technique.)

Hanson, M., and Canfield, J. (1998). *Chicken Soup for the Kids' Soul.* Deerfield Beach, FL: Health Communications. (Inspiring stories to heal.)

————. (1997). *Chicken Soup for the Teenage' Soul.* Deerfield Beach, FL: Health Communications. (Inspiring stories to heal.)

Therapy

Aronson, J., ed., (2000). *3-Minute Consultations with America's Greatest Psychotherapists.* Northvale, NJ: Jason Aronson.

Cade, B., and O'Hanlon, W. H. (1999). *A Brief Guide to Brief Therapy.* Dunmore, PA: Norton.

Dane, B., Tosone, C., and Wolsojn, A., eds. (2001). *Doing More with Less: Using Long-Term Skills in Short-Term Treatment.* Northvale, NJ: Jason Aronson.

O'Hanlon, W. H. (2000). *Taproots: Milton Erickson's Therapy and Hypnosis.* Dunmore, PA: Norton.

O'Hanlon, W. H., and Rowan, T. (1999). *Solution-Oriented Therapy for Chronic and Severe Mental Illness.* New York: Wiley.

Violence

Bloom, S. L., and Reichert, M. (1998). *Bearing Witness: Violence and Collective Responsibility.* Binghamton, NY: Haworth. (Violence and responsibility.)
Prothrow-Stith, D. (1991). *Deadly Consequences.* New York: HarperCollins. (An anti-violence proposal for our schools.)
Garbarino, J. (1997). *Lost Boys.* New York: Free Press. (Proven methods to thwart violent behavior.)

CATALOGS FOR PROVIDERS

The expanding list of books, games, and audio-video materials is in constant flux. Following is a list of a few major catalogs to keep you on top of new publications and other items as they become available.

Courage-to-Change
PO Box 1268
Newburgh, NY 12551
1-800-440-4003
Fax: 1-800-772-6499

Publications Catalog & Resource Guide
NASW Press
750 First Street NE
Washington, DC 90002-4241
Fax: 202-336-8312

Jossey-Bass
250 Sansome St
San Francisco, CA 94104-1342
1-800-956-7739
Fax: 1-800-05-2665

Guilford Publications
72 Spring Street
New York, NY 10012
1-800-365-7006
Fax: 212-966-6708

Hazelden
15251 Pleasant Valley Road
Center City, MN 550121
1-800-328-9000
Fax: 1-651-213-4590

The Haworth Press
10 Alice Street
Binghamton, NY 13904-1580
1-800-HAWORTH
Fax: 1-800-895-0582

KIDSRIGHTS
8902 Otis Avenue
Indianapolis, IN 46216-1033
1-800-892-KIDS
Fax: 877-543-7001

Childswork/Childsplay
135 Dupont Street
PO Box 760
Plainview, NY 11803-0760
1-800-962-1141
Fax: 1-800-262-1886

Self Esteem Shop
32839 Woodward Ave.
Royal Oak, MI 48073
1-800-251-8336
Fax: 248-549-0442

The Center for Applied Psychology
PO Box 61586
King of Prussia, PA 19406
215-277-4020

Western Psychological Services
12031 Wilshire Blvd.
Los Angeles, CA 90025-1251
1-800-648-8857
Fax: 310-478-7838

VIDEO TAPES FOR PROVIDERS

Berry, J. *Casey's Revenge*. Self Esteem Shop, Royal Oak, MI.

———. *Lean Mean Machine—Handling Emotion*, Self Esteem Shop, Royal Oak, MI.

———. *Letter on Light Blue Stationary*. Self Esteem Shop, Royal Oak, MI.

———. *Unforgettable Penpal*. Self Esteem Shop, Royal Oak, MI.

———. *Fair Weather Friend*. Self Esteem Shop, Royal Oak, MI.

———. *High Price to Pay*. Self Esteem Shop, Royal Oak, MI.

Faller, K. *Interviewing for Child Sexual Abuse*. Self Esteem Shop, Royal Oak, MI.

References

Allen, F. H. (1942). *Psychotherapy with Children*. New York: Norton.

American Psychiatric Association. (1994). *Diagnostic and Statistical Manual of Mental Disorders, 4th Ed. (DSM-IV)*. Washington, DC: Author.

Axline, V. (1969). *Play Therapy*. New York: Ballantine.

Azrin, N. H., and Foxx, R. M. (1974). *Dry-Bed Training: Rapid Elimination of Childhood Enuresis*. New York: Simon & Schuster.

———. (1974). *Toilet Training in Less Than a Day*. New York: Simon & Schuster.

Bandler, R. (1985). *Using Your Brain—for a Change*. Moab, UT: Real People Press.

Bandler, R., and Grinder, J. (1982). *Reframing—Neuro-Linguistic Programming and the Transformation of Meaning*. Moab, UT: Real People Press.

Bourne, E. J. (1998). *Overcoming Specific Phobias*. Oakland, CA: New Harbinger.

Bradley, S., and Zucher, K. (1995). *Gender Identity Disorder and Psychosocial Problems in Children and Adolescents*. New York: Guilford.

Bruce, T. J., and Sanderson, W. C. (1998). *Specific Phobias: Clinical Applications of Evidence-Based Psychotherapy*. Northvale, NJ: Jason Aronson.

Carkhuff, R. R. (1969). *Helping and Human Relations*, Vol. 1. New York: Holt, Rinehart & Winston.

Carnes, P. (1992). *Out of the Shadows: Understanding Sexual Addiction*. Center City, MN: Hazelden.

Davis, M., Eschman, E. R., and McKay, M. (1994). *The Relaxation & Stress Reduction Skills Workbook*. Oakland, CA: New Harbinger.

DiCeglia, D. (2000). "Gender Disorder in Young People." In *Psychiatric Treatment* 6:458–466.

Dodds, J. B. (1985). *A Child Psychotherapy Primer*. New York: Human Sciences.

Emery, G. (2000). *Overcoming Depression*. Oakland, CA: New Harbinger.

Erickson, E. H. (1950). *Childhood and Society*. New York: Norton.

Fink, J. (1999). *How to Use Computers and Cyberspace in the Clinical Practice*. Northvale, NJ: Jason Aronson.

Frager, S. (2000). *Managing Managed Care: Secrets from a Former Case Manager*. New York: John Wiley and Sons.

Freud, A. (1965). *Normality and Pathology in Childhood*. New York: International Universities Press.

Freud, S. (1920). *Beyond the Pleasure Principle*. New York: Norton.

Gardner, R. A. (1971). "The Mutual Storytelling Technique in the Treatment of Anger Inhibition Problems. *International Journal of Child Psychoanalysis* 1:34–64.

Goldstein, A. P., and Glick, B. (1987). *Aggression Replacement Training: A Comprehensive Intervention for Aggressive Youth*. Champaign, IL: Research Press.

Gottman, J. M., Gonso, J., and Shuler, P. (1976). "Teaching Social Skills to Isolated Children." *Journal of Abnormal Psychology* 4:179–197.

Gresham, F. M. (1986). "Conceptual Issues in the Assessment of Social Competence in Children. In *Children's Social Behavior: Developmental, Assessment, and Modification*, ed. P. S. Strain, M. J. Gurainick, and H. M. Walker. Orlando, FL: Academic.

Guerin, P. J., Jr., ed. (1976). *Family Therapy: Theory and Practice*. New York: Gardner.

Halberstadt-Freud, L. (1975). "Technical Variations in the Psychoanalytic Treatment of a Pre-School Child." *Israel Annals of Psychiatry and Related Disciplines* 13:162–176.

Harter, S. (1977). "A Cognitive-Developmental Approach to Children's Expression of Conflicting Feelings and a Technique to Facilitate Such Expression in Play Therapy." *Journal of Consulting and Clinical Psychology* 45:417–432.

Hendricks, G., and Wills, R. (1975). *The Centering Book*. Englewood Cliffs, NJ: Prentice-Hall.

Horney, K. (1945). *Our Inner Conflicts*. New York: Norton.

Irwin, E. C. (1983). "The Diagnostic and Therapeutic Use of Pretend Play." In *Handbook of Play Therapy*, ed. C. E. Schaefer and K. J. O'Connor. New York: Wiley.

Jacobs, E. H. (2000). *ADHD: Helping Parents Help Their Children*. Northvale, NJ: Jason Aronson.

Jacobson, E. (1938). *Progressive Relaxation: A Physiological and Clinical Investigation of Muscular States and Their Significance in Psychology and Medical Practice*, 2nd ed. Chicago: University of Chicago Press.

Jozefowski, J. (1999). *The Phoenix Phenomenon: Rising from the Ashes of Grief.* Northvale, NJ: Jason Aronson.

Kadusen, H., and Schaefer, C. E., eds. (1998). *101 Favorite Play Therapy Techniques.* Northvale, NJ: Jason Aronson.

Kelly, G. A. (1985). *The Psychology of Personal Constructs.* Vol. 2: *Clinical Diagnosis and Psychotherapy.* New York: Norton.

Kendall, P. C. (1991). *Child and Adolescent Therapy: Cognitive Behavioral Procedures.* New York: Guilford.

Kendall, P. C., and Braswell, L. (1985). *Cognitive Behavioral Therapy for Impulsive Children.* New York: Guilford.

Klein, M. (1975). *The Psychoanalysis of Children.* New York: Free Press.

Klosko, J. S., and Sanderson, W. C. (1999). *Cognitive-Behavioral Treatment of Depression.* Northvale, NJ: Jason Aronson.

Knell, S. M. (1993). *Cognitive Behavioral Play Therapy.* Northvale, NJ: Jason Aronson.

Krumholtz, J. D., and Thoresen, C. E. (1969). *Behavioral Counseling: Cases and Techniques.* New York: Holt, Rinehart & Winston.

Kurdek, L. A. (1986). "Custodial Mothers' Perceptions of Visitations and Payment of Child Support by Noncustodial Fathers in Families with Low and High Levels of Preseparation Interparent Conflict." *Journal of Applied Developmental Psychology* 9:315–328.

La Greca, A. M. (1983). *Interviewing and Behavioral Observations.*" In *Handbook of Clinical Child Psychology,* ed. C. E. Walker and M. C. Roberts. New York: Wiley.

Lazarus, A. A. (1971). *Behavior Therapy and Beyond.* New York: McGraw-Hill.

Lazarus, A. A., and Abramovitz, A. (1962). "The Use of Emotive Imagery in the Treatment of Children's Phobias." *Journal of Afentat Science* 108:191–195.

McGinn, L. K., and Sanderson, W. C. (1999). *Treatment of Obsessive-Compulsive Disorder.* Northvale, NJ: Jason Aronson.

McGuire, W. J. (1961). "The Effectiveness of Supportive and Refutational Defenses in Immunizing and Restoring Beliefs against Persuasion." *Sociometry* 24:184–197.

McKay, M., Fanning, P., and Paleg, K. (1994). *Couples Skills.* Oakland, CA: New Harbinger.

Moreno, J. (1969). *Psychodrama.* New York: Beacon House.

Moustakas, C. E. (1953). *Children in Play Therapy.* New York: McGraw Hill.

O'Connor, K. (1991). *The Play Therapy Primer.* New York: Wiley.

Piaget, J. (1952). *The Origins of Intelligence.* New York: Norton.

Ramey, C. T., Campbell, F. C., and Ramey, S. L. (1998). "Early Intervention: Successful Pathways to Improving Intellectual Development." Paper presented at the Conference on Dendritic Mechanisms of Mental Retardation and Developmental Disabilities, National Institute for Child Health and Human Development, Bethesda, MD. Available online at *http://www.circ.uab.edu/cpages/Eipath.htm.*

Rapee, R. C., and Sanderson, W. C. (1998). *Social Phobia.* Northvale, NJ: Jason Aronson.

Reinecke, M. A., Dottilio, F. M., and Freeman, A., eds. (1996). *Cognitive Therapy with Children and Adolescents.* New York: Guilford.

Reisman, J. M. (1973). *Principles of Psychotherapy with Children.* New York: Wiley.

Rychlak, J. F. (1973). *Introduction to Personality and Psychotherapy: A Theory-Construction Approach.* Boston: Houghton Mifflin.

Sarnoff, C. (1976). *Latency.* New York: Jason Aronson.

Schaefer, C. E. (1993). *The Therapeutic Powers of Play.* Northvale, NJ: Jason Aronson.

Schaefer, C. E., and Conglosai, D. M., eds. (1997). *Play Therapy Techniques.* Northvale, NJ: Jason Aronson.

Schaefer, C. E., and Millman, H. L. (1977). *Therapies for Children.* San Francisco: Jossey-Bass.

Schwebel, A. I., and Fine, M. A. (1994). *Understanding and Helping Families: A Cognitive-Behavioral Approach.* New Jersey: Lawrence Erlbaum Associates.

Sketekee, G. (1998). *Overcoming Obsessive-Compulsive Disorder.* Oakland, CA: New Harbinger.

Smith, C. D. (1977). "Counter Attitudinal Role-Playing and Attitude Change in Children." *Dissertation Abstracts International* 39:400–B.

Steinberg, M., and Schnell, M. (2000). *The Stranger in the Mirror: Dissociation, the Hiddden Epidemic.* New York: HarperCollins.

Swassing, R. H., ed. (1997). *Teaching through Modality Strengths: Concepts and Practices.* New York: Zanner-Bloser.

Tobin, L. (1999). *What Do You Do with a Child Like This?* Los Angeles, CA: Western Psychological Services.

Tuckfelt, S., Fink, J., and Warren, M. P. (1997). *The Psychotherapists' Guide to Managed Care in the 21st Century.* Northvale, NJ: Jason Aronson.

Value Options. (1999). *Provider Handbook: More Choices for More People.* New York State Department of Civil Services.

Waelder, R. (1933). "The Psychoanalytic Theory of Play." *Psychoanalytic Quarterly* 2:208–224.

Warren, M. P. (2001). *Behavioral Management Guide: Essential Treatment Strategies for Adult Psychotherapy.* Northvale, NJ: Jason Aronson.

White, J. (1998). *Overcoming Generalized Anxiety Disorder.* Oakland, CA: New Harbinger.

Woody, R. H. (1971). *Psychobehavioral Counseling and Therapy. Integrating Behavioral and Insight Techniques.* New York: Appleton-Century-Crofts.

Zuercher-White, E. (1998). *Overcoming Agoraphobia and Panic Disorder.* Oakland, CA: New Harbinger.

Index

ABOUT THE AUTHOR

Muriel Prince Warren, DSW, ACSW, is a psychotherapist, author, and educator. She is engaged in private practice in New York City and Rockland County, New York. Dr. Warren is the Executive Director of the Psychoanalytic Center for Communicative Education as well as a senior training and supervising analyst there. She is past president of the International Society for Communicative Psychoanalysis and Psychotherapy where she has received many awards for excellence. She holds degrees in psychology and social work from Fordham, Columbia, and Adelphi universities, and a certificate in psychoanalysis from Lenox Hill Hospital in New York. Dr. Warren is the author of three books: *A Psychotherapist's Guide to Managed Care in the 21st Century* (with Sondra Tuckfelt and Jeri Fink), *SONS: A Mother's Manual* (with Elise Karlin), and *Behavioral Management Guide: Essential Treatment Strategies for Adult Psychotherapy.*